The RoutledgeFalmer Reader in Sociology of Education

In this new Reader, Stephen J. Ball brings together a carefully selected collection of articles and book chapters to reflect enduring trends in the field of Sociology of Education. Focusing on the major issues confronting education today, this lively and informative Reader provides broad coverage of the field and includes sections on crucial topics such as:

- social class
- globalisation
- gender
- curriculum
- social inequality and social justice
- students and classrooms

With an emphasis on contemporary pieces that deal with issues relevant to the immediate real world, this book represents the research and views of some of the most respected authors in the field today. Stephen J. Ball offers a collection that is theoretically informed, internationally applicable, and universally accessible.

In a specially written introduction, Stephen J. Ball provides a much-needed context to the current education climate. Students of sociology and sociology of education will find the Reader an important route map to further reading and understanding.

Stephen J. Ball is Karl Mannheim Professor of Sociology of Education at the Institute of Education, University of London.

Readers in education

The RoutledgeFalmer Reader in Higher Education
Edited by Malcolm Tight

The RoutledgeFalmer Reader in Language and Literacy
Edited by Teresa Grainger

The RoutledgeFalmer Reader in Psychology of Education
Edited by Harry Daniels and Anne Edwards

The RoutledgeFalmer Reader in Sociology of Education
Edited by Stephen J. Ball

The RoutledgeFalmer Reader in Science Education
Edited by John Gilbert

The RoutledgeFalmer Reader in Multicultural Education
Edited by David Gillborn and Gloria Ladson-Billings

The RoutledgeFalmer Reader in Inclusion
Edited by Keith Topping and Sheelagh Maloney

The RoutledgeFalmer Reader in Teaching and Learning
Edited by Ted Wragg

The RoutledgeFalmer Reader in Sociology of Education

Edited by
Stephen J. Ball

 RoutledgeFalmer
Taylor & Francis Group

LONDON AND NEW YORK

First published 2004
by RoutledgeFalmer
11 New Fetter Lane, London EC4P 4EE

Simultaneously published in the USA and Canada
by RoutledgeFalmer
29 West 35th Street, New York, NY 10001

RoutledgeFalmer is an imprint of the Taylor & Francis Group

© 2004 Selection and editorial matter: Stephen J. Ball

Typeset in Sabon by
Florence Production Ltd, Stoodleigh, Devon
Printed and bound in Great Britain by
TJ International Ltd, Padstow, Cornwall

British Library Cataloguing in Publication Data
A catalogue record for this book is available from the
British Library

Library of Congress Cataloging in Publication Data
The RoutledgeFalmer reader in sociology of education/
  [edited by] Stephen J. Ball.
    p. cm.
    Includes bibliographical references and index.
  1. Educational sociology.   I. Ball, Stephen J.
  LC191.2.R69 2004
  306.43'2–dc22   2003058479

ISBN 0–415–32775–X (hbk)
ISBN 0–415–32776–8 (pbk)

CONTENTS

Preface   ix
Acknowledgements   xi

The sociology of education: a disputational account   1
STEPHEN J. BALL

Turning points 3
The chapters 10

PART 1
Social class   13

1   **The forms of capital**   15
    PIERRE BOURDIEU

    Cultural capital 17
    Social capital 21
    Conversions 24

2   **Finding or losing yourself? Working-class relationships to education**   30
    DIANE REAY

    Introduction: the more things change the more they stay
      the same 30
    Making difficult transitions: choosing hybridity? 33
    Normativity and 'the other' 38
    Finding 'you're a nothing': working-class dilemmas of being
      'found out' 39
    Conclusion 41

PART 2
Globalisation and the economy   45

3   **Education, globalization and economic development**   47
    PHILLIP BROWN AND HUGH LAUDER

    Introduction 47
    Globalization and the new rules of economic competition 48
    The New Right: education in a neo-Fordist 'market' economy 51

Left modernizers: education in a post-Fordist 'magnet' economy 55
Conclusion 67

4   Globalisation, the learning society and comparative education   72
PETER JARVIS

The processes of globalisation 72
Learning societies 74
Comparative education and the learning society 81
Conclusion 83

PART 3
Gender   87

5   The social construction of youthful masculinities: peer group
    sub-cultures   89
MIKE O'DONNELL AND SUE SHARPE

White boys and the social construction of masculinities:
    class and nation 90
White boys, class and ethnicity 98
African-Caribbean boys and the social construction of masculinities 101
Asian boys and the construction of masculinities 117
Conclusion 124

6   The discursive production of the male/female dualism in
    school settings   128
BRONWYN DAVIES

The myth of the unitary person: contradictions and subjectivity 128
Positioning within textual narratives 129
Positioning within lived narratives in the classroom 130
The location of individuals in relation to social structures 133
The possibility of refusing a discourse 137

PART 4
Regulation   141

7   Performativities and fabrications in the education economy:
    towards the performative society   143
STEPHEN J. BALL

Social relations of practice 146
Fabrications 148
The routine selection (or manipulation) of statistics and indicators 149
The stage management of events 150
Constructing accounts of the institution 150
Performance as performativity 151
Individual fabrications 151
The performative society 152

8 The capitalist state and public policy formation. Framework for a
political sociology of educational policy making 156
CARLOS ALBERTO TORRES

Determinants of education policy formation 156
Theory of the state and education 158
State authority and policy formation 160
Production rules of public policy: a theoretical assessment
  and hypothesis 161
Production rules of policy formation: a summary 168
Conclusion: a theoretical approach to public policy formation
  in education 169

PART 5
Curriculum 177

9 Cultural politics and the text 179
MICHAEL W. APPLE

Introduction 179
Whose knowledge is of most worth? 180
Regulation or liberation and the text 183
The politics of cultural incorporation 187

10 Social class and pedagogic practice 196
BASIL BERNSTEIN

The rules of pedagogic practice as cultural relay 197
Generating modalities of pedagogic practice 199
Types of pedagogic practice: visible and invisible 201
Social class assumptions of pedagogic practice 203
Autonomous and market-oriented visible pedagogies 212
Addendum 214

PART 6
Teacher 219

11 The reconstruction of primary teachers' identities 221
PETER WOODS AND BOB JEFFREY

Introduction 221
The primary teachers' Plowden self-identity 223
Challenges to the Plowden self-identity 225
Identity work: meeting the challenges 230
Conclusion 236

12 Teachers doing their 'economic' work 240
JOHN SMYTH AND GEOFFREY SHACKLOCK

An ideology of production or the production of an ideology? 240
Developing a 'reading position' on teaching 246

Discursive pedagogical skill construction in teaching 250
Marketised relationships in schools 255
Management for all seasons: managing teaching through
market consent 256

PART 7
Students and classroom   263

13 **Schools, families and academically able students: contrasting modes**
    of involvement in secondary education   265
    SALLY POWER, GEOFF WHITTY, TONY EDWARDS AND
    VALERIE WIGFALL

    Introduction 265
    Sources of consensus and disaffection in education 266
    Discussion 280

14 **Towards a sociology of learning in primary schools**   285
    ANDREW POLLARD

    The limitations of disciplinary boundaries 285
    Learning in primary schools 286
    Policy and substantive contexts 288
    A longitudinal ethnography 291
    Learning and developing an identity 292
    Towards an analytical framework 294
    Summary and conclusion 297

PREFACE

Any selection of work from the vast output of the sociology of education is bound to be both idiosyncratic and unsatisfactory. The point is does it work, does it do a useful job for the intended readership? Let me explain how these contributions were chosen, that is, make clear the principles of selection involved. It may help to begin with what is not being attempted in the collection. First of all it is not representative, whatever that might mean in terms of the sociology of education. Not every sub-specialism, theoretical position or important figure are included – that would be impossible. Second, there is no attempt to directly represent the 'founding fathers' of sociology or the sociology of education. That sort of approach to the field is adequately dealt with in existing textbooks. Third, I rejected the idea of a collection of classic works – Willis, Lacey, Floud, Jackson and Marsden, Bowles and Gintis, Delamont, Bernstein, M.F.D. Young, Lather, Kenway etc. Again, these can be accessed easily in other ways; although there might be a case for another Reader which does bring these together in one place. Fourth, I am aware that some important sub-specialisms are not foregrounded: race for example and disability. Race, however, is a significant issue in some of the chapters and another Reader in this series (*Reader in Multicultural Education*, edited by David Gillborn and Gloria Ladson-Billings) is devoted to race and education.

So how does this collection work? The emphasis, the bias, is towards contemporary pieces, and towards writing and issues that are relevant to immediate real world issues. But I did not want contributions that simply reported research on contemporary issues, that would have built a fatal obsolescence into the selection. So I have tried to find pieces that were both relevant and had a theoretically informed approach, and that would be transposable to other issues, other times and other locations (although the chapters are mainly English and all are from English-speaking countries). None, however, are irredeemably local: they operate at the level of generality and with a conceptual array which make them readable in, and applicable to, a wide variety of national locations. Having said that, the English bias is also a response to the intended audiences. Nonetheless, there is the unfortunate effect of reproducing the English and Northern biases built into our sociology of education and that is something I shall comment on in the introductory chapter. Furthermore, of course, even the English-speaking countries have their own national sociologies and there are significant differences between the UK and US traditions for example.

Then what? I mainly chose contributions that were broad and in part expository, that is, papers with a pedagogical edge, papers that did not take too much for granted, papers that situated themselves clearly in a tradition or a body of research or ideas and, in some cases, over and against other traditions. Papers, that is, that students would find useful, not simply in their own right but as a way into, an introduction to, the issues addressed. This tended to exclude a lot of potential contributions.

In reading many of the papers which I initially identified as worth considering for inclusion I found them to be locked into a single position, or set very narrowly within the confines of their own project without a sense of how they relate to other work. That is not necessarily a criticism of those papers but it meant that they did less 'work' than I had hoped and took more for granted than I thought was useful for the collection.

I also paid attention to the quality of the writing and while there are a wide variety of styles and forms of expression, they all communicate their ideas effectively; although some are more 'difficult' than others. Sociology is bounded and divided as much by its forms and styles of writing as it is by theories and methods. The make-up of the collection also reflects, to a degree, my own interests and prejudices, my own biography in the sociology of education and my own sense of excitement at major points of transition in the recent history of the field.

I would like to thank Sean Vertigan for his help in editing the papers.

ACKNOWLEDGEMENTS

The following articles have been reproduced with the kind permission of Taylor & Francis Journals (www.tandf.co.uk):

Philip Brown and Hugh Lauder (1996) 'Education, globalization and economic development', *Journal of Education Policy* 11 (1): 1–25.

Bronwyn Davies (1989) 'The discursive production of the male/female dualism in school settings', *Oxford Review of Education* 15 (3): pp. 229–41.

Peter Jarvis (2000) 'Globalisation, the learning society and comparative education', *Comparative Education* 36 (3): 343–55.

Andrew Pollard (1990) 'Towards a sociology of learning in primary schools', *British Journal of Sociology of Education* 11 (3): 241–56.

Sally Power, Geoff Whitty, Tony Edwards and Valerie Wigfall (1998) 'Schools, families and academically able students', *British Journal of Sociology of Education* 19 (2): 157–77.

Diane Reay (2001) 'Finding or losing yourself? Working-class relationships to education', *Journal of Education Policy* 16 (4): 333–46.

Carlos Alberto Torres (1989) 'The capitalist state and public policy formation. Framework for a political sociology of educational policy making', *British Journal of Sociology of Education* 10 (1): 81–102.

Peter Woods and Bob Jeffrey (2002) 'The reconstruction of primary teachers' identities', *British Journal of Sociology of Education* 23 (1): 89–106.

The following texts have been reproduced with the kind permission of the relevant publishers:

Pierre Bourdieu (1986) 'The forms of capital' in John C. Richardson, *Handbook of Theory and Research for the Sociology of Education*, pp. 241–58. Copyright © 1986 John C. Richardson. Reproduced with permission of Greenwood Publishing Group, Inc., Westport, CT.

The following texts have been reproduced with the kind permission of Taylor & Francis Books:

Michael W. Apple (2000) 'Cultural politics and the text' in M. Apple, *Official Knowledge*, 2nd edn. Copyright © 2000, 1993 by Michael W. Apple. London: Routledge, pp. 42–60.

Stephen J. Ball (2001) 'Performatives and fabrications in the education economy' in Denis Gleeson and Chris Husbands (eds), *The Performing School: Managing, Teaching and Learning in a Performance Culture*. Copyright © 2001 Denis Gleeson and Chris Husbands. London: RoutledgeFalmer, pp. 210–26.

Basil Bernstein (2003) 'Social class and pedagogic practice' in *The Structuring of Pedagogic Discourse*, Volume IV: *Class, Codes and Control*. Copyright © 2003 Basil Bernstein. London: Routledge, pp. 63–93.

Mike O'Donnell and Sue Sharpe (2000) 'The social construction of youthful masculinities' in *Uncertain Masculinities: Youth, Ethnicity and Class in Contemporary Britain*. Copyright © 2000 Mike O'Donnell and Sue Sharpe. London: Routledge, pp. 38–88.

John Smyth and Geoffrey Shacklock (1998) 'Teachers doing their "economic" work' in *Re-making Teaching*. Copyright © 1998 John Smyth and Geoffrey Shacklock. London: Routledge, pp. 77–106.

THE SOCIOLOGY OF EDUCATION

A disputational account

Stephen J. Ball

In this introduction I want to put the papers selected into a context and a history. That is to situate them within the discipline and its vicissitudes. In doing this I want to be clear that any attempt to encompass or sum up the sociology of education within a single framework is fraught with difficulties. Indeed, there is no single, unified or stable discipline or intellectual project to which we can refer. As Michael Apple (1996: 125) put it in a review of sociology of education in the US 'what actually counts as the sociology of education is a construction'. More precisely, the sociology of education is made up of a set of dynamic and located constructions. By that I mean the field has a set of disparate, nationally located histories and styles of sociology (Davies, Chapter 6, this volume); each made up of 'shifting amalgamations of sub-groups and traditions' in Goodson's terms (1983: 3).

If there is anything at all which stands as common ground between these traditions, amalgamations and styles it is an orientation to critique and to redemption.

The development and discontinuities within the sociology of education are produced both by the changing patterns of relations within the field and the relations between the sociology of education and adjacent fields or disciplines. The former changes take place on a number of dimensions. On the one hand, the sociology of education has been defined and redefined by a set of theoretical and methodological disputes or 'paradigm wars' (more of which later). On the other, the field has been subject to various breakaways and splits which have created new sub-fields or, in some cases, distinct, new disciplines. This has been markedly the case in the UK in recent years. The latter, inter-disciplinary relations, what Kant called 'the conflict of the faculties' (Bourdieu 1988), are increasingly complex as, especially in the wake of the postmodern 'turn', the boundaries between sociology and philosophy, political science, geography and social psychology have become fuzzy and loose. Postmodernism 'has spread like a virus through the disciplines of the social sciences and humanities eating away at the boundaries between them' (Maclure 2003: 4). Consequently, it is sometimes difficult to say who is a sociologist of education and who is not.

This collection is, itself, an act of construction; a drawing-up of boundaries, a marking-off of divisions, oppositions and positions, a 'carving up and carving out' (Edwards 1996). But it is not a 'policing action' (Apple 1996). I did not set out to deliberately fashion a purist or singular version of the field; although the inclusions and exclusions announced by the collection will have something of that effect. It is by no means an 'innocent text'. All disciplines are fields of struggle and arenas of interest. They are made up of sets of 'discourse communities' which 'produce knowledge and establish the conditions for who speaks and who gets heard' (Brantlinger 1997). These interests have a number of dimensions; there is the personal – related to the satisfactions, reputations and status of those in positions of power and patronage, expressions of identity; there are the vested – the material rewards from career, position and publication; and the ideological – matters of value, personal philosophy and political commitment. Such interests are at stake in decisions, appointments and influences which shape the field of sociology of education and its rewards. For example, they are reflected in the efforts of scholars of colour, women, gay and lesbian and disabled scholars to rework the boundaries, the analytical tools and theoretical bases of the sociology of education; and in doing so, secure positions and grants, become published and take control of key journals or create new ones. Such struggles take place, in an intellectual register, on the floor of conferences and in the pages of journals but they are also played-out, micropolitically (Ball 1987), in editors' offices, in department meetings and in appointing committees. These struggles are also embedded in 'the hidden curriculum in graduate sociology departments' (Margolis and Romero 1998). This hidden curriculum, Margolis and Romero suggest, takes two forms. There is the 'weak' form, which defines and attempts to control what it means 'to be a sociologist'. This is the professionalisation process within which certain methods, topics, concerns and dispositions are validated as 'good sociology'. This is described by Bourdieu (1988: 56) as the 'corporeal hexis'; that is 'the visceral form of recognition of everything which constitutes the existence of the group, its identity, its truth, and which the group must reproduce in order to reproduce itself'. There is also the 'strong' form which works to reproduce stratified and unequal social relations – reinforcing, in particular, the control and influence of white, male scholars (see Bagilhole 1993 and Henry 1990). In part, the point I am making here is that the sociology of education has its own sociology; its own 'collective scientific unconscious', in Bourdieu's words, and its own particular conditions of production, which at different points in time have set different limits upon thought through the deployment of specific sets of theories, problems and categories. It will become obvious from the chapters included here that one very powerful aspect of the sociological unconscious is its 'Westernism'. The European and Anglo-Saxon philosophical traditions, to all intents and purposes, define the sociology of education. Despite the important and lively histories of the sociology of education in Latin America and Japan, Korea and Taiwan in particular, the locus of control over the field is firmly located in 'the north'.

It is the case, clearly, that the development and discontinuities within sociology and the sociology of education, as one would expect, both reflect and respond to changes in society; although I would not want to suggest that there is a uniform and direct relationship between social and political context and the preoccupations and dispositions of the academy. The work of the social sciences also works back on society. It certainly feeds into the social professions; although less directly now than in the past. Many developments within these 'human sciences', like the sociology of education, function politically and are intimately imbricated in the practical management of social and political problems. The idea that human sciences, like sociology, stand outside or above the political agenda of the management of the population or somehow have a neutral status embodied in a free-floating progressive rationalism is a dangerous and debilitating conceit. The 'scientific' or theoretical vocabulary may distance researchers from the subjects of their activity but, at the same time, it also constructs a 'gaze' that renders the 'landscape of the social' ever more visible and produces or contributes to discourses which create 'subject positions' for people to occupy.

Bearing in mind these issues and difficulties, I outline below a brief and schematic 'disputational' history of the sociology of education using a set of key 'turning points' as historical and ideological markers, as gaps and spaces, within which the discipline can be located. I am certainly not attempting to be exhaustive or representative in this history but rather illustrative and indicative. In particular, in focusing on feminism(s) as the 'second turn', I am not intending to demote or marginalise work on 'race', sexuality or disability. Feminism serves as a major 'case in point', a challenge to orthodoxy and a significant re-orienting influence within the sociology of education. Each of the turning points also reflect and refract fashions

and conflicts within mainstream sociological theory. The evolution of the sociology of education is clearly related but, again, not always directly, to developments in the mainstream.
As will become evident, there are a variety of descriptors in play here which represent various
debates, positions and dichotomies in social science more generally – e.g. positivism, naturalism,
critical, interpretative, postmodern, emancipatory, redemptive. These descriptors are used
by sociologists of education to locate themselves, often over and against others, in a field of
dispute and contention. Relations of difference and opposition are established. While some
of the relations among these terms will, I hope, become clear, I do not have the space
here to specify each of these in detail. I refer the reader to the references and the relevant
chapters in the collection.

Turning points

Let me be clear. In focusing on these turning points, these disputational moments, I am not
intending to suggest that what has taken place are the sort of revolutionary paradigm shifts
that Kuhn identifies in the natural sciences. These are not points of thorough-going conversion across the whole discipline, rather they contribute to the proliferation and sedimentation
of perspectives and standpoints, the multiple traditions, within the sociology of education.
They add and re-orient rather than displace. Nor am I intending to construct a simple, linear
'history' here. There are discontinuities and reactions which have to be accounted for as
fields of study are struggled over by 'traditionalists' and usurpers. As in the first turning point,
despite the powerful and sustained criticisms of naturalism, or what Noblit and Pink (1995)
call the *empirical-analytic* tradition, this remains the dominant tradition within US sociology of
education.

> That this is so is evident in the contents of the 'official' journal of the field here, *Sociology
> of Education*. While the journal is a forum for some of the most technically sophisticated
> empirical work . . . it has been much less apt to publish the interpretative, critical and/or
> post-modern traditions.
>
> (Apple 1996: 126)

And, indeed, both in the US and the UK there has been a recent resurgence of interest in,
and support for, empirical-analytic social science, particularly in response to the call for
research to provide 'evidence' for policy and practice (see Oakley 2000).

Interpretivism/anti-naturalism

As the term suggests, the naturalist tradition attempts to equate the social world with the
natural world and to transpose the methods and perspectives of the natural sciences into the
social sciences – correlational research, field experiments, random controlled trials and such
like. These methods are to provide the basis for objectivity-seeking, quantitative research which
would produce fact-like conclusions and law-like generalisations about human behaviour and
social interaction. In its application and development in the field of education, this approach
is sometimes represented as 'educational sociology' (e.g. Coleman and Blau and Duncan)
in the US or in the UK as the 'political arithmetic' tradition (e.g. Halsey, Floud, Heath and
Banks; see Halsey *et al.* (1997) for examples) rather than and as distinct from 'the sociology
of education'. Lynch (1999: 7) calls these researchers 'equality empiricists'. The central concerns of 'educational sociology' are descriptive and structural and focus upon patterns of
educational opportunity and social mobility within industrial democracy – 'the problematics
of social stratification and status attainment' (Apple 1996: 127). That is, the investigation of
the relationships between social origins (almost exclusively social class/SES) and educational

achievement – sometimes termed 'redemptive sociology'. To coin yet another descriptor, this is 'black box' sociology; exclusively focusing upon the inputs and outputs of education and neglecting and, indeed, methodologically unable to access, the processes of educating.

The critique of naturalism and the empirical/analytic tradition in the sociology of education began in earnest in the 1970s from three very different directions which were unified briefly in relation to their object of opposition – the three being; neo-Marxism, interactionism and the sociology of knowledge. These are often rendered together as 'the new sociology of education' (see Young 1971, Whitty 1985 and Wexler 1987 for overviews). At the centre of the new sociology of education (NSOE) was a focus upon the processes of educational transmission. With some simplification, neo-Marxism provided attention to the relationships between forms of schooling experience and the labour process and the reproduction of class relations within schools and classrooms (best represented in Bowles and Gintis' (1976) 'correspondence principle'; see also Torres, Chapter 8); interactionism, via school-based ethnography, offered a way of exploring the construction of students' and teachers' social identities and generating descriptive accounts of the realisation of social control and social selection in classrooms (see Pollard, Chapter 14; O'Donnell and Sharpe, Chapter 5; and Woods and Jeffrey, Chapter 11); the sociology of knowledge problematised subject and school knowledge attending in particular to the underlying rules shaping the social construction of the curriculum and pedagogic practices (see Bernstein, Chapter 10; and Power *et al.*, Chapter 13) and later to the historical and political struggles over subject status and content (see Apple, Chapter 9). Wexler (1982: 275) puts it like this: 'In the early 1970s we applied the sociology of knowledge to education and attacked the surface of liberal knowledge.' These analyses and critiques of liberal knowledge and liberal pedagogies, and their links to inequalities and oppressions, also laid the groundwork for a new 'possibilitarian' sociology of schooling; critical pedagogy and the teacher as transformative intellectual – a new form of cultural politics or what Giroux (1992) terms 'border crossings'.

The NSOE was, to variable extents, 'radical', in contrast to the 'reformism' of the empirical/analytic tradition.

> They saw that the 'old' approach to the sociology of education reinforced the view that social justice has not been well served by comprehensivisation and that the distribution of social possibilities was not being dramatically 'equalised', but they were less willing to accept that nothing could be done about it.
>
> (Green and Whitty 1994: 8)

Significantly also, in relation to the earlier discussion of the sociology of sociology, Green and Whitty (1994: 7) make the point that: 'Sociologically, NSOE was part of a professionalising occupational structure which simultaneously experienced a process of professional segmentation and sharper identity formation as it staked its claim for inclusion in higher education.'

In the ensuing decades, each of the elements of the uneasy alliance which made up the NSOE developed its own intellectual trajectory. And despite various attempts at strategic integration (notably Sharp and Green (1975) *Education and Social Control*, and Willis (1977) *Learning to Labour*, both neo-Marxist ethnographies of schooling) the basic epistemological and ontological tensions between neo-Marxism and interactionism in particular – macro/micro; control/order; negotiated/structured social realities; structure/process – were a source of continuing mutual critique. Moore (1996) refers to a 'fundamental ambiguity' in the relationship between the NSOE and what he calls 'phenomenological sociology'. Again with some simplicity each of these positions has evolved into a more extensive and diverse tradition, what Noblit and Pink (1995) call, respectively, the *critical* and the *interpretative*. In many respects the inheritors of the NSOE are American theorists and researchers like Apple, Giroux, McLaren and Wexler each of whom, in different ways, has fused Marxism, interactionism and the sociology of knowledge into a set of multi-purpose, critical, analytic tools (see Apple (1996) for a discussion). Indeed, theoretical purism in the sociology of education is increasingly rare and what Lather (1991: 7) names 'conjunction' – the 'unprecedented cross-disciplinary fertilisation of ideas' – is more and more common. In the 1990s, the critical tradition has mutated further to incorporate aspects of postmodernism and address the critical analysis of educational policy and educational reform (Ball, Chapter 7).

In several respects, despite the continuing importance of the theoretical differences and tensions outlined above, one key legacy of the first turning point in the sociology of education is methodological – and I mean to use the term in its precise sense. This is the break with the positivist and scientific assumptions and practices of empirical/analytical methods. As Searle (1999: 21) explains it:

> The positivist vision in social research is an optimistic, moral commitment to a realm of ideas felt to have universal validity, located in a world that is independent of local human concerns, though it is ultimately created by human labour.

In contrast, at this stage, qualitative research was grounded in a dual commitment to realism (the discovery and representation of respondents' meanings) and constructivism (the idea that social actors are active interpreters of the social world). The primary concern of the study of social life from this perspective is thus to understand the meanings that people give to their actions and the actions of those others who share their social world. This understanding, it is argued, is best achieved through intimate and prolonged participation in the social settings under study. Thus, in a classic statement of this position, it is argued that: 'No theorising, however ingenious, and no observance of scientific protocol, however meticulous, are substitutes for developing a familiarity with what is actually going on in the sphere of life under study' (Blumer 1969: 39).

The interpretative break with positivism is typically represented, in crude terms, as the opposition between the quantitative and qualitative which is taken to stand for two 'fundamentally opposed approaches to the study of the social world' (Hammersley 1992: 159). Like all binaries, this opposition obscures as much as it reveals – Searle (1999: 49) suggests the division is artificial and rhetorical – but for now it will serve a purpose. To whatever extent these differences are based upon 'creation myths' (Hammersley 1995), they still provide sociologists of education with major sources of epistemological identity. The qualitative legacy also cuts across, in very different ways, the two further turning points discussed below. Hammersley (1992: 11–12) outlines the qualitative challenge to naturalism as resting on five main criticisms:

1 That the structured character of the data collection process involves the imposition of the researcher's assumptions about the social world and consequently reduces the chances of discovering evidence discrepant with those assumptions.
2 That making claims about what happens in 'natural' settings on the basis of data produced in settings that have been specially set up by the researcher – whether experimental or formal interview – is to engage in a largely implicit and highly questionable form of generalisation.
3 That to rely on what people say about what they believe and do, without also observing what they do, is to neglect the complex relationship between attitudes and behaviour; just as to rely on observation without also talking with people in order to understand their perspectives is to risk misinterpreting their actions.
4 That quantitative analysis reifies social phenomena by treating them as more clearly defined and distinct than they are, and by neglecting the processes by which they develop and change.

5   That quantitative analysis assumes that people's actions are the mechanical products of psychological and social factors thereby neglecting the creative role of individual cognition and group interaction.

In contrast, the emphasis in the interpretative tradition as Mehan (1992) puts it, is on 'social agency, cultural mediation and constitutive activity' (p. 1). At the risk of creating confusion, it is of course the case that the interpretative tradition and the qualitative method are each themselves 'conjunctions' of often quite disparate theories and epistemologies – symbolic interactionism, ethnomethodology and phenomenology among others. Furthermore, as qualitative methods have gained in popularity and legitimacy within the sociology of education, there has also been a process of applying the logic of positivism to qualitative research – particularly in relation to achieving validity, reliability and replicability – usually in response to criticisms of the 'softness' of the interpretative method (for example LeCompte and Goetz 1982, Miles and Huberman 1984, and Lincoln and Guba 1985). Nonetheless, the interpretive criticisms of positivism continue and have been given new impetus by both the feminist and postmodern turns.

A final point about the analytical possibilities opened up by the new sociology of education; the role of reflexivity. The NSOE laid the groundwork for auto-critique: 'In rejecting the positivist view of social reality, social scientists are faced with an expansive propagation of contending ideas that raise serious questions about the legitimacy and authority of scholarly practice' (Goodman 1992: 118). These possibilities were taken up and taken in a new direction by the feminist turn.

Feminism/anti-essentialism

If neo-Marxism and interpretivism were the major new elements of the sociology of education of the 1970s, it was the 'minority epistemologies' or what are sometimes called 'standpoint theories' – gender, race, sexuality and disability – that were to the fore in the 1980s. 'Standpoint theory involves the attribution of epistemic privilege to socially marginalised groups, enabling those who have otherwise been objectified to enter the research process as knowledge-makers' (Morley 1996: 236). Importantly then, returning to an earlier theme, the assertion of standpoint theories involved the development of critiques both for and of sociology. Focusing on the absence of gender as a topic and the absence of women from sociological practice: 'The real and symbolic silencing of women has a long history and is inscribed across philosophical, literary, legal, popular cultural, natural and social science discourses' (Luke 1994: 211). Feminist sociologists were seeking to escape these silences and unpick the 'scientific collective unconscious' of the discipline. This challenge included both making the process of research itself, the academic mode of production, into a researchable topic – as part of what Stanley (1990) calls feminist praxis – and setting out to search for the researcher's subjectivity (Peshkin 1988). It also involved a questioning of individualist, competitive modes of research, and masculinist research styles, and their replacement with collaborative feminist styles (Cook and Fonow 1990) and latterly attempting to find participatory and 'non-violent' relationships with the researched (Lather 1997). Harding (1986) extends this further to argue for a form of social inquiry as 'craft work', as against the bureaucratised and industrialised modes of modern social research. In all this is a basic challenge to the male researcher's 'God's eye view' (Nicholson 1991).

In sexing the subject, and the researcher, feminist critiques introduced a new kind of ontological sensitivity into the sociology of education and brought new areas of social life and social activity – sexuality and the emotions in particular – into the purview of the field (see Reay, Chapter 2). That is, feminism made the personal political; feminist research has been described as 'passionate scholarship' (Dubois 1983). In beginning to ask serious questions about the nature of gender and thus, more generally, about the nature of social identity, feminist critiques set in train the demise of essentialism. Substantively in the sociology of education particular attention was given by feminists to gender stereotyping in schools and the reproduction of demarcations between masculine and feminine, the 'creation of opposites', through the curriculum and classroom practices (see Davies, Chapter 6). In this respect, there was a direct taking up of the perspectives and methods of the sociology of knowledge and school ethnography. Also of crucial importance in feminist sociology, and deriving from Marxist and neo-Marxist materialism, is the ideology of 'patriarchy': 'it is patriarchy — the male hierarchical ordering of society, preserved through marriage and the family via the sexual division of labour — that is the core of women's oppression' (Clarricoates 1980). Patriarchy plays a key role in the preparation of labour power for capital and the reproduction of the social order: 'an engine of inequality had emerged by which women's unpaid labour became available to the school system' (Smith 1998: 13). Patriarchy is also embedded in, and reproduced within, sexual relations. Other feminists addressed themselves to the violence against, and sexual harassment of, young women in schools and other educational institutions; what Kenway and Fitzclarence (1997) refer to as 'poisonous pedagogies'.

On the one hand, while it is important to point up the play of multiple epistemologies within feminist sociology of education we can also signal the unity of the feminist project in relation to method — the qualitative method or what Lather (1997) calls generically 'feminist ethnography'. In part, this rests upon the idea of 'giving voice' to the silenced and oppressed, what Marcus (1986) refers to as 'the ethnographer as midwife' and in part involves 'being at risk in the face of practices and discourses into which one inquires' (Harraway 1997: 190). On the other hand, it is also important to underline the interplay and tensions between and within the standpoint positions and, in particular, the critiques of 'mainstream' feminism made by lesbians and women of colour. In opening up new frames of analysis and new lines of enquiry, as the 'new sociology' critics had done before them, feminists were also opening up themselves for critique. To a great extent the theoretical emphasis on sexual difference in much feminist writing rests upon a simple, gendered binary. This gives rise to a preoccupation, as part of the general political project of feminism, with the shared experiences of women across the divisions of race, class, sexual orientation, age or culture. 'In such theories the diversity of women's experience is often lumped into the category "women's experience", or women as a class, presumably in an effort to provide the basis for a collective feminist subject' (Sawicki 1991: 17). Lesbians and women of colour beg to differ! 'Woman', it is argued, frequently stands for white, middle-class, heterosexual females (Knowles and Mercer 1992).

> As a Black, lesbian, feminist, socialist, poet, mother of two including one boy, and a member of an interracial couple, I usually find myself part of some group in which the majority defines me as deviant, difficult, inferior or just plain 'wrong'. From my membership of all these groups I have learned that oppression and the intolerance of difference come in all shapes and sizes and colors and sexualities.
>
> (Lorde 1983)

Elsewhere, Lorde (1984: 115) makes the point that it is not the differences between women that separate them it is 'our refusal to recognise those differences'. The unpacking of feminism, using feminism's own tools, is also an attack upon the notion of a hierarchy of oppressions and has led to a much greater emphasis upon the concept of diversity and the complex interplay of inequalities and oppressions. Diversity is also a key element of postmodernist theorising.

Postmodernism/anti-humanism

> Postmodernity, one may say, is modernity without illusions . . . The illusions in question boil down to the belief that the 'messiness' of the human state is but a temporary and repairable state sooner or later to be replaced by the orderly and systematic rule of reason.
>
> (Bauman 1993: 32)

The postmodern or linguistic turn can be seen, in typical paradoxical fashion, both as an invigoration of, and threat to, the sociology of education, or rather to modernist social science generally. It is 'the end' of social science and a new beginning. As Bloom (1987: 379) describes it, this is 'the last, predictable stage in the suppression of reason and the denial of the possibility of truth in the name of philosophy'. Postmodern theory presents a challenge to a whole raft of fundamental, often dearly cherished but sometimes un-examined, assumptions in sociological practice; most obviously and profoundly the deployment of totalising 'grand narratives'. Large, all-encompassing and systemic 'explanations' of 'the social' are disrupted and eschewed by postmodernism. Lyotard quite simply defines the postmodern as 'incredulity towards meta-narratives'. As a result: 'Over the last two decades "postmodernism" has become a concept to be wrestled with, and such a battleground of conflicting opinions and political forces that it can no longer be ignored' (Harvey 1989: 39).

Once again, but more so, this major 'turn' turns social science back upon itself. In this case it is the very possibility of social science as a meaningful practice that is being challenged (or at least severely chastened). As Lather (1988: 7) explains: 'What is destroyed by the post-structuralist suspicion of the lust for authoritative accounts is not meaning, but claims to the unequivocal dominance of any one meaning.' In the modernist fight-back against the postmodern onslaught, this suspicion of authoritative meaning is subjected to the charge of 'relativism', which is 'everywhere abominated' (Barnes and Bloor 1991: 21). Relativism is often taken to require the removal of any possibility for certainty, especially the ability to make rational and moral judgements but more accurately it is a refusal to accept foundational truth claims; instead, all ontologies and epistemologies are viewed as historically contextual and socially conditioned. Postmodernism eschews the idea of an 'originary position' outside of the social or outside the discourse from which authoritative judgements can be made. Rather *authority* is viewed as 'the prize for which the competing vocabularies vie with one another' (Fish 1994: 10–11). Truth rests on the workings of power and material interests. All of this requires the rigorous scrutiny of the assumptions that shape the meaning of research itself. Taking postmodernism very seriously also means a careful re-examination of structuralism, realism and agency and that keystone of the Western 'enlightenment legacy', the pursuit of better futures – the relationships between knowledge and progress/social criticism and political liberation. As suggested by the quote above from Bauman, postmodernism raises serious doubts about the possibility of sociology as a redemptive enterprise. All of this can produce either a stultifying methodological self absorption or a new creativity in sociological theorising and exciting moments of 'profane illumination' (Benjamin 1978).

The postmodern turn itself should not however be presented 'out of' social and historical context. In particular, postmodernism needs to be distinguished from, and related to, postmodernity – a new state of world affairs – postmodern times. Postmodernism is thus a theory or a cultural attitude or sensibility which is embedded in, or responsive to, 'the end of modernity'. In Jameson's (1984) particular conception postmodernism is 'the cultural logic of late capitalism' or again, for Lyotard (1984: 170), the term postmodern 'designates the state of our culture following transformations which, since the end of the nineteenth century, have altered the game rules for science, literature and the arts'. In another sense, the postmodern world is denoted by the consumption of style, the exchange value of appearance and of pleasure and desire. All of which are particularly susceptible to discursive and textual readings.

Rather than deal with society and culture as 'raw realities', as materialities, postmodern researchers (if that is not an oxymoron) address society and culture as though it were a text or system of signs. In this view texts and language speak through us, they 'author' us, 'make us up', they make our agency possible, and are thus, by definition, the primary object of concern. It is through texts that we recognise ourselves, come to 'be' ourselves. Thus, for example, there is the research interest in 'narratives', the linguistic and stylistic resources we use to 'tell' ourselves, and in 'discourse', the statements which provide a language for talking about and producing knowledge about a topic (see Davies, Chapter 6). Knowledge is then 'a material practice that constitutes the "self"' (Popkewitz and Brennan 1998: 5). All of this rests on a reversal of the relationship between language and the objects language describes – between signifiers and the signified – and on the notion that language brings facts and objects into being, that they have no essence which precedes their linguistic articulation. Again here, once taken seriously, the basic assumptions and practices of sociological method are necessarily subject to critique. Social scientists can no longer claim to act upon or report a social world independent of their descriptions of it, although of course we continue to do so.

Of course, many sociologists do not take postmodernism seriously, in part perhaps because they regard postmodernism itself as lacking seriousness and condemn it as ironic, nihilistic and narcissistic, and apolitical. Indeed, for some feminists postmodernism is 'a problem', even just 'boys' games', particularly in as much as postmodernism critiques the 'oppressions' embedded within the humanist tradition upon which 'women's liberation' draws. For others, postmodernism offers an extension to and new possibilities for critique and for situated struggle. Kenway (1997: 132) goes as far as to argue that: 'In many senses feminist postmodernism has become "The New Way" to approach feminist research, pedagogy and politics'; but also warns that 'when one takes this new way, one confronts many confusions, difficulties, dilemmas and dangers'.

It is important again, even more important in this case, to make the point that postmodern thought is a 'conjunction', a disparate, internally disputatious, range of positions. Generally, Lather (1988) suggests that the names that sociologists use to represent themselves are best referred to in the plural – feminisms, phenomenologies, Marxisms, postmodernisms. In the case of postmodernism there are as many differences between the work, say, of Foucault, Derrida and Baudrillard as there are commonalities. One of the problems with some of the criticisms of postmodernism(s) is a total failure to distinguish such differences and thence a failure of credibility.

In highlighting the importance of these 'turning points' and the disputes and struggles that ensue I am also highlighting, in effect, the differences and discontinuities which play across the sociology of education, and that is important. Nonetheless, there is another 'story' in this history, a set of continuities within difference. Rhoads (1997: 7) for example, notes that: 'The work of postmodernists, feminists and critical theorists has been particularly attentive to issues of positionality and representation'. The history of the sociology of education is also a history of common concerns, elisions and linkages. Despite the essential disputatiousness of the field, a good deal of contemporary work, as noted already, is eclectic and integrationist – conciliatory (see Tamboukou and Ball 2003). Not that this is easily achieved. Apple (1996: 141) writes of 'the difficult problem of *simultaneously* thinking about both the specificity of different practices, and the forms of articulated unity they constitute'. He goes on to argue however that:

> it is exactly this issue of simultaneity, of thinking neo [Marxism] and post [modernism] together, of actively enabling the tensions within and among them to help form our research, that will solidify previous understandings, avoid the loss of collective memory of the gains that have been made, and generate new insights and new actions.

To a great extent the vitality and purposefulness of the project of the sociology of educa-tion, and its attraction for students and practitioners, is underpinned by the continuing cross-play of tensions and disputes, not the least those tensions between, to borrow Moore's (1996: 159) formulation, critical research 'of' education and research 'for' education. However, this cross-play of positions, currents and influences is also a major challenge for a newcomer seeking a sensible grasp of the field. This collection is aimed at making that grasp just a little easier.

The chapters

As you will see the chapters are organised under seven topics, in pairs. This approach seemed a good way of conveying the diversity and debate that are so prominent in soci-ology and the sociology of education. There are different ways of theorising or researching the same issue; different epistemologies and ontologies are deployed; analyses work at different levels and use different methods and conceptual tools. However, not all of the pairs work as contrasts or in terms of their differences, some are complementary.

The collection starts with 'Social class'. Sociology has a long tradition of attempting to link an individual's life chances to clearly defined social locations. Social class has been the central variable in this endeavour, until recently, in UK sociology of education. Pierre Bourdieu's chapter presents a 'non-minimalist' account of social class and class reproduction. It deals with a set of resources, obligations, relationships and constraints which are involved in the day-to-day processes of social reproduction. Diane Reay's chapter is complementary. It uses Bourdieu's framework to unpick some examples of contemporary social class inequality. There is a sense in this pairing of the relationship between theory-work and research-work.

The next pair of chapters, which deal with 'Globalisation and the economy', might well have been better placed first. In different ways they explain the meanings and slippages and disputes that are invested in the term globalisation and offer two very different emphases in terms of the effects of globalisation in education. Brown and Lauder stress economic changes, whereas Peter Jarvis discusses 'cultural convergence'.

The chapters on 'Gender' differ in a variety of ways although both deal with qualitative data. Mike O'Donnell and Sue Sharpe write in a realist, ethnographic mode, and attend to the relationship between structures and identity. Bronwyn Davies offers a discursive analysis, a good example of careful post-structuralist work.

The chapters on 'Regulation', mine and Carlos Alberto Torres', again contrast. His is a classic Marxist account, mine deploys a variety of post-structural theorists: Foucault, Lyotard and Deleuze. His is top-down, mine is capillary, more bottom-up. But I would want to argue that they are complementary rather than oppositional.

The chapters on 'Curriculum' are two heavyweights, Michael W. Apple and Basil Bernstein. Both are structuralists but of very different kinds: Bernstein, a Durkheimian and highly theo-retical; Apple, neo-Marxist and engaged with curriculum politics. Bernstein is more about organisation and Apple more about agents.

The 'Teacher' chapters contrast similarly. Peter Woods and Bob Jeffrey start in classrooms with ethnographic data. John Smyth and Geoffrey Shacklock have a much broader canvas but do relate global economic changes to the teacher in the classroom.

The 'Students and classroom' chapters are just different. The chapter by Sally Power *et al.* uses Bernsteinian concepts to examine home–school relationships. Andrew Pollard relates sociological concerns to social psychology and learning theory but, again, is trying to concep-tualise home–school relations as part of a sociology of learning. Both chapters focus on the student at the centre of socio-cultural processes but they deploy somewhat different research techniques.

References

Apple, M. (1996) 'Power, meaning and identity: critical sociology of education in the United States', *British Journal of Sociology of Education* 17 (2): 125–44.

Bagilhole, B. (1993) 'How to keep a good woman down: an investigation of the role of institutional factors in the process of discrimination against women academics', *British Journal of Sociology of Education* 14 (3): 261–74.

Ball, S. J. (1987) *The Micropolitics of the School: Towards a Theory of School Organization*, London: Routledge.

Barnes, B. and D. Bloor (1991) 'Relativism, rationalism and the sociology of knowledge', in M. Hollis and S. Lukes (eds), *Rationality and Relativism*, Cambridge, MA: MIT Press.

Bauman, Z. (1993) *Postmodern Ethics*, Oxford: Blackwell.

Benjamin, W. (1978) *Reflections*, New York: Harcourt, Brace, Jovanovich.

Bloom, A. (1987) *The Closing of the American Mind: How Higher Education has Failed Democracy and Impoverished the Souls of Today's Students*, New York: Simon & Schuster.

Blumer, H. (1969) *Symbolic Interactionism: Perspective and Method*, Englewood Cliffs, NJ: Prentice Hall.

Bourdieu, P. (1988) *Homo Academicus*, Cambridge: Polity Press.

Bowles, S. and H. Gintis (1976) *Schooling in Capitalist America*, London: Routledge & Kegan Paul.

Brantlinger, E. (1997) 'Using ideology: cases of non-recognition of the politics of research and practice in special education', reprinted in S. J. Ball (ed.) (2000) *Sociology of Education: Major Themes*, London: Routledge.

Clarricoates, K. (1980) 'The importance of being Ernest . . . Emma . . . Tom . . . Jane', in R. Deem (ed.), *Schooling for Women's Work*, London: Routledge & Kegan Paul.

Cook, J. and M. Fonow (1990) 'Knowledge and women's interest', in J. Neilson (ed.), *Feminist Research Methods*, Boulder, CO: Westview Press.

Davies, W. B. (1996) 'Durkheim and the sociology of education in Britain', *British Journal of Sociology of Education* 15 (1): 3–25.

Dubois, E. C. (1983) 'Passionate scholarship: notes on values, knowing and method in feminist social science', in G. Bowles and R. Duelli Klein (eds), *Theories of Women's Studies*, London: Routledge & Kegan Paul.

Edwards, D. (1996) *Discourse and Cognition*, London: Sage.

Fish, S. (1994) *There's No Such Thing as Free Speech . . . and it's a Good Thing Too*, Oxford: Oxford University Press.

Giroux, H. (1992) *Border Crossings: Cultural Workers and the Politics of Education*, New York: Routledge.

Goodman, J. (1992) 'Theoretical and practical considerations for school-based research in a post-positivist era', *International Journal of Qualitative Studies in Education* 5 (2): 117–33.

Goodson, I. (1983) *School Subjects and Curriculum Change*, Beckenham: Croom Helm.

Green, T. and G. Whitty (1994) *The Legacy of the New Sociology of Education: A View from the Institute of Education*, New Orleans: American Educational Research Association Annual Meeting.

Halsey, A. H., H. Lauder, P. Brown, and A. Stuart Wells (eds) (1997) *Education: Culture, Economy and Society*, Oxford: Oxford University Press.

Hammersley, M. (1992) *What's Wrong with Ethnography*, London: Routledge.

Hammersley, M. (1995) *The Politics of Social Research*, London: Sage.

Harding, S. (1986) *The Science Question in Feminism*, Milton Keynes: Open University Press.

Harraway, D. (1997) *Modest-Witness @ Second-Millenium. FemaleMan c-MeetspOncoMouse tm: Feminism and Technoscience*, London: Routledge.

Harvey, D. (1989) *The Condition of Postmodernity*, Oxford: Basil Blackwell.

Henry, M. (1990) 'Voices of academic women on feminine gender scripts', *British Journal of Sociology of Education* 11 (2): 121–36.

Jameson, F. (1984) 'Postmodernism or the cultural logic of late capitalism', *New Left Review* (146).

Kenway, J. (1997) 'Having a postmodern turn or postmodernist angst: a disorder experienced by an author who is not yet dead or even close to it', in A. H. Halsey, H. Lauder, P. Brown and A. Stuart Wells (eds), *Education: Culture, Economy, Society*, Oxford: Oxford University Press.

Kenway, J. and Fitzclarence, L. (1997) 'Masculinity, violence and schooling: challenging "poisonous pedagogies"', reprinted in S. J. Ball (ed.) (2000) *Sociology of Education: Major Themes*, London: Routledge.

Knowles, C. and S. Mercer (1992) 'Feminism and antiracism: an exploration of the political possibilities', in J. Donald and A. Rattansi (eds), *'Race', Culture and Difference*, London: Sage.

Lather, P. (1988) *Ideology and Methodological Attitude*, New Orleans: American Educational Research Association Annual Meeting.

Lather, P. (1991) *Getting Smart Feminist Research and Pedagogy Within/in the Postmodern*, New York: Routledge.

Lather, P. (1993) 'Fertile obsession: validity after poststructuralism', *Sociological Quarterly* 34 (4): 673–93.

Lather, P. (1997) 'Drawing the line at angels: working the ruins of feminist ethnography', reprinted in S. J. Ball (ed.) (2000) *Sociology of Education: Major Themes*, London: Routledge.

Lorde, A. (1983) 'There is no hierarchy of oppressions', *Homophobia and Education* 14 (3–4): 9.

Lorde, A. (1984) *Sister Outsider*, New York: Crossing Press.

Luke, C. (1994) 'Women in the Academy: the politics of speech and silence', *British Journal of Sociology of Education* 15 (2): 211–30.

Lynch, K. (1999) *Equality in Education*, Dublin: Gill and Macmillan.

Lyotard, J.-F. (1984) *The Postmodern Condition: A Report on Knowledge*, Manchester: Manchester University Press.

Maclure, M. (2003) *Discourse in Educational and Social Research*, Buckingham: Open University Press.

Marcus, G. E. (1986) 'Contemporary problems of ethnography in the modern world system', in J. Clifford and G. E. Marcus (eds), *Writing Culture: The Poetics and Politics of Ethnography*, Berkeley, CA: University of California Press.

Margolis, E. and Romero, M. (1998) 'The department is very male, very white, very old, and very conservative: the functioning in the hidden curriculum of graduate sociology departments', reprinted in S. J. Ball (ed.) (2000) *Sociology of Education: Major Themes*, London: Routledge.

Mehan, H. (1992) 'Understanding inequality in schools: the contribution of interpretive studies', *Sociology of Education* 65 (January): 1–20.

Moore, R. (1996) 'Back to the future: the problems of change and possibilities of advance in the sociology of education', *British Journal of Sociology of Education* 17 (2): 145–62.

Morley, L. (1996) 'Interrogating patriarchy: the challenges of feminist research', in L. Morely and V. Walsh (eds), *Breaking Boundaries*, London: Taylor & Francis.

Nicholson, L. (1991) 'Introduction', in L. Nicholson (ed.), *Feminism/Postmodernism*, New York: Routledge.

Noblit, G. and W. Pink (1995) 'Mapping the alternative paths of the sociology of education', in W. Pink and G. Noblit (eds), *Continuity and Contradiction: The Futures of the Sociology of Education*, Cresskill, NJ: Hampton Press.

Oakley, A. (2000) *Experiments in Knowing: Gender and Method in the Social Sciences*, Cambridge: Polity Press.

Peshkin, A. (1988) 'In search of subjectivity – one's own', *Educational Researcher* 17 (7): 17–22.

Popkewitz, T. and M. Brennan (1998) 'Restructuring of social and political theory in education: Foucault and a social epistemology of school practices', in T. Popkewitz and M. Brennan (eds), *Foucault's Challenge: Discourse, Knowledge and Power in Education*, New York: Teachers College Press.

Rhoads, R. A. (1997) 'Crossing sexual orientation borders: collaborative strategies for dealing with issues of positionality and representation', *Qualitative Studies in Education* 10 (1): 7–23.

Sawicki, J. (1991) *Disciplining Foucault: Feminism, Power and the Body*, New York: Routledge.

Searle, C. (1999) *The Quality of Qualitative Research*, London: Sage.

Sharp, R. and T. Green (1975) *Education and Social Control*, London: Routledge & Kegan Paul.

Smith, D. (1998) 'The underside of schooling – restructuring, privatisation and women's unpaid work', *Journal of Just and Caring Education* 4 (1): 11–29.

Stanley, L. (1990) 'Feminist praxis and the academic mode of production', in L. Stanley (ed.), *Feminist Praxis*, New York: Routledge.

Tamboukou, M. and S. J. Ball (2003) *Dangerous Encounters: Genealogy and Ethnography*, New York: Peter Lang.

Wexler, P. (1982) 'Structure, text and subject: a critical sociology of school knowledge', in M. Apple (ed.), *Cultural and Economic Reproduction in Education*, London: Routledge & Kegan Paul.

Wexler, P. (1987) *Social Analysis of Education: After the New Sociology of Education*, London: Routledge.

Whitty, G. (1985) *Sociology and School Knowledge*, London: Methuen.

Willis, P. (1977) *Learning to Labour: How Working Class Kids Get Working Class Jobs*, Farnborough: Saxon House.

Young, M. F. D. (ed.) (1971) *Knowledge and Control*, London: Collier-Macmillan.

PART 1

SOCIAL CLASS

CHAPTER 1

THE FORMS OF CAPITAL

Pierre Bourdieu

Richardson, J., *Handbook of Theory and Research for the Sociology of Education* (1986), Westport, CT: Greenwood, pp. 241–58

The social world is accumulated history, and if it is not to be reduced to a discontinuous series of instantaneous mechanical equilibria between agents who are treated as interchangeable particles, one must reintroduce into it the notion of capital and with it, accumulation and all its effects. Capital is accumulated labor (in its materialized form or its "incorporated," embodied form) which, when appropriated on a private, i.e., exclusive, basis by agents or groups of agents, enables them to appropriate social energy in the form of reified or living labor. It is a *vis insita*, a force inscribed in objective or subjective structures, but it is also a *lex insita*, the principle underlying the immanent regularities of the social world. It is what makes the games of society—not least, the economic game—something other than simple games of chance offering at every moment the possibility of a miracle. Roulette, which holds out the opportunity of winning a lot of money in a short space of time, and therefore of changing one's social status quasi-instantaneously, and in which the winning of the previous spin of the wheel can be staked and lost at every new spin, gives a fairly accurate image of this imaginary universe of perfect competition or perfect equality of opportunity, a world without inertia, without accumulation, without heredity or acquired properties, in which every moment is perfectly independent of the previous one, every soldier has a marshal's baton in his knapsack, and every prize can be attained, instantaneously, by everyone, so that at each moment anyone can become anything. Capital, which, in its objectified or embodied forms, takes time to accumulate and which, as a potential capacity to produce profits and to reproduce itself in identical or expanded form, contains a tendency to persist in its being, is a force inscribed in the objectivity of things so that everything is not equally possible or impossible.[1] And the structure of the distribution of the different types and subtypes of capital at a given moment in time represents the immanent structure of the social world, i.e., the set of constraints, inscribed in the very reality of that world, which govern its functioning in a durable way, determining the chances of success for practices.

It is in fact impossible to account for the structure and functioning of the social world unless one reintroduces capital in all its forms and not solely in the one form recognized by economic theory. Economic theory has allowed to be foisted upon it a definition of the economy of practices which is the historical invention of capitalism;

Originally published as "Okonomisches Kapital, kulturelles Kapital, soziales Kapital," in Soziale Ungleichheiten (Soziale Welt, Sonderheft 2), edited by Reinhard Kreckel. Goettingen: Otto Schartz & Co., 1983, pp. 183–98. [. . .] Translated by Richard Nice.

and by reducing the universe of exchanges to mercantile exchange, which is objectively and subjectively oriented toward the maximization of profit, i.e., (economically) *self-interested*, it has implicitly defined the other forms of exchange as noneconomic, and therefore *disinterested*. In particular, it defines as disinterested those forms of exchange which ensure the *transubstantiation* whereby the most material types of capital—those which are economic in the restricted sense—can present themselves in the immaterial form of cultural capital or social capital and vice versa. Interest, in the restricted sense it is given in economic theory, cannot be produced without producing its negative counterpart, disinterestedness. The class of practices whose explicit purpose is to maximize monetary profit cannot be defined as such without producing the purposeless finality of cultural or artistic practices and their products; the world of bourgeois man, with his double-entry accounting, cannot be invented without producing the pure, perfect universe of the artist and the intellectual and the gratuitous activities of art-for-art's sake and pure theory. In other words, the constitution of a science of mercantile relationships which, inasmuch as it takes for granted the very foundations of the order it claims to analyze—private property, profit, wage labor, etc.—is not even a science of the field of economic production, has prevented the constitution of a general science of the economy of practices, which would treat mercantile exchange as a particular case of exchange in all its forms.

It is remarkable that the practices and assets thus salvaged from the "icy water of egotistical calculation" (and from science) are the virtual monopoly of the dominant class—as if economism had been able to reduce everything to economics only because the reduction on which that discipline is based protects from sacrilegious reduction everything which needs to be protected. If economics deals only with practices that have narrowly economic interest as their principle and only with goods that are directly and immediately convertible into money (which makes them quantifiable), then the universe of bourgeois production and exchange becomes an exception and can see itself and present itself as a realm of disinterestedness. As everyone knows, priceless things have their price, and the extreme difficulty of converting certain practices and certain objects into money is only due to the fact that this conversion is refused in the very intention that produces them, which is nothing other than the denial (*Verneinung*) of the economy. A general science of the economy of practices, capable of reappropriating the totality of the practices which, although objectively economic, are not and cannot be socially recognized as economic, and which can be performed only at the cost of a whole labor of dissimulation or, more precisely, *euphemization*, must endeavor to grasp capital and profit in all their forms and to establish the laws whereby the different types of capital (or power, which amounts to the same thing) change into one another.[2]

Depending on the field in which it functions, and at the cost of the more or less expensive transformations which are the precondition for its efficacy in the field in question, capital can present itself in three fundamental guises: as *economic capital*, which is immediately and directly convertible into money and may be institutionalized in the form of property rights; as *cultural capital*, which is convertible, in certain conditions, into economic capital and may be institutionalized in the form of educational qualifications; and as *social capital*, made up of social obligations ("connections"), which is convertible, in certain conditions, into economic capital and may be institutionalized in the form of a title of nobility.[3]

Cultural capital

Cultural capital can exist in three forms: in the *embodied* state, i.e., in the form of long-lasting dispositions of the mind and body; in the *objectified* state, in the form of cultural goods (pictures, books, dictionaries, instruments, machines, etc.), which are the trace or realization of theories or critiques of these theories, problematics, etc.; and in the *institutionalized* state, a form of objectification which must be set apart because, as will be seen in the case of educational qualifications, it confers entirely original properties on the cultural capital which it is presumed to guarantee.

The reader should not be misled by the somewhat peremptory air which the effort at axiomization may give to my argument.[4] The notion of cultural capital initially presented itself to me, in the course of research, as a theoretical hypothesis which made it possible to explain the unequal scholastic achievement of children originating from the different social classes by relating academic success, i.e., the specific profits which children from the different classes and class fractions can obtain in the academic market, to the distribution of cultural capital between the classes and class fractions. This starting point implies a break with the presuppositions inherent both in the commonsense view, which sees academic success or failure as an effect of natural aptitudes, and in human capital theories. Economists might seem to deserve credit for explicitly raising the question of the relationship between the rates of profit on educational investment and on economic investment (and its evolution). But their measurement of the yield from scholastic investment takes account only of *monetary* investments and profits, or those directly convertible into money, such as the costs of schooling and the cash equivalent of time devoted to study; they are unable to explain the different proportions of their resources which different agents or different social classes allocate to economic investment and cultural investment because they fail to take systematic account of the structure of the differential chances of profit which the various markets offer these agents or classes as a function of the volume and the composition of their assets (see esp. Becker 1964b). Furthermore, because they neglect to relate scholastic investment strategies to the whole set of educational strategies and to the system of reproduction strategies, they inevitably, by a necessary paradox, let slip the best hidden and socially most determinant educational investment, namely, the domestic transmission of cultural capital. Their studies of the relationship between academic ability and academic investment show that they are unaware that ability or talent is itself the product of an investment of time and cultural capital (Becker 1964a, pp. 63–66). Not surprisingly, when endeavoring to evaluate the profits of scholastic investment, they can only consider the profitability of educational expenditure for society as a whole, the "social rate of return," or the "social gain of education as measured by its effects on national productivity" (Becker 1964b, pp. 121, 155). This typically functionalist definition of the functions of education ignores the contribution which the educational system makes to the reproduction of the social structure by sanctioning the hereditary transmission of cultural capital. From the very beginning, a definition of human capital, despite its humanistic connotations, does not move beyond economism and ignores, *inter alia*, the fact that the scholastic yield from educational action depends on the cultural capital previously invested by the family. Moreover, the economic and social yield of the educational qualification depends on the social capital, again inherited, which can be used to back it up.

The embodied state. Most of the properties of cultural capital can be deduced from the fact that, in its fundamental state, it is linked to the body and presupposes embodiment. The accumulation of cultural capital in the embodied state, i.e., in the form of what is called culture, cultivation, *Bildung*, presupposes a process of embodiment, incorporation, which, insofar as it implies a labor of inculcation and assimilation, costs time, time which must be invested personally by the investor. Like the acquisition of a muscular physique or a suntan, it cannot be done at second hand (so that all effects of delegation are ruled out).

The work of acquisition is work on oneself (self-improvement), an effort that presupposes a personal cost (*on paie de sa personne*, as we say in French), an investment, above all of time, but also of that socially constituted form of libido, *libido sciendi*, with all the privation, renunciation, and sacrifice that it may entail. It follows that the least inexact of all the measurements of cultural capital are those which take as their standard the length of acquisition—so long, of course, as this is not reduced to length of schooling and allowance is made for early domestic education by giving it a positive value (a gain in time, a head start) or a negative value (wasted time, and doubly so because more time must be spent correcting its effects), according to its distance from the demands of the scholastic market.[5]

This embodied capital, external wealth converted into an integral part of the person, into a habitus, cannot be transmitted instantaneously (unlike money, property rights, or even titles of nobility) by gift or bequest, purchase or exchange. It follows that the use or exploitation of cultural capital presents particular problems for the holders of economic or political capital, whether they be private patrons or, at the other extreme, entrepreneurs employing executives endowed with a specific cultural competence (not to mention the new state patrons). How can this capital, so closely linked to the person, be bought without buying the person and so losing the very effect of legitimation which presupposes the dissimulation of dependence? How can this capital be concentrated—as some undertakings demand—without concentrating the possessors of the capital, which can have all sorts of unwanted consequences?

Cultural capital can be acquired, to a varying extent, depending on the period, the society, and the social class, in the absence of any deliberate inculcation, and therefore quite unconsciously. It always remains marked by its earliest conditions of acquisition which, through the more or less visible marks they leave (such as the pronunciations characteristic of a class or region), help to determine its distinctive value. It cannot be accumulated beyond the appropriating capacities of an individual agent; it declines and dies with its bearer (with his biological capacity, his memory, etc.). Because it is thus linked in numerous ways to the person in his biological singularity and is subject to a hereditary transmission which is always heavily disguised, or even invisible, it defies the old, deep-rooted distinction the Greek jurists made between inherited properties (*ta patroa*) and acquired properties (*epikteta*), i.e., those which an individual adds to his heritage. It thus manages to combine the prestige of innate property with the merits of acquisition. Because the social conditions of its transmission and acquisition are more disguised than those of economic capital, it is predisposed to function as symbolic capital, i.e., to be unrecognized as capital and recognized as legitimate competence, as authority exerting an effect of (mis)recognition, e.g., in the matrimonial market and in all the markets in which economic capital is not fully recognized, whether in matters of culture, with the great art collections or great cultural foundations, or in social welfare, with the economy of generosity and the gift. Furthermore, the specifically symbolic logic of distinction additionally secures material and symbolic profits for the possessors of a large cultural capital: any given cultural competence (e.g., being able to read in a world of illiterates) derives a scarcity value from its position in the distribution of cultural capital and yields profits of distinction for its owner. In other words, the share in profits which scarce cultural capital secures in class-divided societies is based, in the last analysis, on the fact that all agents do not have the economic and cultural means for prolonging their children's education beyond the minimum necessary for the reproduction of the labor-power least valorized at a given moment.[6]

Thus the capital, in the sense of the means of appropriating the product of accumulated labor in the objectified state which is held by a given agent, depends for its real efficacy on the form of the distribution of the means of appropriating the accumulated and objectively available resources; and the relationship of appropriation between an agent and the resources objectively available, and hence the profits they produce, is mediated by the relationship of (objective and/or subjective) competition between himself and the other possessors of capital competing for the same goods, in which scarcity—and through it social value—is generated. The structure of the field, i.e., the unequal distribution of capital, is the source of the specific effects of capital, i.e., the appropriation of profits and the power to impose the laws of functioning of the field most favorable to capital and its reproduction.

But the most powerful principle of the symbolic efficacy of cultural capital no doubt lies in the logic of its transmission On the one hand, the process of appropriating objectified cultural capital and the time necessary for it to take place mainly depend on the cultural capital embodied in the whole family—through (among other things) the generalized Arrow effect and all forms of implicit transmission.[7] On the other hand, the initial accumulation of cultural capital, the precondition for the fast, easy accumulation of every kind of useful cultural capital, starts at the outset, without delay, without wasted time, only for the offspring of families endowed with strong cultural capital; in this case, the accumulation period covers the whole period of socialization. It follows that the transmission of cultural capital is no doubt the best hidden form of hereditary transmission of capital, and it therefore receives proportionately greater weight in the system of reproduction strategies, as the direct, visible forms of transmission tend to be more strongly censored and controlled.

It can immediately be seen that the link between economic and cultural capital is established through the mediation of the time needed for acquisition. Differences in the cultural capital possessed by the family imply differences first in the age at which the work of transmission and accumulation begins—the limiting case being full use of the time biologically available, with the maximum free time being harnessed to maximum cultural capital—and then in the capacity, thus defined, to satisfy the specifically cultural demands of a prolonged process of acquisition. Furthermore, and in correlation with this, the length of time for which a given individual can prolong his acquisition process depends on the length of time for which his family can provide him with the free time, i.e., time free from economic necessity, which is the precondition for the initial accumulation (time which can be evaluated as a handicap to be made up).

The objectified state. Cultural capital, in the objectified state, has a number of properties which are defined only in the relationship with cultural capital in its embodied form. The cultural capital objectified in material objects and media, such as writings, paintings, monuments, instruments, etc., is transmissible in its materiality. A collection of paintings, for example, can be transmitted as well as economic capital (if not better, because the capital transfer is more disguised). But what is transmissible is legal ownership and not (or not necessarily) what constitutes the precondition for specific appropriation, namely, the possession of the means or "consuming" a painting or using a machine, which, being nothing other than embodied capital, are subject to the same laws of transmission.[8]

Thus cultural goods can be appropriated both materially—which presupposes economic capital—and symbolically—which presupposes cultural capital. It follows that the owner of the means of production must find a way of appropriating either the embodied capital which is the precondition of specific appropriation or the services of the holders of this capital. To possess the machines, he only needs economic capital; to appropriate them and use them in accordance with their specific purpose (defined by the cultural capital, of scientific or technical type, incorporated in them), he must have access to embodied cultural capital, either in person or by proxy. This is no doubt the basis of the ambiguous status of cadres (executives and engineers). If it is emphasized that they are not the possessors (in the strictly economic sense) of the means of production which they use, and that they derive profit from their own cultural capital only by selling the services and products which it makes possible, then they will be classified among the dominated groups; if it is emphasized that they draw their profits from the use of a particular form of capital, then they will be classified among the dominant groups. Everything suggests that as the cultural capital incorporated in the means of production increases (and with it the period of embodiment needed to acquire the means of appropriating it), so the collective strength of the holders of cultural capital would tend to increase—if the holders of the dominant type of capital (economic capital) were not able to set the holders of cultural capital in competition with one another. (They are, moreover, inclined to competition by the very conditions in which they are selected and trained, in particular by the logic of scholastic and recruitment competitions.)

Cultural capital in its objectified state presents itself with all the appearances of an autonomous, coherent universe which, although the product of historical action, has its own laws, transcending individual wills, and which, as the example of language well illustrates, therefore remains irreducible to that which each agent, or even the aggregate of the agents, can appropriate (i.e., to the cultural capital embodied in each agent or even in the aggregate of the agents). However, it should not be forgotten that it exists as symbolically and materially active, effective capital only insofar as it is appropriated by agents and implemented and invested as a weapon and a stake in the struggles which go on in the fields of cultural production (the artistic field, the scientific field, etc.) and, beyond them, in the field of the social classes—struggles in which the agents wield strengths and obtain profits proportionate to their mastery of this objectified capital, and therefore to the extent of their embodied capital.[9]

The institutionalized state. The objectification of cultural capital in the form of academic qualifications is one way of neutralizing some of the properties it derives from the fact that, being embodied, it has the same biological limits as its bearer. This objectification is what makes the difference between the capital of the auto-didact, which may be called into question at any time, or even the cultural capital of the courtier, which can yield only ill-defined profits, of fluctuating value, in the market of high-society exchanges, and the cultural capital academically sanctioned by legally guaranteed qualifications, formally independent of the person of their bearer. With the academic qualification, a certificate of cultural competence which confers on its holder a conventional, constant, legally guaranteed value with respect to culture, social alchemy produces a form of cultural capital which has a relative autonomy vis-à-vis its bearer and even vis-à-vis the cultural capital he effectively possesses at a given moment in time. It institutes cultural capital by collective magic, just as, according to Merleau-Ponty, the living institute their dead through the ritual of mourning. One has only to think of the *concours* (competitive recruitment examination) which, out of the continuum of infinitesimal differences between performances, produces sharp, absolute, lasting differences, such as that which separates the last successful candidate from the first unsuccessful one, and institutes an essential difference between the officially recognized, guaranteed competence and simple cultural capital, which is constantly required to prove itself. In this case, one sees clearly the performative magic of the power of instituting, the power to show forth and secure belief or, in a word, to impose recognition.

By conferring institutional recognition on the cultural capital possessed by any given agent, the academic qualification also makes it possible to compare qualification holders and even to exchange them (by substituting one for another in succession). Furthermore, it makes it possible to establish conversion rates between cultural capital and economic capital by guaranteeing the monetary value of a given academic capital.[10] This product of the conversion of economic capital into cultural capital establishes the value, in terms of cultural capital, of the holder of a given qualification relative to other qualification holders and, by the same token, the monetary value for which it can be exchanged on the labor market (academic investment has no meaning unless a minimum degree of reversibility of the conversion it implies is objectively guaranteed). Because the material and symbolic profits which the academic qualification guarantees also depend on its scarcity, the investments made (in time and effort) may turn out to be less profitable than was anticipated when they were made (there having been a *de facto* change in the conversion rate between academic capital and economic capital). The strategies for converting economic capital into cultural capital, which are among the short-term factors of the schooling explosion and the inflation of qualifications, are governed by changes in the structure of the chances of profit offered by the different types of capital.

Social capital

Social capital is the aggregate of the actual or potential resources which are linked to possession of a durable network of more or less institutionalized relationships of mutual acquaintance and recognition—or in other words, to membership in a group[11]—which provides each of its members with the backing of the collectively-owned capital, a "credential" which entitles them to credit, in the various senses of the word. These relationships may exist only in the practical state, in material and/or symbolic exchanges which help to maintain them. They may also be socially instituted and guaranteed by the application of a common name (the name of a family, a class, or a tribe or of a school, a party, etc.) and by a whole set of instituting acts designed simultaneously to form and inform those who undergo them; in this case, they are more or less really enacted and so maintained and reinforced, in exchanges. Being based on indissolubly material and symbolic exchanges, the establishment and maintenance of which presuppose reacknowledgment of proximity, they are also partially irreducible to objective relations of proximity in physical (geographical) space or even in economic and social space.[12]

The volume of the social capital possessed by a given agent thus depends on the size of the network of connections he can effectively mobilize and on the volume of the capital (economic, cultural or symbolic) possessed in his own right by each of those to whom he is connected.[13] This means that, although it is relatively irreducible to the economic and cultural capital possessed by a given agent, or even by the whole set of agents to whom he is connected, social capital is never completely independent of it because the exchanges instituting mutual acknowledgment presuppose the reacknowledgment of a minimum of objective homogeneity, and because it exerts a multiplier effect on the capital he possesses in his own right.

The profits which accrue from membership in a group are the basis of the solidarity which makes them possible.[14] This does not mean that they are consciously pursued as such, even in the case of groups like select clubs, which are deliberately organized in order to concentrate social capital and so to derive full benefit from the multiplier effect implied in concentration and to secure the profits of membership—material profits, such as all the types of services accruing from useful relationships, and symbolic profits, such as those derived from association with a rare, prestigious group.

The existence of a network of connections is not a natural given, or even a social given, constituted once and for all by an initial act of institution, represented, in the case of the family group, by the genealogical definition of kinship relations, which is the characteristic of a social formation. It is the product of an endless effort at institution, of which institution rites—often wrongly described as rites of passage—mark the essential moments and which is necessary in order to produce and reproduce lasting, useful relationships that can secure material or symbolic profits (see Bourdieu 1982). In other words, the network of relationships is the product of investment strategies, individual or collective, consciously or unconsciously aimed at establishing or reproducing social relationships that are directly usable in the short or long term, i.e., at transforming contingent relations, such as those of neighborhood, the workplace, or even kinship, into relationships that are at once necessary and elective, implying durable obligations subjectively felt (feelings of gratitude, respect, friendship, etc.) or institutionally guaranteed (rights). This is done through the alchemy of *consecration*, the symbolic constitution produced by social institution (institution as a relative—brother, sister, cousin, etc.—or as a knight, an heir, an elder, etc.) and endlessly reproduced in and through the exchange (of gifts, words, women, etc.) which it encourages and which presupposes and produces mutual knowledge and recognition. Exchange transforms the things exchanged into signs of recognition and, through the mutual recognition and the recognition of group membership which it implies, re-produces the group. By the same token, it reaffirms the limits of the group, i.e., the limits beyond which the constitutive exchange—trade, commensality, or marriage—cannot take place. Each member of the group is thus instituted as a custodian of the limits of the group: because the definition of the criteria of entry is at stake in each new entry, he can modify the group by modifying the limits of legitimate exchange through some form of misalliance. It is quite logical that, in most societies, the preparation and conclusion of marriages should be the business of the whole group, and not of the agents directly concerned. Through the introduction of new members into a family, a clan, or a club, the whole definition of the group, i.e., its fines, its boundaries, and its identity, is put at stake, exposed to redefinition, alteration, adulteration. When, as in modern societies, families lose the monopoly of the establishment of exchanges which can lead to lasting relationships, whether socially sanctioned (like marriage) or not, they may continue to control these exchanges, while remaining within the logic of laissez-faire, through all the institutions which are designed to favor legitimate exchanges and exclude illegitimate ones by producing occasions (rallies, cruises, hunts, parties, receptions, etc.), places (smart neighborhoods, select schools, clubs, etc.), or practices (smart sports, parlor games, cultural ceremonies, etc.) which bring together, in a seemingly fortuitous way, individuals as homogeneous as possible in all the pertinent respects in terms of the existence and persistence of the group.

The reproduction of social capital presupposes an unceasing effort of sociability, a continuous series of exchanges in which recognition is endlessly affirmed and reaffirmed. This work, which implies expenditure of time and energy and so, directly or indirectly, of economic capital, is not profitable or even conceivable unless one invests in it a specific competence (knowledge of genealogical relationships and of real connections and skill at using them, etc.) and an acquired disposition to acquire and maintain this competence, which are themselves integral parts of this capital.[15] This is one of the factors which explain why the profitability of this labor of accumulating and maintaining social capital rises in proportion to the size of the capital. Because the social capital accruing from a relationship is that much greater to the extent that the person who is the object of it is richly endowed with capital (mainly social, but also cultural and even economic capital), the possessors of an inherited social capital, symbolized by a great name, are able to transform all circumstantial relationships into lasting connections They are sought after for their social capital and, because they are well known, are worthy of being known ("I know him well"); they do not need to "make the acquaintance" of all their "acquaintances"; they are known to more people than they know, and their work of sociability, when it is exerted, is highly productive.

Every group has its more or less institutionalized forms of delegation which enable it to concentrate the totality of the social capital, which is the basis of the existence of the group (a family or a nation, of course, but also an association or a party), in the hands of a single agent or a small group of agents and to mandate this plenipotentiary, charged with *plena potestas agendi et loquendi*,[16] to represent the group, to speak and act in its name and so, with the aid of this collectively owned capital, to exercise a power incommensurate with the agent's personal contribution. Thus, at the most elementary degree of institutionalization, the head of the family, the *pater familias*, the eldest, most senior member, is tacitly recognized as the only person entitled to speak on behalf of the family group in all official circumstances. But whereas in this case, diffuse delegation requires the great to step forward and defend the collective honor when the honor of the weakest members is threatened. The institutionalized delegation, which ensures the concentration of social capital, also has the effect of limiting the consequences of individual lapses by explicitly delimiting responsibilities and authorizing the recognized spokesmen to shield the group as a whole from discredit by expelling or excommunicating the embarrassing individuals.

If the internal competition for the monopoly of legitimate representation of the group is not to threaten the conservation and accumulation of the capital which is the basis of the group, the members of the group must regulate the conditions of access to the right to declare oneself a member of the group and, above all, to set oneself up as a representative (delegate, plenipotentiary, spokesman. etc.) of the whole group, thereby committing the social capital of the whole group. The title of nobility is the form *par excellence* of the institutionalized social capital which guarantees a particular form of social relationship in a lasting way. One of the paradoxes of delegation is that the mandated agent can exert on (and, up to a point, against) the group the power which the group enables him to concentrate. (This is perhaps especially true in the limiting cases in which the mandated agent creates the group which creates him but which only exists through him.) The mechanisms of delegation and representation (in both the theatrical and the legal senses) which fall into place— that much more strongly, no doubt, when the group is large and its members weak—as one of the conditions for the concentration of social capital (among other reasons, because it enables numerous, varied, scattered agents to act as one man and to overcome the limitations of space and time) also contain the seeds of an embezzlement or misappropriation of the capital which they assemble.

This embezzlement is latent in the fact that a group as a whole can be represented, in the various meanings of the word, by a subgroup, clearly delimited and perfectly visible to all, known to all, and recognized by all, that of the *nobiles*, the "people who are known," the paradigm of whom is the nobility, and who may speak on behalf of the whole group, represent the whole group, and exercise authority in the name of the whole group. The noble is the group personified. He bears the name of the group to which he gives his name (the metonymy which links the noble to his group is clearly seen, when Shakespeare calls Cleopatra "Egypt" or the King of France "France," just as Racine calls Pyrrhus "Epirus"). It is by him, his name, the difference it proclaims, that the members of his group, the liegemen, and also the land and castles, are known and recognized. Similarly, phenomena such as the "personality cult" or the identification of parties, trade unions, or movements with their leader are latent in the very logic of representation. Everything combines to cause the signifier to take the place of the signified, the spokesmen that of the group he is supposed to express, not least because his distinction, his "outstanding-ness," his visibility constitute the essential part, if not the essence, of this power, which, being entirely set within the logic of knowledge and acknowledgment, is fundamentally a symbolic power; but also because the representative, the sign, the emblem, may be, and create, the whole reality of groups which receive effective social existence only in and through representation.[17]

Conversions

The different types of capital can be derived from *economic capital*, but only at the cost of a more or less great effort of transformation, which is needed to produce the type of power effective in the field in question. For example, there are some goods and services to which economic capital gives immediate access, without secondary costs; others can be obtained only by virtue of a social capital of relation-ships (or social obligations) which cannot act instantaneously, at the appropriate moment, unless they have been established and maintained for a long time, as if for their own sake, and therefore outside their period of use, i.e., at the cost of an invest-ment in sociability which is necessarily long-term because the time lag is one of the factors of the transmutation of a pure and simple debt into that recognition of nonspecific indebtedness which is called gratitude.[18] In contrast to the cynical but also economical transparency of economic exchange, in which equivalents change hands in the same instant, the essential ambiguity of social exchange, which presup-poses misrecognition, in other words, a form of faith and of bad faith (in the sense of self-deception), presupposes a much more subtle economy of time.

So it has to be posited simultaneously that economic capital is at the root of all the other types of capital and that these transformed, disguised forms of economic capital, never entirely reducible to that definition, produce their most specific effects only to the extent that they conceal (not least from their possessors) the fact that economic capital is at their root, in other words—but only in the last analysis—at the root of their effects. The real logic of the functioning of capital, the conver-sions from one type to another, and the law of conservation which governs them cannot be understood unless two opposing but equally partial views are superseded: on the one hand, economisn, which, on the grounds that every type of capital is reducible in the last analysis to economic capital, ignores what makes the specific efficacy of the other types of capital, and on the other hand, semiologism (nowa-days represented by structuralism, symbolic interactionism, or ethnomethodology), which reduces social exchanges to phenomena of communication and ignores the brutal fact of universal reducibility to economics.[19]

In accordance with a principle which is the equivalent of the principle of the conservation of energy, profits in one area are necessarily paid for by costs in another (so that a concept like wastage has no meaning in a general science of the economy of practices). The universal equivalent, the measure of all equivalences, is nothing other than labor-time (in the widest sense); and the conservation of social energy through all its conversions is verified if, in each case, one takes into account both the labor-time accumulated in the form of capital and the labor-time needed to transform it from one type into another.

It has been seen, for example, that the transformation of economic capital into social capital presupposes a specific labor, i.e., an apparently gratuitous expenditure of time, attention, care, concern, which, as is seen in the endeavor to personalize a gift, has the effect of transfiguring the purely monetary import of the exchange and, by the same token, the very meaning of the exchange. From a narrowly economic standpoint, this effort is bound to be seen as pure wastage, but in the terms of the logic of social exchanges, it is a solid investment, the profits of which will appear, in the long run, in monetary or other form. Similarly, if the best measure of cultural capital is undoubtedly the amount of time devoted to acquiring it, this is because the transformation of economic capital into cultural capital presupposes an expenditure of time that is made possible by possession of economic capital. More precisely, it is because the cultural capital that is effectively transmitted within the family itself depends not only on the quantity of cultural capital, itself accumulated by spending time, that the domestic group possess, but also on the usable time (particularly in the form of the mother's free time) available to it (by virtue of its economic capital, which enables it to purchase the time of others) to ensure the transmission of this capital and to delay entry into the labor market through prolonged schooling, a credit which pays off, if at all, only in the very long term.[20]

The convertibility of the different types of capital is the basis of the strategies aimed at ensuring the reproduction of capital (and the position occupied in social space) by means of the conversions least costly in terms of conversion work and of the losses inherent in the conversion itself (in a given state of the social power relations). The different types of capital can be distinguished according to their reproducibility or, more precisely, according to how easily they are transmitted, i.e., with more or less loss and with more or less concealment; the rate of loss and the degree of concealment tend to vary in inverse ratio. Everything which helps to disguise the economic aspect also tends to increase the risk of loss (particularly the intergenerational transfers). Thus the (apparent) incommensurability of the different types of capital introduces a high degree of uncertainty into all transactions between holders of different types. Similarly, the declared refusal of calculation and of guarantees which characterizes exchanges tending to produce a social capital in the form of a capital of obligations that are usable in the more or less long term (exchanges of gifts, services, visits, etc.) necessarily entails the risk of ingratitude, the refusal of that recognition of nonguaranteed debts which such exchanges aim to produce. Similarly, too, the high degree of concealment of the transmission of cultural capital has the disadvantage (in addition to its inherent risks of loss) that the academic qualification which is its institutionalized form is neither transmissible (like a title of nobility) nor negotiable (like stocks and shares). More precisely, cultural capital, whose diffuse, continuous transmission within the family escapes observation and control (so that the educational system seems to award its honors solely to natural qualities) and which is increasingly tending to attain full efficacy, at least on the labor market, only when validated by the educational system, i.e., converted into a capital of qualifications, is subject to a more disguised but more risky transmission than economic capital. As the educational qualification, invested with the specific force of the official, becomes the condition for legitimate access to a growing number of positions, particularly the dominant ones, the educational system tends increasingly to dispossess the domestic group of the monopoly of the transmission of power and privileges—and, among other things, of the choice of its legitimate heirs from among children of different sex and birth rank.[21] And economic capital itself poses quite different problems of transmission, depending on the particular form it takes. Thus, according to Grassby (1970), the liquidity of commercial capital, which gives immediate economic power and favors transmission, also makes it more vulnerable than landed property (or even real estate) and does not favor the establishment of long-lasting dynasties.

Because the question of the arbitrariness of appropriation arises most sharply in the process of transmission—particularly at the time of succession, a critical moment for all power—every reproduction strategy is at the same time a legitimation strategy aimed at consecrating both an exclusive appropriation and its reproduction. When the subversive critique which aims to weaken the dominant class through the principle of its perpetuation by bringing to light the arbitrariness of the entitlements transmitted and of their transmission (such as the critique which the Enlightenment *philosophes* directed, in the name of nature, against the arbitrariness of birth) is incorporated in institutionalized mechanisms (for example, laws of inheritance) aimed at controlling the official, direct transmission of power and privileges, the holders of capital have an ever greater interest in resorting to reproduction strategies capable of ensuring better-disguised transmission, but at the cost of greater loss of capital, by exploiting the convertibility of the types of capital. Thus the more the official transmission of capital is prevented or hindered, the more the effects of the clandestine circulation of capital in the form of cultural capital become determinant in the reproduction of the social structure. As an instrument of reproduction capable of disguising its own function, the scope of the educational system tends to increase, and together with this increase is the unification of the market in social qualifications which gives rights to occupy rare positions.

Notes

1 This inertia, entailed by the tendency of the structures of capital to reproduce themselves in institutions or in dispositions adapted to the structures of which they are the product, is, of course, reinforced by a specifically political action of concerted conservation, i.e., of demobilization and depoliticization. The latter tends to keep the dominated agents in the state of a practical group, united only by the orchestration of their dispositions and condemned to function as an aggregate repeatedly performing discrete, individual acts (such as consumer or electoral choices).
2 This is true of all exchanges between members of different fractions of the dominant class, possessing different types of capital. These range from sales of expertise, treatment, or other services which take the form of gift exchange and dignify themselves with the most decorous names that can be found (honoraria, emoluments, etc.) to matrimonial exchanges, the prime example of a transaction that can only take place insofar as it is not perceived or defined as such by the contracting parties. It is remarkable that the apparent extensions of economic theory beyond the limits constituting the discipline have left intact the asylum of the sacred, apart from a few sacrilegious incursions. Gary S. Becker, for example, who was one of the first to take explicit account of the types of capital that are usually ignored, never considers anything other than monetary costs and profits, forgetting the nonmonetary investments (*inter alia*, the affective ones) and the material and symbolic profits that education provides in a deferred, indirect way, such as the added value which the dispositions produced or

reinforced by schooling (bodily or verbal manners, tastes, etc.) or the relationships established with fellow students can yield in the matrimonial market (Becker 1964a).

3 *Symbolic capital*, that is to say, capital—in whatever form—insofar as it is represented, i.e., apprehended symbolically, in a relationship of knowledge or, more precisely, of misrecognition and recognition, presupposes the intervention of the habitus, as a socially constituted cognitive capacity.

4 When talking about concepts for their own sake, as I do here, rather than using them in research, one always runs the risk of being both schematic and formal, i.e., theoretical in the most usual and most usually approved sense of the word.

5 This proposition implies no recognition of the value of scholastic verdicts; it merely registers the relationship which exists in reality between a certain cultural capital and the laws of the educational market. Dispositions that are given a negative value in the educational market may receive very high value in other markets—not least, of course, in the relationships internal to the class.

6 In a relatively undifferentiated society, in which access to the means of appropriating the cultural heritage is very equally distributed, embodied culture does not function as cultural capital, i.e., as a means of acquiring exclusive advantages.

7 What I call the generalized Arrow effect, i.e., the fact that all cultural goods—paintings, monuments, machines, and any objects shaped by man, particularly all those which belong to the childhood environment—exert an educative effect by their mere existence, is no doubt one of the structural factors behind the "schooling explosion," in the sense that a growth in the quantity of cultural capital accumulated in the objectified state increases the educative effect automatically exerted by the environment. If one adds to this the fact that embodied cultural capital is constantly increasing, it can be seen that, in each generation, the educational system can take more for granted. The fact that the same educational investment is increasingly productive is one of the structural factors of the inflation of qualifications (together with cyclical factors linked to effects of capital conversion).

8 The cultural object, as a living social institution, is, simultaneously, a socially instituted material object and a particular class of habitus, to which it is addressed. The material object—for example, a work of art in its materiality—may be separated by space (e.g., a Dogon statue) or by time (e.g., a Simone Martini painting) from the habitus for which it was intended. This leads to one of the most fundamental biases of art history. Understanding the effect (not to be confused with the function) which the work tended to produce—for example, the form of belief it tended to induce— and which is the true basis of the conscious or unconscious choice of the means used (technique, colors, etc.), and therefore of the form itself, is possible only if one at least raises the question of the habitus on which it "operated."

9 The dialectical relationship between objectified cultural capital—of which the form *par excellence* is writing—and embodied cultural capital has generally been reduced to an exalted description of the degradation of the spirit by the letter, the living by the inert, creation by routine, grace by heaviness.

10 This is particularly true in France, where in many occupations (particularly the civil service) there is a very strict relationship between qualification, rank, and remuneration (translator's note).

11 Here, too, the notion of cultural capital did not spring from pure theoretical work, still less from an analogical extension of economic concepts. It arose from the need to identify the principle of social effects which, although they can be seen clearly at the level of singular agents—where statistical inquiry inevitably operates—cannot be reduced to the set of properties individually possessed by a given agent. These effects, in which spontaneous sociology readily perceives the work of "connections," are particularly visible in all cases in which different individuals obtain very unequal profits from virtually equivalent (economic or cultural) capital, depending on the extent to which they can mobilize by proxy the capital of a group (a family, the alumni of an elite school, a select club, the aristocracy, etc.) that is more or less constituted as such and more or less rich in capital.

12 Neighborhood relationships may, of course, receive an elementary form of institutionalization, as in the Bearn—or the Basque region—where neighbors, *lous besis* (a word which, in old texts, is applied to the legitimate inhabitants of the village, the

rightful members of the assembly), are explicitly designated, in accordance with fairly codified rules, and are assigned functions which are differentiated according to their rank (there is a "first neighbor," a "second neighbor," and so on), particularly for the major social ceremonies (funerals, marriages, etc.). But even in this case, the relationships actually used by no means always coincide with the relationships socially instituted.

13   Manners (bearing, pronunciation, etc.) may be included in social capital insofar as, through the mode of acquisition they point to, they indicate initial membership of a more or less prestigious group.

14   National liberation movements or nationalist ideologies cannot be accounted for solely by reference to strictly economic profits, i.e., anticipation of the profits which may be derived from redistribution of a proportion of wealth to the advantage of the nationals (nationalization) and the recovery of highly paid jobs (see Breton 1964). To these specifically economic anticipated profits, which would only explain the nationalism of the privileged classes, must be added the very real and very immediate profits derived from membership (social capital) which are proportionately greater for those who are lower down the social hierarchy ("poor whites") or, more precisely, more threatened by economic and social decline.

15   There is every reason to suppose that socializing, or, more generally, relational, dispositions are very unequally distributed among the social classes and, within a given class, among fractions of different origin.

16   A "full power to act and speak" (translator).

17   It goes without saying that social capital is so totally governed by the logic of knowledge and acknowledgment that it always functions as symbolic capital.

18   It should be made clear, to dispel a likely misunderstanding, that the investment in question here is not necessarily conceived as a calculated pursuit of gain, but that it has every likelihood of being experienced in terms of the logic of emotional investment, i.e., as an involvement which is both necessary and disinterested. This has not always been appreciated by historians, who (even when they are as alert to symbolic effects as E. P. Thompson) tend to conceive symbolic practices—powdered wigs and the whole paraphernalia of office—as explicit strategies of domination, intended to be seen (from below), and to interpret generous or charitable conduct as "calculated acts of class appeasement." This naively Machiavellian view forgets that the most sincerely disinterested acts may be those best corresponding to objective interest. A number of fields, particularly those which most tend to deny interest and every sort of calculation, like the fields of cultural production, grant full recognition, and with it the consecration which guarantees success, only to those who distinguish themselves by the immediate conformity of their investments, a token of sincerity and attachment to the essential principles of the field. It would be thoroughly erroneous to describe the choices of the habitus which lead an artist, writer, or researcher toward his natural place (a subject, style, manner, etc.) in terms of rational strategy and cynical calculation. This is despite the fact that, for example, shifts from one genre, school, or speciality to another, quasi-religious conversions that are performed "in all sincerity," can be understood as capital conversions, the direction and moment of which (on which their success often depends) are determined by a "sense of investment" which is the less likely to be seen as such the more skillful it is. Innocence is the privilege of those who move in their field of activity like fish in water.

19   To understand the attractiveness of this pair of antagonistic positions which serve as each other's alibi; one would need to analyze the unconscious profits and the profits of unconsciousness which they procure for intellectuals. While some find in economism a means of exempting themselves by excluding the cultural capital and all the specific profits which place them on the side of the dominant, others can abandon the detestable terrain of the economic, where everything reminds them that they can be evaluated, in the last analysis, in economic terms, for that of the symbolic. (The latter merely reproduce, in the realm of the symbolic, the strategy whereby intellectuals and artists endeavor to impose the recognition of their values, i.e., their value, by inverting the law of the market in which what one has or what one earns completely defines what one is worth and what one is—as is shown by the practice of banks which, with techniques such as the personalization of credit, tend to subordinate the granting of loans

and the fixing of interest rates to an exhaustive inquiry into the borrower's present and future resources.)

20 Among the advantages procured by capital in all its types, the most precious is the increased volume of useful time that is made possible through the various methods of appropriating other people's time (in the form of services). It may take the form either of increased spare time, secured by reducing the time consumed in activities directly channeled toward producing the means of reproducing the existence of the domestic group, or of more intense use of the time so consumed, by recourse to other people's labor or to devices and methods which are available only to those who have spent time learning how to use them and which (like better transport or living close to the place of work) make it possible to save time. (This is in contrast to the cash savings of the poor, which are paid for in time—do-it-yourself, bargain hunting, etc.) None of this is true of mere economic capital; it is possession of cultural capital that makes it possible to derive greater profit not only from labor-time, by securing a higher yield from the same time, but also from spare time, and so to increase both economic and cultural capital.

21 It goes without saying that the dominant fractions, who tend to place ever greater emphasis on educational investment, within an overall strategy of asset diversification and of investments aimed at combining security with high yield, have all sorts of ways of evading scholastic verdicts. The direct transmission of economic capital remains one of the principal means of reproduction, and the effect of social capital ("a helping hand," "string-pulling," the "old boy network") tends to correct the effect of academic sanctions. Educational qualifications never function perfectly as currency. They are never entirely separable from their holders: their value rises in proportion to the value of their bearer, especially in the least rigid areas of the social structure.

References

Becker, Gary S. *A Theoretical and Empirical Analysis with Special Reference to Education.* New York: National Bureau of Economic Research, 1964a.

—— *Human Capital.* New York: Columbia University Press, 1964b.

Bourdieu, Pierre. "Les rites d'institution." *Actes de la recherche en sciences sociales* 43 (1982): 58–63.

Breton, A. "The Economics of Nationalism." *Journal of Political Economy* 72 (1962): 376–86.

Grassby, Richard. "English Merchant Capitalism in the Late Seventeenth Century: The Composition of Business Fortunes." *Past and Present* 46 (1970): 87–107.

CHAPTER 2

FINDING OR LOSING YOURSELF?

Working-class relationships to education

Diane Reay

Journal of Education Policy (2001), 16 (4): 333–46

[. . .]

Introduction: the more things change the more they stay the same

> Was it possible that the children of the working class, however fortunate, however plucky, could hold their own later with those who in the formative years drank deep and long of every fountain of life? No. It's impossible. Below every strike, concealed behind legislation of every order, there is this fact – the higher nutrition of the favoured few as compared with the balked childhood of the majority. Nothing evens up this gross injustice.
>
> (Margaret McMillan 1912)

Andy Green (1990) in his survey of the rise of education systems in England, France and the USA singles out England as the most explicit example of the use of schooling by a dominant class to secure hegemony over subordinate groups. He argues that the growing middle-class commitment to working-class education in the late eighteenth and early nineteenth centuries 'was different in every conceivable way from their ideals in middle-class education . . . it was rather a way of ensuring that the sub-ordinate class would acquiesce in their own class aspirations' (Green 1990: 248). Adam Smith epitomized the English bourgeois viewpoint regarding working-class education in 'The Wealth of Nations':

> An instructed and intelligent people besides are always more decent and orderly than an ignorant one . . . less apt to be misled into any wanton or unnecessary opposition to due measures of the government.
>
> (Smith 1785: 305)

For Smith, as well as the vast majority of politicians and intellectuals of the day, the schooling of the working classes was always to be subordinate and inferior to that of the bourgeoise; a palliative designed to contain and pacify rather than to educate and liberate.

Writing about the introduction of state education for all, 100 years after the publication of 'The Wealth of Nations', Jane Miller asserts that 'the provision of education for working-class children was thought of by and large instrumentally, rather than as likely to contribute to the life possibilities of the children themselves' (Miller 1992: 2). When the English state schooling system was set up in the late nineteenth century the intention of the dominant classes was still to police and control the working classes rather than to educate them (Purvis 1980, Arnot 1983, Green 1990, Plummer 2000). Robert Lowe, writing in 1867, was representing the views of the vast majority of the middle and upper classes when he argued:

> If the lower classes must now be educated . . . they must be educated that they may appreciate and defer to a higher civilisation when they meet it.
>
> (Lowe 1867: 8–10)

In this chapter I argue that the contemporary educational system retains remnants of these past elite prejudices. We still have an educational system in which working-class education is made to serve middle-class interests.[1]

In England in the twenty-first century, 'those who govern are prisoners of a reassuring entourage of young, white, middle-class technocrats who often know almost nothing about the everyday lives of their fellow citizens and have no occasion to be reminded of their ignorance' (Bourdieu 1993: 627). This elitism has consequences for education as well as every other field of social policy. Within the educational system all the authority remains vested in the middle classes. Not only do they run the system, the system itself is one which valorizes middle- rather than working-class cultural capital. Regardless of what individual working-class males and females are able to negotiate and achieve for themselves within the educational field, the collective patterns of working-class trajectories within education remain sharply different from those of the middle classes, despite over a 100 years of universal state education (Halsey 1992, Egerton and Halsey 1993, Savage and Egerton 1997, Egerton and Savage 2000).

It is not surprising then that education for the working classes has traditionally been about failure; about 'being found out'. And this is not just an English phenomenon. Although class divisions have historically been, and currently remain, more polarized in England than in other countries, in many Western societies class remains a strong predictor of academic success, undermining claims that academic failure is rooted in factors largely unrelated to the social class of individual students (Connell 1995, Apple 1996, Gale and Densmore 2000). Educational systems across Western society:

> universally impose the same demands without any concern for universally distributing the means for satisfying them, thus helping to legitimate the inequality that one merely records and ratifies, while additionally exercising (first of all in the educational system) the symbolic violence associated with the effects of real inequality within formal equality.
>
> (Bourdieu 2000: 76)

However, the focus of this chapter is the English educational system and the class relationships that are played out within it. In England, in the minority of cases when the equation of working class plus education equals academic success, education is not about the valorization of working classness but its erasure; education as escape. As Sandy Brewer argues:

> Each successive generation of working-class children is seen as being both a threat to and hope for what society might be. Progress for the children has been framed in terms of disjunction and movement from – rather than a continuum or reproduction of – the culture and values of their parents.
>
> (Brewer 2000: 76)

We cannot talk about working-class relationships to education without examining dominant representations of the working classes. In Bourdieurian terms, the working classes both historically and currently are discursively constituted as an unknowing, uncritical, tasteless mass from which the middle classes draw their distinctions (Skeggs 2000). According to Carolyn Steedman (1985; 1986) working-class childhood is problematic because of the many ways in which it has been pathologized over the last century and a half. This process of pathologization operates through schooling by representing the children of the poor only as a measure of what they lack: 'they are falling-short of a more complicated and richly endowed "real" child' (Steedman 1986: 127). The lack of positive images of the working classes contributes to them being educationally disqualified and inadequately supported academically.

The working classes have never been in a position to influence dominant representations (Roberts 1999). If we examine historical antecedents of 'class' the term was generated to shore up and consolidate the identity of the bourgeoise and had no meaning for those to whom it was applied (Skeggs 2000). 'Working class' has always had negative connotations apart from a brief hiatus post World War II. When for about 20 years there was what Jon Cook (2000) calls a taste for the working classes – a time when working class histories were histories of plenitude rather than histories of lack. However by the mid-1970s this had begun to disintegrate as the UK saw the inception of a right-wing educational revolution that still continues under Tony Blair's New Labour Government.

Bev Skeggs (2000) argues that the politics of redistribution as a stage in the history of social policy neither lasted very long nor was particularly effective. The recent shift from a politics of redistribution to a politics of recognition has generated significant consequences for the politics of class. The growing gap between the rich and poor has become an accepted part of the 'ways things are' for many in England, often understood through discourses of individualization which attribute material success or failure to either individual effort, individual talent or a mixture of the two. Now in the wake of the working-class hero we have a revalorization of the middle classes. Where until very recently the middle classes opted in significant numbers to call themselves working class, it is now alright to be middle class, to send your child to selective schools and earn vast amounts of money. According to a recent issue of *The Sunday Times* even millionaires are not really rich any more. Making class invisible, which is the direction in which all the dominant discourses are moving, signals a historical stage in which, despite all the babble about risk and insecurity, the identity of the middle classes is assured.

Phil Cohen (2000) argues that the concept of the working class 'for itself' or 'in itself' has been replaced by the phenomenon of the working class 'from itself'. This process has been achieved primarily through education. It is the working classes who have been most affected by the contemporary culture of mass credentialism. Despite the advent of schooling for the masses over 100 years ago, education for a majority of the working classes has remained something to be got through rather than go into. Until now that is! Now we have a situation in which the working classes are rapidly moving from a position of marginalization to an ironic situation, given our consumer culture, in which capitalist privatized education is consuming the working classes rather than the other way round. As Bourdieu argues:

> By putting off, prolonging and consequently spreading out the process of elimination, the school system turns into a permanent home for potential outcasts, who bring to it the contradictions and conflicts associated with a type of education that is an end in itself.
>
> (Bourdieu 1993: 422)

Bourdieu's 'outcasts on the inside' are characterized by an enduring ambivalence about education. This ambivalence surrounding credentialism for the working classes arises from a crucial contradiction: on the one hand – desire for the material benefits increased credentialism brings; on the other hand – the alienation, cultural losses and subordination that continued domination within the educational field involves (Furlong and Cartmel 1997). In the twenty-first century growing numbers of the working classes are caught up in education either as escape, as a project for maximizing and fulfilling the self or a complicated mixture of the two. No longer limited to the advantaged few, education is increasingly positioned within dominant discourses as the new panacea for the masses. The UK Higher Education graduation rate of over 35% (the percentage of students graduating with a first degree at typical graduation age) is now greater than the US (OECD 2000) and the stated policy objective is for 40% of the age cohort to go to university by 2005, and 50% by 2010.

A recent controversy surrounding access to Oxford university (Freedland 2000, Ryle *et al.* 2000, Smithers 2000, Utley 2000) managed to overlook the most striking inequalities embedded in access to higher education. It seemed to indicate that class struggle under the New Labour Government is being misconstrued as competition between professional groupings in society who send their children to state schools and those professionals who pay to educate their children in the private sector. Gordon Brown, the Chancellor of the Exchequer, lambasted Oxford University for not offering a place to Laura Spence, a very high achieving pupil from a state compre hensive school. Yet, Laura from a professional background, with a father who is a senior civil servant and a mother who is a teacher, personifies the traditional applicant to elite universities. Over 80% of pupils with the best GCSE results – whatever sort of school they attend – come from social classes one and two (Ryan 2000).

Making difficult transitions: choosing hybridity?

I want to look more closely at some of the ways in which the current focus on widening participation in Higher Education is being played out in the lives of real nontraditional applicants – the working classes. In the ESRC project on access to higher education I worked on with Stephen Ball and Miriam David part of the qualitative sample of 120 HE applicants included 19 working-class mature students on an Access course in a London FE college.

The mature students were the first generation in their families to aim for university. Most (17) either came from solidly manual working-class backgrounds with parents who were builders, weavers and gardeners or else they had parents who had been employed in the service sector as shop assistants, restaurant managers and waitresses. However, the students themselves were not representative of the traditional working class. Two-thirds were women, one-quarter came from minority ethnic backgrounds, and only one was a white, working-class man who worked in industry. Yet they, rather than the outmoded traditional image of the male industrial labourer, represent the contemporary working classes – lone mothers, benefit recipients and low paid, casualized service workers (Reid 1998). In this section I try and capture some of the flavour of the difficult, sometimes tortuous, relationships these working-class adults had with education:

> There is a sort of community feel about Roehampton. It just seemed more of a community sort of feeling as opposed to a larger sized university and being lost within it. And being the type of person I am I like the idea I am going to be part of a community.
>
> (Debbie)

Debbie's fear of being lost within higher education exemplifies a number of complex issues that, in particular, working-class mature students confronted in relation to the field of higher education. The working-class students were trying to negotiate a difficult balance between investing in a new improved identity and holding on to a cohesive self that retained an anchor in what had gone before – between what Steph Lawler calls escape and 'holding on' (Lawler 2000). Unlike their younger counterparts there was a strong sense in many of the mature students' texts that part of the purpose of going to university was 'to find themselves':

> It's about me going to university, it's about finding out about me.
>
> (Denise)

> I want to find out what I can achieve.
>
> (Angie)

> I'd like to be doing something for me. I'd like to be, just me, well more of me, finding out what I'm capable of. And I don't want some man to give me a piece of paper to type, ever again.
>
> (Janice)

However, this emphasis on discovery, whether of unrealized potential or a more fulfilled self, has a negative tinge for the working-class students. Underlying feelings of hopeful anticipation there are confusions and ambiguities about the sort of self they are seeking, which the middle-class students do not have to deal with to anything like the same extent (Reay *et al.* 2001). We glimpse shadows, hear whispers of what Bourdieu refers to as the most unexpected of all the dramas and conflicts that emanate from upward mobility: 'the feelings of being torn that come from experiencing success as failure, or, better still, as transgression' (Bourdieu 1993: 510). Their transcripts hint at a delicate balance between realizing potential and maintaining a sense of an authentic self. Almost by definition, aspirant working classness is pretentious – a hankering after 'the Other' rather than an acceptance of the self. Bourdieu defines pretension as 'the recognition of distinction that is affirmed in the effort to possess it' (Bourdieu 1986: 251). Pretention according to Steph Lawler is embodied in those who are not what they seem to be, in whom there is a gap between being and seeming. The mature students, in particular the women, are well aware of this gap as one they risk opening up through higher education. While the middle-class mature students can talk easily in terms of becoming 'the real me' through higher education, such ways of relating to higher education are far more difficult for the working-class students. I suggest that among its many promises and possibilities, higher education poses a threat to both authenticity and a coherent sense of selfhood for these working-class mature students. Class hybridity does not sit easily with a sense of authenticity. Feelings of being an imposter are never far away. Yet there is a further double bind because I would also argue that while in the past, authenticity was often associated with working classness it is increasingly the middle-class self that is seen to be authentic. The 'genuine trustworthy solid, working classes' of the 50s and 60s seem to have slipped off the discursive agenda.

Education was, in the main, a world into which these mature students fitted uneasily:

> I don't see the point in spending my time with people who are not going to be able to relate to me and I'm not going to be able to relate to them. We are from different worlds, so I think I've had enough of that in my life ... I don't want to feel as if I have to pretend to be someone I'm not.
>
> (Janice)

When we set prevailing dominant discourses against the localized discourses of the mature, working-class students we can see that 'becoming yourself' within higher education is even more complicated for these students. Political discourses of life-long learning combined with prevalent discourses of individualization work to position the uncredentialed as 'unfinished' and 'incomplete in some way'. The cult of individualism can rapidly collapse into individual pathology (Ball *et al.* 2000). As one of the mature students puts it 'life makes some people drop out of school and for some reason they tend to blame themselves'. Against the backdrop of powerful blaming discourses a lack of credentials can all too easily mark out the individual as a failure. A significant number of the mature students, across class, had been variously confronting and avoiding dilemmas of educational failure most of their lives. Within an endemic culture 'of striving for success' and ruthless individualism the working classes are deemed to have failed educationally because of their own faults: 58.7% of young men and 48.5% of young women, the vast majority of them working class, fail to gain five GCSEs A to C (DfEE 1999). All of these working-class mature students, apart from one, are included in this group of 'failures'. But for many of the working-class students there is an additional dilemma around authenticity which cuts across and confounds dilemmas arising from a sense of educational failure.

As Steph Lawler argues authenticity is a classed concept (Lawler 2000). For the working-class students authenticity most often meant being able to hold onto a self rooted in a working-class past. However, within prevailing discourses the authentic self – the self that has to be realized, is a self seeking to maximize its own powers (Rose 1998). It is also a self seeking to escape the fetters of working-class existence; an existence that contemporary political and academic discourses increasingly represent as robbing the self of its actualization. In the bright meritocratic world of New Labour, the very idea of class is seen as increasingly irrelevant and working-classness becomes an aspect of a discredited past (Benyon 1999).

Yet, despite these dominant discourses and their superficial valorization of meritocracy, if university is too different, too alien, then, in particular for the working-class mature students the threat of losing oneself, as Debbie's words, quoted at the beginning of this section, exemplify, is as likely a prospect as finding oneself. The struggle to find oneself implies finding somewhere where one can have a sense of belonging, however tenuous. This is especially problematic for the working-class mature students. The university sector, more than any other educational sector, epitomizes middle classness (Bourdieu and Passeron 1977). How then can the mature working-class student maintain a sense of authenticity and still hope to fit in? Yet, despite the impossibility of ever attaining a perfect fit, there is evidence in many of the transcripts of an attempt to match the habitus of the home with the habitus of the university:

> UCL is wonderful, but it's a very rich university. Not really my sort of place. LSE was another one that I sort of thought I couldn't really apply to ... They seem to be one of the best so there's an element of will I fit in somewhere like UCL and LSE. I think you have to suit somewhere that suits you. I didn't want to go to a really snobby university. ... I'm not interested in the best universities. It's more a case of what's the best university for me.
>
> (Carly)

Janice talks about her scepticism when one of the other students, Mark, returns from a visit to Roehampton, singing its praises:

> I just said 'Yeah, yeah, yeah', but then I went and the staff were really welcoming, the students were really welcoming. I don't know what it was, it was just that they were on my level. I didn't feel as if I had to grovel to these people for anything.

The importance of a sense of being welcomed in must not be underestimated when a majority of these students have shared Mo's experience of 'being made to feel I wasn't up to it, that I wasn't welcome in education'. Similarly, the powerfully classed theme, Janice explicitly articulated, of being looked down on, of being positioned as a supplicant rather than an applicant also infused the transcripts of other working-class mature students. Many of the working-class students were trying to guard against being made to feel inferior and this generalized fear haunted their descriptions of visits and interviews at traditional universities:

> The interview was like what I imagined to be a conversation around a dinner table in like a real upper-class, middle-class family, about world politics and I was like, oh my God, I'm not ready for this. This is not for me. It was terrifying. I was thinking oh my God, I'm not good enough to be coming here.
>
> (Maggie)

The shadow of earlier academic failure hung over the students' decision making. As Janice asserts 'I don't want to compete with anybody. I don't want to be in any of this competitiveness'. This makes the transition to higher education particularly problematic when, for working-class students like Janice, the field of higher education is constituted as a forum in which 'community is dissolved in the acid bath of competition' (Beck 1992: 94).

It is fashionable for academics to dismiss any notion of working-class communities as fantasized or illusory, yet such 'fantasies' had real efficacy in the choice making of some of these mature students. Debbie's earlier evocation of community may have an unfashionable ring yet there are still traces, in the mature student's narratives, of 'the localized milieux of collective experience out of which develop bounded lifestyles and political solidarities', that Thompson (1968) described over 30 years ago. Describing the area surrounding the college she wants to go to, Maggie explains:

> I am really familiar with it over there. I just felt really comfortable thinking I was going over there in an area that I was familiar with, that I knew really well. . . .

That's one of the reasons I chose East London, not that I think there aren't going to be posh people there but just because I know I feel more comfortable there because I come from that area and I feel more centred, more rooted there.

Glib stories of meritocracy skim over, rather than engage with, the difficult uncomfortable configuration of working classness with academic success. It is interesting that in the 1960s and 1970s when the academically successful working-class lads gave their accounts, what we were presented with were fantasies of seamless transitions mingled with nostalgic working-class histories (Hoggart 1962, Seabrook 1982). Now that once-working-class women are writing about working-class relationships to education (Steedman 1986, Walkerdine and Lucey 1989, Kuhn 1995, Mahony and Zmroczek 1997, Maguire 1997, Hey 1997, Skeggs 1997, Plummer 2000, Walkerdine *et al.* 2001) we have very different tales to contend with: tales of ambivalence and uncertainty but also tales of stronger more urgent emotions, of treachery, collusion, tokenism, disloyalty and guilt. The problematic of reconciling academic success with working-class identity that they all write about is echoed in the mature students' narratives.

The mature students' largely negative, sometimes fragmented educational histories reveal no easy union of the academic with personal satisfaction and achievement. Any attempt at transformation runs all the risks of the academic failure and shame many experienced in their early schooling. As Janice says 'I don't ever want that sick feeling in my stomach again'. Instead, most opt for safety and comfort: a combination of achieving educationally and still being able to be themselves that stops short of transformation. As David asserts 'my initial most important thing is that I'm comfortable. It is pretty much the most important thing for me'. On the basis of this criterion he turns down the offer of a place at King's and opts to go to Roehampton instead. The authentic self does not have to be divested of its working classness. Rather, a majority of the working-class students, like the respondents in Louise Archer and Merryll Hutchings study (2001), were engaged in difficult negotiations around identity in which the potential benefits in terms of improved opportunities, 'improved' self, needed to be balanced against the potential costs of losing one's working-class cultural identity.

Maggie and Rumana's narratives add to, and inform, the difficult issues of working-class subjectivity and education I have been trying to convey. Rumana captures the frequent attempt to achieve a configuration of the academic with a more practical, common sense self:

> I think Roehampton is best because there seems to be a balance between academic studies and practice. And I wouldn't like to go to a place where they might be first in every league table but there's no hands-on experience, only academic. I looked for the balance and Roehampton is best for that.

Maggie's text describes a similar impulse. She has decided, despite her enormous zest for learning, that she is not going to study an academic subject like literature and history because:

> It's going to be a really heavy workload and I just thought I've got 3 kids and I'm not going to, it might just be too much for me. ... So I thought a more practical course cos I want to do something I enjoy as well and that I can get really engrossed in ... I didn't want to be stressed out for three years really. I want to do something that I'm going to enjoy.

In spite of being offered a place at other, far more prestigious, institutions, Maggie has decided to accept a place at a university her tutor advises her 'to not even think of going to because it's got such a poor reputation'. The main basis on which she has made her decision is that she got some very positive feedback from a friend 'who is very like me. ... It isn't a high pressure degree, my friend just thought it was brilliant. She loved it'.

Permeating all of the mature students' transcripts was a negotiation of the balance between safety, risk and challenge. For a majority, a sense of safety was the main priority, understandable in view of the often painful, dislocated schooling many of them experienced. If education has been a source of both discomfort and feelings of inadequacy, then fitting in and feeling happy are especially important. Risk, according to Beck and Giddens is supposed to be an individualized process yet the individual-ization thesis neatly covers over the collective class risk for working-class students considering higher education (see also Archer *et al.* 2001, Hutchings and Archer 2001).

Normativity and 'the other'

Collective class risk is not only played out at the stage of higher education access, it is also evident in the texts of working-class, year 7 students in an ESRC project on primary secondary transition I am working on with Helen Lucey. Shaun is an Irish working-class 11 year-old in an inner-city comprehensive, one of 45 pupils Helen and I are tracing from primary to secondary school. His narrative illuminates the conundrum for the working classes between 'finding' and 'losing' yourself within education that I have been trying to illustrate through the mature students' accounts. He exemplifies the sham for the working classes of a project of 'finding yourself' in any positive sense within education. His text reveals that the working-class struggle for academic success is not about finding yourself but rather losing yourself in order to find a new, shiny, acceptable, middle-class persona:

Shaun: Like now I am different in the class than I am out in the playground. I'm just different.
Diane: Right, so how are you different?
Shaun: In the playground, yeah, in the classroom, should I say, I am not myself, I'm totally different. I am hard working and everything. Out in the play-ground, yeah, I am back to my usual self, wanting to fight and everything, just being normal. Like, when I'm in my school uniform I think – I don't want to fight no more, because I don't want to crease my uniform or what-ever.

A case of putting social control in the working-class boy along with the uniform! But it is not the uniform I want to focus on, rather the recognition of the boy in the uniform that he needs to transform in order to succeed. And, as I have mentioned earlier, transformation is a fraught, risky business if you and your kind have histor-ically been, and are currently positioned as, 'other' to the educated, cultured subject. For Shaun, academic success is not normative and he has to literally think and enact himself as 'other' in order to do well. I want to explore issues of normativity and the 'other' further by reference to some work Helen Lucey and I have been doing on social class and the psyche (Lucey and Reay 2000, Reay and Lucey 2000). I want to bring back the abject (Freud 1908) by looking at how the middle classes deal with the 'other', and in the process begin to work against prevailing orthodoxies by problematizing middle- rather than working-class values. Elsewhere, I have written how, instead of accepting middle-class norms which implicitly problematize the working classes, there is a need to problematize conceptions of meritocracy and social mobility, to deconstruct notions of educational failure and success and, concomitantly middle-class practices (Reay 1997, Reay and Ball 1997).

For many middle-class parents, the imperative to reproduce their privileged class position in their children is profound. And it is in the context of their social class reproduction that middle-class children must prove themselves to be self-regulating, a process that begins in the early years and one which is integral to, and inextricable from, the processes through which the required level of educational success is achieved. However, Helen and I argue that the routine nature of that success and the apparent ease with which many middle-class children perform well academically masks deep fears around failure, fears which are driven underground because they so threaten the very bases on which middle-class subjectivities are founded. But out of sight does not mean out of mind. It is precisely this level of terror about failure that lies behind the numerous strategies which many middle-class parents have for ensuring educational advantage for their children, strategies such as: insisting that the primary school curriculum prepare children for selective entrance exams; campaigning for setting and streaming to be introduced; employing private tutors; and buying properties within catchment areas of high-achieving secondary schools (and when that latter strategy is too expensive, lying about addresses).

Tactics like these, although deriving from individual emotional processes, have had a significant impact in many localities on the educational market place, serving to deepen already existing social divisions in schooling. They are also so widespread as to constitute 'class action' although this kind of class action is not about transformation, but about reproduction (Reay 1998). Middle-class children are learning an important lesson about failure – that it is intolerable, unwanted and belongs somewhere else. That is why contemporary educational policy is so paradoxical. It is nominally about raising working-class achievement although its practices generate the exact opposite, ensuring that educational failure remains firmly located within the working classes. And part of that is because we, the middle classes, do not want to take back those messy expelled aspects of the self – fear, contempt, greed – because what would happen to our tenuous sense of centrality then? As Carolyn Steedman argues, it is the marginality of working-class stories that maintains the centrality of middle-class versions. There is no kind of narrative that can hold the two together. Working-class accounts are rendered outsiders' tales, 'held in oscillation by the relationships of class' (Steedman 1986: 139).

Finding 'you're a nothing': working-class dilemmas of being 'found out'

Finally, I want to refer to an article I wrote with Dylan Wiliam on assessment called, 'I'll be a nothing' which examines how 10 and 11 year-old children's identifications as learners are constructed through the assessment process (Reay and Wiliam 1999). The article argues that assessment procedures are implicated in technologies of the self and the struggle to gain 'intimate and secure' social relations – intimate because they feed into the ordering of subjectivity and secure because of the apparent naturalness of the categories they generate (Donald 1985, Rose 1989). The paradox of our contemporary assessment regime is that while the stated aim is to raise the achievement of all children, it often seems to operate as yet another mechanism for fixing failure in the working classes:

Hannah: I'm really scared about the SATs. Ms. O'Brien [a teacher at the school] came and talked to us about our spelling and I'm no good at spelling and David [the class teacher] is giving us times tables tests every morning and I'm hopeless at times tables so I'm frightened I'll do the SATS and I'll be a nothing.

Diane: I don't understand Hannah. You can't be a nothing.

Hannah: Yes, you can 'cause you have to get a level like a level 4 or a level 5 and if you're no good at spellings and times tables you don't get those levels and so you're a nothing.

Diane: I'm sure that's not right.

Hannah: Yes it is 'cause that's what Ms. O'Brien was saying.

and:

Sharon: I think I'll get a two, only Stuart will get a six.

Diane: So if Stuart gets a six what will that say about him?

Sharon: He's heading for a good job and a good life and it shows he's not gonna be living on the streets and stuff like that.

Diane: And if you get a level two what will that say about you?

Sharon: Um, I might not have a good life in front of me and I might grow up and do something naughty or something like that.

Sharon is talking about herself and one of the two middle-class boys in her class. She provides a poignant summation of class destinies and how they are tied to academic achievement. As I have argued earlier, class has entered psychological categories as a way of socially regulating normativity and pathology (see also Plummer 2000), and Sharon, at age 10, has already internalized an understanding of her low achievement as pathological.

The battle over assessment and triumph of publishable, measurement-based, competitive, pencil and paper tests over diagnostic, open-ended, process-oriented assessments has resulted in the establishment of assessment procedures which operate primarily 'as performance indicators of teacher effectivity' (Ball 1994: 41). However, one side effect has been the further marginalization of the working classes within education. At the macro-level SATs can be seen as regulatory mechanisms that link the conduct of individuals and organizations to political objectives; the assumption being that they will impact powerfully on teachers' subjectivities and practices. However, as white working-class Hannah and Sharon's quotes illustrate, at the micro-level of the classroom there are regular glimpses of the normalizing and regulatory function of the SATs on children. Although children expressed anxieties across class differences it was not the white middle-class boys panicking about being exposed as no good through the new assessment procedures. Rather, it was the black and white working-class girls agonizing that they would be 'a nothing', yet another case of being found out within education! Finding yourself within education, no less than losing yourself, is a problematic enterprise for the working-class individual. Finding yourself is all too often simultaneously a process of being found out. And the risks of finding you have very little value are disproportionately high. The league table culture, the accompanying A to C economy, the failing schools policy and government initiatives like the gifted and talented programmes exacerbate rather than alleviate such dilemmas (Schostak 2000).

Perhaps white working-class Tracey provides the best example of 'the governance of the soul' (Rose 1989):

Tracey: I think even now, at night times I think about it and I think I'm going to get them.

Diane: You think about your SATs at night time?

Tracey: Yeah, lots. When I'm in bed, because I've got stars on my ceiling, I'm hoping and I look up and I go, 'I know I'm gonna get there'. And my mum goes, 'Who's talking in there?' and I goes, 'Nothing mum'.

Diane: So what are you hoping?

Tracey: Um, I think about a three. I dunno. I don't think I'll get a five, I'm hoping to get a five. When I look at the stars I hope I'll get a five.

When later in the year I interviewed Tracey, now in year 7 of an inner city predominantly working-class comprehensive she told me, unsolicited, that she was a 3, 3, 3. When I asked her how she felt about that, she replied that it was better than being a nothing, but still 'rubbish'.

Conclusion

Far from developing a 'classless' society, the English educational system is still prey, in the twenty-first century, to Tawney's 'curse' (1938) of being organized along lines of social class. Historically, the working classes have constantly been 'found out' in education; discovered to be inferior, less cultured, less clever than the middle classes. However, while finding themselves in higher education is a very recent development, a consequence of the increasing expansion and resulting stratification within the university system, processes of finding themselves and being found out have frequently occurred simultaneously within schooling. There have always been 'sink, failing' schools. Now we are beginning to have 'sink, failing' universities. Both finding and losing yourself are about a lack in relation to the academic. A lack originally identified and hollowed out in the bourgeoise imaginary and then fixed in the working classes. Perhaps we need to place that lack somewhere else maybe with the academic. For instance, an argument could be made that the National Curriculum holds little relevance for the complexities of life in the twenty-first century regardless of which class you belong to (MacDonald 2000). But most of all the lack lies in our political elites: those policy makers who fail to care, cynically dissemble and refuse to recognize the connections between educational and wider social contexts. However, I would also like to suggest that that lack lies closer to home – in our lack of care, lack of political will. At the beginning of the twenty-first century we still do not have a valued place within education for the working classes and for that we, the middle classes, must all collectively be held responsible. As Bourdieu asserts:

> Nothing is less innocent than noninterference. If it is true that it is not easy to eliminate or even modify most of the economic and social factors behind the worst suffering, particularly the mechanisms, regulating the educational markets, it is also true that any political programme that fails to take advantage of the possibilities for action (minimal though they may be) that science can help uncover, can be considered guilty of nonassistance to a person in danger.
>
> (Bourdieu 1993: 629)

Who of us then is not guilty?

Note

1   In this chapter I concentrate on social class whilst recognizing the complex, differentiated ways in which it is mediated by both ethnicity and gender. A recent Government sponsored report emphasizes that class inequalities exist across ethnic differences and argues that 'the familiar inequality of attainment between pupils from nonmanual and manual backgrounds is replicated *within* each ethnic group (Gillborn and Mirza 2000: 14, authors' own italics). In relation to gender, Egerton and Savage (2000) found marked class polarization among both men and women and, perhaps surprisingly, point to a more marked class polarization amongst young women than among young men.

References

Apple, M. (1996) *Cultural Politics and Education* (Buckingham: Open University Press).

Archer, L. and Hutchings, M. (2000) 'Bettering yourself'? discourses of risk, cost and benefit in young working class non-participants' constructions of HE, *British Journal of Sociology of Education*, 21 (4), 555–574.

Archer, L., Pratt, S. and Phillips, D. (2001) Working class men's constructions of masculinity and negotiations of (non)participation in higher education, *Gender and Education*.

Arnot, M. (1983) A cloud over coeducation: an analysis of the forms of transmission of class and gender relations, in S. Walker and L. Barton (eds), *Gender, Class and Education* (Basingstoke: Falmer Press).

Ball, S. J. (1994) *Education Reform: a critical and post-structural approach.* (Buckingham: Open University Press).

Ball, S. J., Maguire, M. and MacRae, S. (2000) *Choice, Pathways and Transitions Post-16: new youth, new economies in the global city* (London: Falmer).

Beck, U. (1992) *The Risk Society* (London: Sage).

Beynon, H. (1999) A classless society?, in H. Beynon and P. Glavanis (eds), *Patterns of Social Inequality* (London: Longmans), pp. 36–53.

Bourdieu, P. (1993) 'Postscript' in Bourdieu, Pierre et al. (1993) *Weight of the World: social suffering in contemporary society* (Cambridge: Polity Press), pp. 627–629.

Bourdieu, P. (2000) *Pascalian Meditations* (Cambridge: Polity Press).

Bourdieu, P. and Passeron, J. C. (1977) *Reproduction in Education, Society and Culture* (London: Sage).

Brewer, S. (2000) 'Who do you say I am?' Jesus, gender and the (working-class) family romance, in S. Munt (ed.), *Cultural Studies and The Working Class: subject to change* (London: Cassell), pp. 167–179.

Cohen, P. (2000) Cultural Studies and the Working Classes. Keynote address to Cultural Studies and the Working Class Reconsidered, 29 January, University of East London.

Connell, R. (1995) *Masculinities* (Cambridge: Polity Press).

Cook, J. (2000) Culture, class and taste, in S. Munt (ed.), *Cultural Studies and The Working Class: subject to change* (London: Cassell), pp. 97–112.

DfEE (1999) GCSE/GNVQ and GCE A/AS Examination results 1997/8, *Statistical Bulletin* 8/99 (London: HMSO).

Donald, J. (1985) Beacons of the future: schooling, subjection and subjectification, in V. Beechey and J. Donald (eds), *Subjectivity and Social Relations* (Milton Keynes: Open University Press).

Egerton, M. and Savage, M. (2000) Age stratification and class formation: a longitudinal study of the social mobility of young men and women 1971–1991, *Work, Employment and Society*, 14 (1), 23–50.

Egerton, M. and Halsey, A. H. (1993) Trends in social class and gender in access to higher education in Britain, *Oxford Review of Education*, 19 (2), 183–196.

Freedland, J. (2000) Closing the privilege gap, *Guardian*, 17 June.

Freud, S. (1959) [1908] 'Family Romances' *Standard Edition of the Collected Works*, vol. 9 (London: Hogarth Press).

Furlong, A. and Cartmel, F. (1997) *Young People and Social Change: industrialisation and risk in late modernity* (Buckingham: Open University Press).

Gale, T. and Densmore, K. (2000) *Just Schooling: explorations in the cultural politics of teaching* (Buckingham: Open University Press).

Gillborn, D. and Mirza, H. S. (2000) *Educational Inequality: mapping race, class and gender: a synthesis of research evidence* (London: OFSTED).

Green, A. (1990) *Education and State Formation: the rise of education systems in England, France and the USA* (Basingstoke: Macmillan Press).

Halsey, A. H. (1993) *Opening Wide the Doors of Higher Education: briefings for the Paul Hamlyn Foundation* (National Commission on Education London: Heinemann).

Hey, V. (1997) Northern accent and southern comfort: subjectivity and social class, in P. Mahony and C. Zmrocrek (eds), *Class Matters: working class women's perspectives on social class* (London: Taylor & Francis), pp. 140–151.

Hoggart, R. (1962) *The Uses of Literacy* (Harmondsworth: Penguin).

Hutchings, M. and Archer, L. (2001) 'Higher than Einstein': constructions of going to university among working class non-participants, *Research Papers in Education.*

Kuhn, A. (1995) *Family Secrets: acts of memory and imagination* (London: Verso).

Lawler, S. (2000) Escape and escapism: representing working-class women, in S. Munt (ed.), *Cultural Studies and The Working Class: subject to change* (London: Cassell), pp. 113–128.

Lowe, R. (1960) [1867] Primary and classical education, in B. Simon (ed.), *Studies in the History of Education 1780–1870* (London: Lawrence and Wishart).

Lucey, H. and Reay, D. (2000a) Social class and the psyche, *Soundings*, 15, 139–154.

MacDonald, B. (2000) How education became nobody's business, in H. Altrichter and J. Elliott (eds), *Images of Educational Change* (Buckingham: Open University Press), pp. 20–36.

McMillan, M. (1912) How I became a socialist, *Labour Leader*, 11 July.

Maguire, M. (1997) Missing links: working-class women of Irish descent, in P. Mahony and C. Zmroczek (eds), *Class Matters: working class women's perspectives on social class* (London: Taylor & Francis), pp. 87–100.

Mahony, P. and Zmroczek, C. (eds) (1997) *Class Matters: working class women's perspectives on social class* (London: Taylor & Francis).

Miller, J. (1992) *More has Meant Women: the feminisation of schooling* (London: Tufnell Park Press with The Institute of Education).

OECD (2000) *Education at a Glance* (Paris: OECD).

Plummer, G. (2000) *The Failing Working Class Girl* (Stoke-on-Trent: Trentham Books).

Purvis, J. (1980) Working-class women and adult education in nineteenth-century Britain, *History of Education*, 9 (3), 193–212.

Reay, D. (1997) The double-bind of the 'working-class' feminist academic: the failure of success or the success of failure?, in P. Mahony and C. Zmroczek (eds), *Class Matters: working class women's perspectives on social class* (London: Taylor & Francis), pp. 18–29.

Reay, D. (1998) *Class Work: mothers' involvement in their children's primary schooling* (London: University College Press).

Reay, D. and Ball, S. J. (1997) 'Spoilt for choice': the working classes and education markets, *Oxford Review of Education*, 23 (1), 89–101.

Reay, D. and Wiliam, D. (1999) 'I'll be a nothing': structure, agency and the construction of identity through assessment, *British Educational Research Journal*, 25 (3), 343–354.

Reay, D. and Lucey, H. (2000) 'I don't like it here but I don't want to be anywhere else': children living on inner London council estates, *Antipode*, 32 (4), 410–428.

Reay, D., Ball, S. J., David, M. and Davies, J. (2001) Choices of degree or degrees of choice? Social class, race and the higher education choice process, *Sociology.*

Reid, I. (1998) *Class in Britain* (Cambridge: Polity Press).

Roeberts, I. (1999) A historical construction of the working class, in H. Beynon and P. Glavanis (eds), *Patterns of Social Inequality* (London: Longmans), pp. 147–160.

Rose, N. (1989) *Governing the Soul: the shaping of the private self* (London: Routledge).

Rose, N. (1998) *Inventing Ourselves: psychology, power and personhood* (Cambridge: Cambridge University Press).

Ryan, A. (2000) The Letters page, *Guardian*, 27 May, p. 23.

Ryle, S., Ahmed, K. and Bright, M. (2000) The war of Laura's rejection, *Observer*, 28 May, p. 17.

Savage, M. and Egerton, M. (1997) Social mobility, individual ability and the inheritance of class inequality, *Sociology*, 31 (4), 645–672.

Schostak, J. (2000) Developing under developing circumstances: the personal and social development of students and the process of schooling, in H. Altrichter and J. Elliott (eds), *Images of Educational Change* (Buckingham: Open University Press), pp. 37–52.

Seabrook, J. (1982) *Working-class Childhood: an oral history* (London: Victor Gollancz Ltd).

Skeggs, B. (1997) *Formations of Class and Gender: becoming respectable* (London: Sage).

Skeggs, B. (2000) Rethinking Class: Class Cultures and Explanatory Power. Keynote address to Cultural Studies and the Working-Class Reconsidered, 29 January, University of East London.

Smith, A. (1785) *An Inquiry into the Nature and Causes of the Wealth of Nations*.

Smithers, R. (2000) Third of Oxford colleges still take more independent school pupils, *Guardian*, 5 August, p. 4.

Steedman, C. (1985) 'The mother-made-conscious': the historical development of a primary school pedagogy, *History Journal Workshop*, 20, 151–163.

Steedman, C. (1986) *Landscape for a Good Woman: a story of two lives* (London: Virago).

Tawney, R. H. (1938) *Equality* (London: Allen & Unwin).

Thompson, E. (1968) *The Making of the English Working Class* (Harmondsworth: Penguin).

Utley, T. (2000) We parents are well schooled in class war, *Daily Telegraph*, 31 May, p. 24.

Walkerdine, V. and Lucey, H. (1989) *Democracy in the Kitchen: regulating mothers and socialising daughters* (London: Virago).

Walkerdine, V., Lucey, H. and Melody, J. (2001) *Growing up Girl: Gender and Class in the Twenty-first Century* (London: Macmillan).

PART 2

GLOBALISATION

CHAPTER 3

EDUCATION, GLOBALIZATION AND ECONOMIC DEVELOPMENT

Phillip Brown and Hugh Lauder

Journal of Education Policy (1996), 11 (1): 1–25

[. . .]

Introduction

Since the first oil shock in the early 1970s western societies have experienced a social, political and economic transformation that is yet to reach its conclusion. At its epicentre is the creation of a global economy that has led to an intensification of economic competition between firms, regions and nation-states (Dicken 1992, Michie and Smith 1995). This globalization of economic activity has called into question the future role of the nation-state and how it can secure economic growth and shared prosperity. At first sight this may appear to have little to do with educational policy; however, the quality of a nation's education and training system is seen to hold the key to future economic prosperity. This chapter will outline some of the consequences of globalization and why education is crucial to future economic development. It will also show that despite the international consensus concerning the importance of education, strategies for education and economic development can be linked to alternative 'ideal typical' neo-Fordist and post-Fordist routes to economic development which have profoundly different educational implications.

These neo-Fordist and post-Fordist routes can also be connected to alternative political projects. Since the late 1970s the USA and UK have followed a neo-Fordist route in response to economic globalization, which has been shaped by the New Right's enthusiasm for market competition, privatization and competitive individualism. However, with the election of the Democrats in the 1992 American presidential elections and the resurgence of the British Labour Party there is increasing support for a post-Fordist strategy. Although much has already been written about the flaws in the New Right's approach to education and national renewal, far less has yet been written on what we will call the 'left modernizers'. It will be argued that whilst the left modernizers present a promising programme for reform *vis-a-vis* the New Right, their account of education, skill formation and the global economy remains unconvincing. Therefore, an important task of this paper is to highlight the weaknesses in the left modernizers' account to show that if post-Fordist possibilities are to be realized, it will be essential for those on the left to engage in a more thoroughgoing and politically difficult debate about education, equity and efficiency in late global capitalism.[1]

Globalization and the new rules of economic competition

The significance of globalization to questions of national educational and economic development can be summarized in terms of a change in the rules of eligibility, engagement and wealth creation (Brown *et al.* 2001) First, there has been a change in the rules of eligibility. In the same way that sports clubs run 'closed' events where club membership is a condition of entry, they may also run tournaments 'open' to everyone. Likewise there has been a shift away from the closed or walled economics of the postwar period towards an open or global economy. As a result of this change in the rules of eligibility domestic economies have been exposed to greater foreign competition (Reich 1991, ILO 1995). Changes in the rules of eligibility have also enhanced the power of the multinational corporations (MNCs). The MNCs not only account for a growing proportion of cross-border trade, but are a major source of new investment in technology, jobs and skills. Since the mid-1970s the MNCs have grown more rapidly than the world economy. In 1975, the 50 largest industrial corporations worldwide had sales of US$540 billion and $25 billion in profits. In 1990, sales figures for the top 50 had climbed to $2.1 trillion and their profits had reached $70 billion. In real terms, whereas the US economy was growing at an annual rate of 2.8% (the OECD average was 2.9%), the MNCs' annual sales growth was in the region of 3.5% during the period between 1975 and 1990 (Carnoy *et al.* 1993: 49).

Moreover, the old national 'champions' such as Ford, IBM, ICI and Mercedes Benz have tried to break free of their national roots, creating a *global auction* for investment, technology and jobs. As capital has become footloose, the mass production of standardized goods and services has been located in countries, regions or communities which offer low wage costs, light labour market legislation, weak trade unions and 'sweeteners' including 'tax holidays' and cheap rents. Such investment has significantly increased in the new industrial countries (NICs) such as in Singapore, Taiwan, China and Brazil (Cowling and Sugden 1994). It is estimated that in the 1980s some 700 US companies employed more than 350,000 workers in Singapore, Mexico and Taiwan alone and that 40% of the jobs created by British MNCs were overseas (Marglinson 1994: 64).

In reality, the global auction operates like a Dutch auction. In a Dutch auction corporate investors are able to play off nations, communities and workers as a way of increasing their profit margins, bidding spirals downwards impoverishing local communities and workers by forcing concessions on wage levels, rents and taxes in exchange for investment in local jobs. In order to persuade Mercedes to set up a plant in Alabama, the company received an initial $253 million, with tax breaks over 25 years which have been estimated to be worth an extra $230m. The Swiss Bank Corporation will receive some $120m of incentives over the next 10 years from Connecticut, for moving its US headquarters from Manhattan to the city of Stamford.[2]

In the USA and UK the creation of a global auction has also been linked to the breakdown of the Fordist rules of engagement between government, employers and workers. Although some writers have restricted their definition of Fordism to refer exclusively to the system of mass production, Fordism is a label that can equally be applied to Keynesian demand management in the postwar period referring to the expansion of mass consumption as well as mass production (Lipietz 1987, Harvey 1989). The rapid improvement in economic efficiency which accompanied the introduction of mass production techniques necessitated the creation of mass markets for consumer durables, including radios, refrigerators, television sets and motor cars. In order for economic growth to be maintained, national governments had to regulate profits and wage levels to sustain the conditions upon which economic growth depended. Hence, the development of the welfare state in western industrial societies was seen to reflect efforts on the part of national governments to maintain the Fordist compromise between employers and organized labour. The combination of increased welfare state protection for workers, coupled with full employment and a degree of social mobility, temporarily 'solved' the problem of distribution (Hirsch 1977) under Fordism. The problem of distribution is that of determining how opportunities and income are to be apportioned. Under capitalism this is an ever present problem because it is a system which is inherently unequal in its distribution of rewards and opportunities. However, during the Fordist era the combination of the rewards of economic growth being evenly spread across income levels, increasing social security, occupational and social mobility according to ostensibly meritocratic criteria generated a high degree of social solidarity. However, over the last 20 years the USA and UK have introduced 'market' rules of engagement. Here the nation-state is charged with the role of creating the conditions in which the market can operate 'freely'. Therefore, rather than trying to engineer a compromise between employers and the trade unions the state must prevent the unions from using their 'monopoly' powers to bid-up wages which are not necessarily reflected in productivity gains. Hence, according to the market rules of engagement the prosperity of workers will depend on an ability to trade their skills, knowledge and entrepreneurial acumen in an unfettered global market-place.

Finally, the transformation in western capitalism has entailed new rules of wealth creation. These have undermined the viability of building national prosperity on the Fordist mass production of standardized goods and services.[3] Fordist mass production was based on the standardization of products and their component parts. Many of the tasks previously undertaken by skilled craftsmen, such as making door panels or parts of the car's engine 'by hand', were mechanized by designing jigs, presses and machines able to perform the same operations hundreds, if not thousands of times a day, with the use of a semi-skilled operative. The Fordist production line was characterized by a moving assembly line, where the product passes the workers along a conveyor, rather than the worker having to move to the product as in nodal production. A further feature of Fordism was a detailed division of labour, within which the job tasks of shopfloor workers were reduced to their most elementary form in order to maximize both efficiency and managerial control over the labour process. Hence, Fordism was based on many of the principles of 'scientific management' outlined by Frederick Taylor who offered a 'scientific' justification for the separation of *conception* from *execution*, where managers monopolized knowledge of the labour process, and controlled every step of production.

However, in the new rules of wealth creation economic prosperity will depend on nations and companies being able to exploit the skills, knowledge and insights of workers in ways which can no longer be delivered according to Fordist principles. Enterprises which can deliver a living wage to workers now depend on the quality as much as the price of goods and services, and on finding new sources of productivity and investment. Such 'value added' enterprise is most likely to be found in companies offering 'customized' goods and services in microelectronics, telecommunications, biotechnology, financial services, consultancy, advertising, marketing and the media.[4]

In response to these new rules all western nations, in their domestic economies and foreign affairs, have had to look to their own social institutions and human resources to meet the global challenges they confront (OECD 1989). Lessons learnt from Japan and the Asian Tigers suggest that the 'human side of enterprise' is now a crucial factor in winning a competitive advantage in the global economy. Advantage is therefore seen to depend upon raising the quality and productivity of human capital. Knowledge, learning, information and technical competence are the new raw materials of international commerce.

> Knowledge itself, therefore, turns out to be not only the source of the highest-quality power, but also the most important ingredient of force and wealth. Put differently, knowledge has gone from being an adjunct of money power and muscle power, to being the very essence. It is, in fact, the ultimate amplifier. This is the key to the power shift that lies ahead, and it explains why the battle for control of knowledge and the means of communication is heating up all over the world.
>
> (Toffler 1990: 18)

Although such statements greatly exaggerate the importance of knowledge in advanced capitalist economies, without exception, national governments of all political persuasions have declared that it is the quality of their education and training systems which will decisively shape the international division of labour and national prosperity. Therefore the diminished power of nation-states to control economic competition has forced them to compete in what we call the global *knowledge wars*. In Britain, for instance, the National Commission of Education suggests that:

> For us, knowledge and skills will be central. In an area of world-wide competition and low-cost global communications, no country like ours will be able to maintain its standard of living, let alone improve it, on the basis of cheap labour and low-tech products and services. There will be too many millions of workers and too many employers in too many countries who will be able and willing to do that kind of work fully as well as we or people in any other developed country could do it – and at a fraction of the cost.
>
> (1993: 33)

But how the problem of education and training policies is understood and how the demand for skilled workers is increased is subject to contestation and political struggle. There is no doubt, for instance, that the introduction of new technologies has expanded the range of strategic choice available to employers and managers. However, this has exposed increasing differences, rather than similarities, in organizational cultures, job design and training regimes (Lane 1989, Green and Steedman 1993). There are few guarantees that employers will successfully exploit the potential for 'efficiency', precisely because they may fail to break free of conventional assumptions about the role of management and workers, and cling to the established hierarchy of authority, status and power. As Harvey (1989) has recognized, new technologies and coordinating forms of organization have permitted the revival of domestic, familial and paternalistic labour systems given that, 'The same shirt designs can be reproduced by large-scale factories in India, cooperative production in the 'Third Italy', sweatshops in New York and London, or family labour systems in Hong Kong' (p. 187). This should alert us to the fact that the demise of Fordism in the West does not necessarily mean that the majority of workers will find jobs which exercise the range of their human capabilities. The interests of employers seeking to maximize profits and workers seeking to enhance the quality of working life and wages remain an important source of cleavage given that it is still possible for companies to 'profit' from low-tech, low-wage operations. There is no hidden-hand or post-industrial logic which will lead nations to respond to the global economy in the same way, despite the fact that their fates are inextricably connected. Indeed, we would suggest that the universal consensus highlighting education and training systems as holding the key to future prosperity his obscured fundamental differences in the way nations are responding to the global economy.

Therefore, while recognizing that some of the key elements of Fordism in western nations are being transformed in the global economy, it is important not to prejudge the direction of these changes which must remain a question of detailed empirical investigation (see Block 1990). For analytical purposes it is useful to distinguish two 'ideal typical' models of national economic development in terms of neo-Fordism and post-Fordism (see Table 2). Neo-Fordism can be characterized in terms of creating greater market flexibility through a reduction in social overheads and the power of trade unions, the privatization of public utilities and the welfare state, as well as a celebration of competitive individualism. Alternative, post-Fordism can be defined in terms of the development of the state as a 'strategic trader' shaping the direction of the national economy through investment in key economic sectors and in the development of human capital. Therefore, post-Fordism is based on a shift to 'high value' customized production and services using multi-skilled workers (see also Allen 1992).

In the 'real' world the relationship between education and economic development reveals examples of contradiction as much as correspondence. Moreover, although it is true to say that countries such as Germany, Japan and Singapore come closer to the model of post-Fordism, and the USA and UK approximate neo-Fordist solutions, we should not ignore clear examples of 'uneven' and contradictory developments within the same region or country. It also highlights the fact that there are important differences in the way nation-states may move towards a post-Fordist economy with far-reaching implications for democracy and social justice.

Nevertheless, these models represent clear differences in policy orientations in terms of the dominant economic ideas which inform them and underlying cultural assumptions about the role of skill formation in economic and social development (Thurow 1993). First we will assess the New Right's interpretation of education as part of a neo-Fordist strategy, before undertaking a detailed account of the left modernizers' vision of a post-Fordist high-skill, high-wage economy.

The New Right: education in a neo-Fordist 'market' economy

The New Right interpretation of the Fordist 'crisis' is based on what we call the welfare shackle thesis. In the 19th century it was the aristocracy and the *ancient régime* in Europe who were blamed for 'shackling' the market and free enterprise. In the late 20th century it is the welfare state.[5] The New Right argue that the problem confronting western nations today can only be understood in light of profound changes in the role of government during the third quarter of the 20th century. They assert it is no coincidence that at the same time western governments were significantly increasing expenditure on social welfare programmes, there was high inflation, rising unemployment and economic stagnation (Murray 1984). Western societies have run into trouble because of the extensive and unwarranted interference by the state. Inflation, high unemployment, economic recession and urban unrest all stem from the legacy of Keynesian economics and an egalitarian ideology which promoted economic redistribution, equality of opportunity and welfare rights for all. Hence, the overriding problem confronting western capitalist nations is to reimpose the disciplines of the market.

Table 2 Post-Fordist possibilities: alternative models of national development

Fordism	Neo-Fordism	Post-Fordism
Protected national markets	Global competition through: productivity gains, cost-cutting (overheads, wages)	Global competition through: innovation, quality, value-added goods and services
	Inward investment attracted by 'market flexibility' (reduce the social cost of labour, trade union power)	Inward investment attracted by highly skilled labour force engaged in 'value-added' production/services
	Adversarial market orientation: remove impediments to market competition. Create 'enterprise culture'. Privatization of the welfare state	Consensus-based objectives: corporatist 'industrial policy'. Cooperation between government, employers and trade unions
Mass production of standardized products/low skill, high wage	Mass production of standardized products/low-skill, low-wage 'flexible' production and sweatshops	Flexible production systems/ small batch/niche markets; shift to high-wage, high-skilled jobs
Bureaucratic hierarchical organizations	Leaner organizations with emphasis on 'numerical' flexibility	Leaner organizations with emphasis on 'functional' flexibility
Fragmented and standardized work tasks	Reduce trade union job demarcation	Flexible specialization/ multi-skilled workers
Mass standardized (male) employment	Fragmentation/polarization of labour force. Professional 'core' and 'flexible' workforce (i.e. part-time, temps, contract, portfolio careers)	Maintain good conditions for all employees. Non 'core' workers receive training, fringe benefits, comparable wages, proper representation
Divisions between managers and workers/low-trust relations/ collective bargaining	Emphasis on 'managers' right to manage'. Industrial relations based on low-trust relations	Industrial relations based on high-trust, high-discretion, collective participation
Little 'on the job' training for most workers	Training 'demand' led/little use of industrial training policies	Training as a national investment/state acts as strategic trainer

According to the New Right the route to national salvation in the context of global knowledge wars is through the survival of the fittest, based on an extension of parental choice in a market of competing schools, colleges and universities (Ball 1993). In the case of education, where funding, at least during the compulsory school years, will come from the public purse, the idea is to create a quasi-market within which schools will compete (Lauder 1991). This approximation to the operation of a market is achieved by seeking to create a variety of schools in a mixed economy of public and private institutions. In some cases they will aim at different client groups such as the ethnic minorities, religious sects, or 'high flyers'. This 'variety', it is argued, will provide parents with a genuine choice of different products (Boyd and Cibulka 1989, Halstead 1994). Choice of product (type of school) is seen to be sufficient to raise the standards for all, because if schools cannot sell enough desk space to be economically viable, they risk going out of business. Moreover, the economic needs of the nation will be met through the market, because when people have to pay for education they are more likely to make investment decisions which will realize an economic return. This will lead consumers to pick subjects and courses where there is a demand for labour, subsequently overcoming the problem of skill shortages. Equally, there will be a tendency for employment training to be 'demand led' in response to changing market conditions (Deakin and Wilkinson 1991).

Critics of the marketization of education therefore argue that the introduction of choice and competition provides a mechanism by which the middle classes can more securely gain an advantage in the competition for credentials (Brown 1995). This is because not all social groups come to an educational market as equals (Collins 1979). Cultural and material capital are distributed unequally between classes and ethnic groups. In particular, it is the middle classes which are more likely to have the cultural capital to make educational choices which best advantage their children (Brown 1990, Brown and Lauder 1992). In consequence, the introduction of parental choice and competition between schools will amount to a covert system of educational selection according to social class as middle-class children exit schools with significant numbers of working-class children. The consequence will be that the school system will become polarized in terms of social class and ethnic segregation and in terms of resources. As middle-class students exit from schools with working-class children they will also take much needed resources from those schools and effectively add to already well-off middle-class schools.

What evidence there is about the workings of educational markets suggests that they are far more complex than their critics suggest (Lauder *et al.* 1994). Nevertheless, the evidence so far confirms the prediction that choice and competition tend to lead to social class and ethnic polarization in schools (Willms and Echols 1992, Lauder *et al.* 1994). In nations such as the USA and UK, the overall effect will be to segregate students in different types of school on the basis of social class, ethnicity and religion. The net result will again be a massive wastage of talent as able working-class students once more find themselves trapped in schools which do not give them the opportunity of going to university (Halsey *et al.* 1980). If this is the overall effect then it can be argued that the marketization of education, while appearing to offer efficiency and flexibility of the kind demanded in the post-Fordist era, will in fact school the majority of children for a neo-Fordist economy which requires a low level of talent and skill.

The marketization of education will inevitably have an inverse effect on the ability of nation-states to compete in the global auction for quality inward investment, technology and jobs. Although multinational organizations are always on the look-out to reduce their overheads, including labour costs, investment in 'high-value' products and services crucially depends upon the quality, commitment and insights of the workforce, for which they are prepared to pay high salaries. The problem that nation-states now confront is one of how to balance commercial pressures to reduce labour costs and other overheads whilst mobilizing an educated labour force, and maintaining a sophisticated social, financial and communications infrastructure. This problem has been exacerbated by the fact that the low-skill, high-wage jobs associated with Fordism in North America and Europe are being transplanted to the NICs where labour costs are much lower, leading to a significant deterioration in working conditions in the low-skill jobs remaining in the west (Wood 1994).

In the context of the global auction, the market reforms in education are likely to leave a large majority of the future working population without the human resources to flourish in the global economy. Here the link between market reforms and neo-Fordism is barely disguised in countries which were dominated by New Right governments in the 1980s. The principle objective of economic policy is to improve the competitiveness of workers by increasing labour market flexibility by restricting the power of trade unions, especially in order to bring wages into line with their 'market' value. This philosophy led Britain to reject the Social Chapter of the Maastricht Treaty which provided legislative support for workers, because it was argued that it would undermine Britain's competitiveness in attracting inward investment, despite the poor work conditions this would inflict on employees. In contradistinction, market reforms in education and the economy have ensured the conditions in which highly paid middle-class professionals and elite groups are able to give their children an 'excellent' (*sic*) education in preparation for their bid to join the ranks of Reich's (1991) 'symbolic analysts'.

A different critique, albeit coming to the same conclusions, can be mounted against the introduction of market mechanisms in post-compulsory education and training. A key area of the post-compulsory sector for a post-Fordist economy is that concerned with the education of skilled tradespeople and technicians (Streeck 1989). The New Right has argued that the introduction of market mechanisms into this area will ensure a closer matching of supply and demand for trained labour and hence greater efficiency in the allocation of skilled labour. The argument rests on the assumptions that individuals and employers should bear the cost and responsibility for training. It is assumed that individuals gain most of the benefits from such a training and that they should therefore bear much of the cost (Lauder 1987). Moreover, since they are paying substantially for their training they will choose to train in an area in which there is market demand. In so far as employers should help bear the cost of training and the responsibility for the type of training offered, it is argued that employers are in the best position to assess the numbers of skilled workers required and the kind of skills they should possess. Underlying this observation is an appreciation of employers' short-term interests. Given the assumption that they 'know best' what the levels and nature of skilled labour should be, it follows that they will be reluctant to pay taxes or levies for training undertaken by a third party, such as the state.

While this view, as with other New Right views, is plausible, it has come in for sustained criticism. One of the most cogent is that of Streeck (1989, 1992). He argues that under a free labour contract of the kind found in liberal capitalist societies which gives workers the right to move from one firm to another, skills become a collective good in the eyes of employers. This is because the rewards of training individuals can easily be 'socialized' by the expedient of trained workers moving to another job while the costs of training remain with the original employer. Since employers face a clear risk in losing their investment they are unlikely to invest heavily in training.

Streeck argues that, as a result, western economies are likely to face a chronic skill shortage unless the state intervenes to ensure that adequate training occurs.

Moreover, unless there is state intervention employers will reduce the training programmes they do have when placed under intense competitive pressure and/or during a recession. Streeck (1989) notes that in the prolonged economic crisis of the 1970s, western economies, with the exception of Germany, reduced their apprenticeship programmes. In Germany government and trade union pressure ensured that the apprenticeship programme was extended. Two consequences followed: the apprenticeship system helped to alleviate youth unemployment and it contributed to the technical and economic advantage enjoyed by German industry in the early 1980s.

There are further criticisms that can be made of a market-determined training system. From the standpoint of the individual, it is unlikely that those who would potentially enter a skilled trade or technical training, working- and lower middle-class school leavers, could either afford the costs of such a training or take the risks involved. The risks are twofold: first, given the time lag between entering a training programme and completing it, market demand for a particular type of training may have changed with a resulting lack of jobs. In the competitive global market, such an outcome is all too likely. If the training received were of a sufficiently general nature to produce a flexible worker that might be less of a problem. However, in an employer-led training system the pressure will always exist for training to meet employers' specific and immediate needs. The consequence is that such a training system is likely to be too narrowly focused to meet rapidly changing demand conditions. Second, a further point follows from this, namely that the industries of today are likely to be tomorrow's dinosaurs. As a result, employer-led training schemes may not contain the vision and practice required in order to maintain the high skill base necessary for a post-Fordist economy. Clearly the structure of Germany's training system offers an example of an alternative which can begin to meet the requirements of a post-Fordism economy. This, as Streeck (1992) notes, involves a partnership between the state, employers and trade unions. It is a system which ensures that employers' immediate interests are subsumed within a system concerned with medium and longer term outcomes. Therefore the outcome of the reassertion of market discipline in social and economic institutions has been the development of a neo-Fordist economy characterized by insecurity and the creation of large numbers of temporary, low-skilled and low-waged jobs. We have also argued that the appeal to 'self-interest' and 'free enterprise' serves to mask the political interests of the most privileged sections of society. Indeed, the very notion of a national system of education is called into question as professional and élite groups secede from their commitment to public education and the ideology of meritocracy upon which public education in the 20th century has been founded.

Left modernizers: education in a post-Fordist 'magnet' economy

Over the last decade a new centre-left project has emerged in response to the ascendancy of the New Right. These 'left modernizers' reject much that was previously taken for granted amongst their socialist predecessors, contending that the transformation of capitalism at the end of the 20th century had significantly changed the strategies that the left needs to adopt in its pursuit of social justice *and* economic efficiency. This involves a recognition that the left must develop a credible response to the global economy, which will include economic policy and management as well as dealing with issues of distribution, equity and social policy (Rogers and Streeck

1994: 138). At the top of their agenda is a commitment to investment in human capital and strategic investment in the economy as a way of moving towards a high-skilled, high-waged 'magnet' economy. Underlying these economic forms of investment is a vision of a society permeated by a culture of learning for it is the knowledge, skills and insights of the population that provide the key to future prosperity. The ideas of the 'left modernizers' are to be found in books such as Reich (1991) and Thurow (1993) in the USA, the Commission on Social Justice (1994) and Brown (1994) in the UK. The ideas represented in these works are also consistent with Democratic politics in the USA and have informed the direction of Labour Party policy in Britain.[6]

The modernizers' account of how to create a post-Fordist economy can be summarized in the following way. It begins with a recognition that it is impossible to deliver widespread prosperity by trying to compete on price rather than the quality of goods and services. They therefore advocate a change in policy relating to investment in both physical and human capital. They advocate what has become known as producer capitalism (Dore 1987, Thurow 1993, Hutton 1995) in which low-cost long-term investment is linked to the development of human capital. Producer capitalism stands in stark contrast with market capitalism in which price and short-term profit are the key criteria for enterprises. Not surprisingly, they reject the assertion made by the acolytes of market capitalism that the only route to prosperity is through the creation of greater market 'flexibility' by lowering labour costs or by repealing labour protection laws. The modernizers see that in the new economic competition making those at the bottom end of the labour market more insecure and powerless against exploitative employers is not the way for workers and nations to confront the challenge of the global auction. They recognize that the provision of a floor of protective rights, entitlements and conditions for workers in the context of the global auction is both socially desirable and economically essential. In practice what this means is reinforcing labour laws against the worst excesses of unscrupulous employers and the vagaries of the global auction. This will include a minimum wage and various forms of government intervention to get the long-term unemployed back to work. For modernizers, this is part of building a new high-trust partnership between government, employers and workers. For they argue that it is only through such a partnership that a high-skill, high-wage economy can be created. The role of the state in such a partnership is that of a 'strategic trader' (Krugman 1993) selecting 'winners' or guiding industrial development where appropriate and, most importantly, providing the infrastructure for economic development. Here the development of a highly educated workforce is seen as a priority.

The importance the modernizers attach to education stems from a belief that the increasing wage inequalities in the USA and UK over the last decade are a reflection of the returns to skill in a global auction for jobs and wages. The essence of this idea was captured by Bill Clinton in a major address on education:

> The key to our economic strength in America today is productivity growth . . . In the 1990s and beyond, the universal spread of education, computers and high speed communications means that what we earn will depend on what we can learn and how well we can apply what we learn to the workplaces of America. That's why, as we know, a college graduate this year will earn 70 per cent more than a high school graduate in the first year of work. That's why the earnings of younger workers who dropped out of high school, or who finished but received no further education or training, dropped by more than 20 per cent over the last 10 years alone.[7]

Hence, for all western societies the route to prosperity is through the creation of a 'magnet' economy capable of attracting high-skilled, high-waged employment within an increasingly global labour market. This is to be achieved through sustained investment in the national economic infrastructure including transportation, telecommunications, R&D, etc. alongside investment in education and training systems. In the modernizers' account it is nevertheless acknowledged that there are unlikely to be enough skilled and well-paid jobs for everyone. However, flexible work patterns are assumed to lead to greater occupational mobility permitting people to move from low-skilled jobs when in full-time study, to high-skilled jobs in mid-career back to low-skilled jobs as retirement age approaches. Of course, such a view depends on substantial mobility in both an upwards and downwards direction (Esping-Andersen 1994). Therefore, in the same way that unemployment is tolerable if it only lasts for a few months, being in a low-skilled, poorly paid job is also tolerable as long as it offers progression into something better.

Education and training opportunities are thus pivotal to this vision of a competitive and just society. For not only can education deliver a high value-added 'magnet' economy but it can also solve the problem of unemployment. However, it is a mistake for nation-states to 'guarantee' employment because this harbours the same kind of vestigial thinking that led to previous attempts to protect uncompetitive firms from international competition: they simply become even less competitive. The only way forward is to invest in education and training to enable workers to become fully employable. In this account, social justice inheres in providing all individuals with the opportunity to gain access to an education that qualifies them for a job. Clearly there is a tension here between the idea of flexibility and the need to guarantee a minimum wage, so protecting labour from exploitation. All the indications are that the modernizers will err on the side of caution and provide what could only be described as minimal protection. In the end, the difference between the modernizers and the New Right on this issue may be marginal although, as we shall see, there are good economic reasons why adequate social protection is desirable.

There are several features of the modernizers' account with which we concur, including the need to introduce a version of 'producer' capitalism, but as a strategic policy for education and economic development it is flawed. Our purpose in exposing these flaws is to set the scene for a more radical and thoroughgoing debate about education, economy and society in the early decades of the 21st century. Our criticisms cluster around four related problems: first, the idea of a high-skilled, high-wage magnet economy; second, whether reskilling the nation can solve the problem of unemployment; third, whether it is correct to assume that income polarization is a true reflection of the 'value' of skills in the global labour market; and finally, the problem of how the modernizers propose upgrading the quality of human resources so all are granted an equal opportunity to fulfil their human potential.

How can a high-skilled, high-wage 'magnet' economy be created?

Their view that the future wealth of nations will depend on the exploitation of leading-edge technologies, corporate innovation and the upgrading of the quality of human resources can hardly be quarrelled with. Nations will clearly need to have a competitive advantage in at least some of the major industrial sectors, such as telecommunications, electronics, pharmaceuticals, chemicals and automobiles (Porter 1990, Thurow 1993). There is also little doubt that this will create a significant minority of jobs requiring highly skilled workers. However, the problem with the modernizers' account is that they assume that highly skilled and well-paid jobs will become available to all for at least a period of their working lives. Indeed, this is an essential tenet of their argument given that they suggest that widening inequalities can be overcome through upskilling the nation and that full employment remains a realistic goal. In other words, the modernizers continue to believe that the labour market can act as a legitimate mechanism (through the occupational division of labour) for resolving the distributional question in advanced capitalist societies.

The plausibility of this account hangs on the idea that the global auction for jobs and enterprise offers the potential for western nations to create 'magnet' economies of highly skilled and well-paid jobs. This is an idea which has obvious appeal to a broad political constituency. It serves to replenish the spirits of those who see the USA following the UK in a spiral of economic decline after a period of global dominance. We are presented with the comforting picture of a global economy which, although no longer likely to be dominated by American and European companies, is characterized by prosperous western workers making good incomes through the use of their skills, knowledge and insights. In reality, however, this characterization represents an imperialist throw-back to the idea that innovative ideas remain the preserve of the advanced western nations, with the possible exception of Japan. Reich, for example, assumes that as low-skilled work moves into the NICs and Third World economies, the USA, the European EU countries and Japan will be left to fight amongst themselves for the high value-added jobs. The problem with this view is that it completely misunderstands the nature of the economic strategies now being implemented by the Asian Tigers, who have already developed economic and human capital infrastructures which are superior to those of many western countries (Ashton and Sung 1994). This is partly reflected in the international convergence in education systems, at least in terms of expanding their tertiary sectors. Therefore, whilst we should not rule out the possibility that MNCs, when making inward and outward investment decisions, will judge the quality of human resources to be superior in particular countries, it is extremely unlikely that a small number of nations will become 'magnets' for high-skilled, high-waged work.

They have also overestimated the extent to which even the most successful modern economies depend on the mass employment of highly skilled workers. Indeed, an unintended consequence of the massive expansion of tertiary education may be to create a substantial wastage of talent amongst college and university graduates unable to find a demand for their skills, knowledge and insights. This new 'wastage of talent' is likely to be especially acute in countries which have pursued the neo-Fordist trajectory of labour market deregulation, corporate down-sizing and growth of temporary, casual and insecure work – conditions which arc hardly conducive to the production of high-quality jobs distinguished by worker autonomy and cognitive complexity.

The difficulty for the modernizers is that by concentrating on the question of skill formation rather than on the way skills are linked to the trajectory of economic development, they obscure some of the fundamental problems, relating to educated labour, that need to be confronted. Piore (1990) has, for example, argued that where labour market regulation is weak, there is no incentive for employers to invest and use the new technology in a way which raises the value added and the quality of work. Rather, weak labour market regulations lead to a vicious circle whereby profit is extracted through sweatshop labour, low wages and low productivity. In effect, what regulated labour markets do is to create an incentive for entrepreneurs to invest in capital-intensive forms of production in order to generate the high value added to pay for the wage levels set by regulated labour markets (Sengenberger and Wilkinson 1995). If Piore is correct then we would expect the patterns of future work to develop along different trajectories depending on the degree to which their labour markets are regulated. While projections of labour supply and occupational change need to be viewed with some scepticism the recent OECD (1994) report on this subject certainly supports Piore's position when the USA is compared with Holland. On all indices of social protection and labour-market regulation Holland provides an example of far greater social protection for workers, yet the vast majority of new jobs being created could be classified as 'skilled' (OECD 1994). In the USA approximately half the jobs being created were in service occupations requiring little formal training. The lesson here is obvious: the route to a high value-added economy must involve an analysis of factors affecting the demand for educated labour. The implicit assumption, harboured by the modernizers, that through investing in the employability of workers, employers will automatically recognize this potential and invest in upgrading the quality of their human resources is clearly naive.[8] The historical record in both the USA and UK shows that while there are firms that recognize investment in people to be vital to the medium-term success of their companies, there are many others who equally recognize that fat profits can still be made off the backs of semi-skilled and unskilled, low-waged workers. Equally, the idea that western nations can compensate for the failings of local employers by attracting inward investment from blue-chip MNCs is clearly not going to be sufficient to move from a neo-Fordist to a post-Fordist economy. Therefore, there seems little doubt that although in some important respects the modernizers will succeed in producing some improvement in the quality of employment opportunities, they will not achieve the goals of post-Fordist development because investment in education and training as the focal point of their policy will not lead to the creation of a high-skill, high-wage economy.

Can reskilling the nation solve the problem of unemployment?

The focus on employability rather than employment also leaves the modernizers accused of failing to offer a realistic return to full employment. Indeed, the high-skill, high-wage route may be pursued at the price of high unemployment. This is because neo-classical economists argue that labour market deregulation is the only way to solve unemployment. The theory is that the regulation of the labour market favoured by the modernizers bids up the price of those in work and discourages employers from taking on more workers. With deregulation the price of labour would fall and employers would 'buy' more workers. The debate over labour-market deregulation has given rise to the view that all advanced societies are now on the horns of a dilemma in terms of unemployment. Either labour markets are deregulated as in the USA, where official unemployment is below 5%, but where there is extensive poverty because wages at the bottom end of the labour market are insufficient to live off, or they are more regulated as in the producer capitalist route pursued by Germany, but unemployment is higher – as is the compensation paid to the unemployed (Commission of the European Communities 1993, Freeman 1995). The problem this poses to the modernizers is that on the one hand a majority of workers can expect good quality jobs and a reasonable standard of living but the polarization of market incomes avoided by the producer capitalist route is reproduced between those in work and those unemployed. The divisions in society remain but the source is different.

Unemployment, at the low levels achieved during the postwar period, was historically unique, depending on a contingent set of circumstances (Ormerod 1994). Attempting to create similar circumstances for the early part of the 21st century is likely to prove elusive and in political terms something of a hoax perpetrated by political parties who promise it or something close to it. It is, perhaps, for this reason that the modernizers translate full employment into full employability, thereby throwing the onus on the individual to find a job.

If we examine the profiles of several OECD countries, there are two striking observations that can be made. First, GDP has been divorced from employment in the past 20 years, just as growth has not led to a shared prosperity during the same period. In Spain the economy grew by 93% between 1970 and 1992 and *lost* 2% of its jobs (*Financial Times* 2 October 1993). This is in stark contrast with the postwar period when both incomes and jobs were linked to economic growth. Growth delivered an even rise in income for all occupational groups. Second, the trajectories taken by OECD countries in terms of their main indicators – inflation, growth and balance of payments – vary dramatically, yet unemployment remains around or above 7%, in terms of the official statistics, for every country with the exception of the USA and Japan. This includes countries with high levels of growth such as Canada, New Zealand and Australia.[9]

What appears to have happened in the past 25 years is that a set of economic and social forces have pushed the lower limit of unemployment up substantially from an OECD average well below 5% in the postwar period to an average well above 7%. Clearly the oil price hikes of the early 1970s had much to do with the initial jump in unemployment but since then a series of contingent factors have conspired to lock unemployment in at this high level. The introduction of new technology, which has enabled machines to replace workers, could have had a significant impact on unemployment for both blue- and white-collar workers as the jobless growth in Spain suggests. Similarly the number of blue-collar jobs lost to the developing nations has added to the problem (Wood 1994). However, these factors have to be placed within the wider context of economic regulation in relation to the global economy. It is worth noting that current economic orthodoxy ensures that interest rates rise with economic growth, thereby potentially choking off further investment in productive capacity and hence employment. It may also reduce demand, especially in countries such as the USA and UK with a high proportion of families with mortgages.

There are two mutually consistent explanations for the link between rising interest rates and growth. The first is that in a deregulated global finance market there is a shortage of investment funds, especially at times of growth. After all, with the potential to invest in developing nations, as well as the developed nations, the competition for investment has increased dramatically. Moreover, in a global economy the business cycles of the developed and developing nations are likely to be more synchronized so that an upturn in the global economy is likely to be met by a global demand for increased investment (Rowthorn 1995). The second is that, within nations, the key instrument for the control of inflation is interest rates. As economies overheat, interest rates are raised by central banks to choke off demand. The use of interest rates to control inflation is claimed to be successful in a way in which other measures tried in the 1970s and 1980s, incomes policies and control of money supply, were not. Again, however, we should note the role of the new global economy in defining the control of inflation as a key element in any successful national competitive strategy. If inflation in any one country rises to appreciably higher levels than in competitor countries, its goods are likely to be priced out of the market. Hence the significance accorded to the control of inflation in a global economy. But the cost of using interest rates to this end is that economies are permanently run under capacity (ILO 1995: 163). The rise in interest rates simply chokes off demand before it can appreciably affect unemployment levels.

More recently, studies have argued that it is declining economic growth and hence demand, among the OECD countries, since 1973 which is the fundamental cause of unemployment (Eatwell 1995, ILO 1995). While the trend in economic growth in all OECD countries has declined (ILO 1995: 133) it is unclear whether raising levels to those in the period between 1960 to 1973 would have the same impact on unemployment now as it did then, as the examples of Australia and Canada show. The problem is that in a global economy, growth may be achieved through exports and the benefits of growth spent on imports rather than home-produced goods. Whereas in the postwar Fordist economies a rise in demand would percolate through the economy, thereby creating jobs, a rise in demand now may simply create jobs in some other part of the world. This may be especially so in countries where increases in incomes are accruing to the wealthy who spend their money on luxury goods from overseas.

The alternative to this macro-analysis of the causes of unemployment is the micro-analysis of some neo-classical economists, who argue that it is labour market rigidities, of the kind discussed above, especially the power of trade unions and highly regulated labour markets, which cause unemployment and sustain inflation. There are two elements to their explanation. The first is that these rigidities bid up the price of labour and maintain it at a level higher than desirable to clear the labour market of unemployed. The second is that these rigidities allow the 'insiders' who are employed to bid up their wages even when others are unemployed (Lindbeck and Snower 1986). There are two problems with this theory. First, there appears to be no strong relationship between the degree of social protection, labour market regulation and unemployment, with the exception of the USA (although see Freeman 1995). Historically the lowest levels of unemployment, from 1950–73, have been associated with the highest levels of social protection and labour market regulation, while the present period represents one of the lowest levels of protection and regulation and the highest levels of unemployment. Moreover, even within the current period differences between nations relating to regulation, protection and economic performance hardly bear out this thesis. For example, the UK has one of the lowest levels of labour protection in the OECD and an unemployment rate of 8.4% (OECD 1994: 155). In contrast, Holland, which has an above-average level of protection and regulation, has an unemployment rate of 7.3%. Moreover, their inflation rates are not substantially different. Britain has had an annual rate of 2.4% in the past year and Holland 3%. Second, where labour markets have been deregulated they have not brought about a substantial reduction in unemployment. This is certainly the case in the UK and in New Zealand where unemployment is still about 7%.

Overall, it seems extremely unlikely that the problem of unemployment can be solved by any of the conventional remedies and to pretend otherwise merely holds out false promises to a generation of unemployed. The New Right solution was to price people back into jobs. The modernizers' solution is to create a high-skill, high-wage 'magnet' economy. Neither solution is adequate. The New Right solution manifestly has not worked and it threatens a new cycle of low-wage job creation. The modernizers, whilst having a more sustainable approach to global economic competition, have no answer to unemployment. Therefore, the most important conclusion to be drawn from this discussion is that the modernizers lack an adequate account of how all will share in the future prosperity accrued from the investment in education and national economic growth. Unemployment will remain a structural feature of western societies and the 'distributional' question (Hirsch 1977), temporarily solved under Fordism through full employment and the even spread of the fruits of growth across the occupational structure, must now be addressed by the modernizers. Consequently, we argue elsewhere (Brown *et al.* 2001) that the distributional problem can only be remedied by the introduction of a 'social wage' and that occupational opportunities will have to be shared. Moreover, the question of unemployment is not only one about social justice, but one of economic efficiency. If the economic fate of nations increasingly depends upon the quality of their human resources, it will not be possible to write off a large minority of the population to an 'underclass' existence. Indeed, the issue of long-term unemployment is part of a wider problem of social and economic polarization. Therefore, we need to examine the modernizers' account of skill and income polarization before asking how those people living in poverty are going to acquire the appropriate skills to get high-skilled, high-waged jobs, when research has demonstrated that social deprivation has a profoundly negative impact on academic performance.

Does income polarization reflect the 'value' of skills, knowledge and insights in the global labour market?

Considerable doubt must be cast on the way the modernizers have understood the 'high skill = high wage' equation. This is important to our discussion because growing income inequalities are seen to reflect individual differences in the quality of their 'human capital'. Here their argument is based on trend data which show a widening of income inequalities. There has been a dramatic increase in income inequalities in both the USA and the UK since the late 1970s. Such evidence is taken to reflect the relative abilities of workers to trade their knowledge, skills and insights on the global labour market. According to the modernizers, as low-skilled jobs have been lost to developing economies with cheaper labour, the wages of less skilled workers in the West have declined. By the same token, in the new competitive conditions described above, those workers who have the skills, knowledge and insights that can contribute to 'value-added' research, production, consultancy or service delivery in the global labour market have witnessed an increase in their remuneration. Hence analysis and remedy are closely related in the modernizers' account: if the reason so many workers are in low-paying jobs, or worse, unemployed is that they lack skills, the solution is to give them the skills. It is an appealing analysis but at best it is based on a partial truth.

If increasing income polarization was a consequence of the neutral operation of the global economy we should find the same trend in all the advanced economies. However, the evidence suggests that the increasing polarization in income is far more pronounced in the USA and UK than in any other OECD country (Gardiner 1993: 14, Hills 1995). In Germany there has actually been a decline in income differentials (OECD 1993)!

It could also be expected that if the increased dispersion of income was a result of the changing cognitive and skill demands of work, then nations with the highest levels of technology and investment in research and development would lead the table of income inequalities. Yet, the evidence that does exist suggests quite the opposite. Wood (1994) notes that, 'Japan and Sweden are leaders in applying new technology, while the USA and UK are laggards' (p. 281). He also notes that the work of Patel and Pavitt (1991) suggests that civilian research and development, as a proportion of GDP in the 1980s, was higher in Sweden and Japan than in the USA and UK. Equally, in terms of patenting in the USA, Germany, which experienced declining inequalities of income during this period, greatly outperformed the UK.

One conclusion to be drawn from these considerations is that rather than the returns to skill becoming more responsive to the operation of the global auction, the relationship between skill and income is less direct than the modernizers assume, the reason being that the relationship between income and skills is always mediated by cultural, political and societal factors. This is of course obvious when unpaid child care, undertaken primarily by women, is taken into consideration. Moreover, despite the way skill is used in the current debate about income inequalities and economic performance it has proved extremely difficult to arrive at an agreed definition of skill, which explains why studies comparing labour markets in neighbouring countries such as Germany and France show that the process of training, career progression and reward for skills is intricate, subtle and substantially different in the two countries (Maurice *et al.* 1986). Another study (Dore 1987) has highlighted differences in the way rewards are distributed for work in the USA as opposed to Japan. In the USA it is assumed by neo-classical economists that there is a direct relationship between skill and income. However, Japanese industry, the exemplar of producer capitalism, has not organized the relationship between skill and income in this way. Rather, it has based income on loyalty to the company and length of service, rather than 'skill' in any pristine sense. As Dore has noted, in Japan there is a remarkable 'lack of consciousness of the market price of a skill' (p. 30). This being the case it could be expected that even if the polarization of income in the USA was a response to the changing demand for skill, this would not be the case in Japan. A further glance at the OECD (1993) data also tells us that while there has been some widening of income differentials in Japan, it does not reflect the polarization characteristic of the USA and UK.

What this evidence suggests is that the modernizers' assumption that by raising skill levels there will be a commensurate increase in income regulated through the global labour market is clearly incorrect. The answer is to be found not in the neutral operation of the global labour market as Reich and others have suggested, but in the way the USA and UK have *responded* to global economic conditions. This response, like the global economy itself, has been shaped by the New Right political projects of Reagan and Thatcher (Marchak 1991). Although the debate about what is distinctive about the USA and UK takes us beyond the confines of this chapter, the polarization in income can be explained more convincingly in terms of differences in labour market power rather than returns to skills (although they are not mutually exclusive). A major consequence of market deregulation has been to enhance the power of 'core' workers in down-sized organizations. This is supported by the fact that the most dramatic changes in income distribution are to be found at either end of the income parade. What income polarization in the US and UK also reveals is the way in which the 'casino' economies of these countries in the 1980s enabled company executives and senior managers, along with those who worked in the financial markets, to engage in 'wealth extraction' rather than the development of sustainable forms of 'wealth creation' (Lazonick 1993). This largely explains why a study reported by Bound and Johnson (1995) found that in the USA a large part of the increase in the returns to a university degree was due to an increased premium put to use in the business and law fields. The wages of computer specialists and engineers actually *fell* relative to those of high school graduates.

But if the rising incomes of the work rich are explicable in terms of 'paper entrepreneurialism' (Reich 1984) and corporate restructuring, can the decline in the wages of the unskilled be explained in terms of the neutral operation of the global economy? In addressing this question there is the problem of measuring the extent to which semi- and unskilled work has been transplanted to the developing nations. One estimate is that up to 1990 changes in trade with the South has reduced the demand for unskilled relative to skilled labour in the North by approximately 20% (Wood 1994: 11). However, it is not only that industrial blue-collar jobs were lost, but the perennial threat of relocation to developing world countries which ensured that wages were depressed for remaining unskilled workers. It is, of course, hard to measure the degree to which this threat has been material in keeping down wages. Nevertheless, it is worth noting that there is little correlation between manufacturing competitiveness and low wages. In the most successful industrial economies Germany and Japan, manufacturing wages are higher than anywhere else. However, New Right governments in the USA and UK took the 'lesson' to heart and helped to drive down wages by labour market deregulation. Estimates for the UK (Gosling and Machin 1993) and the USA (Blackburn *et al.* 1990), for instance, calculate that the decline in unionization in the 1980s accounts for 20% of the increase in wage inequality. In addition, making it easier to hire and fire workers enabled companies to achieve numerical flexibility in terms of their wages bills (Atkinson 1985). At times of economic boom workers could be hired while in times of downturn they could be fired. In Britain, for example, in the last three months of 1994, 74,120 full-time jobs disappeared and 173,941 part-time jobs were created. This is a clear example of how to organize a labour market for short-term expedience, but it also suggests that companies have not only externalized the risks associated with unstable market conditions but also their labour costs, especially among low-skilled workers. In such circumstances it is difficult to see how the modernizers can resolve the problem of widening income inequalities when they are judged to reflect the neutral operation of the global economy.

Indeed, high levels of income inequalities are interpreted by the modernizers as a reflection of educational and corporate inefficiency in a global labour market which can only be narrowed through investment in education and training. If inequalities persist it is because the latter are failing to upgrade the quality of human resources. With respect to national systems of education, inequalities become a useful measure of their effectiveness. However, this raises a set of questions and problems for the modernizers with respect to the social conditions under which education can achieve greater equality of opportunity and higher levels of educational achievement for all. It is to this, fourth, problem that we now turn.

How can the quality of human resources be upgraded where all are granted an equal opportunity to fulfil their human potential?

In answering this question the modernizers recognize that the wealth of nations depends upon upgrading the quality of human resources. They recognize that ways must be found to develop the full potential of a much larger proportion of the population than prevailed in the Fordist era. They point to the need to widen access to tertiary education and to create the institutional framework necessary to offer lifelong learning to all. They also recognize a need to improve overall educational standards as US and UK students appear to be falling behind in international comparative tests. A national commitment to investment in the 'employability' of present and future workers is understood by the modernizers to represent a new social contract between the individual and the state, given that such investment is viewed as a condition for economic efficiency and social justice. However, their interpretation of how equity and efficiency are to be achieved in the global economy is politically impoverished. In part, this is because the question of equity has been subsumed within a debate about how to upgrade the overall quality of education and training systems based on an assumption that domestic inequalities of opportunity are largely irrelevant if a nation can win a competitive advantage in the global knowledge wars, permitting all to compete for high-skilled, high-waged jobs. Therefore, the old national competition for a livelihood, based on the principles of meritocratic competition, is of far less importance than that of how to upgrade the quality of the education system as a whole. Again we find the idea of a high-skill, high-wage magnet economy used to extract the political sting from questions of social and educational inequalities.

The reality is that questions of social justice cannot be resolved through the operation of the global labour market. Indeed, if the creation of a post-Fordist economy depends on a general upgrading of the skills of the labour force, tackling the problem of domestic inequalities in income and opportunities has become *more* rather than less important with economic globalization. There are at least two related reasons for this. First, the use of education and training institutions to raise technical standards for all does not resolve the question of 'positional' advantage (Hirsch 1977). In other words, access to elite schools, colleges and universities, along with the credentials they bestow, remains a key factor in determining labour market power. In addition, if our analysis of income inequalities is correct, labour market power has, if anything, become more important as a result of corporate restructuring and the decline of graduate careers (Brown and Scase 1994). Therefore, the question of social justice will continue to depend on how individual nation-states frame the competition for a livelihood.

The question of positional competition has also become more important because there has been a change in the nature of educational selection. Today the institutional expression of a commitment to meritocratic competition in education has been suffocated under the grip of the New Right. A commitment to a unified system of schooling within which students will be educated according to ability and effort has been abandoned in favour of consumer sovereignty based on parental 'choice' and a system of education based on market principles. A consequence of this change in the organization of educational selection from that based on 'merit' to the 'market' (Brown 1995) is, as argued above, that it serves to encourage the creation of under-funded sink schools for the poor and havens of 'excellence' for the rich. Therefore, the school system in both the USA and UK no longer reflects a commitment to open competition but gross inequalities in educational provision, opportunities and life chances. In Washington, DC the wealthy are queuing up to pay as much as $12,000 a year to send their five-year-old children to private schools, while the city is virtually bankrupt and severe cuts to the educational budget are inevitable.[10]

Therefore, although equality of opportunity is recognized as a condition of economic efficiency the modernizers have effectively avoided perhaps the most important question to confront the left at the end of the 20th century, that is, how to organize the competition for a livelihood in such a way that a genuinely equal opportunity is available to all. Avoiding the positional problem by appeals to the need to raise educational standards for all in the global market not only fails to address this question but also offers little insight into how the foundations for social solidarity upon which the institutional expression of meritocratic competition rests, are to be rebuilt. Indeed, their focus on increasing the 'employability' of workers reinforces a sense of the insecure nature of work at the end of the 20th century (Newman 1993, Peterson 1994). It encourages people to watch their backs constantly and to put their child first in the educational and labour market jungle. Without an adequate foundation for material and social security the emphasis on enhanced employability within a culture of competitive individualism becomes translated into the Hobbesian condition of 'all against all'. When education becomes a positional good and where the stakes are forever increasing in terms of income, life-chances and social status, powerful individuals and groups will seek to maximize their resources to ensure that they have a stake in the game by whatever means.[11] Therefore, how the state intervenes to regulate this competition in a way which reduces the inequalities of those trapped in lower socioeconomic groups must be addressed, not only as a matter of economic efficiency but also for reasons of social justice in a post-Fordist economy.

The relationship between equity and efficiency at the end of the 20th century does not only rest on the reassertion of meritocratic competition in education, but on a recognition that the wealth of the nation's human resources is *inversely* related to social inequalities, especially in income and opportunity. Therefore, narrowing such inequalities is likely to be a cost-effective way of investing in human capital, which in turn should lead to improvements in economic efficiency. Hence, we would predict that the polarization of income in nations such as the USA and UK during the 1980s will have led to a wider dispersal of educational achievement than in nations with little or not widening of incomes. We are currently analysing the comparative evidence in order to examine the hypothesis that relative deprivation has an absolute effect on the quality of a nation's human resources (Wilkinson 1994). If our hypothesis proves to be supported by the empirical evidence, it will come as little surprise to sociologists who have consistently found a close relationship between inequality and academic performance.[12] The fact that at least a fifth of children in both the USA and UK now live in poverty is inevitably going to have a detrimental impact on the ability of these children to respond to educational opportunities and to recognize the relevance of formal study when living in neighbourhoods with high unemployment, crime and deprivation. Indeed, the importance of equity to the question of social learning is graphically illustrated in Julius Wilson's (1987) study of the urban under-class in America. He suggests that 'a perceptive ghetto youngster in a neighbourhood that includes a good number of working and professional families may observe increasing joblessness and idleness but he [sic] may also witness many individuals going to and from work; he may sense an increase in school dropouts but he can also see a connection between education and meaningful employment' (1987: 56). He goes on to argue that the exodus of 'respectable' middle- and working-class families from the inner-city neighbourhoods in the 1970s and 1980s removed an important 'social buffer' that could deflect the full impact of prolonged and increasing jobless-ness, given that the basic institutions in the area (churches, schools, stores, recreational facilities, etc.) were viable so long as more economically stable and secure families remained. Hence, the more social groups become isolated from one another the fewer opportunities exist for the kind of social learning which even in the deprived neigh-bourhoods of USA and UK cities could offer role models to children other than those which now exist due to the 'political economy of crack' (Davis 1990).

Moreover, the impact of widening social inequalities is not restricted to children from ghetto or poor backgrounds; it also infects the social learning of the wealthier sections of the population. In a characteristically perceptive discussion John Dewey noted that every expansive period of social history is marked by social trends which serve to 'eliminate distance between peoples and classes previously hemmed off from one another' (1966: 100). At times where the opposite happens it narrows the range of contacts, ideas, interests and role models. The culture of the privileged tends to become 'sterile' to be turned back to feed on itself; their art becomes a showy display and artificial; their wealth luxurious; their knowledge over-specialised; their manners fastidious rather than human' (Dewey 1966: 98).

Hence the view which the modernizers take in assuming that inequalities will narrow once there is proper investment in education and training fails to recognize that the future wealth of nations depends upon a fundamental challenge to inequal-ities in both income and opportunities. Therefore, the role of the nation-state must increasingly become one of balancing the internal competition for a livelihood with a strategy geared towards upgrading the quality of education for all through a reduction in relative inequalities. Moreover, a commitment to equality of opportunity is not only vital to the life-blood of a high-skill economic strategy, but it provides a clear message to all sections of society that they are of equal worth and deserve genuine opportunities to fulfil their human potential.

Conclusion

The increasing importance attached to education in the global economy is not misplaced in the sense that nations will increasingly have to define the wealth of nations in terms of the quality of human resources among the population. The creation of a post-Fordist economy will depend upon an active state involved in investment, regulation and strategic planning in the economic infrastructure alongside a commitment to skill formation through education and training. We have argued that such an economic strategy is necessary because it is the best way of creating a social dividend which can be used to fund a 'social wage' for all givers that the 'distributional' problem can no longer be solved through employment within the division of labour. A social wage which delivers families from poverty thereby becomes an important foundation of a learning society, designed to follow the post-Fordist trajectory to a globally competitive economy and to a socially just society (see Brown *et al.* 2001). Hence, if the potential and limitations of educational reform in the creation of post-Fordist economy are to be adequately addressed by the modernizers there is an urgent need for those on the left to grapple with the issues explored in this chapter.

Notes

1 This chapter develops a number of themes outlined in earlier papers (Brown and Lauder 1992, 1993). It also serves to clarify our interpretation of the relationship between education and post-Fordism which has been criticized by Avis (1993) and Jones and Hatcher (1994).
2 Figures from *Financial Times* Survey 'North American Business Location' 19 October 1994.
3 Antonio Gramsci (1971) used the term Fordism to describe a new system of mass production introduced by the American car manufacturer Henry Ford. Gramsci recognized that the introduction of mass production also required a new mode of social regulation 'suited to the new type of work and productive process' (p. 286). Ford's rise to prominence at the time stemmed from the market success of the Model T motor car which was launched in 1916. The system of mass production enabled him to capture 55% of the US market in the early 1920s by selling the Model T at a tenth of the price of a craft-built car (Braverman 1974, Murray 1989).
4 As it is more difficult for competitors to mass produce the same goods or to offer customers tailored services (see Schumpeter 1961, Collins 1986, Blackwell and Eilon 1991). In such companies improvements in productivity depends upon the 'organic' integration of applied science, technological innovation, free-flow information networks, and high-trust relations between management and multi-skilled workers. The increasing costs of errors, demand for quality control, and for multi-skilled workers with a conceptual grasp of a large section of the production process or office activities has made the specialized division of labour in Fordism a source of organizational inefficiency.
5 The idea of a 'Feudal' shackle is discussed by Hirschman (1986).
6 Given such a diverse range of publications there will inevitably be differences in focus and policy emphasis. The extent to which the Clinton administration in America has attempted to introduce a viable industrial policy has been clearly limited; see Shoch, J. (1994) 'The politics of the US industrial policy debate, 1981–1984 (with a note

on Bill Clinton's "industrial policy")', in D. Kotz, T. McDonough and M. Reich (eds) *Social Structures of Accumulation* (Cambridge: Cambridge University Press).

7   'They are all our children', speech delivered at East Los Angeles College, Los Angeles, 14 May 1992. The modernizers' view contrasts with the rhetoric, if not the practice, of the New Right. There is clearly a tension between New Right views regarding the expansion of tertiary education and the practice of the Conservative Party in the UK, where there has been a rapid expansion of tertiary provision despite the views of influential theorists and journalists such as Friedman, Hayek and Rees-Mogg, suggesting that it is only an élite that needs a university education. It is also worth noting that, in terms of imagery, the New Right do not present the future in terms of a 'learning society' but an enterprise culture, in which a few outstanding captains of industry and commerce, the Bill Gates and Richard Bransons of this world, are feted as the leaders of an economic renaissance.

8   The floor of protective rights for workers as envisaged by the modernizers is, for example, likely to be too weak to act as an incentive to employers to upgrade the quality of work opportunities. Moreover, see Kuttner's response to Rogers and Streeck (1994).

9   Data compiled from the *Independent on Sunday*'s economic indicators 1994–95.

10 The question of equality of opportunity needs to be addressed head on as it is not only essential to economic efficiency, but to the legitimization of a system of educational and occupational selection which is inherently stratified in terms of income, status, work styles and lifestyles. In postwar western societies the reason why a menial labourer is paid $17,000 and a private sector manager $85,000 was legitimized in terms of the outcome of a meritocratic competition based on individual ability and effort. The commitment to open competition found expression in the idea of the socially-mixed-ability high or comprehensive school. Yes, there remained deprived inner-city districts where children, especially from African-American and Hispanic backgrounds, were clearly not getting equality of opportunity but even here 'head start' programmes were launched to try to create a level playing field.

11 Moreover, for those in lower socioeconomic circumstances their exclusion from decent academic provision is compounded by deindustrialization which has created a rust belt across the heartlands of both the USA and UK, sometimes destroying vibrant communities (Bluestone and Harrison 1982). Therefore, although the modernizers assume greater flexibility in the occupational structure as a response to the employment needs of men and women at different stages of their lives, the reality seems more likely to lead to intensive competition and highly restricted opportunities to enter the professional core and a constant flux restricted to jobs which are low skilled, low waged and inherently insecure. This outcome may well be reinforced by the fact that as employers place a premium on employees with the appropriate social and interpersonal skills alongside their technical know-how, the cultural capital of job-seekers assumes greater importance. Without the financial and social resources required to invest in cultural capital those from poorer backgrounds who are more likely to attend less prestigious halls of learning will be at a distinct disadvantage (Brown and Scase 1994).

12 For a discussion of the definition of relative deprivation and poverty see Townsend, P. (1993) *The International Analysis of Poverty* (New York: Harvester Wheatsheaf).

References

Allen, J. (1992) 'Post-industrialism and Post-Fordism'. In S. Hall *et al.* (eds), *Modernity and its Futures* (Cambridge: Polity).

Ashton, D. N. And Sung, J. (1994) *The State, Economic Development and Skill Formation: A New Asian Model*, Working Paper No. 3 (Leicester: Centre for Labour Market Studies, University of Leicester).

Atkinson, J. (1985) 'The changing corporation'. In D. Clutterbuck (ed.), *New Patterns of Work* (Aldershot: Gower).

Avis, J. (1993) 'A new orthodoxy, old problems: post-16 reforms'. *British Journal of Sociology of Education*, 4, 245–260.

Ball, S. (1993) 'Education markets, choice and social class: the market as a class strategy in the UK and the USA'. *British Journal of Sociology of Education*, 14(1), 3–19.

Blackburn, M., Bloom, D. and Freeman, R. (1990) 'The declining economic position of less skilled American men'. In G. Burtless (ed.), *A Future of Lousy Jobs?* (Washington DC: Brookings Institute).

Blackwell, B. and Eilon, S. (1991) *The Global Challenge of Innovation* (Oxford: Butterworth-Heinemann).

Block, F. (1990) *Postindustrial Possibilities: A Critique of Economic Discourse* (Berkeley: University of California Press).

Bluestone, B. and Harrison, B. (1982) *The Deindustrialization of America* (New York: Basic Books).

Bound, J. and Johnson, G. (1995) 'What are the causes of rising wage inequality in the United States?' *Economic Policy Review*, Federal Reserve Bank of New York, 1(1), 9–17.

Boyd, W. and Cibulka, J. (eds) (1989) *Private Schools and Public Policy* (London: Falmer Press).

Braverman, H. (1974) *Labour and Monopoly Capital* (London: Jessica Kingsley).

Brown, G. (1994) 'The politics of potential: a new agenda for Labour'. In D. Miliband (ed.), *Reinventing the Left* (Cambridge: Polity).

Brown, P. (1990) 'The "Third Wave": education and the ideology of parentocracy'. *British Journal of Sociology of Education*, 11, 65–85.

Brown, P. (1995) 'Cultural capital and social exclusion: some observations on recent trends in education, employment and the labour market'. *Work Employment and Society*, 9(1), 29–51.

Brown, P. and Lauder, H. (1992) 'Education, economy and society: an introduction to a new agenda'. In P. Brown and H. Lauder (eds), *Education for Economic Survival: From Fordism to Post-Fordism?* (London: Routledge).

Brown, P., Green, A. and Lauder, H. (2001) *High Skills: Globalization, Competitiveness and Skill Formation*, Oxford: Oxford University Press.

Brown, P. and Scase, R. (1994) *Higher Education and Corporate Realities* (London: UCL Press).

Carnoy, M., Castells, M., Cohen, S. and Cardoso, F. H. (1993) *The Global Economy in the Information Age* (Pennsylvania: Penn State University).

Collins, R. (1979) *The Credential Society* (New York: Academic Press).

Collins, R. (1986) *Weberian Sociological Theory* (New York: Cambridge University Press).

Commission of the European Communities (1993) *Growth, Competitiveness, Employment: The Challenges and Ways Forward into the 21st Century* White Paper, Bulletin of the European Communities 6/93.

Commission on Social Justice (1994) *Social Justice: Strategies for National Renewal* (London: Vintage).

Cowling, K. and Sugden, R. (1994) *Beyond Capitalism: Towards a New World Economic Order* (London: Pinter).

Davis, M. (1990) *City of Quartz* (New York: Verso).

Deakin, S. and Wilkinson, F. (1991) 'Social policy and economic efficiency: the deregulation of the labour market in Britain'. *Critical Social Policy*, 11(3), 40–61.

Dewey, J. (1966) *Democracy and Education* (New York: Free Press).

Dicken, P. (1992) *Global Shift: The Internationalisation of Economic Activity* (London: Paul Chapman).

Dore, R. (1987) *Taking Japan Seriously* (London: Athlone Press).

Eatwell, J. (1995) 'The international origins of unemployment'. In J. Michie and J. G. Smith (eds), *Managing the Global Economy* (Oxford: Oxford University Press).

Esping-Andersen, G. (1994) 'Equity and work in the post-industrial life-cycle'. In D. Miliband (ed.), *Reinventing the Left* (Cambridge: Polity).

Freeman, R. (1995) 'The limits of wage flexibility to curing unemployment'. *Oxford Review of Economic Policy*, 11(1), 63–72.

Gamble, A. (1988) *The Free Market and the Strong State* (London: Macmillan).

Gardiner, K. (1993) A Survey of Income Inequality Over the Last Twenty Years – How Does the UK Compare?, Welfare State Programme, No. 100 (London: Centre for Economics and Related Disciplines, London School of Economics).

Gosling, A. and Machin, S. (1993) *Trade Unions and the Dispersion of Earnings in UK Establishments, 1980–90*, Centre for Economic Performance Discussion Paper No. 140 (London: London School of Economics).

Gramsci, A. (1971) *Selections from Prison Notebooks*, (London: Lawrence & Wishart).

Green, A. and Steedman, H. (1993) *Education Provision, Education Attainment and the Needs of Identity: A Review of Research for Germany, France, Japan, the USA and Britain* (London: NIESR).

Halsey, A. H., Heath, A. and Ridge, J. (1980) *Origins and Destinations* (Oxford: Clarendon).

Halstead, M. (ed.) (1994) *Parental Choice and Education* (London: Kogan Page).

Harvey, D. (1989) *The Conditions of Postmodernity* (Oxford: Blackwell).

Henderson, A. and Parsons, T. (eds) (1974) *Max Weber: The Theory of Social and Economic Organisation* (New York: Oxford University Press).

Hills, J. (1995) *Income and Wealth, Vol 2: A Summary of the Evidence* (York: Joseph Rowntree Foundation).

Hirsch, F. (1977) *Social Limits to Growth* (London: Routledge).

Hirschmann, A. (1986) *Rival Views of Market Society and Other Essays* (London: Viking).

Hutton, W. (1995) *The State We're In* (London: Jonathan Cape).

International Labour Organisation (ILO) (1995) *World Employment* (Geneva: ILO).

Jones, K. and Hatcher, R. (1994) 'Education, progress and economic change: notes on some recent proposals'. *British Journal of Educational Studies*, 42, 245–260.

Krugman, P. (1993) *Peddling Prosperity: Economic Sense and Nonsense in the Age of Diminished Expectations* (NewYork: W.W. Norton).

Lane, C. (1989) *Management and Labour in Europe* (Aldershot: Edward Elgar).

Lauder, H. (1987) 'The New Right and educational policy in New Zealand'. *New Zealand Journal of Educational Studies*, 22, 3–23.

Lauder, H. (1991) 'Education, democracy and the economy'. *British Journal of Sociology of Education*, 12, 417–431.

Lauder, H. and Hughes, D. (1990) 'Social inequalities and differences in school outcomes'. *New Zealand Journal of Educational Studies*, 23, 37–60.

Lauder, H. *et al.* (1994) *The Creation of Market Competition for Education in New Zealand* (Wellington: Ministry of Education).

Lazonick, W. (1993) 'Industry clusters versus global webs: organisational capabilities in the American economy'. *Industrial and Corporate Change*, 2, 1–24.

Lindbeck, A. and Snower, D. (1986) 'Wage setting, unemployment and insider–outsider relations'. *American Economic Review*, 76, 235–239.

Lipietz, A. (1987) *Mirages and Miracles: The Crises of Global Fordism* (London: Verso).

Marchak, M. P. (1991) *The Integrated Circus: The New Right and the Restructuring of Global Markets* (Montreal: McGill-Queen's University Press).

Marginson, P. (1994) 'Multinational Britain: employment and work in an internationalised economy'. *Human Resource Management Journal*, 4(4), 63–80.

Maurice, M., Sellier, F. and Silvestre, J. (1986) *The Social Foundations of Industrial Power* (Cambridge, MA: MIT Press).

McGregor, D. (1960) *The Human Side of Enterprise* (New York: McGraw-Hill).

Michie, J. and Smith, J. G. (eds) (1995) *Managing the Global Economy* (Oxford: Oxford University Press).

Murray, C. (1984) *Losing Ground: American Social Policy 1950–1980* (NewYork: Basic Books).

Murray, R. (1989) 'Fordism and post-Fordism'. In S. Hall and M. Jacques (eds), *New Times* (London: Lawrence & Wishart).

National Commission in Education (1993) *Learning to Succeed* (London: Heinemann).

Newman, K. (1993) *Declining Fortunes* (NewYork: Basic Books).

OECD (1989) *Education and the Economy in a Changing World* (Paris: OECD).

OECD (1993) *Employment Outlook* (Paris: OECD).

OECD (1994) *Employment Outlook* (Paris: OECD).

Ormerod, P. (1994) *The Death of Economics* (London: Faber & Faber).

Parkin, F. (1979) *Marxism and Class Theory: A Bourgeois Critique* (London: Tavistock).

Patel, P. and Pavitt, K. (1991) 'Europe's technological performance'. In C. Freeman, M. Sharp and W. Walker (eds), *Technology and the Future of Europe* (London: Pinter).

Peterson, W. (1994) *Silent Depression: The Fate of the American Dream* (New York: W. W. Norton).

Piore, M. (1990) 'Labor standards and business strategies'. In S. Herzenberg and J. Perez-Lopez (eds), *Labor Standards and Development in the Global Economy* (Washington DC: US Department of Labor).

Piore, M. and Sabel, C. (1984) The *Second Industrial Divide: Possibilities for Prosperity* (New York: Basic Books).

Porter, M. (1990) *The Competitive Advantage of Nations* (London: Macmillan).

Reich, R. (1984) *The Next American Frontier* (Harmondsworth: Penguin).

Reich, R. (1991) *The Work of Nations* (London: Simon & Schuster).

Rogers, J. and Streeck, W. (1994) 'Productive solidarities: economic strategy and left politics'. In D. Miliband (ed.), *Reinventing the Left* (Cambridge: Polity).

Rowthorn, R. (1995) 'Capital formation and unemployment'. *Oxford Review of Economic Policy*, 11(1), 26–39.

Sabel, C. F. (1982) *Work and Politics* (Cambridge: Cambridge University Press).

Schumpeter, J. (1961) *The Theory of Economic Development* (NewYork: Oxford University Press).

Sengenberger, W. and Wilkinson, F. (1995) 'Globalization and labour standards'. In J. Michie and J. G. Smith (eds), *Managing the Global Economy* (Oxford: Oxford University Press).

Snower, D. (1995) 'Evaluating unemployment policies: what do the underlying theories tell us?'. *Oxford Review of Economic Policy*, 11, 110–135.

Streeck, W. (1989) 'Skills and the limits of neo-liberalism: the enterprise of the future as a place of learning'. *Work, Employment and Society*, 3, 90–104.

Streeck, W. (1992) *Social Institutions and Economic Performance* (London: Sage).

Thurlow, L. (1993) *Head to Head: The Coming Economic Battle Among Japan, Europe and America* (London: Nicholas Brealey).

Toffler, A. (1990) *Powershift* (New York: Bantam).

Wilkinson, R. (1994) *Unfair Shares: The Effect of Widening Income Differences on the Welfare of the Young* (Ilford: Barnardo's Publication).

Willms, J. and Echols, F. (1992) 'Alert and inert clients. the Scottish experience of parental choice of schools'. *Economics of Education Review*, 11, 339–350.

Wilson, W. (1987) *The Truly Disadvantaged* (Chicago: University of Chicago Press).

Wood, A. (1994) *North–South Trade, Employment and Inequality: Changing Fortunes in a Skill-Driven World* (Oxford: Clarendon).

CHAPTER 4

GLOBALISATION, THE LEARNING SOCIETY AND COMPARATIVE EDUCATION

Peter Jarvis

Comparative Education (2000), 36 (3): 343–55

[...]

In an earlier piece ... (Jarvis, 1999a), I argued that the universities had to respond to the international division of labour generated through the forces of globalisation in innovative ways. In a sense, that argument reflected the one contained in the logic of industrialisation thesis, first propounded by Kerr *et al.* in the 1960s (Kerr *et al.*, 1973). While that thesis was not totally correct, I want to expand upon that article here and argue that the logic of industrialism thesis contained a basis from which to understand globalisation and, consequently, the learning society. However, the learning society is a contested concept, so that it is also necessary to understand it if we are to examine ways by which comparative education might relate to it.

The general thesis of this chapter is that comparative education needs to continue to adapt and to find its place in studies of the newly emerging learning society, one which is far broader than the educational institutions themselves. Indeed, there are many other providers of learning opportunities than education. But, significantly, the learning society itself might be regarded as an object for comparative study, as the following argument demonstrates. Consequently, the chapter has three parts; the first examines the process of globalisation, the second analyses different interpretations, or dimensions, of the learning society and, finally, comparative education is examined within the context of the learning society.

The processes of globalisation

The logic of industrialisation thesis was first published at the beginning of the 1960s in *Industrialism and Industrial Man* (Kerr *et al.*, 1973). In it the authors argued that the industrialising processes at the heart of society would have a world-wide impact, producing a convergence in the social structures in the different countries of the world, a more open and global society. The driving force of these changes was, they argued, the process of industrialisation. This thesis was widely debated for a number of years and, like many major studies, it had many strengths—but it also had weaknesses. Like Marx, but from an entirely different viewpoint, the authors implied that each society has an infrastructure and a superstructure. The infrastructural driving force of change was the industrialisation process itself and, not surprisingly, education was part of the superstructure, responding to the needs of the infrastructure and being forced to change according to its demands. However, it was the identification of the infrastructural forces that was a major weakness; they did not foresee the changes that were to occur in the 1970s which were to alter the face of industry and commerce itself.

But another aspect of Kerr *et al.*'s argument which is important to this chapter is where they located education in their framework. They were only really concerned about higher education, which they regarded as the handmaiden of industrialism. They wrote of it thus:

> The higher educational system of the industrial society stresses the natural sciences, engineering, medicine, managerial training—whether private or public—and administrative law. It must steadily adapt to new disciplines and fields of specialization. There is a relatively smaller place for the humanities and the arts, while the social sciences are strongly related to the training of the managerial groups and technicians for the enterprise and for government. The increased leisure time, however, can afford a broader public appreciation of the humanities and the arts.
>
> (Kerr *et al.*, 1973, p. 47)

The argument claimed that the educational system would have to expand to meet the needs of industrialisation, and this process would create an increasing level of education for all citizens, albeit there would be greater emphasis on those subjects relevant to the infrastructural demands. The process about which they wrote has now occurred. It is not just higher education that has expanded but the whole of the post-school sector, so this chapter is not only about higher education but it is also about education as a whole and, indeed, for the ways in which lifelong learning and the learning society are being conceptualised. Industrialisation is not now the driving force of change, although there are still infrastructural forces—but they are world-wide rather than country-wide—and education remains part of the superstructure. Indeed, the learning society as a whole is superstructural.

The process of globalisation, as we know it today, can be seen to have begun in the early 1970s. In the face of competition from Japan and the oil crisis, corporations began to relocate manufacturing and to transfer capital around the world, seeking the cheapest places and the most efficient means of manufacturing and the best markets in which to sell, their products. This resulted in the continued decline in manufacturing industries in much of the First World and the need for new occupational structures emerged. Theorists began to suggest that there is actually a world economy (Wallerstein, 1974, *inter alia*) based on the capitalist system of exchange. This theoretical approach was questioned in part by Robertson (1992) who was more concerned to show that globalisation is a cultural phenomenon, and by Castells (1996) who argued that the state still has a place to play in a not completely free global market. Even so, the world market expanded rapidly, aided and abetted by the rapid development of electronic communication systems. The information technology revolution took off, with one development leading to another, as Castells (1996, p. 51f.) demonstrates. He makes the point that 'to some extent, the availability of new technologies constituted as a system in the 1970s was a fundamental basis for the process of socio-economic restructuring in the 1980s' (1996, p. 52).

Another factor that reinforced this process was the Fall of the Berlin Wall for from the time it occurred there has literally been 'no alternative' (Bauman, 1992) to capitalism; the global economic infrastructure was reinforced. Now the world-wide infrastructural driving force of social change is information technology empowered by those who control capital.

Castells (1996, p. 145) argues that this has resulted in three major economic regions, Western Europe, America and the Asian Pacific, with other areas of the world associated with them, although he sees Russia as a fourth potential region.

These processes changed the structure of the work-force, with a decline in manufacturing jobs and an increased demand for knowledge-based workers in some countries, but with new industrial workers in others. Indeed, Reich (1991) postulated that there would be three major groups of workers—knowledge-based, service-based and routine production. He indicated (Reich, 1991, pp. 179–180) that the proportion of symbolic analysts (knowledge workers) in the American work-force increased from 8% in the 1950s to about 20% in the 1980s. He then argued that this will continue to increase. Rifkin (1995) said that knowledge workers are:

> ... the creators, manipulators and purveyors of the stream of information that makes up the post-industrial, post-service global economy. Their ranks include research scientists, design engineers, civil engineers, software analysts, biotechnology workers, public relations specialists, lawyers, investment bankers, management consultants, financial and tax consultants, architects, strategic planners, marketing specialists, film producers and editors, art directors, publishers, writers, editors and journalists.
>
> (p. 174)

Castells (1996, p. 147) also suggests a similar division of labour to Reich, with four main types: the producers of high value (knowledge workers); producers of high volume (based on low-cost labour), producers of raw materials (based on natural products); redundant producers (devalued labour). He maintains that each of these types of workers is to be found in most societies, with differing proportions occurring in each country and region.

It is significant to note that at both the global level, and within the economic regions, there is this division of labour. The wealthiest countries have a large proportion of knowledge workers. As other countries industrialise, they generate more knowledge-based workers but their work-force remains predominantly agricultural and manufacturing. Additionally, other countries are socially excluded with most of their work-force being redundant labour and they have subsistence economies; these are among the world's poorest, for this is the inevitable result of globalisation (Bauman, 1998).

However, it is the fact that there are increasing numbers of workers utilising knowledge that has led to the emergence of the learning society.

Learning societies

Since education is driven by the infrastructural forces, it has to respond to a great extent to the demands of the international division of labour. However, education is social and both public and private, depending upon the provider, whereas learning is something that is individual and private. Education is designed to provide specified learning opportunities and is institutionalised, either as state institutions (public) or as corporate ones (private). Both forms of institution emphasise the knowledge necessary for the work-force to compete in the global market economy. The knowledge societies predominate in the countries of Western Europe, the US and the Asian Pacific (Stehr, 1994). But the term frequently used in these societies is 'the learning society'. Learning can be related to knowledge in two quite distinct ways. The learning is the content of what has been learned; it is, in this sense, the knowledge. But even more significantly, much of that knowledge is changing with great rapidity, as Lyotard (1984) noted when he suggested that knowledge is narrative, and this demands that the members of those societies continue to be taught, or to learn, new information and acquire new knowledge and skill in order to keep abreast with the changes in their society. Significantly, the concept of the learning society does not distinguish between education and learning but the learning society is probably more accurately described as being both educative and learning, as will be discussed below. There are, however, dangers in losing education under the learning umbrella since they are profoundly different concepts.

It should be recognised that there are no real boundaries around learning societies, so that the symbols and practices of a learning society can, and will, be transferred to less developed societies, by the transnational companies amongst others, since they will almost certainly transfer practices from one area of their influence to another. Additionally, there is much more cultural borrowing today as government delegations from one country visit others, as participants in international conferences share knowledge and ideas, and as international consultants take their expertise across the globe.

However, the learning society is, as noted earlier, a contested concept and I want to suggest that there are at least four different interpretations that may be placed upon this term, each emphasising one of its dimensions: futuristic, planned, reflexive and market.

The learning society as a futuristic society

When Hutchins (1968) wrote his classic book on the learning society, he looked to the future and suggested that the learning society:

> ... would be one that, in addition to offering part-time adult education to every man and woman at every stage of grown-up life, had succeeded in transforming its values in such a way that learning, fulfilment, becoming human, had become its aims and all its institutions were directed to this end.
>
> (p. 133)

For Hutchins, education would come into its own and the new learning society would be the fulfilment of Athens, made possible not by slavery but by modern machines. It was the realisation of this computer revolution that led Husen (1974) to very similar conclusions. He argued that '*educated ability* will be democracy's replacement for passed-on social prerogatives' (Hutchins, 1974, p. 238). He recognised that the knowledge explosion would be fostered by a combination of computers and reprographics and he foresaw the possibility of 'equal opportunities for all to receive as much education as they are thought capable of absorbing' (Hutchins, 1974, p. 240). Despite Sweden's long history of adult education, Husen regarded the learning society as being educational and based on an extension of the school system.

A similar position has been adopted by Ranson (1994) who has suggested that:

> There is a need for the creation of a learning society as the constitutive condition of a new moral and political order. It is only when the values and processes of learning are placed at the centre of the polity that the conditions can be established for all individuals to develop their capacities, and that institutions can respond openly and imaginatively to a period of change.
>
> (p. 106)

Ranson's writing does not cite either of the earlier authors mentioned above although he approaches the subject from a similar perspective, starting with school education rather than an adult or lifelong education framework. It is futuristic and rather idealistic. By way of contrast, Boshier (1980), while still looking forward to a learning society, actually started from the position of an adult educator recognising it to be more than school education. He explored the post-school institutions in New Zealand to discover the structural basis of such a society, but he still regarded it as an educational phenomenon.

The learning society as a planned society

In recent years governments have been concerned to plan for the learning society, and there has been a multitude of reports, papers and even legislation throughout the world. This is not the place to review all the official reports published on education that particularly refer to lifelong learning, or indeed of all the reports by commercial and industrial bodies calling for more emphasis to be placed on lifelong learning—that would constitute a book in itself. Nevertheless, there are similar themes running through them all as a result of the significance of the global market—competitiveness, competencies, widening participation, and the need for workers to keep on learning so that countries can maintain their place in the economic world, and their people their standard of living. In addition, most statements make some reference to the need for people to learn so that they can grow and develop and participate more in the democratic processes of their society. For instance, in the introduction to the Organisation for Economic Cooperation and Development (OECD) report (1996) the following comments are made:

> Success in realising lifelong learning—from early childhood education to active learning retirement—will be an important factor in promoting employment, economic development, democracy and social cohesion in the years ahead.
>
> (p. 13)

In the European Union White Paper (European Union, 1995) a similar claim is made:

> The crucial problem of employment in a permanently changing economy compels the education and training system to change. The design of appropriate education and training strategies to address work and employment issues is, therefore, a crucial preoccupation.
>
> (p. 18)

In the European perspectives (Collomb & Seidal, 1998), we read the following:

> For Europe to be competitive, working adults need Lifelong Learning: a continual replenishment of their education. Adult Education and Lifelong Learning are essential ingredients in today's integrated Europe.
>
> (p. 8)

Even in the rather more utopian Delors Report (Delors, 1996), we see that the significance of the economic institution in society is recognised:

> Under the pressure of technological progress and modernization, the demand of education for economic purposes has been constantly on the rise in most countries . . .
>
> (p. 70)

Perhaps it is only in Germany where this relationship has not been fully recognised and developed by theorists. Dohman (1996) makes the point that:

> The fact that Germany's education policy has remained relatively unaffected by international efforts to realize lifelong learning ... appears to be due to the German's tendency to over-rate their educational system, their desire to preserve it and their somewhat apprehensive-skeptical attitude toward unsupervised learning.
>
> (p. 96)

While the German position might be one of over-valuing its education system, the apprehensiveness toward uncontrolled learning is apparent in a number of different reports, for people's learning must be influenced even if it cannot be entirely controlled. Indeed, in the British government's policy, there is certainly more than a sense of focusing the learners on what they should learn, in what they should gain qualifications, and for what they will receive maximum funding. This has become clear in nearly all the reports that have been published in the UK during this period, but recognition that the society is global means that governments cannot regulate such processes entirely, only seek to influence them.

In the Kennedy Report (Kennedy, 1997) into further education, for instance, the relationship between learning for work and learning for life is clearly established but, significantly, the Report questioned whether the learning market is the most efficient distributive mechanism, and suggested a middle way between bureaucratic centralisation and the market:

> We have no desire to return to the centralised and bureaucratic planning approaches of the past. We would wish to see local strategy emerging, developing and being sustained by partnership approaches, involving all the key stakeholders, which recognise both the independence and inter-dependence of partners.
>
> (Kennedy, 1997, p. 39)

The Report recognised that funding is a most important lever for change and, perhaps, for creating some partnership agreements. Nevertheless, the power of funding lies only in as much as neither the providers nor consumers could afford to operate without it and, secondly, that there is no competition between partners to gain student enrolments, etc. While partnerships are to be applauded, there is also, however, a sense in which the funding of partnership arrangements seeks to re-create monopoly type situations. This is clearly illustrated in Kennedy's emphasis on data-gathering in order to provide relevant education. Kennedy, therefore, seeks to offer a rather modern answer to a late modern problem. But the generation of partnership arrangements reflect the fact that the barriers between educational and other providers are being lowered, and this diversity itself reflects a late modern situation.

In the British government report *The Learning Age* (Department for Education and Employment (DfEE, 1998) it is clearly stated that the learning society is something to be created (p. 13) and that it will be educative in nature:

> In the Learning Age we will need a workforce with imagination and confidence, and the skills required will be diverse: teachers and trainers to help us acquire these skills ... All of these occupations ... demand different types of knowledge and understanding and the skills to apply them. That is what we mean

by skills, and it is through learning—with the help of those who teach us—that we acquire them.

(DfEE, 1998, p. 15)

Consequently, educational institutions are being encouraged to introduce new courses leading to vocational qualifications, often at higher degree level, and in this case the learning is certificated and public (see Jarvis, 1999a). However, the lecture hall is not the only site for learning, as the development of work-based learning recognises. More significantly, the laboratory is no longer the main place in which research occurs. Many part-time research students today are writing up research conducted by themselves in the work place—they are practitioner researchers (Jarvis, 1999b) who are recognising that the innovations that they are making in their work are actually research situations. The practitioner researcher has arrived, but not all universities are able to recognise these changes and embrace this new breed of researcher, one which is the epitome of the learning society.

However, the educational institutions are not responding sufficiently rapidly to the demands of the infrastructure. Transnational corporations are, therefore, commencing their own corporate universities (Meister, 1994) which are also planning their education/learning for, not only their work-forces, but for the corporations suppliers and distributors as well. These new universities will play a significant role internationally in the future since some of them, such as Motorola, already have campuses in different countries throughout the world.

This tremendous growth in new information and the very rapid changes that are occurring in society might reflect the idea that the learning society is intrinsic to modernity. Both of these approaches foresee an educative society and, as such, it is a phenomenon of which Illich & Verne (1976) were afraid, since they feared people would become imprisoned within a classroom to be educated rather than being free to learn from different and less restrictive sources. Significantly, they also started their analyses with one part of the public institution—the structures of society, and while it might be unwise to separate structure from agency, once the structures are loosened or weakened, then the agent becomes more significant—or individual learning assumes a more significant place than education, and herein lies the foundation for the other major approaches to the learning society, because the rapid changes that are occurring in society have resulted in the weakening of societal structures.

The learning society as reflexive society

Reflective learning and reflective practice have become commonplace ideas among educators in recent years, echoing the work of Schon (1983). But reflective learning is itself a sign of the times. Underlying this is another approach to society epitomised by Giddens (1990) and Beck's (1992) *Risk Society*. However, Giddens, and others, have argued that reflexivity is fundamental to the nature of modernity, for with its advent modernity overrode tradition of all forms. Giddens (1990) writes:

> The reflexivity of modern social life consists in the fact that social practices are constantly examined and reformed in the light of incoming information about those very practices, thus constitutively altering their character. We should be clear about the nature of this phenomenon. All forms of social life are partly constituted by actors' knowledge of them. Knowing 'how to go on' . . . is intrinsic to the conventions which are drawn upon and reproduced in human activity. In all cultures, social practices are routinely altered in the light of ongoing

discoveries which feed into them. But only in the era of modernity is the revision of convention radicalised to apply (in principle) to all aspects of human life . . .

(pp. 38–39)

Society has become reflexive and the knowledge that people acquire is no longer certain and established for ever—its value lies in its enabling them to live in this rapidly changing society. As society is changing so very rapidly, everybody is required to learn new things in order to keep abreast with everything, but in everyday life a great deal of this non-institutionalised learning is incidental as individuals adapt their behaviour to the changed conditions or the innovations that have been introduced. Since this learning is non-vocational there is a tendency for it to be treated as private and not to be recognised publicly. This is not the case with the knowledge-based occupations (and the service orientated ones as well) which are themselves reflexive within late modern society, so that practitioners are required to keep abreast with the changes occurring in their occupational field and to utilise new techniques and procedures. Much of this occurs in work-based learning, which is slowly leading to educational institutions adopting new attitudes to learning that occurs outside the classroom and the lecture hall. Slowly the public education institutions are beginning to accredit work-based learning, and with it the accreditation of prior experiential learning—learning from prior experience for educational qualifications (Jarvis, 1996). But for how long they will retain their monopoly remains another question. Judging by the direction of recent events, the answer will be that this monopoly will soon be broken and education will be but one more provider of information in the learning market and the educational qualification will become the public recognition of a very private process. However, there is a danger here that the education institutions are assuming a role in a non-educational process and public accreditation penetrates the private world!

In addition, there has been a growth in learning networks, rather like those learning webs advocated by Illich (1973, pp. 75–105). Then he was regarded as radical, but now these ideas are becoming more realistic with the development of the Internet and of all forms of electronic communication. This has led to greater opportunity for those who have the technological knowledge, skill and equipment to access up-to-date knowledge and for those who are knowledge producers to share their ideas and research.

As some forms of knowledge change more rapidly than others (Scheler, 1980) the process of learning is both individuating and fragmenting to society as a whole. Neither is it something which all individuals desire; they sometimes seek an unchanging world (Jarvis, 1992, pp. 206–207), and a harmony with their environment. Endeavouring to discover the certainty of an unchanging world is a reaction to the learning society, as it is to modernity itself.

From the perspective of rapidly changing knowledge, there is a fundamental shift in the conception of knowledge itself, from something that is certain and true to something which is changing and relative. This means that underlying this form of society lies experimentation itself, leading to people reflecting constantly upon their situation and the knowledge that they possess to cope with it. Constantly they need to learn new knowledge, but learning new things and acting upon them always contains an element of risk—for inherent in learning is risk but, paradoxically, learning is also a reaction to the risk, of not always knowing how to act in this rapidly changing world. Reflexivity is a feature of modernity (Beck, 1992). Reflective learning is a way of life rather than a discovery made by educators and something to be taught in educational institutions. The learning society is not then a hope for the future but an ever-present phenomenon of the contemporary world, but one that it is not always recognised because the learning is not accredited!

The learning society as a phenomenon of the market

Contemporary society is also a consumer society and the history of consumerism can be traced back to the 18th century (Campbell, 1987). Campbell traces it back to the romantic period in the 18th century, when pleasure became the crucial means of realising that ideal truth and beauty which imagination had revealed and, significantly, this Romantic Movement 'assisted crucially at the birth of modern consumerism' (Campbell, 1987, p. 206), so that a longing to enjoy those creations of the mind becomes the basis for consuming new phenomena. In other words, there can be no market economy unless there are consumers who want to purchase the products that are being produced. Advertising plays on imaginary pleasure, and learning becomes fun! Now, as Usher & Edwards (1994) point out, one of the features of contemporary society is that of experiencing—it is a sensate society. This is nothing new, as Campbell has shown, but it is the type of society in which the longings of the imagination can be realised through consumption, so that the basis of advertising is the cultivation of desire.

Whilst learning was equated with the educational in people's minds, they remembered their unpleasant experiences at school where it was no fun to learn, a barrier to further education was erected and it was one which every adult educator sought to overcome. But once learning became separated from education, then learning could become fun—and there is a sense in which this has become a more popular thing to do in the UK since the creation of the British Open University. Now people could learn all the things that they had wanted to learn, and they did not have to go to school to do it. They could read books, watch the television, listen to the radio and go and talk with other people if they wanted. The Open University marketed a commodity and other organisations have followed. The Open University's foundation marked a crucial step in this process—it moved education of adults away from the school setting and into the consumer society. Now it is possible for individuals to learn all the things they have wanted to know by purchasing their own multimedia personal computers and surfing the Web, watching the television learning zone programmes, buying their own 'teach yourself' books and magazines and, even, purchasing their own self-directed learning courses. But the providers of these learning materials are now not all educational institutions, and educational institutions are having to change their approach with a great deal of alacrity in order to keep abreast with a market generating information about all aspects of life every minute of the day, so that people have to choose not only what channel they are going to watch but what medium they are going to employ to receive their information!

More significantly, learning has become an aspect of symbolic capital (Bourdieu, 1984):

> Knowledge becomes important; knowledge of new goods, their social and cultural value, and how to use them appropriately. This is particularly the case with aspiring groups who adopt a learning mode towards consumption and the cultivation of a lifestyle. It is for groups such as the new middle class, the new working class and the new rich or upper class, that the consumer-culture magazines, newspapers, books, television and radio programmes which stress self-improvement, self-development, personal transformation, how to manage property, relationships and ambition, how to construct a fulfilling lifestyle, are most

relevant. Here one may find most frequently the self-conscious auto-didact who is concerned to convey the appropriate and legitimate signals through his/her consumption activities.

(Featherstone, 1991, p. 19)

Knowledge production has become an industry, cultivating the desire of people to learn so that they can be seen to be modern. The learning society has now become a learning market. Significantly, information is a public commodity contained in every form of media transmission, but learning remains a private activity and knowledge has become personal knowledge (Polanyi, 1962). Herein lies a problem with private learning since one of the features of the market is that the consumption has to be public—conspicuous consumption—and so offering educational qualifications for private learning has now become an institutional activity.

It is also important to note, especially when we discuss this topic from the perspective of comparative education, that this is a learning society of which education is only one part. This is clear from the four descriptions above—the first two are educative but the final two are learning-based. Education has long been seen as having the monopoly of control of the people's learning; it has acted as a government agency, a public institution, and it has been an agency of social and cultural reproduction (Bourdieu & Passeron, 1977). By way of contrast, learning is private and less amenable to control. Education might be regarded as one institutionalised form of learning but, as we have argued above, in the learning society there are other approaches to learning. The learning society might, therefore, assume varying forms and perform different functions in the different countries, or regions, of the world, so that it becomes a legitimate subject for comparative study.

Comparative education and the learning society

If the above interpretations have any validity, they might point to some new directions for comparative studies, both in education and learning. The following paragraphs do not seek to be either exhaustive or prescriptive but illustrate some of the implications of the arguments detailed above, in which there are both global and learning society perspectives.

The phenomenon of globalisation sets its own agenda for comparative studies. For instance, the global infra-structure is not affecting the whole world uniformly, and the international division of labour means that different sectors of the workforce are making different demands on education and learning. Additionally, the social and cultural reproductive functions of education mean that curricula need to retain specific aspects of a nation's cultural heritage if education is to retain some of its traditional functions, rather than reflect the global infra-structural forces—but none of these things might occur uniformly, if they occur at all.

In addition, Kerr *et al.* (1973) claimed that the curricula of higher education would relate to the infra-structural demands of a society and that the humanities would be relegated to leisure time pursuits. Within the context of the learning society, it will be interesting to explore this idea internationally and comparatively in greater detail, especially since recent findings in the UK suggest that a common reason for undertaking learning, even leisure time learning, is work-related (Bienart & Smith, 1997).

Even so, there has been a tremendous growth in leisure time learning, through such organisations as the universities of the third age. Swindell (1999) has recently begun to compare these institutions in Australia and New Zealand and an extension to his work would allow comparison between those who undertake leisure time learning whilst they are still at work with those who have left paid employment. Universities of the third age are a feature of the learning society and the extent to which they emerge throughout the world raises many issues for comparative education.

The different elements of the learning society itself point to other ways that comparative studies might develop; there are both the educational and other ways people are learning that might be studied. It is impossible to provide a total agenda of new fields open for comparative scholarship but a few of them will be listed here for both the educational and the learning.

Institutionalised education

Within the framework of institutionalised education a variety of different studies might be conducted, such as analyses of: the different government policies and strategies seeking to influence people to learn, and the different laws that are being enacted; the manner in which the control of lifelong learning is institutionalising it into lifelong education; the differing ways in which educational institutions are becoming part of the learning market and how this is affecting the way that they operate; the ways in which the educational system is becoming more open, more accessible and more lifelong; the way that the educational system responds to the demands of the global infrastructure in different countries—especially how the higher education sector responds since it might resist these pressures, as Dohman (1996) suggests Germany is doing; the developing role that transnational corporations will play in the education and training of the work-force; the manner in which cultural differences are being manifested in the educational systems; the ways that educational institutions recognise private learning through systems of accreditation of prior experiential learning; the new forms of partnership between education and other sectors of society, such as the transnational corporation, that emerge; the new institutionalised forms of education that arise, such as the corporate university (Meister, 1994).

Learning

In precisely the same way, comparative studies in learning might be undertaken. Once again, it is impossible to outline an agenda, although it is possible to provide examples, such as analyses of

- the way that different cultural styles influence both the process and the content of learning;
- the extent to which it is necessary for institutions selling their learning materials throughout the world to adjust the content and process of learning in order to make them more relevant to the cultures of their potential learners;
- the place of reflection in learning in different cultural settings;
- the influence of gender on learning style in different countries;
- the extent that varying forms of self-directed and leisure-time learning are occurring;
- the different ways in which the culture of consumption is manifesting itself in learning activities;
- the extent to which lifelong learning is occurring in different countries of the world and whether this is related to the different levels of employment.

It would have been easy, however, to spell out a vast range of new topics that open themselves to comparative study in the future, some of which might examine the extent to which societies are converging and education is being standardised by these global processes, or whether the world is fragmenting and self-directed learning is more relevant because it is more flexible. However, this chapter seeks only to point the way to a new agenda for comparative studies, especially in lifelong education and learning.

Some of the above topics have been studied a little by a small band of adult educators who have been conducting comparative studies on the education of adults since before the Exeter (New Hampshire) Conference of 1966 (Liveright & Haygood, 1968). These studies continued with seminars held at the Ontario Institute for Studies in Education (OISE) in Toronto for a number of years, and are still on-going as an international seminar. However OISE does not publish much of its research in the traditional comparative education journals. They also have to refocus their activities, as does school-based comparative education, on lifelong education and lifelong learning as the educational scene has been transformed. It would be beneficial to the field as a whole if we could see a drawing together of these two perspectives, each enriching the other, in the near future. The question remains, however, why should we undertake comparative education studies in this global village?

Perhaps the answers to this have hardly changed with respect to education from those given by the early pioneers of comparative adult education study:

- to generate international understanding that might lead to peace and brother-hood (and sisterhood);
- to understand some of the barriers to cross-cultural understanding;
- to understand the need to improve the educational level of some countries and ways by which this might be undertaken;
- to understand the place education has in economic development but to recognise that education has wider functions in personal development;
- to see how education might be utilised as a means of solving problems and attacking social ills;
- to understand how education can be used in community development;
- to understand the ways in which new institutional forms of learning respond to people's learning needs;
- to understand how different educational institutions can share responsibility for lifelong learning.

(Liveright & Haygood, 1968, pp. 110–113)

This far-sighted agenda that those early adult educators formulated emerged before the present emphasis on learning, so that there might be other reasons why we might compare learning. Among these are: to develop a greater understanding of the cultural differences between people and to understand how these affect their behaviour; to develop a greater toleration of different peoples and cultures; to develop a critical awareness of difference, etc.

Conclusion

These are broader aims than many formulated by the early comparativists, although they reflect many similar sentiments. But by comparing and understanding difference, both in institutions and cultures, in both education and learning, greater levels of toleration might be developed as we 'learn to live together' (Delors, 1996, pp. 91–93) in this global village. Additionally, it might facilitate the development of a more critically aware people who can play their part as active citizens in formulating policy and creating the more democratic world envisaged by many who look forward to the creation of a global learning society.

References

Bauman, Z. (1992) *Intimations of Postmodernity* (London, Routledge).
Bauman, Z. (1998) *Globalisation: the human consequences* (Cambridge, Polity Press).
Beck, U. (1992) *Risk Society* (trans. M. Ritter) (London, Sage).
Beinart, S. & Smith, P. (1997) *National Learning Survey* Research Report No. 49 (London, Department for Education and Employment).
Boshier, R. (1980) *Towards a Learning Society* (Vancouver, Learning Press).
Bourdieu, P. (1984) *Distinction: a social critique of the judgement of taste* (London, Routledge and Kegan Paul).
Bourdieu, P. & Passeron, J-F. (1977) *Reproduction in Education, Society and Culture*, (trans. R. Nice) (London, Sage).
Campbell, C. (1987) *The Romantic Ethic and the Spirit of Modern Consumerism* (Oxford, Blackwell).
Castells, M. (1996) *The Rise of the Network Society* Vol. 1, *The Information Age: economy, society and culture* (Oxford, Blackwell)
Collomb, B. & Seidel, H. (1998) Foreword in: L. Otala *European Approaches to Lifelong Learning* (Geneva, European University-Industry Forum).
DfEE (1998) *The Learning Age: a renaissance for a new Britain* (London, Stationery Office).
Delors, J. (Chair) (1996) *Learning: the treasure within* (Paris, UNESCO).
Dohman, G. (1996) *Lifelong Learning: guidelines for a modern education policy* (Bonn, Federal Ministry of Education, Science, Research and Technology).
European Union (1995) *Teaching and Learning: towards the learning society* (Brussels, European Union).
Featherstone, M. (1991) *Consumer Culture and Postmodernism* (London, Sage).
Giddens, A. (1990) *Consequences of Modernity* (Cambridge, Polity Press).
Husen, T. (1974) *The Learning Society* (London, Methuen).
Hutchins, R. (1968) *The Learning Society* (Harmondsworth, Penguin).
Illich, I. (1973) *Deschooling Society* (Harmondsworth, Penguin).
Illich, I. & Verne, E. (1976) *Imprisoned in a Global Classroom* (London, Writers and Readers Publishing Co-operative).
Jarvis, P. (1992) *Paradoxes of Learning* (San Francisco, Jossey Bass).
Jarvis, P. (1996) The public recognition of lifetime learning, *European Journal of Lifelong Learning*, 1, pp. 10–17.
Jarvis, P. (1999a) Global trends in lifelong learning and the response of the universities, *Comparative Education*, 35(2), pp. 249–257.
Jarvis, P. (1999b) *The Practitioner Researcher: developing theory from practice* (San Francisco, Jossey Bass).
Kerr, C., Dunlop, J.T., Harbison, F. & Myers, C.A. (1973) *Industrialism and Industrial Man* 2nd edn. (Harmondsworth, Penguin).
Kennedy, H. (Chair) (1997) *Learning Works: widening participation in further education* (Coventry, Further Education Funding Council).
Liveright, A.A. & Haygood, N. (Eds) (1968) *The Exeter Papers* (Brookline, MA, Center for the Study of Liberal Education for Adults at Boston University).
Lyotard, J-F. (1984) *The Post-Modern Condition: a report on knowledge* (Manchester, Manchester University Press).
Meister, J. (1994) *Corporate Quality Universities* (Alexander, ASTD and Burr Ridge, IL, Irwin).
Organisation for Economic Cooperation and Development (OECD) (1996) *Lifelong Learning for All* (Paris, OECD).
Otala, L. (1998) *European Approaches to Lifelong Learning* (Geneva, European University-Industry Forum).

Polanyi, M. (1962) *Personal Knowledge* (London, Routledge & Kegan Paul).

Ranson, S. (1994) *Towards the Learning Society* (London, Cassell).

Reich, R. (1991) *The Work of Nations* (London, Simon & Schuster).

Rifkin, J. (1995) *The End of Work: the decline of the global labour force and the dawn of the post-market era* (New York, G.P. Putnam's Sons).

Robertson, R. (1992) *Globalization* (London, Sage).

Scheler, M. (1980) *Problems of a Sociology of Knowledge* (trans. M. Frings (Ed.) K. Stikkers) (London, Routledge & Kegan Paul).

Schon, D. (1983) *The Reflective Practitioner* (New York, Free Press).

Stehr, N. (1994) *Knowledge Societies* (London, Sage).

Swindell, R. (1999) U3A's in Australia and New Zealand: society's $4million bonanza, *Comparative Education*, 35(2), pp. 235–247.

Usher, R. & Edwards, R. (1994) *Education and Postmodernism* (London, Routledge).

Wallerstein, I. (1974) *The Modern World System* (New York, Academic Press).

PART 3

GENDER

CHAPTER 5

THE SOCIAL CONSTRUCTION OF YOUTHFUL MASCULINITIES

Peer group sub-cultures

Mike O'Donnell and Sue Sharpe

Uncertain Masculinities: Youth, Ethnicity and Class in Contemporary Britain (2000), London: Routledge, pp. 38–88

To a large extent it is within the male peer group that boys construct their masculinities – imitating each other and evaluating themselves against each other. Peer group rivalry and conflict is sometimes sharpened by ethnic difference, which can intensify a youthful 'masculine' aggressiveness which seems to alienate rather than attract a growing number of girls.

Schools engage in what is sometimes a losing battle to counterbalance the collective influence of the peer group, particularly the male peer group. The gap between what teachers are trying to achieve with 15- and 16-year-olds and what some of the boys would rather be doing can create an air of non-communication and a sense of cross purpose in the classroom. Matters can deteriorate in all sorts of ways, sometimes into substantial disorder but more characteristically into student boredom and teacher frustration. Humour and parody is another reaction to such imperfect situations, and we found an example of this among a group of African-Caribbean students at one of the Ealing schools. These boys were aware that, as a group, they obtained poorer academic results than the white and Asian students. They were also aware of the liberal educational jargon routinely used by teachers in referring to this issue. Simultaneously deprecating both themselves and the educational system, they referred to themselves as 'The Underachievers'.

Research has established that a wide range of responses to the educational system – individual and group – occur among students other than simply 'pro-school' or 'anti-school', and that peer group membership and identity is an important mediating factor in shaping response (Ball, 1981; Woods, 1983). Both as a basis of identity and as a unit of collective action, the peer group is an immensely powerful player in school dynamics. The peer group itself, as a specific reference point of generational belonging, can have substantial independent influence on the identities and actions of its members. It is also important as a mediator or conduit of other influences on them, such as class, ethnicity and wider youth culture (which is often the peer group's own main point of subjective reference). For many of the boys, school was not the main, or even a major, factor in the formation of their general attitudes and behaviour, although of course even the most reluctant and disaffected among them tended to acquire some skills and knowledge. Far more important was what their friends were thinking and doing. As Paul Willis put it with reference to the anti-school 'lads' in *Learning to Labour*: 'In some respects school is a blank between opportunities for excitement on the street or at a dance with your mates, or trying to "make it" with a girl' (1977: 38).

The senior teachers we interviewed and many of the boys acknowledged – the former sometimes ruefully – the powerful influence of the peer group, especially on boys. Jane Green, the Deputy Head of a West London school with predominantly Asian pupils, put the point emphatically:

> The children at school only seem to flourish as groups. Any child who doesn't operate within a group ... is seen as isolated ... The group seems a very powerful thing. And to be accepted. Peers seem to be much more important than the family or home in children's eyes ...
>
> (Jane Green)

No doubt her comments reflect a teacher's-eye view, but they were widely repeated not least by some of the boys themselves. Desai, an Indian boy, stated somewhat aphoristically: 'you are who you hang around with'.

This chapter, then, examines several of the main influences which help to shape youthful identities and particularly the formation of masculinities. The peer group is an important influence in itself and a mediator of other influences. Among the many influences on masculine identity formation, this chapter looks particularly at ethnicity. It is therefore the confluence of masculinities and ethnicities that is the central but not exclusive focus here. However, no assumption is made that ethnicity rather than, say, patriarchy, global youth culture, or class, is necessarily the main influence in shaping youthful masculinities. While theoretical analysis requires that their relative influence is weighed, in practice they work together and affect particular individuals and groups differently. Our concentration here on the interaction of ethnicity and masculinity is based on the view that the former is an important influence in the formation of masculinities which is in need of some reinterpretation.[1]

White boys and the social construction of masculinities: class and nation

The title of this section does not imply that there is a fixed form or forms of masculinity specific to white males. Rather, what is being examined is the way in which ethnicity, youth culture and class, as well as other factors, generate flows of influence which contribute to how the boys perceive and construct their gender identities. The reality is one of flux and change around key values, beliefs and images which themselves shift over time. However, it is the case that membership of the dominant and overwhelmingly the most numerous ethnic group in Britain has had a significant effect on the formation of the masculinities of white boys and men over a long historical period. Membership of the white majority both gives some boys a feeling of power and focuses their sense of nationalism and territory. Of course, white ethnicity is a wide term, and one that meant somewhat different things to different boys. Most of the white boys had a sense of local belonging and identity as well. For the most part, the white boys we surveyed were born-and-bred Londoners often with a strong sense of identification with the area of London in which they lived. A few of them came from the North of England and the Celtic countries, and one or two from families of asylum seekers, and this was reflected in their senses of identity.

Many of the non-white boys, of course, were the sons or grandsons of 'immigrants', and to varying extents shared similar cultural interests and identifications with white boys. However, ethnic identification was very strong among African-

Caribbean and Asian boys. In this respect our research supports, albeit more impressionistically, the evidence cited in the fourth PSI survey, which reports that ethnicity is almost as common a self-descriptor as nationality among African-Caribbeans and the main Asian groups across the age range (Modood and Berthoud, 1997: 292). Nationality is the basis of citizenship and, as such, of those crucial rights that include permanent residence and access to work and social security; it is also an indicator of cultural identity that varies greatly between individuals. Quite reasonably, an immigrant (or an asylum seeker) may be far more interested in national membership for practical reasons of access to rights, rather than cultural membership. Given this, it is quite probable that in cultural terms many members – if not a majority of the members of Britain's minority ethnic groups – identify as much or more with their ethnic culture as they do with the British culture of which they are nevertheless a part. This is not to contradict the point made by Stuart Hall and many others that many minority ethnic Britains think of themselves as having dual, or 'hyphenated', or multiple identities, such as British-Pakistani or young black British (Hall, 1992). Nor is there any need systematically to order identities in any hierarchy of subjective preference – people generally prefer living their identities rather than grading them.

Between the mid-1960s and the mid-1980s a substantial body of work was published which shared a broadly common purpose and methodology. Its purpose was to establish why working-class boys achieved far less academic and career success than boys of middle-class origin (the performance of boys of upper-class origin did not receive comparable attention).[2] This body of work will be used here for the different purpose of analysing the main characteristics of youthful, white working-class masculinities, about which it contains an enormous amount of material.

This chapter, then, is . . . discursive and is . . . dependent . . . on secondary sources. The aim is to use this body of work to build up flexible models of youthful masculinities which reflect the interaction of ethnicity, gender and other factors and . . . to relate these models to our own findings.

Most of the works discussed below examined school and classroom processes. The methodologies used in the classroom research were predominantly qualitative with a strong emphasis on participant observation. The backbone of this impressive corpus is a trilogy of studies of the relative failure of working-class students in three types of school – a secondary-modern, a grammar school and a comprehensive. The studies are David Hargreaves's *Social Relations in a Secondary School* (1967), David Lacey's *Hightown Grammar* (1970), and Stephen Ball's *Beachside Comprehensive: A Case-Study of Secondary Schooling* (1981). The first two were studies of single-sex boys' schools. By the time Ball embarked on his study, male sociologists had come to appreciate more fully the importance of researching girls as well as boys in the education system, and so he selected a mixed-sex school for his study. As well as recognising the potential role of the peer group in drawing pupils away from formal education, Ball also stressed the attractions of youth culture in general as an alternative to school work. Further, he observes that at the time he was carrying out his research in the late 1970s, many children of working-class background did not see school as particularly relevant to their goals in relation to their adult lives:

> Out of school, many of these adolescents had jobs, went to pubs and to dances, and were able to make their own decisions or to participate in the decision-making of the social group. They participated in or aspired to much of an adult 'working-class culture'.
>
> (Ball, 1981: 117)

A central theoretical point of all three works is that schools, and particularly classroom teachers, play a significant part in the relative educational failure of working-class children through the labelling process. Specifically, the negative labelling of working-class children can lead to conflict with teachers, loss of confidence and alienation from school – with likely destructive consequences for the children's educational and career success. It is not our intention to replicate these studies. On the matter of the relationship between class and labelling, our impression was that the progressive policy frameworks and managerial regimes in the schools that we researched probably resulted in less negative labelling of pupils on the basis of class – as well as gender and 'race' – than was reported in these studies. However, this impression is based on interviews with the boys and some members of the school management, not on observation. An interesting research study would be systematically to explore whether the negative labelling in schools and classrooms remains as extensive and damaging as is sometimes assumed.

The main relevance of the above trilogy of studies to our own work is the information they contain on youthful masculinities, and particularly on the relationship between class and masculinities. As their authors presented it, their data pertained mainly to class, labelling, the peer group and educational failure, but, cut slightly differently, the data provides a mine of information on young masculinities or, at least, young working-class masculinities. Hargreaves's study is the earliest of the three, and presents a vivid picture of the often hard and bitter conflict between tough, working-class boys who were generally consigned to the lower streams and teachers variously determined to impose their authority on the boys, or being cowed and demoralised by them. The single-sex 'sec mod' where he carried out his study seems at times to have been more like a battleground than a school – a reinforcer of these macho and anti-educational attitudes that characterised much of a generation of working-class lads and which still linger today (see Riseborough's evocatively titled 'GBH: The Gobbo Barmy Harmy', in Bates and Riseborough, 1993).

Lacey's research tells us less about the collective power of the working-class boys' peer group because the boys he researched were relatively isolated in a predominantly middle-class grammar school environment. However, the tendency of these boys to 'stick together' – intensified by the labelling process and to drift back to their own cultural roots, indicates that both the collective and solidaristic values of working-class culture survived the boys' transition to grammar school. These values and associated behaviour played a part in the relative failure of working-class boys to settle or succeed in the grammar school compared to middle-class boys. Lacey's study shows how difficult it could be for working-class boys to break from their class situation even when they clearly had the ability to achieve upward social mobility.

Ball's study had more to say about the complexities of interaction between class culture and labelling, especially with respect to middle-class pupils. The latter were more likely than working-class pupils to be pro-school in a way that was either *supportive* or *manipulative* of the formal school system. Working-class pupils were more likely to be anti-school in that they were *passive towards* or *rejecting of* the formal school system. Ball did not claim that his categories were exhaustive of pupils' possible relationships to the school system, nor that they were entirely generated by the class background of the pupils. He effectively indicated that the variety of potential responses of pupils to the interplay of their own cultural background and the school context, including the way they constructed their masculinities, was considerable.

Macho lads and ordinary kids: Paul Willis and Phil Brown

As far as constructing a typology of white working-class masculinities is concerned, the most comprehensive source of material is Paul Willis's classic, *Learning to Labour* (1977) and the book is used for this purpose later in this section. Here it is relevant to note the main argument of the book which is that it is primarily the culture of 'the lads' which caused their educational failure rather than negative labelling at school. In contrast to the conformist 'ear'oles' (or 'swots') who hoped to 'better themselves', the lads rejected school values in the confident belief they would get the kind of a job they wanted anyway. This analysis represented a significant change of emphasis from Hargreaves and Lacey, who stressed the role of teacher labelling in the 'failure' of working-class boys. However, Ball, perhaps reflecting Willis's influence, saw labelling as reinforcing class and peer group influence in contributing to the underachievement of working-class children rather than as the main cause of it.

From the point of view of this book, Willis's description of the formation of an anti-school sub-culture is less relevant than his more incidental but equally well observed description of a dominant form of youthful working-class masculinity of the time. The term widely adopted in the literature to describe this form of masculinity is 'macho' and the aptness of it will become obvious. Toughness and posturing are common characteristics of this form of masculinity which remains an influential model of youthful 'laddishness' as we enter a new millennium, even though it has frequently become wholly detached from the culture of industrial manual labour in which it developed. Given that identity is partly defined in terms of who one sees as 'different' and 'other', the lads avoided behaving in ways they might have seen to be weak or feminine, routinely talked of girls as sex objects and tried to treat most girls as such, and adopted aggressive and insulting attitudes to gays and to members of other ethnic groups. In short, they were what would be judged now, if not then, sexist and racist. Although such attitudes were by no means shared by all working-class people, they were strong enough in traditional working-class culture to find expression in sex segregated gender roles and sometimes in discriminatory behaviour to people of other 'races'/cultures. However, despite the negative streak of intolerance and exclusion in their culture, the lads were as clear about what they were as what they were not, i.e. they had a strong positive sense of their own identity.

It is possible to abstract from Willis's work a number of core values and related behaviours central to the lads' type of youthful working-class masculinity. Figures in brackets are page references in Willis, 1977.

- *physicality/practicality* 'practice is more important than theory' (56)
- *toughness* 'The fight is the moment when you are fully tested in the alternative culture' (35); 'In a more general way, the ambience of violence with its connotations of masculinity spread through the whole culture' (36)
- *collectivism* (centrality of the informal peer group/loyalty to 'yer mates') 'The essence of being "one of the lads" lies within the group. It is impossible to form a distinctive culture by oneself' (23). 'Solidaristic masculinity' ... is a major characteristic of what Willis calls the boys' 'collectivism'.
- *territoriality/exclusion* The following is a quote from Joey, one of the lads: 'That's it, we've developed certain ways of talking, certain ways of acting, and we developed disregards for Pakis, Jamaicans and all different ... for all the scrubs and the fucking ear'oles and all that ...' (23)
- *hedonism/'having fun'* Another quote from Joey: 'I think fuckin' laffin' is the most important thing in fuckin' everything ... it can get you out of a million things' (29)

- *opposition to authority* This occurs partly because of the lads' determination to have fun and to win enough freedom to do so: 'The most basic, obvious and explicit dimension of counter school culture is entrenched general and personalised opposition to authority'; 'In many respects the opposition ... can be understood as a classic example of the opposition between the formal and the informal' (22)

(All the above quotations are from Willis's own commentary except where otherwise stated.)

A problem in attempting to analyse any form of masculinity is establishing with any precision what influences structure it. This issue will not be fully addressed at this point, but it is worth reiterating that class, generational, patriarchal and ethnic influences all contribute to the formation of masculinities, but not in any predictable or formulaic way. The macho masculinity of the lads reflects clear class and patriarchal influences and also the shared generational experience of school and impending work as well as a strong sense of white ethnic identity. One of our main purposes in writing ... is to tease out the effects of ethnicity on gender formation, and specifically on masculinities. In the case of the above studies, the focus is exclusively or primarily on white youth and, perhaps as a result of this, their ethnicity is taken for granted rather than explored, although it does surface in the form of racism among the lads in Willis's study. In the case of the macho working-class lads, class and ethnic factors seem to converge to reinforce their sense of collective identity and territoriality and their often narrow attitudes to others.

While accepting Willis's view that class culture is crucial in influencing attitudes to education, Phil Brown's *Schooling Ordinary Kids* (1987) criticises the polarised picture of working-class youth he considers Willis presents. As the title of his book suggests, Brown finds that the 'ordinary', just-getting-by, type of behaviour is typical of the majority of the boys and girls in his survey, rather than the aggressive search for excitement of the lads. On the basis of his own research in a South Wales comprehensive school, Brown suggests 'three different ways' among working-class kids 'of being in school and becoming adult' ... 'getting in' (the 'rems' – not all 'rems' were remedials but they tended to be low academic achievers); 'getting out' (the 'swots'); or 'getting on' ('ordinary kids'). Those who adopt the 'getting in' approach want to get into working-class culture and work proper – and out of school; those who adopt the 'getting out' approach aspire to a middle-class job and lifestyle; and those who adopt the 'getting on' approach are the majority of 'ordinary working-class pupils' who 'neither simply accept nor reject school, but comply with it' (Brown, 1987: 31).

From the point of view of how masculinities are constructed by working-class boys, the relevant point from Brown's study is that the majority of lads are not 'extreme macho'. As was suggested ..., historically, working-class men and boys may have benefited from gender inequality but they were not crudely macho. They expressed their masculinities in different ways which, within their own frame of cultural reference, were often supportive to their families as well as their mates. Like Ball, Brown emphasises that most working-class boys and girls, not just the 'rems' or rebels, take part in youth culture but, according to Brown, unlike the 'rems', most of them do not use it as a basis from which to reject school:

> The difference between the ordinary kids and the 'rems' is not that ordinary kids are not exposed to an increasing number of activities and 'outside interests' which may bring them into conflict with the school. It is not the case that ordinary kids will not engage in generational and class youth subcultures, but

rather, that these rarely become full-blown, which would bring them into direct opposition to the school.

(Brown, 1987: 92)

Brown's analysis has some application to our own findings. First, as the extract shows, he does not see a huge gap between the experience of the 'rems' and the ordinary kids, although their different adaptations to school are likely to have future significant effects on career and lifestyles. It is a reasonable speculation that it is the rather more macho 'rems' who are more likely to be unemployed and to fall foul of authority after leaving school. Similarly, most of the boys in our survey were more or less engaged with youth culture – there was no sharp difference in this respect between the more and the less academically oriented, although a variety of differences occurred between the boys in terms of cultural practices.

Second, Brown's more differentiated account of adaptations to school and of school–work transitions is closer to our own findings. . . . So, too, is the implication in Brown's book that working-class boys construct a variety of masculine identities of which being macho is only one. In any case, our data was drawn from individual interviews and questionnaires rather than group observation, and, to that extent, was designed to reflect individual differences. A further point is that the boys in our survey, like Brown's respondents, were faced with an employment market blighted by economic recession in which youth unemployment was even higher than the national average. It no longer made sense for them to adopt the cocksure attitude to job prospects of the lads of Willis's study. Nevertheless, if Brown does not find a sharply polarised 'lads and ear'oles' situation, it is also the case that some of the 'rems' showed typical features of macho culture. Nationally, macho working-class masculinity began to take on a dislocated and even slightly desperate character as the infrastructure of traditional industrial working-class life began to collapse in 1980s Britain.

Beyond macho, other forms of youthful masculinities: Mairtin Mac an Ghaill

Mairtin Mac an Ghaill's *The Making of Men: Masculinities, Sexualities and Schooling* (1994) was the first book to deal substantially and directly with the contribution of schooling to the construction of masculine gender and sexual identities. Previously he had examined aspects of schooling and ethnicity, particularly labelling, in *Young, Gifted and Black* (1988). Mac an Ghaill's full consideration of gender and ethnic factors in the schooling process does not mean he downgrades the influence of class in the formation of identities. In fact he finds that types of masculinity are strongly influenced by class background and seems to see class as the main factor shaping masculinities. Thus, while in no way seeking to be exhaustive, he finds three 'modes' of masculinity among the working-class students in his study and one among the middle-class boys. He identifies the three groups of working-class boys as 'The Macho Lads', 'The Academic Achievers', and 'The New Enterprisers' (although this group appears not to be exclusively working-class); and the middle-class group as 'The Real Englishmen'.

Although sometimes referred to in other terms, the two types of masculinities described by the terms 'Macho Lads' and 'Academic Achievers' occur frequently in the works referred to above. The macho lads were simply called 'the lads' by Willis – the traditional term that friendship groups of working-class men of all ages use to refer to themselves. Macho laddish behaviour is still quite widely adopted by boys of working-class origin, even though the socio-economic context from which this type of masculinity emerged and flourished has largely disappeared. The decline of traditional manual work is the main underlying cause of what Mac an Ghaill refers to as a crisis of white working-class masculinity. The greatest degree of dislocation occurs among those working-class boys (and men) whose self-esteem and identity is based on their ability to perform heavy physical labour. The gendered division of labour which generated this type of masculinity has rapidly changed over the last quarter of a century. For those working-class students who did not want or could not find traditional working-class jobs, the options were increasingly to seek upward mobility into white collar work (Academic Achievers and New Enterprisers) or to face the prospect of low-paid, perhaps irregular employment or longer-term unemployment (Goldthorpe *et al.*, 1987). . . . The real possibility of not getting a job unnerved some of the boys in our survey, and the collective sense of security and confidence of the previous generation had gone. Although some of them were bored with school and wanted badly to move on, few expressed the contempt for education shown by some of the boys in Willis's study.

Until recently, the concerns of many sociologists with educational underachievement have led them to focus more on 'the lads' than the upwardly mobile working-class children ('the lobes') or the more routinely successful middle-class children. Mac an Ghaill's categories of 'Academic Achievers' and 'New Enterprisers' incorporate more adequately both the changing educational and occupational realities of the 1980s and 1990s and the different aspirations of students. He specifically notes that the Academic Achievers contained a high proportion of Asian as well as white boys (Mac an Ghaill, 1994: 59). Mac an Ghaill describes the New Enterprisers as working-class lads who saw an opportunity for upward social mobility in the newly vocationalised curriculum and 'were negotiating a mode of school student masculinity with its values of rationality, instrumentalism, forward planning and careerism' (1994: 63). Although the boys in our survey were younger than those in Mac an Ghaill's sample and had not developed their academic specialisms and career choices to the same extent, the differences he indicates in academic and career orientation among working-class boys were broadly apparent.

Middle-class boys and masculinities: 'The Real Englishman' and 'TechnoMan'

Mac an Ghaill's fourth category, the middle-class 'Real Englishmen', was the least apparent in our survey, although there were boys of similar background and aspiration in our sample. However, Mac an Ghaill's description of this grouping is quite specific:

> A central contradiction for the Real Englishmen was that unlike the Macho Lads' overt rejection of formal school knowledge and the potential exchange value it has in the market place, the Real Englishmen had a more ambiguous relationship to it. They envisaged a future of higher education and a professional career . . . they defined themselves as the younger generation of the professional elite who like modern-day high priests positioned themselves as arbiters of culture.
>
> (Mac an Ghaill, 1994: 65)

Although Mac an Ghaill's four categories of masculinities are conceived as class–gender categories, all the Real Englishmen were white, as might be expected from their collective label, and at the time at which the above quotation applies, were slightly older than the boys we surveyed. Although many of the middle-class boys in our study also 'envisaged a future of higher education and a professional career', we found little sign of the precise cultural pretensions noted by Mac an Ghaill. Perhaps the boys in our study were not yet mature and sophisticated enough to think in these terms. Further, there are more opportunities for sixth formers than fifth formers to develop a reflective sub-culture of this kind. However, one of Mac an Ghaill's observations about the Real Englishmen does strike a chord of recognition. Mac an Ghaill comments that they were at pains to distance themselves from what they saw as the hypocritical liberalism of their well-heeled parents, in particular in their adoption of strongly nationalistic views.

In contrast to the 'Real Englishmen' of Mac an Ghaill's study, some of the white middle-class boys in our survey carried nationalism over into clear prejudice and expressed illiberal attitudes. ... One boy in our research, Bruce, expressed rather aggressive attitudes on 'race' in which he sees himself as a participant in a world of antagonistic racially-based male youth groups. Edward from Hackney was the son of a property surveyor and a nurse. He had stereotypical views about white and African-Caribbean boys as being 'pretty tough' and Asian boys as being weaker. However, his tendency to liberalism more obviously leaked through in his comments on gender. On the sexual division of labour between himself and his future spouse, Edward stated that: 'If she wanted to ... I'd let her stay at home. But if she wanted to work, I'd let her do that as well'. It is Edward's assumption of control that gives away the patriarchal and incipiently authoritarian attitudes behind his attempted gesture of liberality. Edward had expressed similar views on the issue of gender equality and the curriculum. He considered that other boys would consider it 'weird' if one of them opted to study Child Development, and his own attempt to avoid overtly agreeing with this attitude was mild and unconvincing.

A more familiar manifestation of masculinity than that expressed in the attitudes of 'the Real Englishmen' – though not incompatible with them – is the instrumental and hyper-rationality often associated with high- and middle-level businessmen, bureaucrats and technocrats. Both Bob Connell (1995) and Vic Seidler (1997) have explored this cultural formation in men and see it as a major component in their dominating and controlling behaviour, particularly that of middle-class men. This kind of orientation, albeit in embryo, was certainly apparent among the boys in our survey. It was obvious among more ambitious middle-class boys but also among some less advantaged working-class and ethnic minority boys. If one was in the business of inventing labels for categories of masculinity, this one might be termed 'techno-masculinity'. However, the speed of social and cultural change is such that the cultural formations that such categories seek to describe transform very quickly. Too rigid categorisation can give a false sense of stability. Nevertheless, control of technology is likely to become even more important as a means of achieving power, influence and wealth. It is an area in which boys and men are already much more firmly established than girls and women. According to an EOC report, *Gender Equality and the Careers Service* (1999), 67 per cent of school leavers opting for apprenticeships in Information Technology are young men, and this gender inequality is even more marked in respect to higher qualifications.

Although interest in the new technology was even more apparent among middle-class students in our survey, at least in the academic context, to some extent, command of the new technology has become a new benchmark of masculinity among boys regardless of class. Among working-class boys we found that a frequent use of computers was to play exciting and often violent games, and to that extent it may partly have replaced the celebration of physical labour and strength both as an expression of and a symbolic referent for macho. Middle-class boys were more likely to refer to the new technology in an academic and career context, and for them the dividend in masculinity seemed more to be in the hard-edged cleverness associated with this type of skill. However, an equally notable social factor in relation to the new technology was the large number of Asian, especially Indian boys, who expressed both an academic and a career interest in it. Their enthusiasm seemed to be for both the technology itself and the opportunities that mastery of it might offer them. Speculating, it may be that they also felt that the high demand for objective skills in this area would ensure that employers could not afford the luxury of racial discrimination. The perceived importance of technological mastery in contemporary masculine success can be viewed as a variation and extension of the long association of masculinity with rationality. . . . 'Techno man', then, would seem to be a sub-species of 'rational man' – a mutant survivor!

White boys, class and ethnicity

The body of work referred to and partly reinterpreted above is not intended to be a comprehensive analysis of youthful white masculinities as they have developed in relation to the educational system. The majority of the authors referred to were not primarily concerned with masculinity, although all of them had to confront it, given its impact on formal education and the socialisation of youth. The picture of white youthful masculinities they collectively present is only partial. Mac an Ghaill's *The Making of Men* is directly concerned with the construction of masculinities and offers by far the fullest account. Even so, he selects from observation just four groups of young males, each of which is characterised by a more or less identifiable 'mode' of masculinity. Again, it is worth stressing that his categorisation systematically prioritises class over ethnicity as an influence on the formation of gender identities, whereas a key argument of this chapter is that no particular influence should necessarily be privileged in this way. Nevertheless, Mac an Ghaill's work does offer a coherent example of how masculinities can be analysed in relation to socio-economic context as well as developing a typology of youthful masculinities that is specific to his data but is clearly open to some generalisation.

As far as working-class boys are concerned, he adds to the familiar categories of Macho Lads and Academic Achievers that of New Enterprisers. We came across many boys in our survey who could be included in this category, not only white but Asian and, though less so, African-Caribbean. It would be very surprising if a strong orientation of this kind to the new, higher-status vocational curriculum and related jobs had not developed. Although their competitive and instrumental attitudes are hardly novel among young men, the socio-economic context in which they strive to assert themselves is very different from that of their fathers' generation as is the anxiously keen timbre of their response. Although not seeking to be comprehensive, Mac an Ghaill describes only one middle-class grouping of young males, the Real Englishmen. While we found no clear evidence of such a form of white youthful masculinity, it is highly likely that it occurs more widely than just in the institutions which Mac an Ghaill researched. However, we did find that some white middle-class boys as well as some white working-class boys were sometimes uneasy in their attitudes to ethnic minorities, and that their sense of identity was sometimes strongly ethnocentric.

Later sections in this chapter argue that, in certain circumstances, ethnicity can play as strong – or even stronger – a role in the construction of masculinities as class. This is specifically the case in relation to African-Caribbean boys and arguably so in relation to Asian boys, particularly those of Muslim background. Mac an Ghaill's theoretical model seems to prioritise the class–gender axis of influence somewhat at the expense of that of ethnicity–gender. We have no *a priori* theoretical view of this kind and, in the cases just mentioned, the balance of empirical evidence seems to point away from Mac an Ghaill's assumptions. Historically, the British class system has operated in a sharply divisive way, including within the education system, but it has always been open to ameliorating influences. We found some evidence that traditional class divisions may have influenced the boys in our survey rather less than was the case with previous generations of boys from roughly similar backgrounds. Even among white boys, who might have been expected to be most influenced by the British class system in their attitudes to education, we found a mix of middle- and working-class boys with an interest in either or both academic areas and higher-status vocational courses. This seemed more likely to result in a reduction in class cultural differences between them, including the way they perceived themselves as masculine, than to accentuate differences. Even granted that attitudes associated with differential educational choice are likely to harden in the sixth form, there were few signs among the boys in our survey of the contempt that Mac an Ghaill reports the middle-class Real Englishmen had for the working-class Achievers (Mac an Ghaill, 1994: 66–7). Mac an Ghaill's concentration on class as apparently the key influence on the formation of 'modes of masculinity' results in an underemphasis on the influence of ethnicity. In particular he does not consider that the Indian boys who adopt the New Enterprisers approach to educational advancement and self-presentation do so because of pressure and support from their families and community, which is more reflective of ethnicity than class. Of course, there is no doubt that in the lived reality of everyday life, ethnic and class influences are inseparable, but it is still necessary to weigh their respective effects.

For several reasons, then, the relationship between class and masculinities appears to be weakening. First, as is consistently argued here, post-war immigration has complicated the class-derived working-, middle- and upper-class-influenced modes of masculinity of pre-war Britain. Second, the British occupational and class structure has changed and become more differentiated. It is increasingly difficult to 'read off' boys' or men's class background from the way they present themselves as masculine. This is because the effect of class background on gender identities is weaker, while other influences on them are stronger. The education system reflects this greater complexity both in their gender styles and in that boys from different class backgrounds seem somewhat less differentiated by the types of courses they want to do. This is perhaps less a process of embourgeoisement and more one of increasing diversity and complexity. Third, educationalists themselves may well have contributed to the extent to which young people seem to be able to think and act outside of class boundaries. In particular, comprehensive reform sought in part to diminish the socio-cultural boundaries of Britain. Reformers may have achieved more in undermining the cultural than the material influence of class.

In addition to the factors mentioned above, the media has also played a relatively independent role in generating new masculine or 'masculinised' images and styles. In the 1980s and 1990s, the most popular youthful masculine style was neither genuine working-class macho nor a youthful version of the often understated but confident and 'rational' masculinity of the managerial and professional middle class. What emerged quite pervasively was the 'laddish' style, the origins of which seem quite various. Often this new laddishness took the form of a purportedly classless yobbish-ness and collective male self-celebration which nevertheless had an element of shaky self-reassurance about it. No doubt this style was partly motivated by a sense of threat from increasingly assertive females as well as from the prospect of unemployment. The style was even adopted by many middle- and upper-class young males who, however, were generally much less willing to give up their wealth and privilege than they were the manners and accent that had been associated with them.

Although 'laddishness' affects to be a classless cultural style, its main origin may lie with the achievement of money and status by upwardly mobile working- and lower-middle-class males in the 1980s and 1990s. In retaining their accents and abrasive attitudes and in rejecting total cultural assimilation to the wealthy, these young men perhaps showed a degree of integrity and undermined some of the pretensions and affectations for which the established British upper-middle and upper class is notorious. Whether their own preferred style offered anything much better is debatable, although it probably generated more intentional humour. Perhaps because economic success and upward social mobility were most associated with London and the South East, the most widely adopted accent taken to portray the laddish style was a slightly flattened Cockney which became known as 'Estuary English'. On some lips it came to seem even more forced and false than did received pronunciation. Like all widely adopted modern youth styles, the media played a significant role in purveying and popularising new laddishness. . . . Like many youth styles, 'laddishness' as a media and market reference point was beginning to look in need of an injection of energy by the late 1990s. In an effort to provide this, the magazine 'for lads' ZN created the 'whopper', who turned out to be a new type of lad with all the old characteristics!

Upper-class boys and masculinities

Historically, upper-class youthful masculinity has been as distinctive as working-class macho masculinity and, partly because it also served as a model for the professional middle classes, more influential than the working-class version. The traditional masculine demeanour and behaviour of upper-class men and boys is closely associated with the exercise of power, influence and authority. Acceptance of this authority runs deep in Britain's common culture, but so does resistance to it, not least in the form of parody and mockery. A more complete account of the formation and types of masculinities than is required here would need to analyse upper-class masculinity at some length. However, the public schools which, from the mid-nineteenth century, have forged this type of masculinity are remote from the immediate experience and considerations of the boys in our survey, even though the national elites that public schools substantially produce disproportionately shape the conditions in which less advantaged boys live. The public schools continue to inculcate upper-class and patriarchal values among the offspring of the traditionally and newly rich. It would be a gross mistake to underestimate either how formidable the more successful products of public schools are or the extent of their power in national life. The notorious 'public school type' or 'public school man' was and is disciplined, tough, self-confident to the point of arrogance, accustomed to the notion of leadership, and elitist in the highest degree. These were the types of men who ran the British Empire, and the current generation remains powerfully positioned. To a large extent, grammar schools were modelled on the public school system. They usually adopted prefectorial and house systems and emphasised the character building potential of sporting activities all of which aped public school practice. Successful grammar school pupils were likely to become members of local elites, with a minority gaining access to the national elite dominated by ex-public school pupils.

The introduction of the comprehensive school system was intended to challenge the patent non-egalitarianism of the grammar/secondary-modern school system. It is still too early to say whether the comprehensives have improved the relative chances of upward social mobility of children of working-class origin. However, it is now the case that there is a much greater variety and range of social background among Britain's wealthy and powerful, and correspondingly the dominance of the traditional upper-class masculine style has diminished (see successive annual editions of 'The *Times* Rich List' for an illustration of the accelerated decline of traditional wealth). Whether matters of cultural style and self-presentation are of much importance against the reality of a rapidly increasing wealth gap between the rich and the poor and the continuing, if slightly decreasing, patriarchal control of wealth and power is open to debate. Whatever their contribution to a materially more equal society, the comprehensives can better enable more mixing and social exchange to occur between various socio-cultural groups than might otherwise take place. Further consequences of this exchange in relation to different ethnic groups will emerge as this chapter progresses.

African-Caribbean boys and the social construction of masculinities

Understanding African-Caribbean masculinities: the boys' view

African-Caribbean boys talking about themselves

Perhaps reflecting the post-modern interest in difference and diversity, much recent literature on youthful identities has emphasised the influence of ethnicity. Although Mac an Ghaill's theoretical perspective is predominantly a class–gender one, in practice he gives considerable weight to the effect of ethnicity in the formulation of masculinities. Thus, in his earlier book *Young, Gifted and Black* (1988) he adopts as his own descriptors the ethnically-based self-designated names of two groups of boys – 'The Rasta-heads' and 'The Warriors' – and explains much of their respective behaviour in terms of their response to labelling. ... The categories Mac an Ghaill uses to refer to various groups of boys in *The Making of Men* (1994) are not ethnically based. Even 'The Real Englishmen' are clearly indicated and interpreted as a middle-class group. Nevertheless, it is difficult – although not impossible – to envisage non-whites gaining 'membership' of this group. As its title suggests, Les Back's *New Ethnicities and Urban Culture* emphasises the role of ethnic identity in the lives of the inner urban young people he researched (Back, 1996). However, Back sees ethnic culture among the young as fluid and porous, and as inter-playing with class and other factors such as neighbourhood identification and culture. For instance, he describes the admiration of some white boys for African-Caribbeans as sometime based on a selective and egocentric identification with the latter's much vaunted macho characteristics. In general, Back's stress on diversity is based on the extent and dynamism of cultural inter-change and is the antithesis of a rigidified multi-culturalism.

Like many other researchers, we found that the 'macho' image is a pre-dominant style among African-Caribbean boys (see page 111). This was not only true in terms of many of the African-Caribbean boys' self-perception, it was a view of them commonly taken by boys from other ethnic backgrounds. Before exploring the macho identification, however, it is necessary to introduce some qualifying comment. First, not all the African-Caribbean boys either saw themselves as 'macho' or aspired to be so. Second, even among some of the more obviously macho types, there were some hesitations and qualifications. These two points are illustrated in parts of the remainder of section. Third, for understandable reasons, discussions of the macho style of masculinity often tend to be emotive and judgemental. Some see it as threatening and invasive. Here the emphasis will be on analysis and interpretation.

Courtney, whose parents were from Grenada and who was big enough to wear the macho style with ease, rejected it – although he then expressed some attitudes towards housework which slightly smacked of macho. Courtney rejected the macho label not only in terms of himself but also in relation to most of his African-Caribbean peers:

> From what people think of me – 'He's a nutter, he's a hard one' – I'm not like that, no. Maybe the image is like that. I find that a lot of my West Indian friends, they are relatively sensitive, they see both points of view. I find that some of my friends who are not Afro-Caribbean are more closed up. They don't reveal their sensitivity, so it looks as though they're macho and everything, whereas possibly they aren't. Me, I don't try to confine it.
>
> (Courtney)

Courtney is saying that, as far as he himself is concerned – and perhaps by implication his African-Caribbean friends – superficially they may seem macho but in fact they are more openly sensitive than his non-African-Caribbean friends. However, Courtney was quite clear that sensitivity did not involve egalitarian attitudes towards a partner. To a question on the 'new man', he replied: 'Rubbish! It's never going to be. You might get more sensitive, help a bit more, but you're not going to be the "househusband", it's not going to get like that, no.'

Courtney came from a single parent family and his mother did secretarial work. In Mac an Ghaill's terms, Courtney might be classified as a working-class Achiever. He was keen to go on to do A-levels and get a professional job. His smart but conventional self-presentation reinforced this message. It may have been because of his serious academic and career ambitions that he rejected the macho identity, although, at a less instrumental, more personal level, he did give indications of practising the sensitivity he claimed. His father was dead and he clearly had an active concern for his mother and siblings. Further, despite his rubbishing of the househusband concept, like many of the African-Caribbean boys we interviewed he considered it normal and fair that he should do 'his share' of the housework. One of the most interesting points he raised is that, behind the macho facade some of his African-Caribbean friends are prepared to be more emotionally open – suggesting that African-Caribbean macho may be less 'closed off' than white macho.

Franklin's parents were both born in Jamaica. He said that most of his friends were quite macho and tough and that 'occasionally' he was also. Yet Franklin did not give an unqualified endorsement to the macho style. Asked why some boys adopt a macho image, he replied:

Franklin: I don't know. To impress, to show off. I don't know.
Interviewer: Do you think it attracts girls?
Franklin: Not all the time. Most of them like a new man, sensitive approach.

Another African-Caribbean boy, Adam, also took the view that boys should be able to show sensitivity, but again this was not part of an overall ideology of gender equality. In fact, like Courtney, he combined his endorsement of sensitivity with quite a traditional and patriarchal view of gender roles:

Adam:	I think that a man should be strong, but on the other hand he should show his emotions. Some people say that if a man cries he's a sissy, but why do you have tears – they're meant to come out at some time or another. A man should be able to look after his children, look after his wife. And the wife should be able to look after the husband and children.
Interviewer:	So you could cry if you wanted?
Adam:	Yes.
Int:	Do you think men are more violent?
Adam:	Most men, yes.
Int:	Is it nature or do you think they've learnt to be that way?
Adam:	I think it's nature.

All three boys appreciate that masculine behaviour can have a sensitive side, but they are also attached to more traditional notions of masculinity. . . . They are attracted by the idea of being able to show a range of emotions but not by an egalitarian sharing of power and labour. It is possible that, in an interview situation, face-to-face with an adult, the boys felt defensive about being seen as macho, and this may partly account for their slightly ambiguous responses on the subject. Still, there is no expectation that 16-year-olds should display ideological consistency!

White boys talking about African-Caribbean boys

Although some African-Caribbean boys themselves show some unease about the macho aspects of their own behaviour, the most negative constructions came from members of other ethnic groups. Given the negative image of young African-Caribbean boys still prevalent in much of the British press and the public perception, it is important to establish as precisely as possible how boys from other ethnic groups do see African-Caribbean boys. Some, such as Terry and Paul – white boys from two different Ealing schools – expressed mixed but predominantly negative opinions. Terry's ambiguity on matters of 'race' can be gauged by his observation that, although he had 'a few' African-Caribbean friends, he would 'probably not' go out with an African-Caribbean girl because of 'the stick' he would get from his white friends. The following was his response to the question of whether he saw 'any signs at all of racial tension in the school':

Terry:	Yes there is. Groups of people. In the year below, there's a group of coloured people, they go around hassling people.
Interviewer:	You say 'coloured' – what group are you talking about?
Terry:	Afro-Caribbeans. Basically, they're loud and they've no respect for anything. Some of them are fine. Just this particular group, and you get the odd person calling names. And people call them names.
Interviewer:	Who do you see as starting the aggro?
Terry:	Both parties really. You've got them asking for it. Some people should ignore it.

Terry makes an effort to be fair in apportioning blame for the 'aggro', but he clearly inclines to the view that it is mostly the African-Caribbean boys' fault. Despite indicating that not all African-Caribbean boys get involved, there is a strong sense in which he is condemning African-Caribbean boys collectively as distinct from merely some individuals. Such perceptions and attitudes are characteristic of stereotyping and occur among adults as well as younger people. However, it is also possible that there is some empirical substance in the perception of Terry and others. The possibility that the macho style of some African-Caribbean boys is particularly confrontational – even by comparison with macho white working-class boys – is an issue which will be further discussed.

Paul, a white boy, was himself almost classically stereotypical in his views of African-Caribbean boys:

> There's quite a lot of racism in our school. Most of the kids are half-caste or coloured. The coloured kids try to be hard, better than the white people. The white people don't like that, and call them names. Things like that. It ends up in a fight. I don't get into that. I had a couple of fights last year which I got suspended for . . .
>
> (Paul)

Paul expressed the quite common view among white boys that African-Caribbean boys went around threateningly in groups. He blamed 'blacks, Jamaicans', for going round 'in gangs, groups of fives' and claimed that they 'come over and start all the fights'.

Then in a sudden apparent about-turn, he said: 'Most of my friends are Jamaican. I like playing football with them'.

It is not unusual for white boys to sustain seemingly incompatible opinions and feelings about black boys. Les Back (1996) suggests that some white working-class boys tend to select aspects of macho masculinity from the African-Caribbean boys' culture that fit well with their own macho aspirations and self-image.[3] This seems likely and could well be the case with Paul. Sport is an area of conspicuous achievement for some African-Caribbeans, and we found other examples where it provided a positive meeting point for black and white boys. Back further suggests that the selective acceptance and adoption by some white boys of African-Caribbean macho culture may not dislodge the underlying racism and hostility which can flare at times of conflict, sometimes bringing friendships to an end. He also notes that white macho boys are unlikely to select Asian boys as friends on the basis of the latter's perceived (non-) macho qualities. We also found that, in the world of youth culture, the popular stereotype of Asians as passive and even as victims was widely accepted – although not by many Asian boys themselves. Several Asian boys had an interest in martial arts, but in the mid-1990s this did not seem to be providing a frequent basis for friendship with white boys. Of course, as Back himself recognises, the pattern of inter-ethnic friendship just indicated is simply one among many. As he illustrates, shared experience in leisure, work or in the neighbourhood can provide the foundation of much deeper and more lasting relationships for people of different ethnic backgrounds.

James was another white boy we interviewed who regarded African-Caribbean boys as particularly aggressive and in the habit of going around in groups. James went to a West London school which has a large majority of Asian pupils. Therefore, in the context of this school, he was a member of a minority. It is interesting that what he perceived was consistent with Terry's and Paul's observations about which group 'starts the trouble'. Contrary to what some others boys said, he claimed that there was 'a lot' of racial tension within the school:

Interviewer: Do you think one group more than another causes it [racial tension]?
James: Sometimes. Usually West Indian people start it. They go around in groups.

Interviewer: Being in a group doesn't start a racial incident.
James: No. They start it because they're in a big group and they cause a fight.

The repeated perceptions of some white boys that black boys 'go around in groups' and are sometimes 'loud' and even threatening require some comments. First, some white boys behave in pretty much the same way, and which ethnic group does it the most may well be to a considerable extent in the eye of the beholder. Second, African-Caribbean boys are still disproportionately likely to be working-class compared to white and Asian boys, and working-class culture, including working-class youth culture, has historically tended to be social and even 'street' oriented. Third, and perhaps most convincingly, until recently African-Caribbean culture has been overwhelmingly public – in the sense of communal – and oral. Again, given the minimal education available to black people during and for long after slavery, it was allowed to be little else. Even the strong musical tradition of African-Americans and African-Caribbeans has a notable element of the poetic and rhetorical about it. The continuing dominance of rap in youth music in the late 1990s owed much to this powerful tradition of audience engagement. That much of white and, increasingly, Asian youth is also engaged is obvious, although this does not always lead to a wider mutual acceptance.

Not all the white and Asian boys we interviewed saw society in an ethnically polarised way. Dick, the son of white parents, sustained a thought-through anti-racism from which he had not been dislodged even though he had once 'been mugged by three black youths, Afro-Caribbeans'.

Interviewer: Who do you think causes it [racism]?
Dick: Probably the white youths. I suppose the media as well . . .
Interviewer: So you haven't been generally embittered against African-Caribbeans?
Dick: No. There are some Afro-Caribbeans here who are quite bad and annoy you. I was walking up here and somebody just decided to swing the door, like that, just to give you a bit of a fright. No point. There are a lot of people who are a bit stupid like that. A lot of Afro-Caribbeans are nice and fine. I don't see any reason why you should hate the whole race, just because of a couple of people . . .

Although, as one would expect, there was a range of opinion among white boys about the extent to which African-Caribbean boys 'started trouble', the view that they did so was a common one. As was suggested earlier in this chapter, some of this was little more than finger-pointing by white boys who were just as involved as the African-Caribbean boys. In particular, many of the white working-class boys with whom the African-Caribbean boys most came into direct conflict also cultivated a macho style. It is probably impossible to say with certainty which group is the more macho and confrontational. However that may be, the weight of evidence clearly shows that an element in the confrontational macho style of some African-Caribbean boys reflects ethnic rather than simply class experience. To the extent that this is the case, then the African-Caribbean boys' macho style is a genuinely collective ethnic phenomenon rather than simply a matter of individual behaviour. In other words, as Ken Pryce effectively argued over twenty years ago (see Pryce, 1986), 'black macho' behaviour is culturally learnt and elaborated. A form of collective behaviour that is inter-generational and culturally embedded cannot sensibly be regarded as merely the product of negative labelling, however much the latter may occur.

The contribution of racism to the formation of African-Caribbean masculinities

This section will argue that, for African-Caribbean boys and men, racism, including the racist system of slavery, and their response to it, has been relatively more influential than class in forming their masculinities. The relationship of class, ethnicity and gender presents somewhat different issues in respect to young African-Caribbean males than is the case with young white males. The history and cultural experience of African-Caribbeans in relation to white people has deeply affected many aspects of African-Caribbean masculinities. The masculinities of young African-Caribbean boys cannot be understood without contextualisation in relation to white racism and patriarchy in both their contemporary and historical manifestations. Slavery and the plantation system oppressed and humiliated African-Caribbeans in every aspect of their lives. Of course, as is the case with any system of domination, members of the subordinate group were organised and controlled on the basis of different degrees of oppression and 'privilege', but overall, slavery is about as 'total' a system of social domination as it is possible to devise. Slavery was abolished in the British empire only about three lifetimes ago, and in the United States about two lifetimes, periods of time well within 'folk' or group memory. As far as black men are concerned, perhaps the symbolic image is that of ritual castration and burning carried out well into the twentieth century in some of the former slave states. As recently as 1998, three white racists tied a black man to the back of their truck and dragged him along for several miles. Later they painted his decapitated head black. No immediate motive for the murder appeared to exist other than that the man was black. This is an extreme example, but it does dramatise widely typical attitudes and behaviour. In any case, history and contemporary events suggest that it is not wise to understate the degree of hatred and brutality that focuses on 'race' and ethnicity.

American examples of racism are relevant to the British context because, as Paul Gilroy and others have shown, the cultural consciousness of African-Caribbeans embraces the United States as well as, of course, Africa – the 'black Atlantic' as Gilroy evocatively refers to it (1993b). In any case, slavery operated at comparable levels of brutality in the former British West Indies (Thomas, 1997: 221). However, it is not necessary to plumb history to illustrate white racism against people of African heritage. There is a mountain of evidence of both individual and institutional racism against African-Caribbeans in Britain since their large-scale immigration began in the early post-Second World War period. As it happens, on the day on which this section is being drafted, two national newspapers led with headlines indicative of evidence of racism in policing and schooling in Britain. The case of policing is the most clear-cut. The *Guardian* headline is 'Stop and Search leaps by 20' (8.3.99: data based on research published by Statewatch). The lead article then goes on to give the extraordinary statistics behind the headline: African-Caribbean people are 7.5 per cent more likely to be stopped and searched than white people and 4 times more likely than them to be arrested. Asians were just under three times more likely to be stopped and searched than white people. Overall, 10 per cent of those stopped and searched are arrested and no further proceedings are taken against one in five of these. To put it mildly, 'stop and search' seems to be widely operated in a way likely to inflame a sense of injustice among African-Caribbeans already made sensitive by a long history of discriminatory practices. As far as this study is concerned, it is particularly relevant to younger people, and especially young men, who are the ones most likely to be stopped and searched.

The other headline relevant to the argument that African-Caribbean masculinities tend to be created in the context of struggle and adverse circumstances was 'Schools Failing Black Pupils', and occurred in the *Daily Express* (8.3.99). The headline complemented two articles in the same edition, one written by David Blunkett, then Secretary of State for Education and Employment, and the other by a journalist, Dorothy Lepkowski. Quite fairly, accusations of racism were not bandied about in the coverage, but again the question of control and conflict was raised. Lepkowski noted the disproportionate rates of expulsion among children of African-Caribbean origin. Citing a 1997 report from the Commission for Racial Equality as her source, she went on to observe that these expulsions were usually not for the more obvious and clear-cut breaches of discipline:

> Two years ago the Commission for Racial Equality reported that exclusions had reached 'crisis' proportions, with youngsters in some ethnic groups being six times more likely to be expelled than their white class mates. Of these, three out of four were disciplined not for violence or bullying – the most common cause of expulsion – but for insolence or bad attitude. Many dropped out of education and failed to gain any qualifications . . .
>
> (*Daily Express*, 8.3.99)

From the point of view of the argument being presented in this section, the significant phrase in this extract is 'insolence or bad attitude'. To the extent that what is referred to as 'insolence or bad attitude' does occur among young African-Caribbean males, it reflects an understandable sensitivity to authority, particularly authority exercised by whites, and a demand for 'respect'. As will be discussed later, the need for 'respect' is common among African-Caribbean boys and young men (Pryce, 1986; Sewell, 1997). ('Respect' is to some extent a quality in life also desired and mentioned by young people in general, in a variety of youth studies.) The educational system needs to cope with and positively accommodate this cultural phenomenon among young black males, and certainly not by directing them to predominantly sporting and musical activities. Of course, it is easy to write in critical terms about schools excluding black boys for what is perceived as 'insolence and bad attitude' – it is much harder to deal with challenging and aggressive behaviour in practice. This chapter is not in the business of blaming teachers either individually or en masse for the problems under discussion. There is doubtless some individual racism among teachers, but perhaps rather less than in other occupational groupings. It is primarily at the cultural and institutional level that the educational system is failing to produce curricular and organisational frameworks that genuinely engage and tap the potential of African-Caribbean boys, just as the system significantly failed and still fails many working-class white boys. African-Caribbean boys are likely to be caught by a dual disadvantage – class inequality and racism – and now perhaps by a third – gender disadvantage – reflecting negative masculine stereotypes and the erosion of traditional 'male' work.

Because of their sense of injustice due to racism and disadvantage, many black boys are suspicious of white authority and power. Because their group and sometimes individual experience is even more acutely disadvantaged than that of white working-class boys, their response is correspondingly even more intense. Implicitly, and sometimes explicitly, they sometimes reject its legitimacy. That is hardly surprising. However, when carried into the school context, the boys' anti-authority attitudes – in combination with whatever individual or institutional racism might characterise a particular school – can contribute to conflict and discontent. Darcus Howe, the black

British writer and broadcaster, gives an account of African-Caribbean boys' alien-ation from school based on close observation – and it is interesting that he refers to processes and experiences outside rather than inside school in his explanation. The boys he refers to in the following passage include his sons:

> The boys begin that way [getting obediently down to work like their sisters] at primary school, but soon realise that there are other immediate issues: racial attacks by whites, the police, the local shopkeeper who thinks that every black boy is a shoplifter. Soon the boy is transformed because he has to face directly the weight of the society that surrounds him. He moves into a warrior stance, using language that transforms ordinary English into a series of confrontational metaphors and similes. By secondary school he is mature beyond his years.
>
> The school system tries to tame the instincts of survival and offers a smooth edge that bears no relation to reality. I have seen it unfold in my own house. Black Caribbean boys are a new and growing social force and they cannot be compared to OFSTED's mould of who a child is and what he or she is required to learn.
>
> (Howe, 1999: 23)

The next section begins to examine how various modes of black masculinity are historically constructed and how they relate to African-Caribbean boys' wider social experience, including education.

The effects of slavery, both at the time and after, on black masculine identities

The starting point for understanding African-Caribbean masculine identities is racism and the responses to it. This is then followed by class. It is against the harsh inter-face of imperial conquest and oppression that African-Caribbean men and boys have fought to shape their masculine identities. Prior to slavery, their gender identities were formed within indigenous African cultures, but within the modern epoch it was not until the mid-twentieth century that they achieved sufficient freedom to assert and develop relatively autonomous, as distinct from largely imposed, self and collec-tive identities. It was virtually inevitable that when this opportunity came, black masculinities would develop often in angry reference to white oppression, particu-larly white racist patriarchal oppression. Slavery drove at the heart of black masculinity, separating men from their wives and children and abusing both. The exploitation and stereotyping of black women – as domestic 'maids' and objects for sexual use – took significantly different forms than for black men. As these brief examples show, the various forms of black gender identity, including 'black macho', widely recognised as a dominant form of contemporary black masculinity, cannot be properly understood without reference to historical context. The origin of contem-porary black macho can be understood partly as an expression of cultural *resistance*, sometimes developing into more conscious political activism, including *rebellion* (although rebellion is not necessarily political in character).

Both during and after slavery a wide range of identities and lifestyles were devel-oped by men of African origin which embodied the adoption of different strategies for coping with the system to which they found themselves subject. A similar range of identities occur among black men and boys today, as they struggle in different ways to deal with a society that to a greater or lesser extent they still see as racist, although changed circumstances are reflected in a shift towards more overtly assertive strategies. Of course, their struggle for identity in the face of slaughter and abuse was not only, and probably not even mainly, a gender one. Because African slaves had been brutalised and humiliated as a 'race', their primary struggle was to reassert their 'racial'/ethnic humanity, dignity, competence and achievement. This struggle occurred both at the individual and the general or collective level. There was a quantitative leap forward in this long and difficult process in the 1960s when positive black images began to be asserted, starting with 'black power'. In the terminology of Miles and Solomos, African slaves had been negatively 'racialised', and it is scarcely surprising that one of their responses was to reassert 'racial'/ethnic pride and worth (Miles, 1989; Solomos, 1989). How ethnic struggle for pride and identity related to the desire of individuals to achieve economic success and social mobility is an important question which is addressed on pages 116–17.

Slavery, an extreme system, provoked a range of responses, some of them also extreme. The following typology of coping strategies is presented here not as definitive nor exhaustive but merely as indicative of a range of responses adopted to cope first with slavery and then with a freer but still highly racist society. It is not based on specific empirical research but reflects a broad range of historical and contemporary data. It is similar to Weber's description of an ideal type model, in that it attempts to abstract the main possible types or formations of a phenomenon – in this case patterns or strategies of coping or survival negotiable by black men and boys. As the following account indicates, the balance of strategic options shifted as African-Caribbeans emerged from a context of severe oppression into relative freedom. A range of identities and lifestyles can be loosely associated with the various coping strategies – these are ways of acting and self-presentation which embody the intention behind the strategies. The style/identity column has been gendered to capture styles particularly associated with men and boys (although in principle there is no reason why they cannot be associated with women and girls – as in practice some, to a degree, are). In two cases, the strategies/identities can be said to harden into consciously-held political positions: rebellion–political activism, and separatism–nationalism. The strategies and related identities are:

Coping strategies	*Related (masculine) identity/style*
Submission	Uncle Tomism
Conformity/accommodation	Low key
Imitation	'More English than the English'
Resistance/rebellion	Macho Culture/Political Activism
Retreatism	Drug Dependency, Drop-out
Separatism	Rastafarianism, Black Muslims, Nationalist

A response to oppression which has become much despised within black culture was submission, the related cultural style of which is 'Uncle Tomism'. In this case, the definitions of the oppressor are internalised and domination and power accepted. An acceptance by a black man of his own or his people's inherent inferiority in relation to white people is a form of such submission. Others adopted a conformist approach to the demands of the slave system without necessarily accepting its legitimacy or succumbing to it psychologically. In Erving Goffman's terms, some must have 'played it cool' – secretly rejecting the slave system, if not actively planning to overthrow it (see Goffman, 1968). The term *accommodation* conveys a lesser degree of overt conformity to the system but still a willingness to 'do business' with it, if only for lack of an alternative. In our view the term *robust* or *critical accommodation* is a coping strategy more typically adopted by contemporary African-Caribbean girls and women than by boys and men. What underlies it in their case is the practical need to get educated and to get on with paid and domestic work (a higher proportion of African-Caribbean women than white women are in full-time work).

Given the chasm in power and position between the 'slave-owner' and the slave, there must have been few meaningful opportunities for full-scale *imitation* other than in surreptitious ridicule. Nevertheless, the terrible dislocation and cultural trauma experienced by African slaves left them open to cultural impression by the dominant group. Contemporary British African-Caribbean culture reflects many aspects of the Western-Christian tradition as well as more specifically British and English cultural elements. During the early years of post-war immigration, the middle-class ideal, often with smart clothes and an accent to match, represented a model of imitation for some immigrants with aspirations to acceptance by indigenous Britons and perhaps with aspirations to upward social mobility. These tended to be from Asia and Africa rather than the predominantly rural and working-class African-Caribbeans. However, this approach does highlight the interesting issue of how a person from a minority ethnic group negotiates mobility in a class system still heavy with white cultural reference and symbolism. . . .

Unsurprisingly, *resistance* to 'whitey', both as cultural lifestyle and as an embryo political strategy, has attracted more kudos than more conformist orientations. Resistance has had tremendous appeal to young black people in both Britain and the United States since the 1960s. Resistance to white authority, such as is embodied in the educational and police systems, burst into rebellion in 1981, 1985 and again in 1995. The strength of contemporary black macho and the resistance of many young African-Caribbean boys to 'white' authority can be explained partly by the humiliation and repression of their forebears under slavery. Control was exercised over black men's sexuality and over their children and partners to a degree that was almost bound to provoke an assertive, highly masculinised reaction – when the opportunity emerged. Overt resistance to white domination and abuse – individual or collective – under slavery was only possible to a limited degree. As is the case with the women's movement, it is since the 1960s that the most sustained and powerful resistance has occurred.

Retreatism and *separatism* both represent attempts to escape from white power and oppression rather than to negotiate with it in some way. Within sub-cultural theory, retreatism is usually associated with psychological breakdown, often as a result of inability to cope with social pressures. Cloward and Ohlin use the category to describe those criminals – the least effective – who are able to organise themselves neither in relation to the dominant society nor in relation to those who deviate from it (Cloward and Ohlin, 1961). Such a model of 'normals and deviants' is transparently inappropriate here, given that it is the majority or at least the oppressive majority culture that merits censure rather than the minority. However, it would be surprising if there were not significant numbers of black people who did give up either trying to prosper in a substantially racist society or trying to change it and retreat into marginal activities. What is perhaps more surprising is that resilience and resistance are much more characteristic of black youth culture than retreatism, although doubtless many individuals mix or move in and out of these cultural modes. The belief that only separating from white society will ensure equality has a long history among black people. Most recently it has been expressed by a group within the American Black Panther Party and by the Rastafarians. Although some have a literal belief in separatism, for many it can be taken as symbolic of their disillusionment and alienation from white society.

This model of coping strategies and related identities spans a long historical period, and the practically available options changed greatly in relation to shifts in the wider socio-economic system. The economic and cultural options for black men changed somewhat after their transition from slaves to wage-labourers. Once they became more integrated into the capitalist system, the possibility of various class identities emerged. This occurred in the United States in the late nineteenth and the twentieth century, and in Britain after the immigration which followed the Second World War. However, white racism in both the United States and Britain meant that the cultural identities and conflicts initially generated within slavery remained relevant. To some extent, these established identities and conflicts were projected onto the capitalist class system. Thus, for a black person to become middle-class raised the spectre of a new form of 'Uncle Tomism'. How could an ethnic/'racial' identity forged under oppression survive 'success' in the system of the oppressor? Some found the notion of being black and middle-class unproblematic, but others struggled with it. A so-called young black underclass developed, partly because of white racism and exclusion and partly as a cultural choice on the part of young black people. Arguably, it is this group that has been the dynamic and charismatic centre of black youth culture. Other young black people sought conventional success within the capitalist system but bought into 'black flash' – a stream of extrovert and assertive cultural styles which reflect black rather than white identities.

The typology of African-Caribbean masculinities is no more than a rough guide to the range of gender identities constructed or negotiated by black men and boys. The danger with such models is that they can be taken to imply that social reality and forms of identity are simpler and more clear-cut than they are. In practice, people's identities may shift in one direction or another and they may hold contra-dictory identities simultaneously. A day-time conformist at work might be a night-time rebel. Broad typologies can indicate the direction and flow of collective identities, especially when such typologies adopt the labels of the social actors themselves.

The pride in, and insistence on, self-autonomy of many black boys and men, their *resistance* to white power and authority, can therefore partly be understood in terms of the group experience of slavery and subsequent exploitation. However, these qual-ities are also often found among African-Caribbean girls and women, and it is too simple to categorise them as exclusively gendered 'masculine' (Phoenix, 1987; Mirza, 1992). Further, the majority of African-Caribbean boys are working-class or the off-spring of parents who are irregularly employed. The masculinity of young African-Caribbean males is similar in some aspects to that of white working-class boys, and this is no doubt partly due to similarities in socio-economic experience and back-ground. It is an arguable point whether class or ethnicity plays the greater part in the formation of youthful African-Caribbean masculinities, although the latter case is strongly maintained here.

Making sense of macho

A main argument so far suggested in this section and further developed below is that the macho style prominently adopted by some African-Caribbean boys and men is only in part the product of negative stereotyping; it is also generated by some African-Caribbeans in response to aspects of their historical and contemporary experience. Given what African-Caribbeans have had to 'fight against', this is an historically highly plausible argument and, further, there is no lack of evidence for it. However, perhaps because such an analysis may be – wrongly – taken as 'blaming the victim' it has tended not to be explored. Even recent work which fully explores and acknowledges the power and pervasiveness of the African-Caribbean macho style fights shy of fully recognising that it is now an embedded cultural characteristic which is generationally reproduced and not mainly a reaction to negative stereotyping. Thus both Clair Alexander (1996: 137–8) and Tony Sewell (1997: 126–7), especially the former, describe macho behaviour among black boys as substantially an internalisation of negative stereotypes which have been generated by the dominant culture.

Here, we argue an alternative thesis without any sense either of censure or of liberal guilt, neither of which are appropriate or constructive to analysis. This is that black macho is now an established mode of masculinity which is generated and contested from within the African-Caribbean culture just as working-class macho was and to some extent still is in working-class culture. The parallel with working-class macho is an extremely fruitful one. There are many reasonably unbiased studies of macho style among white working-class males which locate this somewhat similar type of masculinity to black macho firmly within working-class culture. Willis's definitive work shows that, although the lads are positioned in subordination, their values and actions must be understood as reflective of their own culture rather than as merely reactive. In principle the same level of dispassionate analysis ought to be achievable with respect to the study of African-Caribbean culture, including black macho. Just as the conditions of industrial labour experienced by the working-class male provoked tough, sometimes embattled and uncompromising collective resistance, so the experience of slavery generated a culture of injured pride, anger and resistance among many black men. Macho may be regarded as an extreme, and in some expressions an unacceptable, form of resistance, but as an element in a tough and assertive strategy for coping with oppression and brutality it is comprehensible. Where macho is most pointlessly destructive is when it is expressed collectively in intra-group or gang rivalry, or individually as a form of domination of a partner. What is being offered here is not a celebration of macho but an interpretation of it as a constructed response rather than mainly as a label imposed by white society. Ultimately, interpretation of this issue is one of emphasis and, given that cultural orientations are the product of continuous interaction, black macho should not be regarded as static, however embedded it may currently be. Just as the decline of industrial culture has seen a decline of working-class macho and of the more widely shared solidaristic masculinity, so black macho could become a semi-redundant cultural mode should racism decline and the opportunity structure become more open to African-Caribbean boys.

Predictably, some of the resistance of African-Caribbean boys and men to exploitation and racism has been categorised as deviant by the dominant society, just as working-class men routinely fell foul of the law and official censure. Partly because it was made even more difficult for black people than for the working class to organise and institutionalise their resistance to oppression, black resistance has tended to be predominantly individual and cultural rather than institutional and political. Resistance embodied in lifestyle is probably easier to characterise as deviant or even pathological than organised political dissent.

Class, ethnicity and racism in the making of African-Caribbean resistance

Within the traditional Marxist paradigm, ethnicity is generally seen as a less significant form of identity than class. However, the recent writings of Stuart Hall and Paul Gilroy have to some extent rendered ethnic identity, in its more positive and tolerant formulations, as respectable within radical theory and action. Initially, in the Thatcher period, Hall queried whether the political Right should be allowed to extol the virtues of the dominant white ethnic group while ethnic minorities adopted a low-key approach to their own cultural achievements – many of them wrought through resisting racism and discrimination (1992). However, while Hall acknowledges a legitimate basis for the celebration of ethnic identity, he is understandably chary in the extreme of ethnic chauvinism and intolerance. Nor does he consider that ethnic identity should be exclusionary or static. On the contrary, he considers that a dynamic identity is open to other influence and images and so is itself likely to be constantly shifting and changing – albeit usually on an axis of values and self-presentations that have a degree of recognisable continuity. Further, Hall argues that individuals tend to have multiple identities – including, for instance, gender and sexual identities, and perhaps varieties of each, as well as ethnic. Paul Gilroy is equally emphatic that ethnic identity is subject to constant flux. Indeed, his study of black identity, *The Black Atlantic* (1993b), treats not only the huge variations within black identity but acknowledges the variety of influences on black experience from other cultural sources.

A key question at issue here is the extent to which the macho style of many young African-Caribbean males is a product of their class experience or of their ethnic experience. In fact, although this matter is often posed in this slightly polarised way, to do so risks oversimplification. It is the interplay of these and other factors that contributes to the formation of African-Caribbean macho. It is a misleading assumption that, because macho behaviour occurs frequently among both white and black working-class males, African-Caribbean macho can be defined primarily in class cultural terms. Of course, in psycho-behavioural terms, all macho behaviour is fairly similar. It involves the assertion of power and control, or frustration at the lack of them. However, because these characteristics typify macho behaviour regardless of the social origins of the actors involved, they provide little clue about what is specific to African-Caribbean macho. A more precise understanding of what is distinctive about African-Caribbean culture, including African-Caribbean masculinities, is better achieved with reference to historical context rather than on the basis of theoretical assumption.

The historical experience of African-Caribbeans prior to immigration to Britain was typically that of economic struggle and uncertainty – sharpened by recent recession in the countries from which immigration occurred; and most of the population other than the elites were very poor by comparison with Britain. While many immigrants to Britain were skilled workers, work was often insecure and wages low. As was the case in the United States, the abolition of slavery in Britain's ex-colonies in the Caribbean had little effect on the extent to which society was stratified by 'race' – for which colour was the most obvious signifier. The hierarchies of class and 'race' closely coincided. In more technical terms – and this is a crucial point of analysis – status, in the form of 'race' and ethnic identity, influenced class position as much and perhaps more than class influenced status. In this respect, matters proved little different for African-Caribbean immigrants to Britain, and the experience of 'racial' and ethnic prejudice no doubt partly explains the sense of injury and anger which characterises African-Caribbean macho masculinity.

The second and third post-war generations of African-Caribbeans in Britain have been more prepared than the first to resist and confront rather than to accommodate to injustice and disadvantage. Whereas the white working-class boys who were the main subject of *Resistance Through Rituals* (Hall and Jefferson, 1975) were expressing a diffuse anger against authority or, at most, what they experienced as 'the system', young African-Caribbean men had a very specific focus of grievance – racism and racial discrimination. They increasingly resisted 'racial' oppression in all kinds of ways. Although the style and manner of the working-class boys' resistance reflected their class situation, few of them specifically focused on members of the capitalist class or any other class as the clearly perceived object of their aggravation and ridicule. Individuals were objected to at a lifestyle and personal level rather than for ideological reasons. Thus, more middle-class people might be targeted because they were seen as 'posh' or because their apparent power was resented, but otherwise almost anybody different would do as a target – 'JAs, poofs or 'ippies' – as long as they were not part of the immediate gang of lads. In contrast, for African-Caribbean boys it was the symbols and institutions of white, rather than class, domination that irked – and white, like black, is highly visible. Almost any institution in 'white' society could become a specific object of resentment because hard experience taught that racism could occur anywhere. What African-Caribbean youth was resisting was both more easily generalised about and more easily specified than what white working-class boys were resisting. African-Caribbean youth culture manifests a much greater awareness and resentment of racial than of class oppression, and to that extent is far more anti-racist than it is anti-capitalist. Indeed, there is a strong theme of conspicuous consumption in African-Caribbean youth culture which often resonates positively with capitalist consumption.

The young black 'underclass' debate: the excluded

The location in the system of stratification of African-Caribbeans in Britain and of African-Americans in the United States has been referred to by a number of commentators as that of an 'underclass', and the term has often been given a specific application to youth, and especially minority youth.[4] However, perhaps because it is sometimes used in a stigmatising way, the term has become less often used. The Blair government prefers to use the term 'excluded' to apply to a wide range of people, of whatever ethnic background, who in one way or another struggle to achieve an adequate independent life. Although the term 'underclass' is best discarded, a review of the underclass debate does usefully set up some key issues in relation to the opportunity structure as it affects black people and, in particular, black youth. The term 'black underclass' effectively conveys the extent to which people of African descent have been socially and economically marginalised, mainly as a result of racial discrimination. The term implies that black people experience significant disadvantage not routinely experienced by white people, and that established class terminology, including the term 'working-class', is not in itself sufficient to describe their position in the system of stratification. The use of the term 'black underclass' also indicates, albeit ambiguously, that status differentiation, in this case perceived racial or cultural difference, can play a major role in the stratification of black people in white-dominated societies.

John Rex argues that racial discrimination was the main cause of the development of a black underclass in Britain (Rex and Tomlinson, 1979; Rex, 1986). In the context of suggesting a much wider usage of the term, Ralf Dahrendorf correctly states that 'the underclass is not a class' but is comprised of a variety of people who for various reasons are excluded from the social mainstream (1992: 57). For Rex, status disadvantage does not preclude class disadvantage – he considers that in Britain they have converged and reinforced each other. In the United States, Douglas Glasgow used the term 'black underclass' to apply specifically to black youth, particularly to young men. Like Rex, Glasgow considers racial discrimination to be the main factor underlying the emergence of a black underclass (Glasgow, 1981). Writing some 20 years ago, Glasgow noted with some prescience that, in the United States, the underclass was in danger of becoming inter-generational. He further observed that alienation and disillusionment, which had its roots in discrimination and exclusion from the opportunity structure, was in danger of being culturally internalised by young black people who were increasingly turning away from the dominant white society.

The term 'underclass' has been adopted by some on the political Right as well as a number of non-Marxist, radicals and liberals, including those mentioned above. The best known of these is the American social policy advisor Charles Murray, who later turned his article 'Underclass: A Disaster in the Making' (1989) into an influential book. Murray directed his comments especially at African-American youth, particularly fingering the roles of young mothers and fathers. The direction of Murray's analysis is perhaps apparent in his summary of what he sees as early indicators of the emergence of an underclass:

> There are many ways to identify an underclass. I will concentrate on three phenomena that have turned out to be early warning signs in the United States: illegitimacy, violent crime, and drop-out from the labour force.
>
> (C. Murray, 1989)

Murray went on to argue that the main cause of the development of the American underclass was 'welfare dependency'. During his 1989 visit to Britain, Murray had some contact with leading members of the Conservative government – thus his concern with warning signs which he did indeed think were present in Britain. He noted that, in the British context, the issues he raised might apply on a wide scale to less educated and employable white young men as well as to young black men in the same position.

There is nothing in Murray's essay which gives much weight to the impact of discrimination, particularly in employment, in the formation of a black underclass. His solution to the so-called dependency culture is equally narrow in scope and imagination – withdraw welfare from single parents who cannot independently support their children and, where the latter cannot be supported by family, have them fostered or put into care.

Murray misses entirely the historical and still relevant explanation for the exclusion of many black people in Britain and the United States. As a group, they are at a structural disadvantage in the first instance because of racial discrimination. The prime responsibility for this situation lies with individual and institutional white racism, not with black people or their culture. A large part of any solution must be in firm public opposition to and practical policies against racism. Despite inequality of opportunity, a sizeable African-American middle class has developed, and there are signs that one is also emerging in Britain – albeit as yet on a relatively smaller scale. Unless this process continues and accelerates, it is evident that a disproportionate number of young black men will continue to be in long-term unemployment. While some young black men do 'give up' on the system, research in Liverpool carried out by Michelle Connolly and her colleagues (1991) found that a large majority of them wanted settled work.

Young black men's negotiation of identity in a majority white society

Clair Alexander's *The Art of Being Black* (1996) includes a number of young, middle-class African-Caribbean and African-British males in her study of 'the creation of black British youth identities'. The point of including a reference to her book here is that it deals with a rather older group of men than those in our survey. The two case studies discussed below can be regarded as examples of the sort of experiences that might subsequently happen to boys in our study, although they are not presented here as necessarily typical. Although not a macro-scale study of stratification issues, Alexander's work offers many useful insights on how racial discrimination can affect opportunities for occupational mobility and class status. She also provides many illustrations of the varied and creative responses to discrimination and frustration of the young black men.

Of the two groups that Alexander researched, it is the first – whom she referred to as 'the boys' – that we will concentrate on here. The nine members of this more or less loosely knit group of friends were all between 22 and 24 years of age – young men as compared to the mid-teenagers we interviewed. Of the boys, four were of Jamaican origin, three of Nigerian origin, one from Ghana, and one, Satish, who was born in India and had lived in Britain since he was twelve. His girlfriend, Dion, was 'not officially a member of the group' but 'had known all the boys for many years' and was a rich source of information about them. Dion was of Jamaican origin and Satish himself would sometimes pretend he was from the Caribbean and generally presented himself as 'black'. Clair Alexander is of Asian origin, and the twelve months she spent doing ethnographic research as 'one of the boys' were not without interesting incident!

Alexander's study shows that, as a result of being black, the young men of both Caribbean and African origins have to deal with a common issue – racial discrimination and often negative images of black males and masculinities. They responded in a variety of ways.

Malcolm, of Jamaican origin, and Clive, of Nigerian origin, adopted lifestyles which reflected a degree of conformity or accommodation, but which were also quite assertive in their extravagant style and consumerism. Their experiences illustrate how many ambitious young black men feel that they must 'look the part' as well as also be competent to do a given job. Thus what is sometimes referred to as 'black flash' has become an established style among ambitious black males.

Malcolm was self-employed in the family tropical foodstuffs retailing business. He regarded racial abuse as inevitable in his line of work but countered it by seeking to achieve an image of success and wealth within the work environment. He drove a new Audi car, wore handmade suits and a large quantity of gold jewellery, and not only owned two mobile phones but also a message pager! Malcolm explained that he was keen to avoid the stereotype of black failure, although in doing so he perhaps veered towards the stereotype of 'black flash'. As Alexander sympathetically puts it, '(t)his external image, based upon the expression of material wealth, can perhaps be seen as an attempt to carve out a model for black achievement' (Alexander, 1996: 89). Thus she implies that 'the manipulation' of 'class' symbols can be an attempt to combat the stereotype of black economic failure. However, a relevant point to add here is that both economically successful and unsuccessful black males often adopt assertive forms of masculinity which involve conspicuous display, including display of clothes, jewellery and possessions. Those who have 'made it' can usually differentiate themselves through the scale and quality of their consumption, but are still connected in aspects of style and aspiration to their 'black brothers'. White 'polite middle-class' disdain for 'black flash' is somewhat schizophrenic and ethnocentric and creates a potential catch-22 for black people. The image of black failure is riddled with stereotypes, but the black celebration of black success may be resented or somehow seen as 'not quite right'. On the other hand, many young black people seem to ride these potentially complex tensions very effectively and ... they gain great kudos from their leadership in areas of youth culture.

Clive, who was of Nigerian origin, was the most conventionally successful of the young men. He deliberately set out to avoid the fate of many of his friends who did 'silly things: postmen, train-drivers, bus-drivers, or you see them loafing around the street' (Alexander, 1996: 77). Clive chose to side-step issues of racism and adopt a strategy of individual competition and conformity in order to achieve career success. He sought to render the issue of 'race' irrelevant in his working life, although his social life was overwhelmingly among black people. Alexander's account acutely observes the interplay of class and 'race', and in particular Clive's inability to neutralise 'race' in the eyes of others:

> He utilized all the external images to portray a facade of conformity; he wore designer suits to work, owned a new Alfa-Romeo, carried a message pager, and cultivated an appropriate accent ... Although there is undoubtedly a 'class' element to Clive's situation, the primary identity which was negotiated was signalled by phenotype ... When Clive was 'made redundant' just after I left London, the reason given was that the Company felt that Clive would be unable to adapt to future developments in technology. Although no overt reference was made to 'race', it is interesting that the company used lack of intellectual capacity as a reason for dismissal.
>
> (Alexander, 1996: 87)

Conclusion: the construction of young African-Caribbean masculinities

This section has not sought to establish which factor – class, 'race', ethnicity or age – is 'dominant' or, in lumbering Althusserian terms, 'determinant in the final instance' in the lives of young black males, including in the structuring of their masculinities. To postulate the relationship between these factors in this way is highly misleading. There is no absolute relationship between these powerfully formative forces, and their interplay will vary from individual to individual and, at a higher level of generality, from group to group. Young African-Caribbean and African-British males are aware of, and to various degrees affected by, the racism and racial discrimination that has hampered their parents and may hamper their own socio-economic opportunities. They have responded to oppression and to the challenge to achieve with energy and imagination. Ethnic culture, including particular images of masculinity, is a major resource drawn on by young black males in the development of their identities and in coping with problems and challenges.

Asian boys and the construction of masculinities

In the previous two sections it was argued that the masculinities of white boys are decisively structured by class, and those of African-Caribbean boys by racism and their ethnically mediated response to it. The Asian boys in our survey were the children or grandchildren of people who were born in traditional societies which were predominantly stratified by castes rather than by industrial classes. Their primary socialisation, therefore, occurred in the context of families and communities of a much more traditional (including religious) kind than most of the white boys. The Asian boys differed from the African-Caribbeans in that their forbears were not slaves and their culture had not been forged largely in response to that most extreme and repressive of social systems. Even so, subjection to imperialism and racism has ensured that a certain hardened defensiveness, already present in some traditional concepts of Asian masculinity, has developed further.

Asian boys experience two main flows of cultural influence: the traditional ethnic and the modern British. It is too much of a cliché to say that the boys – or, for that matter, Asian girls – are 'caught' between two cultures. Some boys did experience conflicting cultural influences and pressures, but others seemed to adjust relatively easily and without undue stress to the complexities of their situation. The term 'negotiation' is a better and more neutral descriptor of the process by which individual boys worked out their cultural identities and relationships than one which implies constant angst and struggle. Here the focus is on how the boys negotiated their masculine identities in admittedly often demanding contexts.

Cultural images and perceptions of Asian masculinities in the dominant culture

The Asian boys themselves often had a positive, if sometimes traditionally patriarchal, notion of what becoming and being a man involved. Although the precise detail of the gendered division of labour varies across the wide range of Asian cultures, patriarchy, in the minimal sense of men having much more power than women, is universal or nearly so. Among Muslims, the power and authority of men, although not without qualification, is particularly strongly established in relation to women and children. The right to self-defence is well established both philosophically and practically in many Asian cultures and was quite often evoked by the boys in our survey. It would be a crude simplification to call the tradition of self-defence 'macho', although in the context of peer group interaction in Britain it sometimes takes on a macho aura.

There are a number of perceptions or typings and related images of Asian men and boys in the dominant culture in Britain which are partly accurate and partly exaggerated and stereotypical. Stereotypes can lead to victimisation if they form the basis on which members of the stereotyped group are treated. Three perceptions will be referred to here – each of which occurred among the boys. Oversimplifying somewhat, these can be referred to as 'the weakling', 'the warrior' and 'the patriarch'. First is the notion of Asian men and boys as 'passive' or even 'weak'. The main reference here seems to be one of perceived physical weakness, including lack of aptitude for 'tougher' sports such as football and lack of robust athleticism in general. Edward, a white boy from a West London school, typifies this perception:

> Asian guys aren't seen to be that strong and hard really. Probably because there aren't many of them in our school ... quite a lot ... but they aren't seen to be that strong.
>
> (Edward)

In the world of macho, to be weak physically tends to be elided with weakness of character as expressed in such phrases as 'bottling out' and 'lacking guts', and the status and treatment of Asian boys can suffer accordingly. Sometimes the Asian boys were compared unfavourably to black boys, whose macho behaviour was more overtly combative. The apparent tendency of Asian boys to be physically smaller has fed this stereotype. However, perhaps a higher protein diet and fitness/weight training are already evening out this apparent physical difference between the ethnic groupings.

A second typing of Asian males is in some contrast to the first, although it also has a complementary aspect. In this case, the perception is that some young Asian men possess a disciplined and trained capacity for violence, mainly in the cause of self-defence. Mastery of technique is perceived as compensating for an assumed lack of physical strength. This is an image which has become heavily loaded with stereo-types, but it has a real basis in the oriental tradition of martial arts and self-defence. Among the associations conveyed by this image are a certain latent exoticism and mystery – a power not fully understood by 'Westerners' but felt as potentially threat-ening to them. The high level of technical control and the complex and sometimes elaborate ritual involved in the advanced practice of martial arts and self-defence contrasts with the relatively simple framework of, for example, boxing and wrestling. The philosophical underpinnings of these practices adds to their mystique. Not surpris-ingly, practices associated with physical and technical control as well as with the exotic have had considerable appeal to some Asian British boys – not least, at one remove from reality, in films and computer games. . . .

A third image of Asian males, particularly Muslims, is that they exercise strong domestic and family control. This is part of a much wider understanding of Asian culture, again particularly Islam, as being patriarchal and traditional. In general, these perceptions are well founded, but they have sometimes led to dramatic and unsym-pathetic media presentations of conflict and male oppression of women and children within Asian families and communities – presentations which in turn have fed nega-tive stereotypes of Asians within popular culture. Our research interest mainly focused on the effect on Asian boys of their own family and parental experience, which by no means always conformed to popular stereotype. . . .

Each of the above images of Asian masculinity is part of the stock of cultural 'knowledge' and reference in mainstream society which the Asian boys in our study were themselves able to draw on. Not surprisingly – given their 'inside' knowledge – the boys rarely drew on these referents in a way which crudely endorsed domi-nant stereotypes. Their own ideas about their masculinity were part of larger constructions of their identity, about which their ideas were often provisional and still in the course of development. One further aspect of Asian youth needs to be mentioned because it certainly played a significant part in the thinking of a relatively large number of the Asian boys in our study. This is the commitment of Asian school-children to education and relatedly to career success. As we discuss in the next section, to some extent this enthusiasm for education is a class as well as an ethnic cultural characteristic, but in the case of the Asian boys in our survey it seemed to cross class lines.

Education and 'masculine' career orientations

The strong orientation towards educational and career success among many boys of Hindu, Sikh and Muslim ethnic background was often related to their sense of appro-priate masculine achievement. . . . Answers to the question, 'Have you got a career in mind?', were often along the lines of the following examples:

I want to go into the financial side, hopefully into the Stock Exchange. Or Merchant banking.

(Desai)

I'll go to college to do B. Tech, in electronics. After the HND in electronics.

(Wakar)

Not all the Asian boys were prospective high flyers, but many did have clear ideas about vocational courses they wanted to take and careers they hoped to pursue. Some saw success in highly materialistic terms – Desai, again:

> ... I admire those who achieve ... You need to be good at practical life ... I think without money you can't do many things. That's a fact. You can't do anything. Friendship, love, relationships ... But there's always a price on it.
>
> (Desai)

Mac an Ghaill's term 'New Enterprisers', or simply 'Enterprisers', is an appropriate description of those Asian boys who had a strong interest in higher-status vocational courses and careers in technology and/or business. Mac an Ghaill used this term to describe working-class boys of various ethnic backgrounds who had this orientation (Mac an Ghaill, 1994). However, a large proportion of the Asian boys in our survey for whom this term is appropriate came from backgrounds in which their father was self-employed rather than from the manual working class. Like a substantial number of children from the post-war white working class, these boys aspired to salaried middle-class occupations, although the route they were frequently adopting – the higher-status vocational courses – reflected the impact of the Thatcher reforms on education. Labour Force Survey figures (as published annually in *Social Trends*) show that nationally there is already a sizeable Indian professional and managerial middle class and a smaller Pakistani one. Compared to the national picture, relatively few of the Asian boys in our survey came from backgrounds in which either parent was a member of the middle-class salariat. Proportionately far more were self-employed – a trend which reflects the national situation. For their sons to achieve salaried middle-class jobs in substantial numbers would be something of a breakthrough for Asian parents. So far the real basis of their economic success has been within their own community or as vendors of their own ethnic and other goods to the larger national community. Many of the Asian boys seemed ready to build farther on this achievement and have their sights set on careers in technology, finance or the professions.

If self-employment seemed to induce a certain inter-generational dynamism, this needs to be balanced by the fact that unemployment among the fathers of the Asian boys in our sample was proportionately much higher than among whites (a majority of whom were in service industries or intermediate occupational categories) and somewhat higher than among African-Caribbeans (who were still well represented in their traditional areas of employment – skilled and semi-skilled manual work). There was also a relatively high concentration of Asian fathers, particularly Pakistani and Bangladeshi, in unskilled work. Boys from these backgrounds must have been aware of the obstacles to upward mobility that their parents had faced, some of which they might face themselves. Although some of the boys from these backgrounds expressed little in the way of a clear sense of educational or career direction, others shared in what appeared to be a strong education/career orientation among Asians.

What prompts the ambitions of these Asian boys and how are their masculinities formed by them? To a degree, career ambition requires little explanation, although the extent of it varies between social groups. Immigrant groups in particular are often especially concerned to improve their economic situation or at least to provide the means for their children to do so. ... Many of the Asian boys had hopes of 'doing better' than their parents, although such aspirations were usually negotiated in close reference to their parents' wishes and feelings.

Surprise at the aspirations to upward mobility of Asian boys is therefore inappropriate. What perhaps needs more explanation is the apparently limited ambition of many white working-class lads in the 1960s and after. As is indicated by Willis and other chroniclers of working-class male youth sub-cultures, the explanation appears to lie in their assumption that the 'normal thing' to do was to get a job doing manual work – just like dad and very probably like grandad had done before him. That assumption was exploded by the recessions of the 1980s and the development of widespread unemployment. In any case, the extent to which even 'solid' working-class children harboured ambitions to achieve at least lower middle-class status is perhaps understated in the literature. In fact, many millions did make just such a transition. By the mid-1980s and 1990s, the realities of deindustrialisation were apparent to new generations of working-class youngsters. Mac an Ghaill's well observed groupings of 'achievers' and 'new enterprisers' were working-class boys of white and Asian background. The masculine identities of these boys were interwoven with the success and status they aspired to, and if this sometimes had a modern technological gloss to it, it was not greatly different from the typical ambition of upwardly mobile working-class and middle-class boys throughout the post-war period.

Macho – reaction

Mac an Ghaill also observed that a macho working-class sub-culture persisted among some white boys. It became increasingly clear in the 1990s that a macho culture has developed among some Asian boys, particularly those of Bangladeshi origin. This is less a working-class youth sub-culture than it is one of social exclusion. It is difficult to attempt precise quantification, but compared to earlier decades there were far more cases of 'Asian' youth gangs reported in the 1990s than in earlier decades. There were also several cases of gang attacks by predominantly Asian boys, some of which resulted in the deaths of their victims. The latter were extreme cases, but they were indicative of a trend to aggressive and antisocial behaviour among some Asian boys. Other than in Southall we found little direct evidence of this phenomenon, but it is now widespread enough to require comment. These Asian boys have very different lifestyles and prospects than the more academically and career motivated Asian boys, although there are junctures in school and leisure life where the two 'types' might interact.

The reasons why this macho sub-culture has developed among some Asian youth are not hard to find. Impoverished backgrounds, likely experience of racism, and in some cases difficulties in the use of the English language, would be expected to produce a sense of exclusion and possibly of victimisation. Individual and group frustration and aggression is only one, though perhaps the most predictable, of several possible patterns of reaction to such experience. Whereas working-class youthful macho is, as Miller (1962) and Willis (1977) have demonstrated, indigenous to the parent class culture, that of socially excluded Asian boys appears to be largely reactive. Of course, once a pattern of aggressive and posturing behaviour has been stimulated, it can easily turn from the defensive to the aggressive – particularly among inexperienced young males. In this respect there is some similarity between the behaviour of some second-generation Asian youth and that of some second-generation African-Caribbean youth a decade or so before them. Although some Asian youth do appear to be going through a period of poorly focused anger and even sociocultural disorientation, this does not mean they are wholly isolated from other streams of youth cultural influence. . . . Nor does it appear that even the most delinquent of Asian youth are typically completely adrift from their families, although these may have significant gaps of knowledge about their sons' activities. What emerged in one celebrated case involving murder and multiple acts of violence by several young Asian men was that their parents had no idea of their generally delinquent behaviour. A chasm of communication and information of this kind between the generations is often a sign of rapid and deep cultural change.

In general, the Asian boys we interviewed, especially those of Indian origin, often referred to their parents' and families' influence. Parental influence often occurred in a negotiated rather than in an authoritarian way. The boys seemed motivated by respect for their parents and a concern not to hurt their feelings, rather than by anything resembling fear. These motives seem uppermost in the decision of Asif, a Bangladeshi student, not to pursue his own ambition to be an air-pilot:

Asif: They really wanted me to study medicine, so I'm going for it now. I hope everything goes well for me.

Interviewer: Do you really feel that you're doing it for them? If they hadn't felt like that about piloting?

Asif: No, I think I'm doing it for myself, and for them in a way. It's OK for me. My parents thought that being a pilot could be quite dangerous. Anything could happen in a plane. But being a doctor is more safe and more established.

Self-defence and low-key masculinity

It may be that the influence of family and their traditional cultures had a moderating effect on how many Asian boys envisaged and presented their masculinity. Two boys of Muslim background, Wakar, a Pakistani, and Asif, the Bangladeshi just referred to, talked with insight and sophistication about how they presented their own gender style and how others reacted. Wakar was not impressed by macho peacockery, nor did he think that girls were, but neither was he naive about what gains respect from other boys:

Wakar: . . . I don't approve of fighting in the first place, but I do train for self-defence to use as a last resort.

Interviewer: Do you think that fighting is important to show you are macho?

Wakar: To girls? I don't know. I think most girls tend to go for boys who have a good build. They talk about having good attitudes, or 'I like talking to you because you're fun', or something like that . . . 'You've got a good sense of humour'.

Interviewer: Somebody said people respect you if you're good at fighting.

Wakar: The way I get out of that . . . because I've got a lot of respect in my own year and other years, and the way I get out of that is by doing self-defence . . .

It is obvious that Wakar has thought through his approach to matters such as fighting and how to gain respect. It is impressive that he maintains his view about not approving of fighting even when presented with the opposite proposition – that fighting gains respect. It is true that this view is a basic principle of self-defence, but Wakar has integrated it into his own self-development.

Asif, the Bangladeshi boy, rejects altogether the idea that the macho style has much charisma as far as girls are concerned. In answer to the question 'Is it still important to give a macho image in school?', he replied:

Not really, it doesn't help much. Not like you're 'the tough boy' and everybody respects you. Nowadays, they really respect the clever ones more than the macho big bully types. If you're macho they're not going to be with you or like you, but if you can prove it on paper, that's OK really.

(Asif)

Although they are responding to general questions, both Wakar and Asif speak from personal experience. In Bob Connell's terms, they are reflexively constructing their own gender identities (Connell, 1995), or in Giddens's terms they are consciously developing their own 'life history project' (Giddens, 1991). No doubt people have always pieced together their own identities in this reflexive way, and in the context of the boys' lives such concepts may sound inflated. However, both Connell and Giddens see an increased potential in late modernity for both greater subjective freedom and greater variety and difference in identities. Perhaps Wakar and Asif in their avoidance of gender stereotypes modestly illustrate this trend.

Tariq, a boy of Indian Sikh origin, might be considered macho, but he also was hardly stereotypical. He presented himself as very much 'his own man' and street-wise, but was not anti-academic and intended to go on to study A-levels. He differentiated between boys like himself who mixed work and pleasure and a handful of 'basic dossers' in his class. However, he did comment that at times his social life took priority over his school work. Tariq had a girlfriend and most of his friends were a few years older than himself. He had been 'caught' by the police 'for mari-juana and also joy-riding'. He drank alcohol in pubs and occasionally got involved in fights – some of which had racist overtones. However, he said that racism was not a problem for him at school.

Although prone to chauvinism, Tariq's masculinity was understated and assured. He wore earrings and commented that 'the only real difference' in the way teachers treated boys and girls was 'that girls get away with earrings and styles and stuff'. When asked about his attitude to homosexuality, Tariq's cool momentarily unfroze – 'Gays? They should be shot first.' However, his more considered attitude was slightly less intolerant – 'If they want to do it that's their problem.' When asked what well-known person he admired, Tariq had no instant answer, but when pressed he came up with Linford Christie. Tariq was one of a number of Asian boys who stated their admiration for an individual of African origin – something which did not happen in reverse. However, his real hero was his uncle, a man who had lived a wild youth, spent some time in prison, but had emerged to become manager of a motor-servicing business, earning £35,000 a year and owning a BMW.

An explanation for Tariq's physical self-confidence became clear towards the end of the interview:

Interviewer: Do you do any sports, leisure things?
Tariq: Yes, I'm British kick-boxing champion.
Interviewer: So you can handle yourself?
Tariq: You could say that.

However, although Tariq enjoyed his 'kicks', the life of his uncle seems a better guide to his longer-term agenda. Tariq wanted to make money.

Conclusion: the construction of Asian masculinities

The various images of Asian males discussed at the beginning of this chapter are not wholly unreflective of aspects of Asian masculinities. However, as extreme stereotypes they rarely provide much insight into how individuals act and think, or how members of peer groups collectively behave. In fact, such stereotypes can do great damage. They function not as a basis of sympathetic understanding of others but as a means of objectifying others. Stereotypes define the other as different, often as 'essentially' different and – crucially – usually as inferior or threatening, or in some other way as unacceptable. Stereotypes such as 'Asian males are weak' or 'Asian males are chauvinistic' are not only racist (or ethnically prejudiced) in themselves, they tend to be part of wider patterns of racist thought and behaviour. The step from prejudice of this kind to active discrimination and, in some instances, violence is easily and frequently taken. Virtually all surveys into racist acts, including racial violence, report that Asians are more likely to be the victims of this kind of behaviour than African-Caribbeans.

In general, young Asian men seem resourceful in using their own cultures and their experience of the dominant culture to build viable masculine identities. Given the racism and the provocation and discrimination that Asian boys routinely experience, it is perhaps a tribute to their traditions of restraint that self-defence and self-help, rather than revenge and resentment, seem to be their preferred patterns of response.

Conclusion

This chapter has explored some aspects of the interplay of school, ethnicity and the peer group in the formation of the masculinities of boys in year eleven in four London schools. Large as this frame of reference is, it has also been necessary to refer constantly to the role of other factors in forming the identities of the boys, including, of course, class and, to a lesser extent, locality. There is a significant difference between how the boys behaved under the authority of the school, particularly in the classroom, and their behaviour in the space and time between school and home. The break between the formal sphere of school and the informal but still normatively-structured sphere of play and peer group is not total, but it is substantial in the life of the boys. In school the boys learnt the values and behaviours associated with anti-sexism and anti-racism. Outside school, some of the boys sustained these values to varying degrees while others did not. There is a sense in which, outside of school, free from the constraint of teachers, the boys were able to express their 'real' values. Some of the boys were ethnically and racially tolerant both in and out of school, whereas others were ethnocentric and intolerant. Most boys tended to revert to more ethnically based peer groups and friendships outside school and ethnic/racial awareness in a non-politically correct sense was part of their everyday life. However, it would be a serious mistake to underestimate the possible positive effects of equal opportunities education and socialisation. The concept of equality – gender and 'racial' – was implicitly present in our conversations, even with some of the more racist boys. Somehow the message had impressed itself that people should be treated as equal in their humanity and that racism was therefore wrong. Even the more overtly racist among our boys tended to be uncomfortable in their racism. It is perhaps on the basis of such apparently modest successes that the difference rests between achieving a liberal society or something much worse.

Although social class-based anti-school sub-cultures were clearly not a main focus of our research, it is of some interest that these did not appear to have strongly developed in the schools in our survey. The boys referred to individual or small groups of troublemakers, but suggested nothing on the scale observed by Hargreaves in the 1960s and Willis in the 1970s. If this is the case, it is probably because the boys formed social groups partly if not primarily along ethnic lines, thus weakening potentially class-based sub-cultures. It is significant that the one apparently anti-school sub-culture that did come to our attention was the ethnically-based, self-styled 'Underachievers'. It is also possible that social class-based anti-school sub-cultures are, in any case, generally less strong than previously. This would reflect the numerical and cultural decline of the working class and perhaps the highly controversial policy of excluding 'troublesome' pupils adopted in many schools.

While a variety of masculine orientations occurred among the boys, the extent to which many young men still desire to dominate – either in reality or symbolically – was notable. There was a minority who viewed partner relationships democratically, and a minority of 'male chauvinist pigs'. However, more common than 'new man' or 'mcp' was 'mixed up man' – who had learned something from the gender equality agenda but still retained significantly patriarchal and sexist attitudes and patterns of behaviour. The situation in relation to 'race' was similarly mixed. Often, tendencies to tolerance and intolerance were present in the same person. The main explanations for this inconsistency and confusion probably do not lie within the education system itself. In respect of both patriarchy and class, schools alone cannot change society – at least not very much, especially in the short term. In this matter, teachers' sense of helplessness against the influence upon children of the home, media and peer group is more realistic than that of more optimistic social engineers who would use the education system as a mechanism for fundamental change. The various models of masculinity learnt by the boys in our survey are generated mainly in the economic and occupational structure and reinforced in a culture that itself is increasingly driven by commercial considerations. To challenge these forces effectively would require much more centralised control of the education system even than has developed under the Thatcher/Blair governments, and probably more than is compatible with liberal values. Education can and does play a part in the cause of gender equality, but the latter will only be achieved if change occurs on a much wider front.

The real axis on which patriarchy turns is the gendered division of labour. It is developments in families and relationships and in paid work that are at the heart of the re-shaping of the gender order currently underway. The growing confidence of girls and the uncertainties of many boys are both reflected in and largely caused by changes in these areas. The next two chapters present and analyse evidence of tension and fragmentation at the core of patriarchy, with clear signs that a different gender order is being constructed by younger people, particularly young women.

Notes

1 In addition to Mac an Ghaill's and Back's work, frequently cited here, see Tony Sewell's *Black masculinities and schooling: how black boys survive modern schooling* (1997).
2 The most authoritative empirical account of the relationship between class and educational attainment is probably still A H Halsey, A F Heath and J M Ridge (1980) *Origins and destinations: family, class and education in modern Britain*, Clarendon Press. The literature cited in the main text, like our own research, is intended to illuminate the processes of cultural reproduction rather than establish statistical associations.
3 Like Paul Gilroy and Vic Seidler, Les Back was until recently based at Goldsmith's College in London, which achieved a quality of work in cultural studies in the 1990s comparable to that achieved at the Centre for Contemporary Cultural Studies at Birmingham in the 1970s.
  [...]
4 For a useful discussion of the pros and cons of the term 'underclass', particularly in relation to youth, see K Roberts, *Youth employment in modern Britain* (1995: 98–104).

References

Alexander, C (1996) *The art of being black: the creation of black British youth identities*, Oxford: Clarendon Press

Back, L (1996) *New ethnicities and urban culture: racism and multiculture in young lives*, London: UCL Press

Ball, S (1981) *Beachside comprehensive: a case-study of secondary schooling*, Cambridge: Cambridge University Press

Bates, I and Riseborough, G (eds) (1993) *Youth and inequality*, Buckingham: Open University Press

Brown, P (1987) *Schooling ordinary kids: inequality, unemployment and the new vocationalism*, London: Tavistock

Cashmore, E and Troyna, B (eds) (1982) *Black youth in crisis*, London: George Allen and Unwin

Cloward, B A and Ohlin, L E (1961) *Delinquency and opportunity*, Glencoe: The Free Press

Connell, R W (1995) *Masculinities*, Cambridge: Polity Press

Connolly, M, Roberts, K, Ben-Tovim, G and Torkington, P (1991) *Black youth in Liverpool*, Culemborg: Giordano Bruno

Dahrendorf, R (1992) 'Footnotes to the discussion', in D J Smith (ed.) *Understanding the underclass*, London: Policy Studies Institute

EOC (1999) *Gender equality and the careers service*, Manchester: Equal Opportunities Commission

Fuller, M (1982) 'Young, female and black', in E Cashmore and B Troyna (eds) *Black youth in crisis*, London: George Allen and Unwin

Giddens, A (1991) *Modernity and self identity: self and society in the late modern age*, Cambridge: Polity Press

Gilroy, P (1993b) *The black Atlantic: modernity and double consciousness*, London: Verso

Glasgow, D (1981) *The black underclass*, New York: Vintage Press

Goffman, E (1968) *Asylums*, Harmondsworth: Penguin

Goldthorpe, J H, Llewellyn, C and Payne, C (1987) *Social mobility and class structure in modern Britain* second edn, Oxford: Clarendon Press

Hall, S (1992) 'New ethnicities', in J Donald and A Rattansi, *'Race', culture and difference*, London: Sage

Hall, S, Critcher, C, Jefferson, T, Clarke, J and Roberts, B (1979) *Policing the crisis*, London: Macmillan

Hall, S and Jefferson, T (eds) (1975) *Resistance through rituals: youth subcultures in postwar Britain*, London: Hutchinson

Hargreaves, D (1967) *Social relations in a secondary school*, London: Routledge and Kegan Paul

Hebdige, R (1979) *Subculture: the meaning of style*, London: Methuen

Howe, D (1999) 'Why black boys fail their exams', *New Statesman*, 19 March

Jones, S (1988) *Black culture, white youth: the reggae tradition from JA to UK*, London: Macmillan

Lacey, C (1970) *Hightown Grammar*, Manchester: Manchester University Press

Man an Ghaill, M (1988) *Young, gifted and black: student-teacher relations in the schooling of black youth*, Buckingham: Open University Press

Mac an Ghaill, M (1994) *The making of men: masculinities, sexualities and schooling*, Buckingham: Open University Press

Miles, R (1989) *Racism*, London: Routledge

Miller, W B (1962) 'Lower class culture as a generating milieu of gang delinquency', in M Wolfgang, L Savitz and N Johnson (eds) *The sociology of crime and delinquency*, New York: John Wiley

Mirza, H S (1992) *Young female and black*, London: Routledge

Modood, T and Berthoud, R (eds) (1997) *Ethnic minorities in Britain: diversity and disadvantage*, London: Policy Studies Institute

Murray, C (1989) 'Underclass: a disaster in the making', *Sunday Times Magazine*, 26 November

Phoenix, A (1987) 'Theories of gender and black families', in G Weiner and M Jacques (eds) *Gender under scrutiny: new enquiries in education*, London: Hutchinson

Pryce, K (1986) *Endless pressure: a study of West Indian lifestyles in Bristol*, Bristol: Classic Press [first edition 1979, Harmondsworth: Penguin]

Rex, J (1986) *Race and ethnicity*, Buckingham: Open University Press

Rex, J and Tomlinson, S (1979) *Colonial immigrants in a British city*, London: Routledge and Kegan Paul

Rowntree Foundation (1999) *We can't all be white*, York: Rowntree Foundation

Seidler, V J (1997) *Man enough: embodying masculinities*, London: Sage

Sewell, T (1997) *Black masculinities and schooling: how black boys survive modern schooling*, Stoke: Trentham Books

Solomos, J (1989) *Race and racism in contemporary Britain*, London: Macmillan

Thomas, H (1997) *Slave trade: the history of the Atlantic slave trade 1440–1870*, London: Picador

Willis, P (1977) *Learning to labour: how working class kids get working class jobs*, Farnborough: Saxon House

Woods, P (1983) *Sociology and the school: an interactionist viewpoint*, London: Routledge and Kegan Paul

CHAPTER 6

THE DISCURSIVE PRODUCTION OF THE MALE/FEMALE DUALISM IN SCHOOL SETTINGS

Bronwyn Davies

Oxford Review of Education (1989), 15 (3): 229–41

[. . .]

The myth of the unitary person: contradictions and subjectivity

We are beginning to understand, largely as a result of the thinking that is being done within the post-structuralist paradigm, that the individual is not so much the product of some process of social construction that results in some relatively fixed end-product but is constituted and reconstituted through the various discursive practices in which they participate (cf. Weedon, 1987). Within this model, who one is is always an open question with a shifting answer depending upon the positions made available within one's own and others' discursive practices and within those practices, the stories through which we make sense of our own and others' lives. Stories are located within a number of different discourses, and thus vary dramatically in terms of the language used, the concepts, issues and judgements made relevant, and the subject positions made available within them.

Each of these possible selves can be internally contradictory or contradictory, with other possible selves located in different story-lines. Like history, the person is disjointed until and unless located in a story. Since many stories can be told even of the same event, then we each have many possible coherent selves. Production of our own sense of who we are, of our subjectivity, involves the following processes.

1   Learning of the categories which include some people and exclude others e.g. male/female, father/daughter.
2   Participating in the various discursive practices through which meanings are allocated to those categories. These include the story-lines through which different subject positions are elaborated.
3   Positioning of self in terms of the categories and story-lines. This involves imaginatively positioning oneself as if one belongs in one category and not in the other (e.g. as girl and not boy, or good girl and not bad girl).
4   Recognition of oneself as having the characteristics that locate one as x or not x—i.e. the development of 'personal identity' or a sense of oneself as belonging in the world in certain ways and thus seeing the world from the perspective of one so positioned. This recognition entails an emotional commitment to the category membership and the development of a moral system organised around the belonging.

In making choices between contradictory demands there is a complex weaving together of:

- the categories (and the cultural/social/political meanings that are attached to those categories) that are available within any number of discourses;
- the emotional meaning attached to each of those categories which have developed as a result of personal experiences of being located as a member of each category, or of relating to someone in that category;
- the stories through which those categories and emotions make sense; and
- the moral system that links and legitimates the choices that have been made.

Generally, when we ask the question "who am I?", we tend to hear it as referring to a fixed knowable identity, as if it were possible to have made a set of consistent choices located within only one discourse. And it is true we do struggle with the diversity of experience to produce a story of ourselves which is unitary and consistent. If we do not, others demand of us that we do so. We have also learned to define ourselves as separate from the social world and in contrast are not taught to be aware of the way in which the taking up of one discursive practice or another (not originating in ourselves) shapes the knowing or telling we can do. Thus, our subjectivities are experienced as if they were entirely our own because we take on the discursive practices and story-lines as if they were our own and make sense of them in terms of our own particular experiences. The sense of continuity that we have in relation to being a particular person are more continuities of shared discourses and of shared interpretations of the subject positions and story-lines available within them. How to be a particular non-contradictory person within a consistent story-line is probably learned, to a large extent, through textual rather than lived narratives.

Positioning within textual narratives

One of the most intriguing findings in my work with pre-school children (Davies, 1989a) emerged when I read them feminist stories. In these stories, some aspect of the traditional patterns is disrupted. For example, the female characters are heroic and the male characters choose not to take up dominant forms of masculinity or else their attempts at dominance are portrayed as unacceptable. In listening to these stories the children usually imaginatively positioned themselves as the same sex character (where there was a male/female pair) and heard the story from the viewpoint of that character. One such story was *The Paper Bag Princess* (Munsch, 1980). This is an amusing story about a princess called Elizabeth who goes to incredible lengths to save her prince from a fierce dragon. At the beginning of the story, Princess Elizabeth and Prince Ronald are planning to get married, but then the dragon comes along, burns Elizabeth's castle and clothes and flies off into the distance carrying Prince Ronald by the seat of his pants. Elizabeth is very angry. She finds a paper bag to wear and follows the dragon. She tricks him into displaying all of his magic powers until he falls asleep from exhaustion. She rushes into the dragon's cave to save Ronald, only to find that he does not want to be saved by a princess who is covered in soot and only has an old paper bag to wear. He tells her to go away and come back when she looks like a real princess. Elizabeth is quite taken aback by this turn of events, and she says "Ronald, your clothes are really pretty and your hair is very neat. You look like a real prince, but you are a bum". The last page shows her skipping off into the sunset alone and the story ends with the words: "They didn't get married after all".

The apparent intention here is to present a female hero who is not dependent on the prince in shining armour for her happiness, nor for confirmation of who she is. It also casts serious doubt on the concept of the prince who can provide eternal happiness. In this story Elizabeth is not a unitary being. She experiences the multiple and contradictory positionings we each experience in our everyday lives. She is portrayed at the beginning as the uncomplicated, happy and loving princess, living out the romantic narrative of love and happiness ever after. She is then portrayed as the dragon's victim, but she rejects this and becomes the active, heroic agent who is in control of the flow of events. She is then positioned as victim again by Ronald and again refuses this positioning, skipping off into the sunset, a free agent.

When the dragon burns Elizabeth's castle and steals Prince Ronald, he also burns her clothes off and makes her very dirty. Most children see her at this point as having magically changed into a bad princess, as if the dragon had cast a spell on her. That badness, because of her nakedness, has negative sexual overtones. Some of the boys are fascinated by her naked and bereft state, but generally it is not Elizabeth who holds their interest so much as the large, powerful and destructive dragon who has devastated her castle and later goes on to devastate entire land-scapes. Other boys perceive Ronald as a hero. They comment on his tennis outfit and the medallion around his neck which they perceive as a tennis gold medal. One boy even managed to see Ronald as heroic, that is as a central agent in control of his own fate, even at the point where he was sailing through the air, held by a dragon by the seat of his pants:

> I'm glad he held onto his tennis racquet so hard. When you've done that, well, you just have to hold onto your racquet tight and the dragon holds you up.

Many of the children to whom I read this story were unable to see Elizabeth as a genuine hero, and were equally unable to see her choice to go it alone at the end as legitimate or positive. The dragon, for most, is the powerful lascivious male, whose power remains untainted by Elizabeth's trickery. In this hearing of the story, Elizabeth clearly loses her prince, not because she chooses to leave him, but because she is lacking in virtue. Most children believed Elizabeth should have cleaned herself up and then married the prince.

What happens with these children who do not hear a story in which Elizabeth is the hero, is that the idea of dualistic oppositional maleness and femaleness which is embedded in the usual stories that they hear, and in the narrative structures which inform their everyday lives, intervenes, precluding a feminist hearing of the text. The story is heard as if it were a variation of a known story-line in which males are heroes and females are other to those heroes. Elizabeth thus becomes a 'normal' (unitary non-contradictory) princess who just got things a bit wrong.

Positioning within lived narratives in the classroom

Probably the majority of teachers these days believe that there should be equitable treatment of the sexes, though precisely what that means in practice is open to inter-pretation. What I plan to do in this section is examine some of the ways in which teachers' discursive practices position girls such that the beliefs about the male–female dualism embedded in the usual stories that children hear and read become a lived reality in the classroom.

There are many beliefs, narratives, images and metaphors located in everyday discursive practices that are not immediately recognisable as constituting inequitable practice. Even when they are recognised as such, it is often perceived as impossible to let go of them since the development of alternative discursive practices has not yet taken place. Sometimes the development of an alternative discourse precedes the recognition of the fault in the old. The naming of 'sexual harassment', for example, was a critical step in the recognition of those practices in which 'boys are just being boys' as not only not amusing but offensive and objectionable. More often, it is possible to see teachers setting out to teach equitably and failing to do so because their discourse constitutes the pupils in exactly the ways that they are saying is no longer appropriate. I have analysed elsewhere and in detail a year seven lesson in which a teacher set out to teach a lesson on sex roles and on the equality of the sexes in today's world, and yet provided a lesson which confirmed the 'fact' of inequality and difference (Baker & Davies, 1989). In part, the disjunction was due to the very mechanism of his teaching style, in part to a lack of knowledge about history, and in substantial part to his use of the concept 'sex role' with its attendant assumptions about biology. Within sex-role theory, what men and women are socially is derived in large part from what they are biologically (Davies, 1988, 1989a,b): gender difference is grounded in sex difference, and sex differences form the unquestioned and unexamined base on which gender is constructed. The effect of this assumption is obvious at many points in the lesson on sex roles. One example is as follows:

Teacher: What are the differences?
Beck: Well, a woman is capable of, um, having children and so she is expected to stay home and look after the kids?
Teacher: What's that called? There's a name given to that expectation of a woman to be a mother. Adam?
Adam: Stereotype?
Teacher: Right it is. It is a stereotype—I think. What is the instinct [. . .] the name given to [. . .]
Pupil: Maternal?
Teacher: Right. Is that the sort of thing you mean, Beck?
Beck: Yeah
Teacher: Maternal instinct. [Writes on board for five seconds] What is that again, Beck, please? What does that mean?
Beck: Um, the woman is expected to stay home and look after the kids because she had them?
Teacher: Had them. She is probably better able to do that. Has anybody heard of paternal instinct? We usually talk about that, don't we, the maternal instinct? . . .

What is happening here is that the pupils, in response to the teacher's question, are raising a social difference to do with beliefs (expectations, stereotypes) and the teacher is legitimating those beliefs in terms of what he understands about biology (instinct). He then further embeds the biological base in a moral base (she should mind the children because she is better able to do it). Interestingly, the justification for the biological argument is linguistic. We do not hear anyone talk about paternal instinct, he says. We only talk about maternal instinct and, by implication, the fact that only women have this instinct becomes, in their talk, a biological fact with moral implications—moral implications which lock women into the existing social order. The absence of an appropriate alternative discourse leads the teacher, unwittingly, to knit back up the fabric of the patriarchal social order faster than he can unpick it. As well he positions Beck as one who is making the same claim that he is. He uses his teacher rights to ask questions and to determine meanings, and thus to set his interpretation up not as one that lies in opposition to hers, but as one that stems directly from hers. Beck is positioned as one who sees the direct and inevitable link between expectation and practice.

This process is not only present in formal instructional talk. Teachers chatting to their pupils can equally constitute the world in inequitable ways. This can be seen in another classroom that I have videotaped. This class is an upper-primary family group. The teacher is an exceptionally competent teacher whom the children like very much. His consciously articulated ideals for his pupils make no distinction between girls or boys. He wants, for all of them, social competence combined with the ability to bring about social change, particularly in relation to 'traditional' (presumably sexist) values. He says:

> Ultimately I'd like to see them as beings that are going to fit fairly well into society, however, still giving them the tools, equipping them with the tools to challenge society, and perhaps even change society. . . . I don't want to see them as just sort of 'normal' type people who go to work, come home, that's it. I'd like to see them, you know, contributing to society and probably changing a few things in society too. The old traditional values for a start.

The children are all observably comfortable in this classroom, and I even found myself at the time I made the video of the classroom imaginatively positioning myself as a girl in his class, wishing I could be one of them and receive the kind of caring attention that he gave each individual person. But the care I found myself desiring is, on analysis, incompatible with a positioning of myself as one who would be able to take myself up as having the same access to educational opportunity as the boys. The images and narratives through which maleness and femaleness are constituted in the teacher's talk undermine that possibility. In the following episode, for example, the children are sitting on the floor, chatting and laughing with the teacher about what they did over the holidays. Some children are new to the group and are being introduced in the process of this first informal lesson. Two of the children, a brother and sister, have been on a plane trip to Sydney:

1	*Teacher:*	Tell us about your trip to Sydney, mate.
2	*John:*	Umm, umm, went down to Sydney with Aunty Sue on the plane and, and we came back on the plane by ourselves.
3	*Teacher:*	Bit of a thrill! Was that the first time you've been on an aircraft?
4	*John:*	It was the first time I'd been on one by myself, ah, back by ourselves.
5	*Teacher:*	And Deb. Deb, sorry I didn't mention you being new to the group. How did you like it on the aircraft?
6	*Deb:*	Really good.
7	*Teacher:*	Hostesses look after you well? Were they good lookin'? Pretty? (smiles and raises eyebrows and rolls eyes upward in a humorous manner. The students laugh. He looks back in John's direction.) Pretty hostess makes a flight very nice doesn't it?

If we examine this brief and friendly interchange in detail we find, as in much of the rest of the teacher–pupil talk in this classroom, the boy positioned as the teacher's 'mate', thus highlighting his equivalence with the male teacher, while the girl is made peripheral, even outside the male teacher–male pupil talk. The teacher construes

John's flight as a thrilling solitary adventure. (In 1 and 3, "your" can be heard in the singular.) Though John indicates in 2 that Deb was there too, he slips, in 4, into the same story-line as the teacher's but corrects himself. At this point the teacher, apparently not having heard the earlier plural reference, expresses some surprise (5) as he remembers not only that Deb was included in the trip, but that he had not earlier introduced Deb to the class when he was introducing other new members to the group. The teacher then turns to Deb but constitutes her experience quite differently from John's. The images relevant to the male heroic narrative form are no longer brought into use. Instead, in 7, images relevant to a romantic narrative are evoked with the male, still located as the hypothetical central character who is being made happier on the flight by the presence of pretty females. Deb becomes at one and the same time someone who was vulnerable and needed looking after by the hostesses (since called flight attendants), and someone who can herself imagine being one of those attractive hostesses who look after men and make their adventures more exciting by adding a sexual dimension. In both of these images there is no place for Deb as one who has agency, one who can be thrilled by the daringness of the adventure of flying in a plane without familiar adults. Her fragility and her future capacity to attract and care for men have been the only subject positions made available to her in the discourse through which her story is told. Further, the joking question at the end can only make sense if it is understood as addressed to the boys, and so for that moment Deb and the other girls are positioned as outside the male discourse which is shared by the teacher with the boys.

The psychic organisation of fantasy and desire thus derives not only from the imaginary placement of oneself as male or female within textual narrative structures but also through one's experience of the subject positionings made available in the everyday discourse of others. The imagined self and the self made possible through interactions are closely woven together, each lending meaning to the other.

The location of individuals in relation to social structures

Current understandings of what it means to be a person require individuals to take themselves up as distinctively male or female persons, these terms being meaningful only in relation to each other and understood as essentially oppositional terms. The opposition embedded in the terms is not an opposition of equals, but one in which part of the definition of one is its dominance over the other. So deeply is the linguistic division assumed to be reflective of a 'real' state of affairs that the idea that a person could be other than male or female is almost unthinkable, though each of us has probably experienced more than one moment in which we were aware of not correctly achieving ourselves as an appropriately gendered person. That fear can be particularly acute for individuals who do not achieve the heterosexual element of their maleness or femaleness and who are not therefore 'correctly' defining themselves in relation to the other sex/gender. Maleness and femaleness thus defined are a constraint on each individual person's practice. Boys are obliged to take themselves up imaginatively as forceful and dominant and girls as other to any manifestation of 'masculine' power. The assumption of the 'realness' of the world represented in people's talk makes it difficult to see power as not inherent in masculinity itself, but as a possibility available to each person depending on the discursive practices they and others take up and their positioning within those practices.

New practices can shift perceptions: "practice can be turned against what constrains it" (Connell, 1987, p. 95). But discursive practices are not just an external constraint (or potentiation), they also provide the conceptual framework, the psychic patterns, the emotions through which each individual takes themselves up as male or female and through which they privately experience themselves in relation to the social world. As well, they provide the vehicle through which others will recognise that taking up as legitimate, as meaningful, as providing the right to claim personhood. The development and practice of new forms of discourse, then, is not a simple matter of choice, but involves grappling with both subjective constraints and the constraints of accepted or habitual discursive practices.

That relation between the subjective and social/linguistic constraints is beautifully illustrated in the following biographical passage from Garrison Keillor's *Lake Wobegon Days*. In the episodes he describes, he reveals the relation between an individual's idea of themselves—the sort of person they take themselves to be—and the manner in which they sustain that belief through their discursive practices:

> In August, Coach Magendanz gets in his Chevy wagon and drives around recruiting Leonards for football season. . . . "You coming out for football?" he says to a big boy he's found mowing hay in a ditch. The boy is not sure. "You queer?" Coach asks. "If you are I don't want you." The boy thinks he may after all. . . . In football it's kill or be killed, and he needs some killers. "There is an animal in you and I intend to bring it out", he tells the team on the first day of practice. . . . He picks out two big boys to stand up and face each other. "Okay Stuart," he says, "rip his shirt off" Stuart advances. "You gonna let him rip your shirt off stupid?" Coach yells. Stupid isn't. They go at it in the hot sun, fooling around at first but then the animal in them comes out. They grunt and pant, rolling in the dirt getting wrist holds, leg holds, ripping each other's shirts off, until Coach calls them off. "That's football," he says. "Any pansies in the bunch can get up and leave right now".

> Some of us who are more sophisticated drift by the practice field on our bikes. . . . We wave to them, on our way to go swimming. He looks at us and we don't hear what he says to them; he says, "I gueth they can't take their eyeth off you guyth." We hear about it later, and far from being sophisticated, we are filled with terror. All those afternoons we went skinny-dipping, the curiosity about what each other looked like—is something terrible going on? Are we that way? Perhaps we are, otherwise why are we so uncertain about girls? [. . .] We don't talk about this. But each of us knows that he is not quite right. Once, at the river, Jim made his pecker talk, moving its tiny lips as he said "Hi, my name's Pete. I live in my pants." Now it doesn't seem funny at all.

> *If it's not wrong, why were we worried that someone would come along and see?* . . .

> When I was about fourteen, [my Uncle Earl] came up to bat one hot July afternoon in the father son softball game and looked at me playing third base and pointed his bat at me. I crouched; my mouth was dry and my heart pounded. He waited for a low pitch and drove it straight down the base line—a blazing swing, a white blur, a burst of chalk dust—I dove to my right just as the ball nicked a pebble—it bounced up and struck me in the throat, stopping my breath, and caromed straight up in the air about fifteen or sixty five feet. Blinded by tears, I hit the ground face first, getting a mouthful of gravel, but recovered in time to catch the ball and, kneeling, got off a sharp throw in the vicinity of

first which caught him by a stride. I was unable to speak for twenty minutes. That play was some proof that I was alright. Everyone saw it and said it was great; even guys who didn't like me had to say that because it was.

(Keillor, 1986, pp. 230–231)

The most obvious element of this narrative is the work that people like football coaches do to establish and maintain amongst schoolboys a certain idea and practice of heterosexual masculinity. More interesting for the purposes of this chapter is the process of self-examination and self-definition that the passage reveals. Through the agonising of the author, we see the ways in which theories embedded in the discursive practices of the football coach are brought to bear on the constitution of self. At first, riding on their bikes, the boys feel 'superior', the 'animal' nature of football is beneath them. But the coach's discourse is capable of disrupting that sense of superiority by defining their non-engagement in football as an indicator of homosexuality, and thus by positioning them as 'queer', as watching not from a superior viewpoint but with illegitimate sexual desire.

Since it is possible to find evidence to support either theory, then the boys find themselves threatened by the 'evidence' in their practices that they can find to support the coach's theory. Thus there is the extraordinary dilemma raised by the question "who am I really?". But the author does not have an attitude towards language which allows its constitutive force to be recognised. Instead of such questions as "which discourse do I take to be legitimate?" and "how can I resist a discourse that positions me in a way that I do not wish to be positioned?", the author is stuck with a view of language as something which portrays reality. He thus looks for elements of his experience which might count as 'proof' that he is homosexual and counterbalances them with proofs of heterosexuality. By engaging in an act which can only be construed as heroic within the coach's terms he gets himself off the hook in one sense (he is definitely not 'queer'), but is caught in another, because he has taken on the coach's discourse, with its attendant assumptions and practices of masculinity, as his own. Precisely because of the metaphysical nature of maleness and femaleness (with their requirement of oppositeness to the other), the coach has the power to frighten the boys into taking on his discourse as their own along with its assumption that maleness cannot be taken for granted—it must continually be achieved by being demonstrated in quite specific ways. If Keillor was undubitably male (if male genitals were taken as sufficient proof) then the coach's words would have been a nonsense that the author could laugh off. Or if masculinity was 'normal', then the evoking of distorted definitions of homosexuality would not be necessary to frighten boys into fervent displays of 'non-homosexual' practices.

Far from 'sex' naturally giving rise to certain gendered practices, it would seem that the possession of a particular set of genitals obliges the possessor to achieve the ways of being that appear to be implicated in the particular set of genitals they happen to have. Teachers who attempt to stretch the boundaries of what will and will not be taken to be masculine and feminine in the interests of establishing nonsexist educational practices must contend with this specific understanding on the part of the children they teach. Take, for example, the following incident that took place in a pre-school in Ohio:

Michael was four years old at the time and profoundly deaf (a sign language user). The children found some nail polish in their teacher's belongings and wanted to try it on. A variety of children (mostly girls) spent the next twenty minutes playing with the polish. Michael painted his nails bright red. Michael came in the next day with an angry note from his father requesting that Michael not be allowed to play with the nail polish. Michael explained to us that "he was a good boy" and "boys don't wear nail polish". We agreed that boys don't wear nail polish but that some of the boys here like to try things when they play that are different, just for fun. "No, no, no, I am a boy, a boy, a boy" he said. We agreed he was a boy but it still seemed O.K. to us. At this point Michael pulled down his pants, pointed to his genitals and exploded with obvious impatience "Here, look, I am a *Boy*!".

(Rebecca Kantor, Ohio State University,
personal communication)

The teachers were introducing one form of discourse here in which the possession of male genitals and 'feminine' behaviour were compatible. The child's father found this a serious threat to the boy's achievement of masculinity as he understood that term (presumably having taken on as his own the discourse of his own Coach Magendanz) and explained to the child that the links between the possession of male genitals, goodness and 'masculine' forms of behaviour are incorrigible. If the child constitutes himself in terms of his father's discourse then the behaviour that the teachers condone is wrong, and he understands their error in terms of their failure to understand that he is genitally male. By providing this evidence, according to the assumptions embedded in his father's discourse, they will see the error of their ways.

In the process of learning the available discursive practices, the individual takes on as his or her own not only the attendant beliefs and emotions as illustrated above, but also the narrative forms, the metaphors, the visual and auditory images, through which stories are told and lived out, through which individuals discursively position themselves and are positioned and re-positioned. Although the various discourses and narratives through which we variously position ourselves provide a shifting nexus of possible positionings, possible interpretations of who we are, and constant challenges to the authenticity of whatever claims we might make about ourselves in our attempts to establish some kind of coherent, consistent identity, individuals build up histories of who they are, and in the maintenance of those histories lies a commitment to the discursive practices and narratives through which they are lived out.

Of critical importance here is the understanding that individuals have access to many forms of discursive practice and many possible ways of positioning themselves and being positioned within those practices. Alongside the kinds of experience cited above, boys have access to other, often contradictory, ways of being. As the author of *Lake Wobegon Days* comments about his school experience "you don't get to specialise: one day Coach Magendanz is trying to bring out the animal in you, and then you are Ernest in *The Importance of Being*, and then you are defending the negative in the question of capital punishment, and the next day you're attempting a sixteenth century polyphony" (Keillor, 1986, p. 279). But each of us is also presented with the ideal, and generally, within current discourses, the moral obligation, to be consistent and non-contradictory. Out of the magnitude of conflicting and often contradictory possibilities, each person struggles, then, to make themself a unitary rational being, whose existence is separate from others and yet makes sense to those others. In learning the discursive practices, we learn the categories, the relations between categories and the fine conceptual and interactive detail with which to take up our personhood, and with which to interpret who we are in relation to others. Taking oneself up as person within the terms made available within a particular social order in turn creates and sustains that social order. But it is not an internally consistent order. As we are exposed to competing discourses, so we are positioned in different ways and have the opportunity to see ourselves in different ways. This fact leads to a certain fragility of self, requiring constant maintenance work on self. As well, the choice-points between one discourse and another are the critical moments in the development of each individual identity. Having made choices, there is, then, the task of maintaining the preferred discursive practices through which one takes who one is to be meaningful. Taking oneself up as unequivocally male or female, and taking that to mean opposite to the other, then requires maintenance of the forms of discourse which sustain that oppositional difference. At the same time, the fact that a consistent and unitary self is never finally achieved makes it possible for new and radically different discourses and positionings to be established and taken on as one's own.

The possibility of refusing a discourse

What I have argued here is that masculinity and femininity are not inherent properties of individuals; they are inherent or structural properties of our society: that is, they both condition and arise from social processes. Each of us, as a member of society, takes on board as our own the 'knowledge' of sex and of gender as they are discursively constituted. As children learn the discursive practices of their society, they learn to position themselves correctly as male or female, since that is what is required of them to have a recognisable identity within the existing social order (Davies, 1987). Not to do so, in fact to resist, can lead to a perception of oneself as a social failure (de Beauvoir, 1972; Haug, 1987; Walkerdine & Lucey, 1989).

So much of everyday discourse structures individuals into a dualistic maleness or femaleness that is quite incompatible with principles of equity and yet is not recognised by the speakers as doing so. Images, metaphors, narrative structures, terms of address, teaching practices, can all function to position girls as marginal within educational discourse, to constitute them as fragile and incapable of agency, while boys are being constituted through the same discourses as aggressively masculine, taking their meaning of who they are in opposition to what girls are and therefore must be.

The language through which dualistic maleness and femaleness is constituted is both external and coercive, a structure through which one is shaped, and at the same time it is experienced as intensely personal in so far as one's thoughts, emotions and desires are understood as one's own. But language cannot be understood simply in terms of structure. It is primarily a process. Language is spoken or written, heard or read. There is a speaker and a listener, a writer and a reader. Where one is positioned and where one positions oneself in the speaking and hearing, or writing and reading of an utterance, has a significant effect on how the utterance or text is understood (Davies & Harré, 1990). What the person positioned as speaker intends with a particular utterance may not at all be what is heard by the person positioned as listener. Coach Magendanz's *intention*, for example, may have been to get an effective football team together, and the reference to homosexuality may have been intended by him as a joking means of focusing the attention of the team on to their training rather than on the boys going for a swim. The boys who were positioned by him as outsiders to, or objects of, his talk were nonetheless profoundly affected by his words *whether he intended that or not*. Similarly, the teacher in the conversation about the flight to Sydney intended that his students all be constituted as agentic regardless of gender, but in that specific moment at least, the girl was deprived of a position with any agency.

The solution is not simply for teachers to clean up their talk and for textbooks and story books to be rewritten. These are both necessary, but the students are treated in such 'solutions' as passive recipients of social structure, and that, as I hope I have shown, is not the way that it works. Students have already acquired a personal baggage of images and metaphors based on their own experience of being positioned within the many and contradictory discursive practices that they have encountered. They have developed their own emotions and patterns of desire as a result of being positioned in different ways and through taking on certain discursive practices as their own. More like than not, the girls in the classroom mentioned above both believed in the commitment to equity and agency espoused by their teacher *and* in being the attractive supportive other evoked in his talk. In the process of taking up those beliefs as their own they would also have developed, or be in process of developing, both the relevant emotions and the discursive practices through which those ideals could be made manifest.

We each learn to operate within multiple discourses that are in conflict with each other. Furthermore, we position ourselves and are positioned differently within each different form of discourse depending on the power and resources that we have at hand. One central and critical resource in this context is the understanding of the constitutive force of language. Another is access to different forms of discourse. If we can see the way in which the discursive practices within a particular text or used by a speaker (including oneself) locate or position us, then the possibility of refusing that positioning, or even the particular discursive practice itself, and taking up another becomes more readily available. Students have multiple forms of resistance to the imposition of unreasonable or demeaning authority. They use, for example, subversive laughter (Woods, 1976), or direct confrontation (Werthman 1971; Davies, 1982), or retribution (Rosser & Harré, 1976). Very few of these are constructive resistances, however, in so far as they leave the original discursive practices through which they were attacked or demeaned unchallenged. At most they develop their own discursive practices through which they can accord themselves a sense of self-respect or self-worth, but that 'alternate' discourse exists outside the meaning structure recognised and legitimated by the school authorities. As well, as I have shown elsewhere, school students are readily able to recognise, and operate within the terms of the many different discursive practices that they encounter in any one day (Davies, 1982). It is not a massive further step, then, to set up a programme in which students are empowered to refuse sexist and oppressive discourse. What they need is to:

(1) learn to recognise the constitutive force of spoken and written language, and, in particular in this context, the metaphysical nature of the male female dualism;

(2) learn to recognise and articulate the multiple and contradictory ways in which they position themselves and are positioned in the various discourses that they encounter and to analyse the personal and social implications of these various positionings;

(3) learn to recognise the constitutive force of the images and metaphors through which sex/gender is taken up as their own, and to make choices about refusing the discursive practices and structures that disempower them or that constitute them in ways they do not want.

(4) and (5) The fourth and fifth steps, which I see as critical, are the development or taking up of alternative discourses and the gaining of the right to refuse old ones. Teachers and teaching techniques allow students little room for articulating their own ideas where these do not fit with teachers' preconceived ideas of what a lesson is about or for developing alternatives to the discourse that

the teacher is using (Baker & Davies, 1989). To the extent that this is the case, empowering the students is not enough since their resistance may only serve to marginalise them. Teachers, too, need to go through steps 1–3 above, and to develop teaching strategies which involve listening to students and making room within their teaching for a genuine incorporation of what students say, *particularly* where this appears to run counter to the images and metaphors through which the lesson is being constituted. Finally, both students and teachers need access not only to textual material in each of the substantive and discipline-based areas with which they are concerned in which non-sexist discourses have been developed, but also to resource material that shows them how to go about providing a critique of existing material that has not yet been rewritten.

References

Baker, C. & Davies, B. (1989) A lesson on sex roles, *Gender and Education*, 1, pp. 59–76.
Beauvoir, S. de (1972) *The Second Sex* (Harmondsworth, Penguin).
Connell, R. W. (1987) *Gender and Power* (Sydney, Allen & Unwin).
Davies, B. (1982) *Life in the Classroom and Playground. The Accounts of Primary School Pupils* (London, Routledge & Kegan Paul).
Davies, B. (1987) The accomplishment of genderedness in pre-school aged children, in: A. Pollard (Ed.) *Children and their Primary Schools* (London, Falmer Press).
Davies, B. (1988) *Gender, Equity and Early Childhood*, pp. 1–42 (Canberra, Curriculum Development Centre, Schools Commission).
Davies, B. (1989a) *Frogs and Snails and Feminist Tales. Preschool Children and Gender* (Sydney, Allen & Unwin).
Davies, B. (1989b) Education for sexism: moving beyond sex role socialisation and reproduction theories, *Educational Philosophy and Theory*, pp. 1–19.
Davies, B. & Harré, R. (1990) Positioning conversation and the production of selves, *Journal for the Theory of Social Behaviour*, 20(1).
Haug, F. (Ed.) (1987) *Female Sexualization* (translated by Erica Carter) (London, Verso).
Keillor, G. (1986) *Lake Wobegon Days* (New York, Penguin).
Munsch, R. (1980) *The Paper Bag Princess* (Toronto, Annick Press Ltd).
Rosser, E. & Harré, R. (1976) The meaning of trouble, in: M. Hammersley & P. Woods (Eds) *The Process of Schooling* (London, Routledge & Kegan Paul).
Walkerdine, V. & Lucey, H. (1989) *Democracy in the Kitchen* (London, Virago).
Weedon, C. (1987) *Feminist Practice and Poststructuralist Theory* (Oxford, Basil Blackwell).
Werthman, C. (1971) Delinquents in schools: a test for the legitimacy of authority, in: B. Cosin *et al.* (Eds) *School and Society* (London, Routledge & Kegan Paul).
Woods, P. (1976) Having a laugh: an antidote to schooling, in: M. Hammersley & P. Woods, *The Process of Schooling* (London, Routledge & Kegan Paul).

PART 4

REGULATION

CHAPTER 7

PERFORMATIVITIES AND FABRICATIONS IN THE EDUCATION ECONOMY

Towards the performative society

Stephen J. Ball

Gleeson, D. and Husbands, C. (eds), *The Performing School: Managing, Teaching and Learning in a Performance Culture* (2001), London: RoutledgeFalmer, pp. 210–26

> Each time I have attempted to do theoretical work it has been on the basis of elements from my experience – always in relation to processes that I saw taking place around me. It is in fact because I thought I recognised something cracked, dully jarring or disfunctioning in things I saw in the institutions in which I dealt with my relations with others, that I undertook a particular piece of work, several fragments of autobiography.
>
> (Foucault, cited in Rajchman, 1985 p. 36)

This chapter joins in a burgeoning conversation concerned with performativity in education and social policy. It looks at both the capillary detail and the bigger picture of performativity in the public sector. Ideally it should be read in relation to the multitude of performative texts and 'texts of performativity' with which we are continually confronted and which increasingly inform and deform our practice. The chapter is intended to be both very theoretical and very practical, very abstract and very immediate.

Performativity is a technology, a culture and a mode of regulation, or even a system of 'terror' in Lyotard's words, that employs judgements, comparisons and displays as means of control, attrition and change. The performances of – individual subjects or organisations – serve as measures of productivity or output, or displays of 'quality', or 'moments' of promotion or inspection. They stand for, encapsulate or represent the worth, quality or value of an individual or organisation within a field of judgement. 'An equation between wealth, efficiency, and truth is thus established' (Lyotard, 1984 p. 46). The issue of who controls the field of judgement is crucial. 'Accountability' and 'competition' are the lingua franca of this new 'discourse of power' as Lyotard describes it. A discourse which is the emerging form of legitimation in post-industrial societies for both the production of knowledge and its transmission through education. My aim is to begin work on and towards an analytics of this discourse of power, and the resistances and accommodations to it. This is both an exercise in critical ontology and the analysis of new regulative forms.

In referring to various texts or data, I am not attempting in any simple sense to mobilise proof of my arguments. I am trying to establish the existence of an attitude and an ethical framework within which teachers and researchers in schools, colleges and universities are having to work and think about what they do and who they are. I am interested in the way in which these texts play their part in 'making us up' (Hacking, 1986 p. 231) by providing 'new modes of description' and 'new possibilities for action'. Thus are new social identities created – what it means to be educated; what it means to be a teacher or a researcher. This remaking can be enhancing and empowering for some but this has to be set over and against the various inauthenticities discussed, below.[1] It is productive as well as destructive. There are 'winners' and 'losers' in the 'struggle for the soul of professionalism' (Hanlon, 1998), which is embedded in this remaking. We make ourselves up within the information we provide and construct about ourselves. We articulate ourselves within the representational games of competition, intensification and quality.

The argument focuses upon a struggle over visibility. I shall explore a paradox, arguing that tactics of transparency produce a resistance of opacity, of elusivity; but that this resistance is also paradoxical and disciplinary. In general terms I want to outline a new mode of social (and moral) regulation that bites deeply and immediately into the practice of state professionals reforming and 're-forming' meaning and identity, producing or making up new professional subjectivities. This new mode involves, as Deleuze (1992) puts it, a shift from 'societies of discipline' to 'societies of control': 'controls are a modulation, like a self-deforming cast that will continuously change from one moment to the other, or like a sieve whose mesh will transmute from point to point' (Deleuze, 1992).

Within this new mode of regulation, the organisation of power within definite forms of time-space (e.g. factory or office production systems) is now less important. It is the database, the appraisal meeting, the annual review, report writing and promotion applications, inspections, peer reviews that are to the fore. There is not so much, or not only, a *structure* of surveillance, as a *flow* of performativities both continuous and eventful – that is *spectacular*. It is not the possible certainty of always being seen that is the issue, as in the panopticon. Instead it is the uncertainty and instability of being judged in different ways, by different means, through different agents; the 'bringing off' of performances – the flow of changing demands, expectations and indicators that make us continually accountable and constantly recorded – 'giving the position of any element within an open environment at any given instant' (Deleuze, 1992 p. 7). This is the basis for the principle of uncertainty and inevitability; it is a recipe for ontological insecurity, posing questions such as – are we doing enough? are we doing the right thing? how will we measure up?

Nonetheless, clearly, controls overlay rather than displace disciplines in most educational organisations even if the emphasis is shifting. There is at work here a combination of two things: first, of *rituals* (grandiloquent pronouncements and spectacular events) which serve to naturalise the discourses of control (such as inspections, audits, promotion applications, job interviews); second, of *routines* (record-keeping, committee and taskforce meetings, interactions) which address forms of identity by treating people in terms of the identities of the discourses of performativity (Corrigan and Sayer, 1985).

Different identities and performances are more or less possible, more or less available, in different locations (Blackmore and Sachs, 1999). However, whatever our location, we now operate within a baffling array of figures, performance indicators, comparisons and competitions – in such a way that the contentments of stability are increasingly elusive, purposes are contradictory, motivations blurred and self worth slippery. Constant doubts about which judgements may be in play at any point mean that any and all comparisons have to be attended to. What is produced is a state of conscious and permanent visibility (or visibilities) at the intersection of government, organisation and self-formation. And one key aspect of the steering effects of judgement and comparison is a gearing of academic production to the requirements of national economic competition, which are in turn supported by: 'Policies which pursue the general goal of reorganizing, maintaining and generalising market exchange relationships' (Offe, 1984 p. 125).

Performativity works from the outside in and from the inside out. As regards the latter, performances are, on the one hand, aimed at culture-building, the instilling of pride, identification with and 'a love of product or a belief in the quality of the services' provided (Willmott, 1992 p. 63). On the other hand, ratings and rankings, set within competition between groups *within* institutions, can engender individual feelings of pride, guilt, shame and envy – they have an emotional (status) dimension, as well as (the appearance of) rationality and objectivity. As regards the former, we can consider a teacher who appears in Jeffrey and Woods' powerful, moving and indeed terrifying book *Testing Teachers* which deals with the UK regime of school inspections and examines teachers' experience of these inspections as a conflict of values, a colonisation of their lives, and deprofessionalisation of their role:

> I don't have the job satisfaction now I once had working with young kids because I feel every time I do something intuitive I just feel guilty about it. 'Is this right; am I doing this the right way; does this cover what I am supposed to be covering; should I be doing something else; should I be more structured; should I have this in place; should I have done this?' You start to query everything you are doing – there's a kind of guilt in teaching at the moment. I don't know if that's particularly related to Ofsted but of course it's multiplied by the fact that Ofsted is coming in because you get in a panic that you won't be able to justify yourself when they finally arrive.
>
> (Jeffrey and Woods, 1998 p. 118)

Here then is guilt, uncertainty, instability and the emergence of a new subjectivity[2] – a new kind of teacher. What we see here is a particular set of 'practices through which we act upon ourselves and one another in order to make us particular kinds of being' (Rose, 1992 p. 161). Crucially, and this is central to my argument, together, these forms of regulation, or governmentality,[3] have a social and interpersonal dimension. They are folded into complex institutional, team, group and communal relations – the academic community, the school, the subject department, the university, for example. *We* sit on peer reviews, *we* write the accountability reports, *we* assign grades to other departments, *we* berate our colleagues for their 'poor' productivity, *we* devise, run and feed departmental and institutional procedures for monitoring and improving 'output'.

Within this economy of education, material and personal interests are intertwined in the competition for resources, security and esteem and the intensification of public professional labour – the changing conditions of and meanings for work.[4] The focus here is primarily on performance itself as a system of measures and indicators (signs) and sets of relationships, rather than on its functions for the social system and the economy. The starting point is Lyotard's concept but my use of the concept of performativity moves beyond his presentation of the principle of performativity 'as the optimising of performance by maximising outputs (benefits) and minimising inputs (costs)'. For I also want to differentiate between perform*ativity* in Lyotard's sense, to 'be operational (that is, commensurable) or disappear' (Lyotard, 1984 p. xxiv); and in Butler's (1990) sense, as enactment or perform*ance*. That perverse form of response/resistance to and accommodation of performativity that I call *fabrication* is also a major concern.

While at times I will talk about schools and school teachers in this chapter, and refer to other public sector organisations, I can claim no luxury or objectivity of distance in all this. My daily practice within a university is the most immediate reality for what I am attempting to analyse. Thus, some of my illustrations are taken from documents, events and observations within my own institution. Some of the oppressions I describe are perpetrated by me. I am agent and subject within the regime of performativity in the academy. As signalled by the opening quotation, this is in part an exercise in autobiography.

Social relations of practice

As represented by Lingard and Blackmore (1997 p. 13) the policy duality of accountability and enterprise in higher education produces tensions which 'are played out in the everyday/everynight lives of individual academics, in the form of demands made upon their time to provide feedback and accountability upwards to their institutions, through performance management, quality assurance and research quantums and productivity agreements under enterprise bargaining'. Two points follow from this. First, there is the contradiction – what Lyotard calls the law of contradiction. This arises between intensification, as an increase in the volume of first-order activities, and the 'costs' of second-order activities themselves, like performance monitoring and management. Thus, as a number of commentators have pointed out, acquiring the performative information necessary for perfect control, 'consumes so much energy that it drastically reduces the energy available for making improvement inputs' (Elliott, 1996 p. 15; also Blackmore and Sachs, 1997). Survival and competitive advantage in the economy of education rests equally upon the energy of first-order activities and the energy of second-order activities – producing what Blackmore and Sachs (1997) call 'institutional schizophrenia'. However, there is no simple 'realist' relationship between the former and the latter and they are mediated by the effort devoted to the production of personal and institutional 'fabrications'. Furthermore, as noted already, it is important to recognise the extent to which these activities enter into our everyday relations. These are most apparent in the pressures on individuals, formalised by appraisals, annual reviews and databases, to make their contribution to the performativity of the unit. Again in this there is a real possibility that authentic social relations are replaced by judgemental relations wherein persons are valued for their productivity alone. In Deleuze's terms, 'individuals have become "dividuals" and masses, samples, data, markets or "banks"' (Deleuze, 1992 p. 5). This is part of what Lash and Urry (1994 p. 15) call the 'emptying out' of relationships, which are left flat and 'deficient in affect'.

In relation to individual practice we can also identify the development and ravages of another kind of 'schizophrenia'. There is the possibility that commitment, judgement and authenticity within practice are sacrificed for impression and performance. There is a potential *splitting* between the teacher's own judgements about 'good practice' and students' 'needs' on the one hand and the rigours of performance on the other. Again this can be illustrated by quoting teachers from Jeffrey and Woods' study of UK school inspections. One teacher, Veronica, talked about resenting 'what I've done. I've never compromised before and I feel ashamed. It's like licking their boots'; and another, Diane, talked about a loss of respect for herself:

My first reaction was 'I'm not going to play the game', but I am and they know I am. I don't respect myself for it; my own self respect goes down. Why aren't I making a stand? Why aren't I saying, 'I know I can teach; say what you want to say', and so I lose my own self-respect. I know who I am; know why I teach, and I don't like it: I don't like them doing this, and that's sad, isn't it?

(Jeffrey and Woods, 1998 p. 160)

There is a lot here. There is an indication of the particular performativity – the management of performance – which is called up by the inspection process. What is produced is a spectacle, or what we might see as an 'enacted fantasy' (Butler, 1990), which is there simply to be seen and judged. And as the teacher also hints the heavy sense of inauthenticity in all this may well be appreciated as much by the inspectors as the inspected; Diane is 'playing the game' and 'they know I am'. Nonetheless, the effects here in terms of discipline and control are powerful indeed; as are the costs to the self. Jeffrey and Woods note the 'most dramatic' example of Chloe:

She was the only year 6 teacher at Trafflon and after criticism of their SATs results she resolved to go down the path of 'improvement of results'. She changed her curriculum, and achieved her aim by getting the second best results the following year in her LEA. She justified this by saying that she was 'now just doing a job'; and had withdrawn her total involvement to preserve her 'sanity'. 'The results were better because I acted like a function machine'.

(Jeffrey and Woods, 1998 p. 163)

Again the alienation of self is linked to the incipient 'madness' of the requirements of performativity: the result, inauthentic practice and relationships. We also see here the emergence of 'new forms of social relations' – social structures are replaced by 'information structures' (Lash and Urry, 1994 p. 111).

We might find a similar splitting and personal and social inauthenticity as teachers and researchers in higher education when we apply for grants in which we have no academic interest but will look good on departmental returns or earn income; or give conference papers or submit journal articles which are unready or unoriginal in order to chalk up another count in the annual output review. This may exemplify a situation that Giddens sees as endemic in late modernity. Where there is an institutionalised 'existential separation' from 'the moral resources necessary to live a full and satisfying existence' (Giddens, 1991 p. 91). He suggests as a result the individual may experience personal meaninglessness. However, there are mixed motives at work here – we tell ourselves 'necessary fictions' winch rationalise our own intensification or legitimate our involvements in the rituals of performance.

Nonetheless, this tension, this structural and individual 'schizophrenia', and the potential for inauthenticity and meaninglessness is increasingly an everyday experience for us all. The activities of the technical intelligentsia drive performativity into the day to day practices of teachers and into the social relations between teachers. They make management ubiquitous, invisible, inescapable – part of, embedded in, everything we do. We choose and judge our actions and they are judged by others on the basis of their contribution to organisational performance. And in all this the demands of performativity dramatically close down the possibilities for 'metaphysical discourses', for relating practice to philosophical principles like social justice and equity. And 'fables' of promise and opportunity such as those which attend democratic education are also marginalised. Even so, we are all expected to make our contribution to the construction of convincing institutional performances. Which brings us to the issue of fabrication.

Fabrications

The fabrications that organisations (and individuals) produce are selections among various possible representations – or versions – of the organisation or person. Complex organisations like schools and universities are multi-faceted and diverse, indeed they are sometimes contested and often contradictory. Clearly, particular groups or individuals will be able to privilege particular representations. However, these selections and choices are not made in a political vacuum. They are informed by the priorities, constraints and climate set by the policy environment. To paraphrase Foucault, fabrications are versions of an organisation (or person) which does not exist – they are not 'outside the truth' but neither do they render simply true or direct accounts – they are produced purposely 'to be accountable'.

Truthfulness is not the point – the point is their effectiveness, in the market or for the inspection, as well as the work they do 'on' and 'in' the organisation – their transformational impact. As Butler (1990 p. 136) puts it, in a rather different context: 'Such acts, gestures, enactments, generally construed, are *performative* in the sense that the essence or identity that they otherwise purport to express are *fabrications* manufactured and sustained through corporeal signs and other discursive means'. However, as Butler is swift to point out, such fabrications are paradoxical, and deeply so. In one sense organisational fabrications are an escape from the gaze, a strategy of impression management that in effect erects a facade of calculation. But in another sense the work of fabricating the organisation requires submission to the rigours of performativity and the disciplines of competition – resistance *and* capitulation. It is, as we have seen, a betrayal even, a giving up of claims to authenticity and commitment, it is an investment in plasticity. Crucially and invariably acts of fabrication and the fabrications themselves act and reflect back upon the practices they stand for. The fabrication becomes something to be sustained, lived up to. Something to measure individual practices against. The discipline of the market is transformed into the discipline of the image, the sign.

All of this keeps the gaze in place – the 'professional' teacher and lecturer are here defined by their grasp of and careful use of systems and procedures, and by the particular rewards and new identities that this delivers through a regressive, self-regulation. It is in these ways that we become more capable, more efficient, more productive, more relevant; we become user-friendly; we become part of the 'knowledge economy'. We learn that we can become more than we were. There is something very seductive about being 'properly passionate' about excellence, about achieving 'peak performance'.[5]

Apart from their official functions, as responses to accountability, both main aspects of educational performativity – comparison and commodification – are linked to the provision of information for consumers within the education market forum. And they are thus also different ways of making schools and universities more responsive or appear to be more responsive to their consumers.

However, the work of fabrication points to a second paradox. Technologies and calculations which appear to make public sector organisations more transparent may actually result in making them more opaque, as representational artefacts are increasingly constructed with great deliberation and sophistication.

Within all this (some) educational institutions will become whatever seems necessary to become in order to flourish in the market. The heart of the educational project is gouged out and left empty. Authenticity is replaced by plasticity. Within the education market institutional promotion and representation take on the qualities of postmodern depthlessness – yet more floating signifiers in the plethora of semiotic images, spectacles and fragments that increasingly dominate consumer society. Indeed, the particular disciplines of competition encourage schools and universities to fabricate themselves – to manage and manipulate their performances in particular ways. Increasingly educational institutions are taking the position that part of what they offer to choosers/consumers is a physical and semiotic context which is no longer 'left to chance, but has to be heavily designed' (Lash and Urry, 1994 p. 204). Certainly, schools have become much more aware of and attentive to the need to carefully organise the ways in which they present themselves to their current and potential parents through promotional publications, school events, school productions, open evenings, websites (Abbott, 1999)[6] and local press coverage. Furthermore, there is a general tension or confusion in the education market between information-giving and impression management and promotion. This blizzard of hype and (pseudo) information also contributes to opacity rather than transparency.

Again, individually, we also fabricate ourselves. We produce versions of ourselves for and at job interviews – and increasingly may have to 'perform' a presentation for our potential colleagues – for promotion and for grant-getting.

Let me try to be even more specific with some more examples, and in doing so begin to develop an analysis of the 'poetics of fabrication'. This might allow us to think about how plausibility and believability are achieved, or brought off, both tactically and creatively. It might be useful to distinguish between trivial or *representational* fabrications (which is not meant to underplay their effects) and those which are *constitutive* and arise from *organising* principles.

The routine selection (or manipulation) of statistics and indicators

Systems of calculability almost always leave latitude for representational variation (Ball 1997):

> I'm rushing around like a loony today trying to put together this exam results display she [the headteacher] wants ... I didn't have any data to do it with and I've had to collect that and then I've had to find a way of presenting the results in a way that looks good ... GCSEs and A level results against the national average ... that's presented us with some problems, because obviously with four subjects the results are uneven ... I've found a way of doing the A-level that looks alright, I'm struggling a bit with the GCSE.
>
> (Secondary School Head of Faculty)

In higher education the dual-authoring of papers with less productive colleagues is another fairly innocuous method of massaging publications returns. Leo Walford, Journals Editor at Sage Publications, has recently talked about the research assessment exercise (RAE) in the UK leading to what he calls the 'salami-slicing of strong research papers in several thinner articles' (Headline 'RAE can "corrupt" research', *THES*, 26 March 1999). In addition the republication of just slightly different versions of essentially the same paper seems to be becoming more common. Publishers are harassed to organise their production schedules to ensure publication before the RAE cut-off date. The choice of indicators, where more than one is available, is another routine act of fabrication. And in the UK the run-up to each RAE is now marked by a flurry of transfers of star performers to institutions wanting to boost their chances of a better grade – another form of instant fabrication.

In the school sector we can point to the introduction of baseline testing in UK schools as another point of struggle over and manipulation of indicators. Primary schools are eager to test early – despite advice to 'let the children settle down' – to produce maximum 'under-performance', against which 'value-added' gains can be made, and attributed to the schools. Some parents on the other hand are preparing their children for the tests to ensure a good showing, or are shocked by the poor performance of their 'unprepared' children. The interests of good schooling and good parenting are made antithetical by the demands of performativity. And the way in which performativity can easily become totally divorced from service is dramatically demonstrated by a UK private rail company which on several occasions has reportedly run trains without stopping at scheduled stations to ensure that they meet their punctuality targets. Or we might note the impact of the publication of the morbidity rates of individual surgeons in the USA which has led to many doctors refusing to operate on difficult or high-risk cases. The same may happen in the UK – 'Surgeons may refuse high-risk cases' was a headline in *The Independent* newspaper (*The Independent*, 7 October 1999).

The stage management of events

A colleague in London described to me a situation where two schools rented extra computers for their open evening, the idea being to give parents the impression of a hi-tech learning environment. Another colleague at the Chinese University of Hong Kong described a practice in mainland China in which schools about to be inspected rented plants and bushes from local nurseries, in order to meet the requirement that they should provide a pleasant and conducive learning environment for students. In both cases, the rented items were returned once the event was finished. Jeffrey and Woods (1998) again, describe a school preparing for inspection by rehearsing the inspectors' questions: 'We practised ensuring that we presented a consensus for any interviews we had. It was very helpful. I want them to say that the Senior Management Team has a shared clear view' (Grace, quoted p. 155). School open evenings are now typically carefully choreographed events, sometimes with professional support.

Constructing accounts of the institution

Increasingly, public sector institutions are required to construct a variety of textual accounts of ourselves in the form of development plans, strategic documents, sets of objectives etc. (as are individuals). Symbolism is as important as substance here, in at least two senses. First, such texts symbolise and stand for the corporate consensus of the institution, and indeed these exercises in institutional extrapolation can also work as a means of manufacturing consensus (Ball, 1997), the focusing of activities around an agreed set of priorities. Second, they provide a touchstone of shared endeavour which displaces or subsumes differences, disagreements and value divergences. Of course they are also a version of the institution constructed for external audiences. They may deploy discursive tactics to convey order and coherence, consensus and dynamism, responsiveness and careful self-evaluation or, to other audiences, a synthetic personalism, 'a caring institution'. By such means the organisation is written into being.

Performance as performativity

All of these examples of what I have called *representational* fabrications do in different ways have *organising* effects. As I argued more generally earlier fabrications act back on their producers. And indeed as technologies of accountability some of the requirements referred to here are intended to work as much as formative interventions as they are as summative indicators. The other sense of fabricating an institution as *constitutive* – in relation to certain organising principles – is the way in which performativities are achieved by the adoption of particular policies and practices. One way in which we can see this, which also points up the relationship between market incentives, market values and market information, is in the generation of GCSE examination results and league table positions in certain UK schools. The logic of market incentives would suggest that any school or university which can select its clients will do so – either formally or informally. Those schools which do select their students, either formally or informally, are more able to control their league table position and their reputation generally. Furthermore, those students who offer the best chance of GCSE success tend to be the cheapest to teach, and easiest to manage. Students who threaten the reputation or performance of the school will be deselected (excluded) and indeed we have seen a massive growth in the number of students excluded from school in the UK since 1991. Generally, as explained by headteachers in our research on many occasions, the most effective long-term strategy for improving GCSE performance is to change the student intake. Thus, GCSE attainment percentages and local league table positions do not in any simple sense represent the outcomes of 'good' teaching and 'effective' learning; they are instead artefacts produced out of a complex set of policy strategies and practical tactics which underpin the fabrication of performance.

Individual fabrications

In addition to these organisational fabrications, as noted earlier, we are increasingly required to fabricate ourselves. While there have always been performance and 'impression-management' aspects of rituals like interviews and lectures, they are increasingly a part of organisational routines, in annual appraisal interviews, in students' assessments of their tutors, and in promotion and job applications. The point is to make yourself different and, in the case of representational texts, to express yourself in relation to the performativity of the organisation. This is an aspect of what Blackmore and Sachs call self-management – 'the issue was as much what was seen to be done, rather than substantively what was done' (Blackmore and Sachs, 1999 p. 10).

The application or promotion text is increasingly an artifice of high order. A career is reconstructed within these texts as a seamless, developmental progression to the present, with lines of further development, a potential value-added, streaming off into the future. We rehearse our national and international reputation, quote from reviews of our books, highlight the excellence of our teaching and our contributions to administration and the institutional and academic communities. We become rounded paragons with multiple strengths and infinite possibilities for further work, adept in the studied art of convincing exaggeration. We make fantasies of ourselves,[7] aestheticise ourselves. Appraisal documents can be equally fantastical in setting and reporting on personal targets. But again we are increasingly caught up in the logic of our own representations. We are engaged in an indexing, a tabularising, of the self. Increasingly we represent and enact our academic selves in terms of productivities and tables of performance. We work on ourselves and each other, through the micro practices of representation/fabrication, judgement and comparison. A new kind of practical ethics is articulated and realised. In all this, what we are seeing, I want to argue, is 'a general change in categories of self-understanding and techniques of self-improvement' (Rose, 1992 p. 161).

The performative society

> . . . the generalisation of an enterprise form to all forms of conduct may of itself serve to incapacitate an organisation's ability to pursue its preferred projects by redefining its identity and hence what the nature of its project actually is.
>
> (Du Gay, 1996 p. 190)

This is also Lyotard's point. It is not that performativity gets in the way of real academic work, it is a vehicle for changing what academic work is! At the heart of Lyotard's thesis is his argument that the commodification of knowledge is a key characteristic of what he calls 'the postmodern condition'. This involves not simply a different evaluation of knowledge but fundamental changes in the relationships between the learner, learning and knowledge, 'a thorough exteriorization of knowledge' (Lyotard, 1984 p. 4). Knowledge and knowledge relations, including the relationships between learners, are desocialised.

Underlying this is the dissemination of the market or enterprise form as the master narrative defining and constraining the whole variety of relationships within and between the state, civil society and the economy. As far as public sector activities are concerned: '. . . the emphasis shifts from the state as provider to the state as regulator, establishing the conditions under which various internal markets are allowed to operate, and the state as auditor, assessing their outcomes' (Scott, 1995 p. 80). As Bernstein (1996 p. 169) puts it 'contract replaces covenant'. Within the public sector this process of exteriorisation also involves a profound shift in the nature of the relationship between workers and their work. Service commitments no longer have value or meaning and professional judgement is subordinated to the requirements of performativity and marketing; though obviously there is an important element of cynical compliance at work in the processes of individual and institutional fabrication. This is part of a larger process of ethical retooling in the public sector which is replacing concern for client need and professional judgement with commercial decision-making. The space for the operation of autonomous ethical codes based on a shared moral language is colonised or closed down. Embedded here is what Hanlon calls 'a struggle for the soul of professionalism' (Hanlon, 1998 p. 50) – a contest over the meaning of professionalism which has at its centre the issue of trust – 'who is trusted, and why they are trusted is up for grabs' (Hanlon, 1998 p. 59). The ethos of traditional professionalism is no longer trusted 'to deliver what is required, increasing profitability and international competitiveness' (Hanlon, 1998 p. 52) and is being replaced by a 'new commercialised professionalism' (Hanlon, 1998 p. 54).

The new structures and roles for organisational management with a central core for policy, audit and regulation and separate 'service delivery units' – the rim and the hub – increasingly mirror the steering-at-a-distance role of the 'small state' or what Neave (1988) calls 'the new evaluative state'. In this way, the state also provides a new ethical framework and general mode of regulation, a much more hands-off, self-regulating regulation, which nonetheless enables and legitimates the dissemination of the commodity form as we are required to commodify ourselves and our academic productions. This is, in Aglietta's (1979 p. 101) terms, a new 'regulative ensemble' or a 'particular mode of social coherence', a historically distinct form of labour organisation. This ensemble of performative technologies is an improvised and polyvalent mix of physical, textual and moral elements which 'make it possible to govern in an "advanced liberal" way' (Rose, 1996 p. 58).

Within the framework of performativity, academics and teachers are represented and encouraged to think about themselves as individuals who calculate about themselves, 'add value' to themselves, improve their productivity, live an existence of calculation. They are to become 'enterprising subjects', who live their lives as 'an enterprise of the self' (Rose, 1989). This is not simply a set of changes in the nature of public sector professionalism and social relations. Rather these changes encapsulate a more general and profound shift in the way we are coming 'to recognise ourselves and act upon ourselves as certain kinds of subject' (Rose, 1992 p. 161) and 'the nature of the present in which we are' (Rose, 1992 p. 161); and thus a certain form of life in which 'one could recognise oneself' (Foucault, 1988 p. 49) is threatened or lost. Instead we are presented with other ways of saying who we are and representing ourselves. We have an opportunity to be enthused. We also have everyday opportunities to refuse these ways of accounting for ourselves, not as apathy, rather as 'a hyper- and pessimistic activism'. As Foucault puts it: 'I think that the ethico-political choice we have to make every day is to determine which is the main danger' (Foucault, 1983, p. 232).[8]

Notes

1   The idea of authenticity, as a discursive practice in its own right, needs to be worked upon. It is deployed here in a neutral sense or at least as a 'nonpositive affirmation ... an affirmation that affirms nothing' (Foucault, 1997 p. 197) – an act of exiting. However, I might go as far as saying that while 'authenticity' is certainly not intended as a normative condition it is intended to indicate a stance towards, an anticipation of the effects of, the discourses we employ 'a refusal to be mindlessly complicitous' (Pignatelli, 1993 p. 430), the generation of 'inventive responses' and an honouring of 'disqualified knowledges' (Foucault, 1980; see also Ball, 1999).

2   Subjectivity is: 'patterns by which experiential and emotional contexts, feelings, images and memories are organised to form one's self-image, one's sense of self and others, and our possibilities of existence' (De Lauretis, 1986 p. 5).

3   As Mitchell Dean explains: 'The notion of governmentality implies, then, first a project for the analysis of the state which would no longer rely on the juxtaposition of micro and macrolevels of power, and the conceptual autonomy of an analytics of micro-power and the theory of sovereignty' (Dean, 1994 p. 160).

4   The pressures of performativity and performance act, in particular and heightened forms, on those academic workers who are without tenure or on fixed-term contracts.

5   Erica McWilliam pointed out to me the importance of trying to capture a sense of the seductive possibilities of performativity. See McWilliam, Hatcher *et al.* (1999) on the role of awards in higher education.

6   Abbott distinguishes between those sites which are promotional and those which are educative.

7   A colleague in another university recently described her application for promotion to me 'as a form of prostitution'.

8   An extended version of this paper was given as the Frank Tate Memorial Lecture at the Australian Association for Research in Education conference in Melbourne, 1999. It was later published in the *Australian Educational Researcher* 27 (2), 1–24.

References

Aglietta, M. (1979), *A Theory of Capitalist Regulation: The US Experience*, London: New Left Books.

Ball, S. J. (1997), 'Good School/Bad School', in *British Journal of Sociology of Education*, Vol. 18 (3), pp. 317–36.

Ball, S. J. (1998), 'Performativity and Fragmentation in "Postmodern Schooling"', in J. Carter (ed.), *Postmodernity and the Fragmentation of Welfare*, London: Routledge.

Ball, S. J. (1999), 'Global Trends in Educational Reform and the Struggle for the Soul of the Teacher!', Education Policy series: Occasional Paper. Chinese University of Hong Kong.

Baudrillard, J. (1998), *The Consumer Society*, London: Sage.

Bernstein, B. (1996), *Pedagogy, Symbolic Control and Identity*, London: Taylor & Francis.

Blackmore, J. and Sachs, J. (1997), 'Worried, Weary and Just Plain Worn Out: Gender, restructuring and the psychic economy of higher education', Brisbane: AARE Annual Conference.

Blackmore, J. and Sachs, J. (1999), 'Performativity, Passion and the Making of the Academic Self: Women leaders in the restructured and internationalized university', in A. McKinnon and A. Grant (eds), *Academic Women*.

Butler, J. (1990), *Gender Trouble*, London: Routledge.

Corrigan, P. and Sayer, D. (1985), *The Great Arch: English State Formation as Cultural Revolution*, Oxford: Basil Blackwell.

Dean, M. (1994), ' "A Social Structure of Many Souls": Moral regulation, government, and self formation', in *Canadian Journal of Sociology*, Vol. 19 (2), pp. 145–68.

De Lauretis, T. (1986), 'Feminist Studies/Critical Studies: Issues, terms and contexts', in T. De Lauretis (ed.), *Feminist Studies/Critical Studies*, Bloomington: University of Indiana Press.

Deleuze, G. (1992), 'Postscript on the Societies of Control', October, Vol. 59, pp. 3–7.

Du Gay, P. (1996), *Consumption and Identity at Work*, London: Sage.

Elliott, J. (1996), 'Quality Assurance, the Educational Standards Debate, and the Commodification of Educational Research', BERA Annual Conference: University of Lancaster.

Foucault, M. (1977), *Language, Counter-Memory Practice: Selected Essays and Interviews*, Ithaca, NY: Cornell University Press.

Foucault, M. (1979), *Discipline and Punish*, Harmondsworth: Penguin.

Foucault, M. (1980), Two Lectures. *Power/Knowledge*, New York: Pantheon Books.

Foucault, M. (1981), *The History of Sexuality: An Introduction*, Harmondsworth: Penguin.

Foucault, M. (1983), 'On the Genealogy of Ethics: An overview of work in progress', in H. Dreyfus and P. Rabinow (eds), *Michel Foucault: Beyond Structuralism and Hermeneutics*, Chicago: University of Chicago Press.

Gewirtz, S. and Ball, S. J. (1999), 'Schools. Cultures and Values: the impact of the Conservative education reforms in the 1980s and 1990s in England', ESRC Values and Cultures project paper, King's College London.

Gewirtz, S., Ball, S. J. *et al.* (1995), *Markets, Choice and Equity in Education*, Buckingham: Open University Press.

Hacking, I. (1986), 'Making People up', in T. Heller, M. Sosna and D. Wellbery (eds), *Autonomy, Individuality and the Self in Western Thought*, Stanford CA: Stanford University Press.

Hanlon, G. (1998), 'Professionalism as Enterprise', in *Sociology*, Vol. 32 (1), pp. 43–63.

Jeffrey, B. and Woods, P. (1998), *Testing Teachers: The Effect of School Inspections on Primary Teachers*, London: Falmer Press.

Lash, S. and Urry J. (1994), *Economies of Signs and Space*, London: Sage.

Lingard, B. and Blackmore, J. (1997), 'The "Performative" State and the State of Educational Research' (Editorial), in *The Australian Educational Researcher*, Vol. 24 (3), pp. 1–20.

Lipietz, A. (1985), *The Enchanted World, Credit and World Crises*, London: Verso

Lyotard, J.-F. (1984) *The Postmodern Condition: A Report on Knowledge*, Minneapolis: University of Minnesota Press and Manchester: University of Manchester Press.

McCollow, C. and Lingard, B. (1996), 'Changing discourses and practices of academic work', in *Australian Universities' Review*, Vol. 39 (2), pp. 11–19.

McWilliam, E., Hatcher, C. *et al.* (1999), 'Developing Professional Identities: Re-making the academic for corporate time', Queensland: Queensland University of Technology.

Neave, G. (1988), 'On the Cultivation of Quality, Efficiency and Enterprise, an Overview of Recent Trends in Higher Education in Western Europe 1986–88', in *European Journal of Education*, Vol. 23 (1), pp. 7–23.

Offe, C. (1984), *Contradictions of the Welfare State*, London: Hutchinson.

Pignatelli, F. (1993), 'What Can I do? Foucault on Freedom and the Question of Teacher Agency', in *Educational Theory*, Vol. 43 (4), pp. 411–32.

Rajchman, J. (1985), *Michel Foucault: The Freedom of Philosophy*, New York: Columbia University Press.

Rose, N. (1989), *Governing the Soul: The shaping of the private self*, London: Routledge.

Rose, N. (1992), 'Governing the enterprising self', in P. Heelas and P. Morris (eds), *The Values of the Enterprise Culture*, London: Routledge.

Rose, N. (1996), 'Governing "Advanced" Liberal Democracies', in A. Barry, T. Osborne and N. Rose (eds), *Foucault and Political Reason: Liberalism, neo-liberalism and rationalities of government*, London: UCL Press.

Scott, P. (1995), *The Meanings of Mass Higher Education*, Buckingham: Open University Press.

Slater, D. (1997), *Consumer Culture and Modernity*, Cambridge: Polity Press.

Willmott, H. (1992), 'Postmodernism and Excellence: The de-differentiation of economy and culture', in *Journal of Organisational Change and Management*, Vol. 5 (1), pp. 58–68.

CHAPTER 8

THE CAPITALIST STATE AND PUBLIC POLICY FORMATION

Framework for a political sociology of educational policy making

Carlos Alberto Torres

British Journal of Sociology of Education (1989), 10 (1): 81–102

[. . .]

Determinants of education policy formation

In comparative research in political science and public administration, determinants of public policy have been cataloged from a vast array of contrasting perspectives. Siegel & Weinberg, for instance, have emphasized the following domestic, internal influences in policy making: (a) environmental determinants of public policy (e.g. economic factors, physical environment, and social and demographic factors), and (b) political system determinants of public policy (e.g. political community, political regimes and the authorities). Among external influences in policy making, they have distinguished the following: (a) international development forces (e.g. military and political developments), and (b) international organizational cooperation, assistance and pressures (which certainly have proven to be very relevant for some areas of educational policy making in various countries) (Siegel & Weinberg, 1997). An alternative schema has been substantiated by H. Leichter for use in analyzing public policy. He has distinguished between *situational factors* (divided into six complementary sets of factors which extend from economic circles to technological change); *structural factors* (which include the political structure and the economic structure); *cultural factors* (distinguishing between political culture and general culture); and finally *environmental factors* (distinguishing between international political environment, policy diffusion, international agreements and multinational corporations) (Leichter, 1979).

These are merely a few examples of common trends in the empirical analysis of public policy. Unfortunately, there are very few studies which address themselves to an analysis of educational policy formation in capitalist states which at the same time try to overcome the narrow and technical point of view commonly used in studies of policy making and planning.

Policy making, for instance, has been commonly analyzed as: (1) the production of interaction between political controllers and professional providers of services (Saran, 1973); (2) the focus on timing and feasibility as crucial elements in policy making (David, 1977); (3) research such as Wirt & Kirst (1982) which, by assuming that schools are miniature political systems, falls into the contradiction of accepting a pluralist power structure in the United States, but ends up portraying schools as a world of harmony and consensus; (4) research that deals with local state policy making, and the development of educational policies taxonomies, especially basic control mechanisms available to state-level policy makers, in which the independent (explanatory) variable would be the political culture and educational assumptions of policy makers (Peabody Journal of Education, 1985); or (5) an Eastonian-system analysis perspective that focuses on education units as parapolitical subsystems that include the processing of demands, the generation of support by authorities, regime and the political community, and the feedback response factor (Howell & Brown, 1983). All of these fairly conventional approaches lack an understanding of theory of the state, and a critical conceptualization of issues such as domination, power, rules and political representation in analyzing policy making. But perhaps they are especially faulty in that the methodological individualism of these studies led to an underestimation of the constraints (or restraints) on policy-makers' actions, and particularly their conspicuously naive worldviews. In short, these types of studies lack the theoretical sophistication needed to understand a very complex and rather sophisticated political process of educational decision making in capitalist societies. As Richard Bates has said, "Underlying this onslaught of criticism was a clear impatience with the value neutrality of classical public administration and its tendency to distance itself from complex and controversial issues while focusing on narrow empiricist studies of administrative processes" (Bates, 1985, p. 15). They also lack a holistic approach to determinants of policy making, i.e. an ability to link what happens in schools and nonformal education settings with what happens in terms of accumulation and legitimation processes in the overall society. Above all, they have a practical–pragmatic bias in which the guiding knowledge interest (borrowing the term from Habermas, 1968) of the research is exclusively empirical–analytical, thus oriented toward potential technical control, rather than, or in addition to, an historical–hermeneutic interest or a critical–emancipatory one.

Hence, prevailing methodological individualism in social theory, and pragmatic–empiricist epistemological assumptions in educational administration have defined the study of policy making as a political process "in which constraints and opportunities are a function of the power exercised by decision-makers in the light of ideological values" (Child, 1973 cited in Clegg & Dunkerley, 1980, p. 338).

In this chapter, I shall argue that a critical theory of power and the state is a necessary starting point to study educational policy making—hence, moving the analysis from the strict realm of individual choice and preference, somehow modeled by organizational behaviour, to a more historical–structural approach where individuals indeed have choices, but they are prescribed or constrained by historical circumstances, conjunctural processes, and the diverse expressions of power and authority (at the micro and macro levels) through concrete rules of policy formation. Also, I will argue that any study of education as public policy should deal with the issues of the organizational context in which power (as an expression of domination) is exercised. The relationships between power, organization and the state should be understood from a combined perspective of the political economy and a political sociology of educational policy making.

I shall argue that policy making should be studied in the context of a theory of politics. Following Clegg (1975), I assume that the concept that articulates political life is domination which has manifold expressions, from economic dominance of one class over others in the material production and reproduction of social life, to patriarchal relations and intersubjective, male to female domination in the household (Morrow & Torres, 1988). Similarly, the distinction between surface/deep

Table 1 Power structures

Structure	Concept	Objective processes
Surface structure	Power	Exchanges
Deep structure	Rules	Rationality
Form of life	Domination/exploitation	Economic activity

Source: adapted from Clegg (1975, p. 78).

structure models of rules, borrowed from structural linguistics, could be very useful as a starting point in understanding power in decision making (Clegg, 1975, p. 70). Chomsky (1968) has distinguished between 'deep structure' (a semantic interpretation of sentences) and 'surface structure' (which implies the phonetic interpretation of sentences) where they both constitute the dynamics of language structure as a vehicle of meaning.

The deep structure is composed of a set of *restrictive* and *enabling* rules, "those which operate to modify independently existing forms of behaviour and activity, and those which create new forms of behaviour and activity" (Shwayder, in Clegg, 1975, p. 75). At the level of deep structure, a given combination of rules constitute different rationalities as, for instance, in Weber's three modes of legitimate authority or domination (e.g. traditional, charismatic and bureaucratic). At the level of surface structure, observable exchanges between individuals and institutions would constitute exchanges of power (which in turn, as Marx pointed out in Chap. 23 of Vol. I of *The Capital*, will inhibit or contribute to the simple and complex reproduction of economic exploitation/domination structures in social life). Clegg has graphically described the articulation of these categorical–analytical relationships (Table 1). In Clegg's terms: "Power is about the outcomes of issues enabled by the rule of a substantive rationality which is temporally and institutionally located. Underlying this rule is a specific form of domination. The progression is from domination → rules → power" (Clegg, 1975, p. 78).

This approach to rules, power and domination, which are essential stand-points to the study of policy making, has to be complemented with a discussion of a theory of the state in order to understand what I have called, following Claus Offe, the production rules of public policy. The next section attempts, first, to highlight the importance of a theory of the state for the study of educational policy making, and second, to introduce the notion of state authority in capitalist societies. For the sake of clarity, the theoretical, analytical and political differences between the theories and authors that are discussed below, and that inspired our framework (e.g. the state derivationists, Poulantzas, Offe, Therborn, Gramsci, etc.), will not be discussed in great detail. Similarly, illustrations and examples that may bring to life this theoretical framework will not be extensively used due to space restrictions.

Theory of the state and education

A common thread that runs through Marxist and Marxist-influenced educational research is the analysis of education as part of the state-administered reproduction of fundamental societal relations (Broady, 1981, p. 143). It has been discussed elsewhere that, in general, the notion of social reproduction (a) presupposes theories of society as a complex totality which develops through contradictions; (b) takes relatively complex societies as the object of inquiry within which formal and specialized educational institutions play a significant role; (c) argues these educational institutions constitute strategic sites for the stability and further development of these societies; (d) studies the relations of mutual interaction between these institutions and the larger society which provides the basis for sociologies of education; (e) suggests that policy formulation within the educational sphere constitutes a crucial context of negotiation and struggle which may have decisive effects on the capacity of society to maintain or transform itself, hence, educational settings are a microscopic representation of the larger macroscopic societal dynamics; and (f) paradoxically considers education to be either a powerful (and somehow a unique) tool for socialization into a given social order or to challenge and resist a hegemonic culture or social practice. In short, theories of social reproduction in education are linked with power, race, gender, class, knowledge and the moral bases of cultural production and acquisition (Morrow & Torres, 1988).

Although the relationship between education and the State is at the core of the definition of education's reproduction function in capitalist societies, it has rarely been thoroughly analyzed in contemporary social theory. Research questions concerning the capitalist state and its class-based proceedings, state impingements on educational structures, practices, codes, and especially educational planning and policy making, still lack sound theoretical understanding and appropriate methodological procedures for their study.

For instance, the influential book *Schooling in Capitalist America* focused on the notion of capital and its intervention in the educational system, particularly in the preparation of students as future workers at the various levels in the hierarchy of capitalist production (Bowles & Gintis, 1976). Bowles & Gintis have suggested a *correspondence principle* which explains educational development. In brief, there is a perceived correspondence between the social relations of production and the social relations of education (Bowles & Gintis, 1981, p. 225). Responding to the critics, they have argued that this correspondence principle depicts five main features of capitalist schooling: (a) the surprising lack of importance of the cognitive aspects of schooling in the preparation of good workers and in the intergenerational reproduction of social status; (b) an assessment of the limits of progressive education which is social rather than biological or technological; (c) a focus on the experience of schooling, which provides a consistent analytical framework for understanding the school as an arena of structured social interaction, and the school curricula as an outcome of these interactive processes; (d) a larger framework to integrate the effects of schooling on individuals (e.g. skills, attitudes, scholastic achievement) into a broader process of structural capitalist transformation and reproduction; and finally (e) Bowles & Gintis claim their analysis shows that, in order to understand the structure of schooling, it is not the ownership but the control of the means of production that matters (Bowles & Gintis, 1981, pp. 226, 227).

The emphasis here is on the general, class-based social determination of educational policy and schooling which is expressed in the correspondence principle. In a more recent contribution, Carnoy & Levin (1985) have emphasized that this earlier analysis of education and reproduction lacks a concrete theory of the State. Similarly, although it is important to consider the process of correspondence between education and capital accumulation, it is even more important to focus on the process of state mediation of contradictions. It is argued that the major problem with the type of analyses produced by Bowles & Gintis and Boudelot & Establet is, "... that it does not account for the contradictory trends towards equality and democracy in education ... Indeed, Bowles and Gintis argue that the 'laws of motion' of correspondence are so dominant that democratic or egalitarian reforms must necessarily fail or be limited in their impact" (Carnoy & Levin, 1985, p. 22).

To understand these complex relationships of correspondence and contradiction in education an explicit theory of the State and politics is necessary. I will argue that to study public policy formation, one must identify concretely the institutional apparatus of the State and who directly controls this apparatus. Similarly, it is of fundamental importance to identify the roles of the capitalist state (and education) in regard to the process of capital accumulation and social legitimation (Curtis, 1984).

Before I turn to discuss the notion of the State and policy making, I would like to assume that the capitalist state has a relative autonomy from the social classes, which seem to be recognized by Marxist and non-Marxist scholars alike (Archer & Vaughan, 1971, pp. 56–60; Offe & Ronge, 1975; Bourdieu & Passeron, 1977, p. 199; Alvater, 1979; Skocpol, 1980, pp. 155–201; Fritzel, 1987, pp. 23–35). Indeed, this relative autonomy is structural and is built into the very foundations of the capitalist mode of production (Boron, 1982, p. 47). Similarly, I will assume that state intervention in civil society has become one of the State's crucial features which takes different forms in different countries, involving such diverse issues as: (a) the articulation and/or independence of the capitalist state and the bloc-in-power, to use the expression developed in Poulantzas's writings (Poulantzas, 1969a, pp. 237–241), (b) the articulation of the State–subordinate class relationships; (c) the degree of direct and indirect state action in the regulation of capital accumulation (i.e. the State's role in the economy); (d) the State–Nation relationship in the context of the World System—as a macrocosmic condensation of broader dynamics and strains built into this structural relationship, particularly in the case of peripheral dependent states; and (e) the issue of the crisis of the capitalist states, with its implications in terms of hegemony and legitimation processes.

State authority and policy formation

The concept of the State has become a fashionable term in political science. However, many authors would refer to political authority and policy making as the role of the Government or the public sector, and some may even be inclined to use a more comprehensive notion such as the 'political system' rather than the State. This is not the place to argue on behalf of the usefulness of the concept. I shall point out that I share the rationale of Daniel Levy (1986, pp. 12–25) regarding the advantages of using the concept of the State.

I use the notion of the State, first of all as a reaction against liberal–pluralist political approaches that for many decades worked within a 'stateless' theoretical framework; and second, in order to highlight particularly, the role of the state as an actor in policy making with purposeful and relatively independent action while at the same time becoming a terrain where public policy is negotiated or fought over.

I propose to consider the State, at the highest level of abstraction, *as a pact of domination and as a self-regulating administrative system.* Cardoso has suggested that the state should be considered "The basic pact of domination that exists among social classes or factions of dominant classes and the norms which guarantee their dominance over the subordinate strata" (Cardoso, 1979, p. 38). Similarly, Claus Offe (1972a, b, 1973, 1974, 1975a, 1975b, 1984) conceptualizes state-organized governance as a selective, event-generating system of rules, i.e. as a sorting process (Offe, 1974, p. 37).

Offe views the State as comprising the institutional apparatuses, bureaucratic organizations, and formal and informal norms and codes which constitute and represent the 'public' and 'private' spheres of social life. The primary focus, then, is neither the interpersonal relations of various elites nor the decision-making process *per se*. Therefore, the class character of the State[1] does not reside in the social origin of the policy-makers, state managers, bureaucracy or the ruling class, but in the internal structure of the state apparatus itself due to its necessary selectivity of public policy; a selectivity that is "built into the system of political institutions" (Offe, 1974, p. 37).

In a similar vein, Goran Therborn identifies two main sources of determination of policy formation in the capitalist states. On the one hand, those determinations which originate at the level of state power, that is, the specific historical crystalliza- tion of relations of forces condensed into a pact of domination which acquires expression in a set of policies concerning the productive process, and, on the other hand, those determinations which originate in the structure of the state apparatus and the class bias of its organizational form (Clegg & Dunkerley, 1980, pp. 433–480; Therborn, 1980, pp. 144–179).

In summary, the emphasis here is on the dual character of the capitalist state and its organizational forms. That is to say, while the state claims to be the official repre- sentative of the Nation as a whole,[2] it is at the same time the object, product and determinant of class conflict. Through its policies directed toward the constitution and reproduction of the capitalist system, it is protected from various threats and guides its transformation: yet by acting as a factor of cohesion, the State's long-term planning synthesizes the goals of economic and social reproduction of capitalism as a system of commodity production, despite the sectoral or factional short-term needs and disputes of individual capitalist or corporative groups (Altvater, 1973; Offe, 1973; Skocpol, 1982, pp. 7–28).

Having outlined in very abstract terms the use of the notion of the State, I turn now to advance a set of working hypotheses on the production rules of public policy.

Production rules of public policy: a theoretical assessment and hypothesis

Is public policy formation mainly a response or anticipation to social threats?

At the highest level of generalization, the first hypothesis advanced here will stress that any mode of state intervention is linked to a changing pattern of potential or actual threats, or to structural problems that emerge out of the process of accumu- lation of capital. Thus, the modes of state activity[3] (which will be identified in the next section) can be seen as responses to these social threats and problems (Offe, 1975b, pp. 137–147; O'Donnell, 1978a, b, 1982; Wright, 1978, p. 277; Curtis, 1984, p. 12).

Obviously, this pattern of perceived social threat and state response should not be taken mechanically. As Goran Therborn has so aptly argued in studying the origins of welfare state policies in Europe and the strengthening of class activism:

> What is being argued is, (1) that a threat from the working-class movement, perceived by the political rulers, was a necessary (but not sufficient) condition for welfare-state initiatives; (2) that there is a structural affinity between the first major welfare-state initiatives and the modern labour movement; and (3) that there is a chronological relationship between the emergence of the modern labour movement and the beginning of the welfare state, which makes it probable

that there is a causal link between the two, the nature of which remains to be demonstrated.

(Therborn, 1984, p. 12)

However, after saying that, Therborn claims that there is always a certain tension between the identified historical processes and the analytical categories used for its study. Arguing that public policy is made out of opposing social-policy perspectives, Therborn cautiously emphasizes that

> the forms and principles of public social commitments have been politically controversial. These controversies have not been merely conjunctural, and have not only pitted individual politicians or civil servants and political parties and interest groups against each other. They have also developed along class lines, and the various specific issues are to a significant degree intelligible in terms of opposite class perspectives. Classes are not decision-making bodies, which is a fundamental reason why policy making is inherently irreducible to class conflict and class power. Yet a class analysis provides an explanatory framework that can make the study of politics and policy into something more than a modernized *histoire événementielle* of strings and episodes acted out by individual policy-makers.

(Therborn, 1984, p. 25)

The extent to which these changing social patterns of threats alter not only public policy formation, but also the very same form of the capitalist state, is not our immediate concern here. However, there seem to be certain affinities between the perceived pattern of threat and the pattern of state response/transformation. For example, recent political sociology argues that the emergence of a highly repressive form of political regime, e.g. the Bureaucratic–Authoritarian State in Latin America, is causally related to the internalization of the production in Latin America and the perceived threats from the subordinate social classes. Guillermo O'Donnell argues that the emergence of such regimes is linked to a particular phase or crisis of capital accumulation encountered in the maturation of dependent, industrializing economies. In short, this is the phase in which 'easy' import-substitution possibilities have been exhausted and further expansion seems to depend upon new investments in capital intensive, technologically advanced industries. Included with this 'economic framework' of the explanation, there is an increased activation of the popular sector and working classes which threatens the political stability of the capitalist regime (what Huntington has termed the "praetorianization" of the masses); finally, there is an increased importance of technocratic roles in the State. The evolution of these two major variables, namely the 'deepening of industralization' and the so-called 'background variables', lead the societal situation to an elective affinity between advanced industrialization and bureaucratic authoritarianism (Collier, 1979, pp. 3–26, 380; O'Donnell, 1982).

Why is this issue of social threats so important, and how are they dealt with by advanced capitalist states? The so-called 'German Debate' (Holloway & Picciotto, 1979, pp. 19–31; Jessop, 1982; Carnoy, 1984) will give us some clues. A prominent participant in this debate. Eltmar Altvater, pointed out that capital is unable, as a result of its existence as many factionalized and mutually antagonistic capitalists, to produce the social preconditions of its own existence. State interventionism is derived (deduced) as a particular state form working toward shortening and overcoming those deficiencies of private capital by organizing individuals into a viable body (namely, a general capitalist interest).

Altvater derives the nature of state interventionism from the four general functions of the State which he has envisaged.

> There are essentially four areas in which the State is primarily active, namely, 1) the provision of general material conditions of production ('infrastructure'); 2) establishing and guaranteeing general legal relations, through which the relationships of legal subjects in capitalist society are performed; 3) the regulation of the conflict between wage labour and capital and, if necessary, the political repression of the working class, not only by means of law but also by the police and the army; 4) safeguarding the existence and expansion of total national capital on the capitalist world market.
>
> (Altvater, 1979, p. 42)

Claus Offe not only explicitly recognizes his agreement with Altvater (Offe 1973a, p. 110) in their mutual criticism of the State Monopoly Capitalism Thesis: (STATEMOP Thesis).[4] Offe also adds to Altvater's formulation that state domination should be understood as a regulating system or as a system of filters with the specific selective mechanisms of: (a) extracting a general class interest from many fractionalized capital units, and (b) oppressing or suppressing any anti-capitalist interest which could arise in any capitalist social formation (Offe, 1975b, pp. 125–144).

Hence, social threats are dealt with by social policies and state institutions as part of this preventive and regulative role of the State. In regard to these state functions, Therborn's comment on the need to look at the State's everyday routines would show a fundamental activity that has not been highlighted so far, the welfare activities which seem to dominate everyday state routine (Therborn, 1984, p. 32). In support of this, Therborn shows that since education is at the core of welfare policies—and since education and also health systems are labour intensive, they employ a sizable majority of the total public servants—school employees in 1970, at the time of the Vietnam War, for the first time since the US turned into an imperial world power, became significantly more numerous than military and civilian defense personnel (Therborn, 1984, p. 35). A similar argument could be developed for a dependent society such as Mexico where slightly more than half of the total increase in federal employment between 1970 and 1976 was allocated to education (Torres, 1984, p. 156).

In societies in social transformation, recent research (Carnoy & Samoff, 1988) has shown that, on the one hand, a new political regime must respond to mass demands for more schooling, better health care, and the redistribution of agricultural land. On the other hand, a fundamental task of these regimes is to accumulate capital in order to expand the national material base. It seems that while, hypothetically, social demands and the accumulation of capital are complementary since healthier, more educated people will have higher productivity and therefore will increase output, to choose one to the relative exclusion of the other may mean, in the worst case, to risk failure of the political project itself. Carnoy, Samoff and co-workers have demonstrated how in all of the case studies, which included Cuba, Nicaragua, China, Tanzania and Mozambique, the expansion of public services such as education and health care also have ideological implications, and that the legitimacy, of the State in both low- and high-income countries is therefore affected by its capability to deliver such services to the population at large.

Patterns of state activity: the pursuit of abstract systemic interests or single-class-based interests? On modes and methods of state intervention

Claus Offe recognizes four main guiding patterns of state action. First, *exclusion*: since the State has no authority to order production or to control it, State and accumulation are somehow divorced in such a way that production and accumulation cannot be separated. Second, *maintenance*: the State does not have the authority but rather has the mandate to create and sustain conditions of accumulation, as well as to avoid, regulate or repress social threats. Threats may come from other accumulating units (e.g. interfirm, interindustry and international competition), from non-capitalist entities (e.g. the working class, social movements), or from criminal or 'deviant', behaviour. Third, *dependency*: the power relationship of the capitalist state and its main decision-making powers depend, like any other relationships in capitalist society, upon the presence and continuity of the accumulation process. A last guiding pattern of state activity is the *legitimation* function of the capitalist state The State can only function as a capitalist state by appealing to symbols and sources of support which conceal its true nature (Offe, 1975b, pp. 126, 127). In a more crude economic analysis of the advanced capitalist societies, Offe has suggested a structural discrepancy between abstract, surplus-value-related forms and concrete, use-value-related forms used in the implementation of state functions. Thus, this discrepancy can be maintained, if not solved, over time only by a system of legitimacy. Indeed, it is likely that as state power acquires more functions, it also requires an increase in legitimation (Offe, 1973b, p. 74).

Considering the above-mentioned fundamental parameters of state intervention, what remains to be clarified is the analytical distinction between *modes* of state intervention and *methods* of state intervention. The former refers to state action *vis-à-vis* state expected functions under the logic of commodity production, while the latter refers to a somehow abstract analytical distinction which embraces those several state alternatives (methods) to choose from in the process of public policy formation.

The principal *modes* of state intervention can be divided into allocative modes and productive modes. Offe has proposed the following schematic description of these types of activities:

1   *Allocative* a) allocation of State-owned resources, b) response to demands and laws ("politics"), c) demands which are positive and specific in regard to time, space, group, type, and amount of state resources, and d) decisions reached by politics.

2   *Productive* a) production of inputs of accumulation (organized production process required) in response to perceived threats to accumulation; b) conflicting or incompletely articulated demands that cannot be eliminated without threatening the overall process of accumulation; c) decision reached by policies based on State-generated decision rules.

(Offe, 1975b, p. 133)

Using allocative activities, the State creates and maintains the conditions of accumulation by means that simply require the allocation of resources which are already under state control (e.g. taxes, repressive forces, land, mass media). The productive mode represents state action which supplies a variable and a constant capital which the units of private capital are unable to produce. Beyond areas of competence or types of policies considered, what really differentiates these two modes is that the allocative mode is usually controlled and thereby reinterpreted by its inputs while the productive mode is generally controlled and thereby evaluated by its outputs (Offe, 1972a, p. 128).

The principal methods of state intervention are the following: (a) *state regulation* through a set of positive and negative sanctions connected with a certain behaviour of social categories (e.g. bureaucracy) or social classes, (b) *infrastructure investment* either as a *partial* or supplementary method to private capital activity (e.g. building roads, bridges, airports) or as a *total* method with which to replace private capital activity (e.g. the case of mass public compulsory education in some countries, law enforcement or the administration of justice. In these cases, the participation of private initiative is negligible in terms of the amount of investment and the probability of a high and consistent degree of control of systemic outcomes); (c) *participation* as the co-determination of policy making and policy-operation through consent building in decision-making bodies which incorporate several interest groups or corporative units.

Considering these modes and methods, it is important to propose a second hypothesis regarding the process of policy formation. Thus far, it has been suggested that the State's motivational force is the pursuit of an abstract systemic interest rather than any particular interest; however, it is equally important to distinguish between short-term, conjunctural processes and long-term, historical or organic processes in policy formation. The Gramscian dictum is in this regard very insightful and clear, and deserves to be quoted at length:

> A common error in historical–political analysis consists in an inability to find the correct relation between what is organic and what is conjunctural. This leads to presenting causes as immediately operative which in fact only operate indirectly, or to asserting that the immediate causes are the only effective ones. In the first case, there is an excess of 'economism', or doctrinary pedantry, in the second an excess of 'ideologism'. In the first case there is an overestimation of mechanical causes, in the second an exaggeration of the voluntarist and individual element. The distinction between 'organic' movement and facts, and 'conjunctural' or occasional ones must be applied to those in which a regressive development or an acute crisis takes place, but also to those in which there is a progressive development or one towards prosperity, or which the productive forces are stagnant. The dialectical nexus between the two categories of movement, and therefore research, is hard to establish precisely.
>
> (Gramsci, 1980, p. 178)

Are the 'form' and the 'content' of policy making two distinct dimensions?

A third working hypothesis regards the distinction between *form* and *content* in the production rules of public policy which results from the same analytical distinction between deep/surface structure models of rules. For instance, analyzing welfare state politics, Therborn has argued that: "One important reason for the intricate complexity of welfare-state history is the fact that public social-policy commitments can take a number of different forms, and questions of form have often aroused more controversy and conflict than the principle of public social responsibility *per se*" (Therborn, 1984, p. 16).

First of all, at a lower level of abstraction, it is not to be expected that a situation in which a stated intention of a policy and its actual outcome faithfully coincide could ever be found. Even though at first glance this point seems to be a trivial one, nonetheless it presents a formal comparison—so common in educational studies —between the State's alleged goals and the practical results. In general, such comparisons are too formal and generic to be worthwhile. Therefore, there will always be a gap between what is declared, what is implemented, and what is the actual policy outcome.

Second, at a higher level of abstraction, if the rationality behind a policy decision is treated as an analysis of language-in-use, any conversation will have a basic grammar, but the linguistic rules will not have entire control over the quality, intensity and meaning of the message. Similarly, "The organization structure can be conceived in terms of the selectivity rules which can be analytically constructed as an explanation of its social action and practice (its surface detail, what it does). The rules collected together, may be conceived of as a mode of rationality" (Clegg, 1979, p. 122). This mode of rationality, that is expressing selectivity rules, could be of different origins. Clegg has distinguished four types of rules: *technical rules* (know-how to carry out a particular administrative task), *social regulative rules* (any intervention to repair social solidarity in an organization, such as the implementation of human relations), *extra-organizational rules* (e.g. discriminatory practices based in racism, sexism, etc.) and *strategic rules* (social contracts, and wages and income policies).

It should be mentioned in passing that an example of a related type of analysis, although applied to education discourses (which influence and inform educational policies), can be found in Giroux when he compares different views of cultural production, pedagogical analysis and political action in the teacher–student experiences. Giroux distinguishes different pedagogical discourses (or logics-in-use in education), namely the discourse of management and control, the discourse of relevance and integration (progressivism), and the discourse of cultural politics—critical affirmative language; hence, using Giroux's terminology, a discourse that moves from a language of criticism to a language of possibilities (Giroux, 1985, pp. 22–41).

In short, the distinction between form and content of public policy is similar and related to the distinctions between rationality and social action, and between deep/surface structures. In fact, if we take into account all the possible combinations of different selectivity rules (and the fact that all of them may be co-existent at some point, or conversely, given a particular historical and organizational setting, one may predominate over the rest) with inputs (including rationalities), processes of transformation, and outputs (including social action) of policy, a simple distinction of form and content will vanish in front of our eyes; every policy form may or may not have a particular policy content if we take into account selectivity rules.

Is the State a problem-solving agent?

As a result of these theoretical explorations, the fourth hypothesis rejects the notion of the State as simply a *problem-solving agent*, an approach that in general places too much emphasis on the analysis of policy content and on the predominance of 'technical rules' among selectivity rules. The main assumptions of this common approach to policy making are the following: (i) the State seems to be analyzing those processes which occur in the political arena, and through a diagnosis of the chief problems, organizes its political agenda for action; (ii) from this standpoint, it is important for researchers to focus mainly upon which interests are involved in the determination of policy making; and (iii) as soon as this identification has been done, the corollary of the analysis will be to check those interests against the material outcomes and the distribution of tangible benefits which result from policies and implementation (Lindblom, 1968, pp. 12, 13). In general, these shared assumptions are used in the basic approaches to policy planning in education, including such areas as the estimation of social demand, needs analysis, manpower planning, cost-effectiveness analysis or rate-of-return analysis (Russel, 1980, pp. 1–15; Simmons, 1980, pp. 15–33; Weiler, 1980).

Is social control built into the selectivity rules?

A fifth hypothesis suggests that any organizational structure has controls which are built into the system of political institutions. Following Clegg, an organization-structure is a set of sedimented (i.e. historically laid down and superimposed) selection rules: "The organization-structure can be conceptualized as a structure of sedimented selection rules. Those prescribe the limits within which the organization-structure might vary" (Clegg, 1979, p. 97). Furthermore, those rules of policy formation depend upon the main guiding patterns of state action, the main state resources to carry out its functions, and the principal modes of state intervention.

The central guiding patterns of state activity have been identified as (a) exclusion, (b) maintenance, (c) dependency, and (d) legitimacy. The political puzzle, then, for the capitalist state is how to reconcile those patterns in the production of public policy. I have maintained, following Offe, that the motivational and structural force underlying policy making is the attempt to reconcile these four elements. To carry on its functions, the State resorts to four principal means: fiscal policies, administrative rationality, law enforcement and repression (which should not be considered only as a special case of administrative rationality) and mass loyalty. In the case of the dependent state,[5] perhaps the most significant feature is that the exercise of coercion and organized repression overlaps (and sometimes will have more prominence than) the other three standard means.

These main resources enable the capitalist state to perform its principal roles of executing preventive crisis management, determining priorities embodied in social needs, social threats and civil society problem-areas (for example in Canada, a typical case of a problem-area is the native question), and devising a long-term avoidance strategy for further threats and conflicts. In this regard, contradictions can no longer be plausibly interpreted simply as class antagonism. They must, as Offe insists, at least be regarded as necessary by-products of an integral political system of control (Offe, 1975a, pp. 4, 5). To this extent, the fiscal crisis of the State,[6] which appears to be the inevitable consequence of the structural gap between state expenditure and revenues, is at the same time a lively testimony and expression of systemic constraints.

Can functional interaction and interdependency be differentiated according to different political regimes?

A last hypothesis will stress that the different forms of functional interaction and interdependency within a bureaucratic organization can be analytically differentiated; and similarly, the form that this interaction assumes will vary according to the type of political regime considered.

For instance, Oscar Oszlak in analyzing political regimes in Latin America has identified three main types: *bureaucratic-authoritarian*, *democratic-liberal* and *patrimonialist*; similarly, Oszlak identifies three main types of bureaucratic interdependency: *hierarchical*, *functional* and *material* or *budgetary* (Oszlak, 1980).

Before exploring determinants of policy formation, it will be necessary to identify and carefully characterize the type of political regime and capitalist state, and which dominant form of bureaucratic interdependency comes into the discussion.

Production rules of policy formation: a summary

(1)   The capitalist state has been defined as an arena, a product and a determinant of class and social conflict. Hence, any mode of state intervention is linked to a changing pattern of threats, potential or actual, or to structural problems that emerge out of the process of capital accumulation and political domination. Particularly in dependent states but also in industrial advanced social formations, class struggle and the political practice of social movements give shape to the state structure at the same time that an institutionalized set of selectivity rules alter the intensity, degree and level (character) of class and social conflict. Two implications can be drawn. On the one hand, the form and content of state policies give shape to the forms and content of the class and social struggles, while, conversely, class and social struggles are shaping the form and content of state policies (Sardei-Bierman *et al.*, 1973, pp. 60–69). On the other hand, there is a practical tension between consensus-oriented practices and coercion-oriented practices in the planning and implementation of state policies.

(2)   There are modes and methods of state intervention which deal with those patterns and threats raised in the class and social struggles; the former (divided into allocative and productive modes) refers to a wide range of probable activities regarding the use of state resources while the latter (distinguishing between state regulations, infrastructure investment and participation) refers to the range of probable courses of action undertaken by the State. Both, methods and modes of state intervention, give substance to the process of public policy formation.

(3)   At the most abstract level, the main determinant of public policy formation is not the pursuit of any particular interest, but of an abstract systemic interest. Nonetheless, two different kinds of historical processes underpin public policy. On the one hand, there are structural determinants which have a historical–organic origin; on the other hand, there are conjunctural determinants which do represent, at a particular point in time, the short-term crystallization of a peculiar constellation of forces in class and social struggles.

(4)   Particularly in liberal-democratic societies, the State always will try to reconcile its contradictory guiding patterns of activity within a concrete corpus of state policies. Then, the process of policy formation will never reach a steady-state situation nor will it be completely coherent; it will always express conflicts, imbalances, contradictions and a fragile stability in policy formation.

(5)   In this regard, there always will be a gap between the publicly stated goals and targets of state policies and the actual outcomes, as well as there will be a practical and analytical difference between rationalities (as selectivity rules) and social action. Then, to consider the State (and state policies) as *only* a problem-solving agent would be grossly misleading. However, this seems to be the dominant approach in educational policy planning. This framework of the State as a problem-solving agent (needless to say, an argument usually advanced by technocratic-minded and not historically-minded scholars and administrators) fails to recognize the internally-produced and the externally-originated determinants of policies—especially those with the most causal weight in non-statistical terms. Secondly, this framework omits the display of the basic regularities, what Offe has termed the basic 'laws' of public policy formation.

(6)   By combining the modes and methods of state intervention, three main laws of motion of public policy can be suggested here. These are the law of motion of bureaucracy, the purposive-action law of motion, and the participatory-consensus building law of motion. In order to study these policy laws of motion, it would be necessary to consider not only a political framework and a theory of the State, but also an organizational approach to policy making. In this regard, any public policy, in its form and content, is bounded by a system of inputs, processes of transformation, and outputs, all of them related to deep/surface structures (rationales) expressing not only social action but domination and power.

(7)   Looking particularly at the dependent state, a decisive landmark is the State's bureaucratic encapsulation of policy making. In this sense, there are different forms of functional interaction within a bureaucratic organization; those forms of interaction can be analytically differentiated; and the form this interaction assumes will vary according to the type of political regime considered. This point leads us to recognize several common traits in the historical evolution of state apparatuses, for example in Latin America (Oszlak, 1981, pp. 3–32); traits that are of paramount importance in the study of educational policy formation in a corporatist state such as the Mexican State, with the complex interaction between a ruling party in power for more than 40 years, the forceful action of corporative trade unions and capitalist associations, and the ideology of efficiency held by the organic bureaucracy of the state (Pescador & Torres, 1985).

(8)   Since capitalism did develop differentially in each country, the configuration of the State will sharply differ across countries. I have assumed here that it is crucial to characterize the type of state, its historical traits and main features as a mode of political control and political organization, and the balance of power established in the society by the on-going confrontation between social and political forces, prior to undertaking an empirical analysis of educational policy making. Without such a historical and political background, it would be difficult to understand the particular rationale of resource assignment and the underlying motives for the creation (or elimination) of institutions, services, plans or policies. Finally, turning now to education in greater detail, it is necessary to clarify theoretically education's particular role in capital accumulation and political domination. By considering a theory of the State and education, it will be possible to assess in detailed fashion the politics of educational policy making, and policy making as politics.

Conclusion: a theoretical approach to public policy formation in education

It has been suggested here that the inquiry about policy formation must be in light of the following dimensions: (1) *the main actors of policy formation*, including the bureaucracy, administrative agents and social constituencies and clienteles; (2) in terms of organizational studies, there are the main systemic elements which can be found within a given educational setting—I will name them inputs, processes of transformation and outputs; (3) *the main institutional phases, stages and/or units of policy formation* (the levels of policy planning, policy making, policy operation and even the policy outcome)—these distinctions are useful in analytical terms for undertaking case studies; finally (4), the intellectual, institutional and ideological atmosphere where those decisions are made (the policy framework). Additionally, I shall argue that those dimensions are offset or shaped by *the general framework of organizational rules*, historically embedded within a particular organization. At a second, but

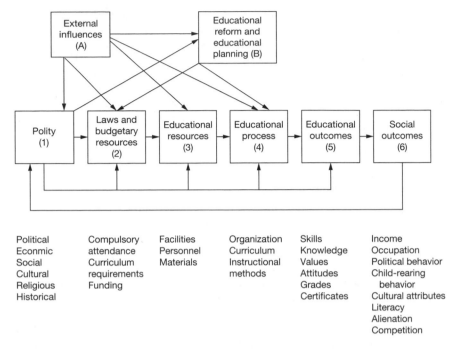

Figure 1 Henry Levin's policy-planning analytical framework.

nonetheless determinant, level of generalization in the analysis, it may be said that the production rules of public policy identified above would offer a theoretical bridge with which to understand educational relationships between the political society and the civil society at a particular point of time.

Henry Levin (1980) has offered a concise and highly stimulating analytical framework with which to study educational policy planning. Figure 1 constitutes a good synthesis of his model of analysis which needs no further explanation.

Combining Levin's analytical dimensions, although modified, and the theoretical framework devised in this chapter, Fig. 2 gives a graphic representation of the main analytical dimensions to be taken into account in analyzing educational policy formation.

By and large, in an analysis of educational policy making, the following concerns could be highlighted: (1) as regards *inputs mechanisms*, I will suggest the need to emphasize specially those principles regulating the type of task dealt with by the State, which is related to bureaucratic ideology and the state self-producing values and ideologies; (2) regarding *processes of transformation*, the emphasis will be placed on modes of decision making rather than on the handling of tasks. In addition, other important analytical dimensions for this study are: patterns of organizational positions and of relations among their incumbents, and the competing models of resource allocation; (3) regarding *output mechanisms*, those that should be explored and analyzed are as follows: (a) patterning of decisions and practices of the State toward the civil society (especially the educational clientele), and (b) modes of outflow of material and non-material resources from the State, understood as concrete processes of transformation of the social relations addressed generally toward particular social classes (Therborn, 1980, pp. 37–48).

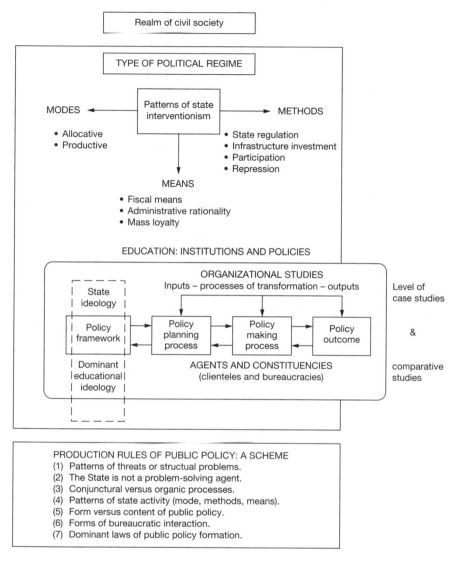

Figure 2 A theoretical approach to public policy formation.

While the study of policy formation should take into account the form and content of rule production and the predominant laws of motion of educational policy formation, any empirical research should confine itself, in its initial stages, to analyze specific levels and modalities in order to avoid simplistic generalizations not based on deep observation and analysis of empirical (quantitative and qualitative) data. Similarly, the production rules of public policy identified should be checked against concrete policy content and policy output in order to substantiate the main hypotheses regarding processes of transformation oriented toward the civil society.

In summary, if the main concern is to study policy formation, a preliminary attempt to do so should offset such distinct analytical dimensions as: (a) the State's goals and policy targets—the social history of state apparatus and the ebb and flow of class and social struggle; (b) modes and methods of operation in educational policy formation in dealing with social threats or problems that arise out of capital accumulation problems and/or political legitimation practices, policies and outputs; (c) the extent and type of bureaucratic organization; (d) the educational bureaucracy's ideologies contained in policy planning—as internal determinants of policy making; (e) material and non-material policy outcomes; perhaps a fundamental issue that ought to be discussed from a post-Marxist perspective is education's (and welfare activities in general) role in the production and reproduction of productive and unproductive labor, and education's contribution to production and realization of surplus-values; (f) capitalist and non-capitalist units of policy formation (Clegg & Dunkerley, 1980, pp. 486–492), which brings to light the important distinction between use-value and exchange-value as distinct goals of policy making in education (and other welfare activities and institutions); (g) the role of the educational policy within the overall state public policy, particularly (although not exclusively) at the level of legitimation practices. For instance, Miller (1986, p. 244) classifies within accumulation expenditures for social investment the levels and modalities of higher education and other non-elementary or secondary school education. Elementary and secondary education's expenditures are classified under accumulation expenditures for social consumptions. Perhaps adult and non-formal education expenditures, always neglected by the analysts, can also be classified, following the original O'Connor's taxonomy as social expenses; (h) and the struggles by groups and social classes to resist the hegemonic practices of the capitalist state. However, if resistance groups have some visible presence and are somehow inserted within the state apparatus, the task will then be to study how they have tried to consolidate or enlarge their position, and to promote specific policies, in the presence of restricting and enabling rules.

Notes

1   As a pact of domination and as a corporate actor who assumes the representation of popular sovereignty and as the political authority that enforces the democratic rule, the State becomes also a terrain for struggle of national and socio-political (class) projects. These contradictory functions summarize the contradictory unity and inherent complexity of capitalist states. Also, it highlights a crucial problem for Marxist analysis: the class character of the State—a question addressed by the neo-Marxist analysis which tries to overcome the impasse that resulted from the instrumentalist–structuralist debate and was exemplified in the exchanges between Poulantzas and Miliband almost two decades ago (Poulantzas, 1969a, pp. 237–241, 1969b, pp. 67–78; Miliband, 1970a, b).

2   The foremost penetrating pieces of research on state policies, have in one way or another pointed out this essential feature. For instance, Weber views the State as not only instrumental but immanent, that is, the State as the monopoly of force and site for exchange of services and community benefits (Weber, 1969, Vol. I, pp. 210–215).

3   Eric Olin Wright (1978, p. 15) has suggested a schema of structural causality distinguishing diverse *modes of determination* and organizing them into several *models of determination*. Modes of determinaton are considered to be distinct relationships of determination among the structural categories of Marxist theory and between these categories and the appearances of empirical investigation. Models of causal determination are schematic representations of the complex interconnections of the various modes of determination involved in a given structural process. Wright has outlined six main modes of causal determination: (a) structural limitation, (b) selection, (c) reproduction/non-reproduction, (d) limits of functional compatibility, (e) transformation, and (f) mediation.

4   The STATEMOP thesis advocates that Marx's political economy was dealing with competitive capitalism. However, the development of productive forces has progressed and large monopolies have thwarted competition in such a way that the State and 'monopoly capital' has become intertwined. This new phase of 'monopoly capitalism' is seen to invalidate the general laws advanced by Marx, particularly the laws of commodity exchange, capital accumulation and the falling rate of profit. Therefore, as in this theory, the analysis of modern capitalism must build on Lenin's analysis of the State and imperialism rather than on orthodox applications of Marx's methodology. The STATEMOP main thesis and critiques are thoroughly discussed in Holloway & Piccioto's book. A very good piece of criticism is Margaret Wirth's article (1977).

5   Since the early formulation of dependency theory, there has been a challenge to the notion that international dependency relies on a set of countries which constitute a central core (industrial advanced countries) and a set of countries which constitute a periphery. Certain countries that have been identified as 'Newly Industrialized Countries' (NIC) have assumed new functions in the world division of labour by constituting industrial platforms of development through their labour–cost advantages (e.g. India, Singapore, Korea, Hong Kong, Pakistan, Brazil and perhaps Mexico). In spite of these changes, the notion of the 'dependent state' could be analytically useful if we assume that it refers to states where (i) the majority or a sizeable proportion of the labour force still remains linked with agriculture production; (ii) in many cases, most of the country's exports are essentially non-manufactured goods, (iii) there is not a political structure resembling the welfare state; (iv) and this state is subject to important constraints for future autarchic economic and political development due to a raising external debt, a continuous outflow of domestic capital and labour, and a huge 'underground' informal, non-taxable, economical exchanges; (v) in this political structure, the role of the Armed Forces is usually prominent in national politics, and it is the ultimate resort for conducting repression activities; (vi), and finally, this state is further constrained by its operation in a given orbit of geopolitical power and the presence of an imperial ruling country—in spite of the global exchangeability of commodities and the international division of labour due to the World System.

6   The first premise of James O'Connor's analysis of the fiscal crisis of the State is that the State must try to fulfil two main functions: the accumulation and the legitimation functions. Therefore, at the same time that the State involves itself in the process of capital accumulation, it also tries to win the support of the economically exploited and socially oppressed classes for its programs and policies (O'Connor, 1973b, pp. 64–96). What is initially stressed in 'Connor's claim is that these two functions are mutually contradictory inasmuch as the growth of the state sector and state spending is increasingly the basis for the growth of the monopoly sector of the economy and the total production. Reciprocally, the growth of state spending and state programs is also the result of the growth of the monopoly industries, and "the greater the growth of the monopoly sector, the greater the State's expenditures on social expenses of production" (O'Connor, 1973b, pp. 13–39, 1973a, pp. 81–82). This, for many years the standard neo-Marxist explanation, is now being critically assessed. As an example of new financial estimates and theoretical developments in radical political economy, see Miller's extension of O'Connor's analysis. Miller (1986, pp. 237–260) argues that although it seems clear that the state fulfils an accumulation and legitimation function, they should be better formulated to explain the state's ability to promote accumulation in the 1970s and 1980s.

References

Altvater, Elmar (1979) Some problems of state interventionism, in: J. Holloway & S. Piccioto (Eds) *State and Capital. A Marxist Debate* (Austin, Tex., University of Texas Press).

Altvater, Elmar (1973) Notes on some problems of state interventionism, *Working Papers on the Kapitalistate*, 1, pp. 96–108, pp. 76–83.

Archer, Margaret & Vaughan Michalina (1971) Domination and assertion in educational systems, in: E. Hooper (Ed.) *Readings in the Theory of Educational Systems* (London, Hutchinson).

Bates, Richard (1985) *Public Administration and the Crisis of the State* (Victoria, Deakin University).

Boron, Atilio (1982) *The Capitalist State and its Relative Automony: arguments regarding limits and dimensions* (Mexico, CIDE, mimeograph).

Bourdieu, P. & Passeron, J.-C. (1977) *Reproduction in Education, Society and Culture* (London, Sage).

Bowles, Samuel & Gintis, Herbert (1976) *Schooling in Capitalist America* (New York, Basic Books).

Bowles, Samuel & Gintis, Herbert (1981) Education as a site of contradictions in the reproduction of the capital–labor relationship: second thoughts on the 'correspondence principle', *Economic and Industrial Democracy*, 2, pp. 223–242.

Broady, Donald (1981) Critique of the political economy of education: the prokla approach. Apropos of a tenth anniversary, *Economic and Industrial Democracy*, 2, pp. 141–189.

Cardoso, F.H. (1979) On the characterization of authoritarian regimes in Latin America, in: D. Collier (Ed.) *The New Authoritarianism in Latin America* (Princeton, N.J., Princeton University Press).

Carnoy, Martin (1984) *The State and Political Theory* (Princeton, N.J., Princeton University Press).

Carnoy, Martin & Levin, Hank (1985) *Education and Work in the Democratic State* (Stanford, Stanford University Press).

Carnoy, Martin & Samoff, Joel (Eds) (1988) *Education and Social Transformation in the Third World* (unpublished manuscript).

Chomsky, Norman (1968) *Language and Mind* (New York, Harcourt, Brace & World).

Clegg, Stewart (1975) *Power, Rule and Domination* (London, Routledge & Kegan Paul).

Clegg, Stewart (1979) *The Theory of Power and Organization* (London, Routledge & Kegan Paul).

Clegg, Stewart & Dunkerley, David (1980) *Organization, Class and Control* (London, Routledge & Kegan Paul).

Collier, David (1979) Overview of the bureaucratic–authoritarian model, in: D. Collier (Ed.) *The New Authoritarianism in Latin America* (Princeton, N.J., Princeton University Press).

Curtis, Bruce (1984) Capitalist development and educational reform, *Theory and Society*, 13, pp. 41–68.

David, M.E. (1977) *Reform, Reaction and Resources, the Three Rs of Educational Planning* (Windsor, NFER).

Fritzell, Christer (1987) On the concept of relative autonomy in educational theory, *British Journal of Sociology of Education*, 8, pp. 23–35.

Giroux, Henry (1985) Critical pedagogy, cultural politics and the discourse of experience, *Boston University Journal of Education*, 167(2), pp. 22–41.

Gramsci, Antonio (1980) *Selections from the Prison Notebooks* (edited and translated by Quintin Hoare & Geoffrey Nowell Smitt; New York, International Publishers).

Habermas, Jurgen (1968) *Knowledge and Human Interests* (edited and translated by Jermy J. Shapiro; Boston, Mass., Beacon).

Holloway, John & Picciotto, Sol (Eds) (1979) *State and Capital. A Marxist Debate* (Austin, Tex., University of Texas Press).

Howell, D.A. & Brown, Roger (1983) *Educational Policy Making. An Analysis* (London, Heinemann).

Jessop, Bob (1982) *The Capitalist State* (New York, Academic Press).

Leichter, Howard M. (1979) *A Comparative Approach to Policy Analysis: health care policies in four nations* (Cambridge, Cambridge University Press).

Levin, Henry (1980) The limits of educational planning, in: Hans N. Weiler (Ed.) *Educational Planning and Social Change* (Paris, IIEP–UNESCO).

Levy, Daniel C. (1986) *Higher Education and the State in Latin America. Private Challenges to Public Dominance* (Chicago, Ill., University of Chicago Press).

Lindblom, Charles E. (1968) *The Policy-Making Process* (Englewood Cliffs, N.J., Prentice-Hall).

Miliband, Ralph (1970a) The capitalist state—reply to Nicos Poulantzas, *New Left Review*, 59, pp. 53–60.

Miliband, Ralph (1970b) Poulantzas and the Capitalist State, *New Left Review*, 82, p. 93.

Miller, John A. (1986) The fiscal crisis of the State reconsidered: two views of the State and the accumulation of capital in the postwar economy, *Review of Radical Political Economics*, 18, pp. 236–260.

Morrow, Raymond & Torres, Carlos Alberto (1988) *Social theory, social reproduction, and education's everyday life: a framework for analysis*, paper prepared for the Western Association of Sociology and Anthropology (WASA) Annual Meeting, University of Alberta, 17–20 February.

O'Connor, James (1973a) Summary of the theory of the fiscal crisis, *Working Papers on the Kapitalistate*, pp. 79–83.

O'Connor, James (1973b) *The Fiscal Crisis of the State* (New York, St Martin Press).

O'Donnell, Guillermo (1978a) Reflections on the patterns of change in the bureau-cratic–authoritarian state, *Latin American Research Review*, 12, pp. 3–38.

O'Donnell, Guillermo (1978b) Apuntes para una teoría del estado, *Revista Mexicana de Sociología*, 40, pp. 1157–1199.

O'Donnell, Guillermo (1982) *El Estado Burocrático-Autoritario: Argentina 1966–1973* (Buenos Aires, Editorial de Belgrano).

Offe, Claus (1972a) Political authority and class structures—an analysis of late capitalist societies, *International Journal of Sociology*, 2, pp. 73–108.

Offe, Claus (1972b) Advanced capitalism and the welfare state, *Politics and Society*, 2, pp. 488–497.

Offe, Claus (1973) The abolition of market control and the problem of legitimacy, *Working Papers on the Kapitalistate*, (a) 1, pp. 109–116; (b) 2, pp. 73–75.

Offe, Claus (1974) Structural problems of the capitalist state: class rule and the political system. On the selectiveness of political institutions, in: Von Beyme (Ed.) *German Political Studies* (Beverley Hills, Calif., Sage).

Offe, Claus (1975a) *Notes on the laws of motion of reformist state policies* (mimeograph).

Offe, Claus (1975b) The theory of the capitalist state and the problem of policy forma-tion, in: Lindberg *et al.* (Eds) *Stress and Contradiction in Modern Capitalism* (Toronto, Lexington Books).

Offe, Claus (1984) *Contradictions of the Welfare State* (London, Hutchinson).

Offe, Claus & Ronge, V. (1975) Theses on the theory of the State, *New German Critique*, Fall, pp. 137–147.

Oszlak, Oscar (1980) *Políticas Públicas y Regimenes Políticos: reflexiones a partir de algunas experiencias latinoamericanas* (Buenos Aires, Estudios Cedes).

Oszlak, Oscar (1981) The historical formation of the State in Latin America: some theo-retical and methodological guidelines for its study, *Latin American Research Review*, 16(2), pp. 3–32.

Peabody Journal of Education (1985) State politics of education, 62, 4.

Pescador, J.A. & Torres, C.A. (1985) *Poder Político y Educación en Mexico* (Mexico, Uthea).

Poulantzas, Nicos (1969a) *Poder Político y Clases Sociales en el Estado Capitalista* (Mexico, Siglo XXI Editores).

Poulantzas, Nicos (1969b) The problem of the capitalist state, *New Left Review*, 58, pp. 67–78.

Russell, David G. (1980) *Planning Education for Development* (Cambridge, Harvard University Press—CRED).

Saran, R. (1973) *Policy Making in Secondary Education* (Oxford, Oxford University Press).

Sardei-Bierman, Christiansen, Jens & Dohse, Knuth (1973) Class domination and the political system. A critical interpretation of recent contribution by Claus Offe, *Working Paper on the Kapitalistate*, 2, pp. 60–69.

Siegel, R. & Weinberg, Leonard B. (1977) *Comparing Public Policies: United States, Soviet Union and Europe* (Homewood, Ill., Dorsey Press).

Simmons, John (1980) *The Educational Dilemma* (Oxford, Pergamon Press).

Skocpol, Theda (1980) Political responses to capitalist crisis: neo-Marxist theories of the state and the case of the New Deal, *Politics and Society*, 10(2), pp. 155–201.

Skocpol, Theda (1982) *Bringing the State back in. False leads and promising starts in current theories and research*, a working paper prepared for discussion at a Conference on States and Social Structures, Seven Springs Conference Center, Mount Kisco, New York, 25–27 February.

Therborn, Goran (1980) *What does the Ruling Class do when it Rules?* (London, Verso).

Therborn, Goran (1984) Classes and states. Welfare state developments, 1881–1981, *Studies in Political Economy*, pp. 7–41.

Torres, Carlos Alberto (1984) *Public Policy Formation and the Mexican Corporatist State: a study of adult education policy making and policy planning in Mexico, 1970–1982*, PhD dissertation, Stanford University.

Weber, Max (1969) *Economía y Sociedad* (Mexico, Fondo de Cultura Económica).

Weiler, Hans H. (Ed.) (1980) *Educational Planning and Social Change: report on an IIEP seminar* (Paris, UNESCO–IIEP).

Wirt, F. & Kirst, M.W. (1972) *The Political Web of American Schools* (Boston, Mass., Little, Brown & Company).

Wirt, F. & Kirst, M.W. (1982) *Schools in Conflict: the policies of education* (Berkeley, McCutchan).

Wirth, Margaret (1977) Towards a critique of the theory of the state monopoly capitalism, *Economy and Society*, 6, pp. 284–313.

Wright, Erik Olin (1978) *Class, Crisis and the State* (London, NLB).

PART 5

CURRICULUM

CHAPTER 9

CULTURAL POLITICS AND THE TEXT

Michael W. Apple

Official Knowledge, 2nd edn (2000), London: Routledge, pp. 42–60

Introduction[1]

For most people, literacy has a nonpolitical function. It is there supposedly to help form the intellectual character of a person and to provide paths to upward mobility. Yet, the process of both defining what counts as literacy and how it should be gained has always had links to particular regimes of morality as well. Literacy was often there to produce economic skills and a shared system of beliefs and values, to help create a "national culture." As the author of a recent volume on newly emerging redefinitions of literacy in education has put it, it served as something of a "moral technology of the soul."[2]

An emphasis on literacy as both "moral technology" and economically driven skills is of course not the only way one could and should approach the issue, no matter what the Right keeps telling us. The value of writing, speaking, and listening should not be seen as access to "refined culture" or to "life skills" for our allotted (by whom?) places in the paid and unpaid labor market, but as a crucial means to gain power and control over our entire lives. In responding to the dangers posed by the conservative restoration, I argued that our aim should not be to create "functional literacy," but *critical* literacy, *powerful* literacy, *political* literacy which enables the growth of genuine understanding and control of all of the spheres of social life in which we participate.[3]

This involves a different vision of knowledge and culture. Neither of these concepts refers to a false universality, a pregiven consensus that is divorced from patterns of domination and exploitation. Rather they refer to the utterly complex struggles over who has the right to "name the world."

Take the word "culture." Culture—the way of life of a people, the constant and complex process by which meanings are made and shared—does not grow out of the pregiven unity of a society. Rather, in many ways, it grows out of its divisions. It has to *work* to construct any unity that it has. The idea of culture should not be used to "celebrate an achieved or natural harmony." Culture is instead "a producer and reproducer of value systems and power relations."[4]

The same is true for the way we think about knowledge. Speaking theoretically, John Fiske reminds us of this:

> Knowledge is never neutral, it never exists in an empiricist, objective relationship to the real. Knowledge is power, and the circulation of knowledge is part of the social distribution of power. The discursive power to construct a common-sense reality that can be inserted into cultural and political life is central in the

social relationship of power. The power of knowledge has to struggle to exert itself in two dimensions. The first is to control the "real," to reduce reality to the knowable, which entails producing it as a discursive construct whose arbitrariness and inadequacy are disguised as far as possible. The second struggle is to have this discursively (and therefore sociopolitically) constructed reality accepted as truth by those whose interests may not necessarily be served by accepting it. Discursive power involves a struggle both to construct (a sense of) reality and to circulate that reality as widely and smoothly as possible throughout society.[5]

Fiske's language may perhaps be a bit too abstract here, but his points are essential. They point to the relationship among what counts as knowledge, who has power and how power actually functions in our daily lives, and, finally, how this determines what we see as "real" and important in our institutions in general and in education in particular. In this chapter, I focus on one particular aspect of education that helps define what "reality" is and how it is connected to critical, powerful, and political literacy in contradictory ways, ways the Right has recognized for years.

Whose knowledge is of most worth?

Reality, then, doesn't stalk around with a label. What something is, what it does, one's evaluation of it—all this is not naturally preordained. It is socially constructed. This is the case even when we talk about the institutions that organize a good deal of our lives. Take schools, for example. For some groups of people, schooling is seen as a vast engine of democracy: opening horizons, ensuring mobility, and so on. For others, the reality of schooling is strikingly different. It is seen as a form of social control, or, perhaps, as the embodiment of cultural dangers, institutions whose curricula and teaching practices threaten the moral universe of the students who attend them.

While not all of us may agree with this diagnosis of what schools do, this latter position contains a very important insight. It recognizes that behind Spencer's famous question about "What knowledge is of most worth?" there lies another even more contentious question, "*Whose* knowledge is of most worth?"

During the past two decades, a good deal of progress has been made on answering the question of whose knowledge becomes socially legitimate in schools.[6] While much still remains to be understood, we are now much closer to having an adequate understanding of the relationship between school knowledge and the larger society than before. Yet, little attention has actually been paid to that one artifact that plays such a major role in defining whose culture is taught: *the textbook*. Of course, there have been literally thousands of studies of textbooks over the years.[7] But, by and large, until relatively recently, most of these remained unconcerned with the politics of culture. All too many researchers could still be characterized by the phrase coined years ago by C. Wright Mills, "abstract empiricists." These "hunters and gatherers of social numbers" remain unconnected to the relations of inequality that surround them.[8]

This is a distinct problem since, as the rightist coalition has decisively shown by their repeated focus on them, texts are not simply "delivery systems" of "facts." They are at once the results of political, economic, and cultural activities, battles, and compromises. They are conceived, designed, and authored by real people with real interests. They are published within the political and economic constraints of markets, resources, and power.[9] And what texts mean and how they are used are fought over by communities with distinctly different commitments and by teachers and students as well.

As I have argued in a series of volumes, it is naive to think of the school curriculum as neutral knowledge.[10] Rather, what counts as legitimate knowledge is the result of complex power relations and struggles among identifiable class, race, gender, and religious groups. Thus, education and power are terms of an indissoluble couplet. It is at times of social upheaval that this relationship between education and power becomes most visible. Such a relationship was and continues to be made manifest in the struggles by women, people of color, and others to have their history and knowledge included in the curriculum. Driven by an economic crisis and a crisis in ideology and authority relations, it has become even more visible in the past decade or so in the resurgent conservative attacks on schooling. Authoritarian populism is in the air, and the New Right has been more than a little successful in bringing its own power to bear on the goals, content, and process of schooling.[11]

[. . .] The movement to the right has not stopped outside the schoolroom door, as you well know. Current plans for the centralization of authority over teaching and curriculum, often cleverly disguised as "democratic" reforms, are hardly off the drawing board before new management proposals or privatization initiatives are introduced. Similar tendencies are more than a little evident in Britain, and in some cases are even more advanced.

[. . .] All of this has brought about countervailing movements in the schools. The slower, but still interesting, growth of more democratically run schools, of practices and policies that give community groups and teachers considerably more authority in text selection and curriculum determination, in teaching strategy, in the use of funds, in administration, and in developing more flexible and less authoritarian evaluation schemes is providing some cause for optimism in the midst of the conservative restoration.

Even with these positive signs, however, it is clear that the New Right has been able to rearticulate traditional political and cultural themes. In so doing, it has often effectively mobilized a mass base of adherents. Among its most powerful causes and effects has been the growing feeling of disaffection about public schooling among conservative groups. Large numbers of parents and other people no longer trust either the institutions or the teachers and administrators in them to make "correct" decisions about what should be taught and how to teach it. The rapid growth of evangelical schooling, of censorship, of textbook controversies, and the emerging tendency of many parents to teach their children at home rather than send them to state-supported schools are clear indications of this loss of legitimacy.[12]

[. . .]. The ideology that stands behind this is often very complex. It combines a commitment to both the "traditional family" and clear gender roles with a commitment to "traditional values" and literal religiosity. Also often packed into this is a defense of capitalist economics, patriotism, the "Western tradition," anticommunism, and a deep mistrust (often based on racial undercurrents) of the "welfare state."[13] When this ideology is applied to schooling, the result can be as simple as dissatisfaction with an occasional book or assignment. On the other hand, the result can be a major conflict that threatens to go well beyond the boundaries of our usual debates about schooling.

Few places in the United States are more well known in this latter context than Kanawha County, West Virginia. In the mid-1970s, it became the scene of one of the most explosive controversies over what schools should teach, who should decide, and what beliefs should guide our educational programs. What began as a protest by a small group of conservative parents, religious leaders, and business people over the content and design of the textbooks that had been approved for use in local schools, soon spread to include school boycotts, violence, and a wrenching split within the community that in many ways has yet to heal.

There were a number of important contributing factors that heightened tensions in West Virginia. Schools in rural areas had been recently consolidated. Class relations and country/city relations were increasingly tense. The tack of participation by rural parents (or many parents at all, for that matter) in text selection or in educational decision making in general also led to increasing alienation. Furthermore, the cultural history of the region, with its fierce independence, its fundamentalist religious traditions, and its history of economic depression, helped create conditions for serious unrest. Finally, Kanawha County became a cause celebre for national right-wing groups who offered moral, legal, and organizational support to the conservative activists there.[14]

Though perhaps less violent, many similar situations have occurred since then in a number of districts throughout the country. For instance, the recent experiences in Yucaipa, California—where the school system and largely conservative and fundamentalist protesters have been locked in what at times seemed to be a nearly explosive situation—document the continuing conflict over what schools are for and whose values should be embodied in them. Here, too, parents and community members have raised serious challenges over texts and over cultural authority, including attacks on the material for witchcraft and occultism, a lack of patriotism, and the destruction of sacred knowledge and authority. And here, too, nationally based conservative organizations have entered the fray.

It is important to realize, then, that controversies over "official knowledge" that usually center around what is included and excluded in textbooks really signify more profound political, economic, and cultural relations and histories. Conflicts over texts are often proxies for wider questions of power relations. They involve what people hold most dear. And, as in the cases of Kanawha County and Yucaipa, they can quickly escalate into conflicts over these deeper issues.

Yet, textbooks are surely important in and of themselves. They signify, through their content *and* form, particular constructions of reality, particular ways of selecting and organizing that vast universe of possible knowledge. They embody what Raymond Williams called the *selective tradition*: someone's selection, someone's vision of legitimate knowledge and culture, one that in the process of enfranchising one group's cultural capital disenfranchises another's.[15]

Texts are really messages to and about the future. As part of a curriculum, they participate in no less than the organized knowledge system of society. They participate in creating what a society has recognized as legitimate and truthful. They help set the canons of truthfulness and, as such, also help recreate a major reference point for what knowledge, culture, belief, and morality really *are*.[16]

Yet such a statement, even with its recognition that texts participate in constructing ideologies and ontologies, is basically misleading in many important ways. For it is not a "society" that has created such texts, but specific groups of people. "We" haven't built such curriculum artifacts in the simple sense that there is universal agreement among all of us and this is what gets to be official knowledge. In fact, the very use of the pronoun "we" simplifies matters all too much.

As Fred Inglis so cogently argues, the pronoun "we"

> smooths over the deep corrugations and ruptures caused precisely by struggle over how that authoritative and editorial "we" is going to be used. The [text], it is not melodramatic to declare, really is the battleground for an intellectual

civil war, and the battle for cultural authority is a wayward, intermittently fierce, always protracted and fervent one.[17]

Let me give one example. In the 1930s, conservative groups in the United States mounted a campaign against one of the more progressive textbook series in use in schools. *Man and His Changing World* by Harold Rugg and his colleagues became the subject of a concerted attack by the National Association of Manufacturers, the American Legion, the Advertising Federation of America, and other "neutral" groups. They charged that Rugg's books were socialist, anti-American, antibusiness, and so forth. The conservative campaign was more than a little successful in forcing school districts to withdraw Rugg's series from classrooms and libraries. So successful were they that sales fell from nearly 300,000 copies in 1938 to only approximately 20,000 in 1944.[18]

We, of course, may have reservations about such texts today, not least of which would be the sexist title. However, one thing that the Rugg case makes clear is that the *politics* of the textbook is not something new by any means. Current issues surrounding texts—their ideology, their very status as central definers of what we should teach, even their very effectiveness and their design—echo the past moments of these concerns that have had such a long history in so many countries.

Few aspects of schooling currently have been subject to more intense scrutiny and criticism than the text. Perhaps one of the most graphic descriptions is provided by A. Graham Down of the Council for Basic Education.

> Textbooks, for better or worse, dominate what students learn. They set the curriculum, and often the facts learned, in most subjects. For many students, textbooks are their first and sometimes only early exposure to books and to reading. The public regards textbooks as authoritative, accurate, and necessary. And teachers rely on them to organize lessons and structure subject matter. But the current system of textbook adoption has filled our schools with Trojan horses—glossily covered blocks of paper whose words emerge to deaden the minds of our nation's youth, and make them enemies of learning.[19]

This statement is made just as powerfully by the author of a recent study of what she has called "America's textbook fiasco."

> Imagine a public policy system that is perfectly designed to produce textbooks that confuse, mislead, and profoundly bore students, while at the same time making all of the adults involved in the process look good, not only in their own eyes, but in the eyes of others. Although there are some good textbooks on the market, publishers and editors are virtually compelled by public policies and practices to create textbooks that confuse students with non sequiturs, that mislead them with misinformation, and that profoundly bore them with point-lessly and writing.[20]

Regulation or liberation and the text

In order to understand these criticisms and to understand both some of the reasons why texts look the way they do and why they contain some groups' perspectives and not others', we also need to realize that the world of the book has not been cut off from the world of commerce. Books are not only cultural artifacts. They are economic commodities as well. Even though texts may be *vehicles of ideas*, they still have to be "peddled on a market."[21] This is a market, however, that—especially in the national and international world of textbook publishing—is politically volatile, as the Kanawha County and Yucaipa experiences so clearly documented.

Texts are caught up in a complicated set of political and economic dynamics. Text publishing often is highly competitive. In the United States, where text production is a commercial enterprise situated within the vicissitudes of a capitalist market, decisions about the "bottom line" determine what books are published and for how long. Yet, this situation is not just controlled by the "invisible hand" of the market. It is also largely determined by the highly visible "political" hand of state textbook adoption policies.[22]

Nearly half of the states—most of them in the southern tier and the "sun belt"— have state textbook adoption committees that by and large choose what texts will be purchased by the schools in that state, a process that is itself contradictory in its history. . . . It too has signified losses and gains at the same time. The economics of profit and loss of this situation makes it imperative that publishers devote nearly all of their efforts to guaranteeing a place on these lists of approved texts. Because of this, the texts made available to the entire nation, and the knowledge considered legitimate in them, are determined by what will sell in Texas, California, Florida, and so forth. This is one of the major reasons the Right concentrates its attention so heavily on these states (though, because of resistance, with only partial success). There can be no doubt that the political and ideological controversies over content in these states, controversies that were often very similar to those that surfaced in Kanawha County, have had a very real impact on what and whose knowledge is made available. It is also clear that Kanawha County was affected by and had an impact on these larger battles over legitimate knowledge.

Economic and political realities structure text publishing not only internally, however. On an international level, the major text-publishing conglomerates control the market of much of the material not only in the capitalist centers, but in many other nations as well. Cultural domination is a fact of life for millions of students throughout the world, in part because of the economic control of communication and publishing by multinational firms, in part because of the ideologies and systems of political and cultural control of new elites within former colonial countries.[23] All of this, too, has led to complicated relations and struggles over official knowledge and the text, between "center" and "periphery," and within these areas as well.[24] Thus, the politics of official knowledge in Britain and the United States, where rightist policies over legitimate content are having a major impact, also can have a significant impact in other nations that also depend on British and U.S. corporate publishers for their material.

I want to stress that all of this is not simply of historical interest, as in the case of newly emerging nations, Kanawha County, or the Rugg textbooks. The controversies over the form and content of the textbook have not diminished. In fact, they have become even more heated in the United States in particular, as Yucaipa demonstrates. The changing ideological climate has had a major impact on debates over what should be taught in schools and on how it should be taught and evaluated. There is considerable pressure to raise the standards of texts, make them more "difficult," standardize their content, make certain that the texts place more stress on "American" themes of patriotism, free enterprise, and the "Western tradition," and link their content to statewide and national tests of educational achievement.

These kinds of pressures are not only felt in the United States. The text has become the center of ideological and educational conflict in a number of other countries as well. In Japan, for instance, the government approval of a right-wing history textbook that retold the story of the brutal Japanese invasion and occupation of China and Korea in a more positive light has stimulated widespread international antagonism and has led to considerable controversy within Japan as well.

Along these same lines, at the very time that the text has become a source of contention for conservative movements, it has stood at the center of controversy for not being progressive enough. Class, gender, and race bias have been widespread in the materials. All too often, "legitimate" knowledge does not include the historical experiences and cultural expressions of labor, women, people of color, and others who have been less powerful.[25]

All of these controversies are not "simply" about the content of the books students find—or don't find—in their schools, though obviously they are about that as well. The issues are also about profoundly different definitions of the common good[26] about our society and where it should be heading, about cultural visions, and about our children's future. To quote from Inglis again, the entire curriculum, in which the text plays so large a part, is "both the text and context in which production and values intersect; it is the twist-point of imagination and power."[27] In the context of the politics of the textbook, it is the issue of power that should concern us the most.

The concept of power merely connotes the capacity to act and to do so effectively. However, in the ways we use the idea of power in our daily discourse, "the word comes on strongly and menacingly, and its presence is duly fearful."[28] This "dark side" of power is, of course, complemented by a more positive vision. Here, power is seen as connected to a people acting democratically and collectively, in the open, for the best ideals.[29] It is this dual concept of power that concerns me here, both at the level of theory (how we think about the relationship between legitimate knowledge and power) and practice (how texts actually embody this relationship). Both the positive and the negative senses of power are essential for us to understand these relationships. Taken together, they signify that arguments about textbooks are really a form of *cultural politics*. They involve the very nature of the connections between cultural visions and differential power.

This, of course, is not new to anyone who has been interested in the history of the relationship among books, literacy, and popular movements. Books themselves, and one's ability to read them, have been inherently caught up in cultural politics. Take the case of Voltaire, that leader of the Enlightenment who so wanted to become a member of the nobility. For him, the Enlightenment should begin with the "grands." Only when it had captured the hearts and minds of society's commanding heights, could it concern itself with the masses below. But, for Voltaire and many of his followers, one caution should be taken very seriously. One should take care to prevent the masses from learning to read.[30]

For others, teaching "the masses" to read could have a more "beneficial" effect. It enables a "civilizing" process, in which dominated groups would be made more moral, more obedient, more influenced by "real culture."[31] We can, of course, hear echoes of this today in the arguments of the cultural conservatives. And for still others, such literacy could bring social transformation in its wake. It could lead to a "critical literacy," one that would be part of larger movements for a more democratic culture, economy, and polity.[32] The dual sense of the power of the text emerges clearly here.

Thus, activities that we now ask students to engage in every day, activities as "simple" and basic as reading and writing, can be at one and the same time forms of regulation and exploitation *and* potential modes of resistance, celebration, and solidarity. Here, I am reminded of Caliban's cry, "You taught me language; and my profit on't is, I know how to curse."[33]

This contradictory sense of the politics of the book is made clearer if we go into the classrooms of the past. For example, texts often have been related to forms of bureaucratic regulation both of teachers' lives and those of students. Thus, one teacher in Boston in 1899 relates a story of what happened during an observation by the school principal in her first year of teaching. As the teacher rather proudly watched one of her children read aloud an assigned lesson from the text, the principal was less than pleased with the performance of the teacher or her pupil. In the words of the teacher:

> The proper way to read in the public school in 1899 was to say, "page 35, chapter 4" and holding the book in the right hand, with the toes pointing at an angle of forty-five degrees, the head held straight and high, the eyes looking directly ahead, the pupil would lift up his voice and struggle in loud, unnatural tones. Now, I had attended to the position of the toes, the right arm, and the nose, but had failed to enforce the mentioning of page and chapter.[34]

Here, the text participates in both bodily and ideological regulation. The textbook in this instance is part of a system of enforcing a sense of duty, morality, and cultural correctness. Yet, historically, the standardized text was struggled *for* as well as against by many teachers. Faced with large classes, difficult working conditions, insufficient training, and even more importantly, little time to prepare lessons for the vast array of subjects and students they were responsible for, teachers often looked upon texts not necessarily as impositions but as essential tools. For young women elementary school teachers, the text helped prevent exploitation.[35] It solved a multitude of practical problems. It led not only to deskilling, but led to time to become more skilled as a teacher as well.[36] Thus, there were demands for standardized texts by teachers even in the face of what happened to that teacher in Boston and to so many others.

This struggle over texts was linked to broader concerns about who should control the curriculum in schools. Teachers, especially those most politically active, constantly sought to have a say in what they taught. This was seen as part of a larger fight for democratic rights. Margaret Haley, for instance, one of the leaders of the first teachers union in the United States, saw a great need for teachers to work against the tendency toward making the teacher "a mere factory hand, whose duty it is to carry out mechanically and unquestioningly the ideas and orders of those clothed with authority of position."[37] Teachers had to fight against the deskilling or, as she called it, "factoryizing" methods of control being sponsored by administrative and industrial leaders. One of the reasons she was so strongly in favor of teachers' councils as mechanisms of control of schools was that this would reduce considerably the immense power over teaching and texts that administrators then possessed. Quoting John Dewey approvingly, Haley wrote, "If there is a single public school system in the United States where there is official and constitutional provision made for submitting questions of methods, of discipline and teaching, and the questions of curriculum, textbooks, etc. to the discussion of those actually engaged in the work of teaching, that fact has escaped my notice."[38]

In this instance, teacher control over the choice of textbooks and how they were to be used was part of a more extensive movement to enhance the democratic rights of teachers on the job. Without such teacher control, teachers would be the equivalent of factory workers whose every move was determined by management.

These points about the contradictory relationships teachers have had with texts and the way such books depower and empower at different moments (and perhaps at the same time) document something of importance. It is too easy to see a cultural practice or a book as totally carrying its politics around with it, "as if written on its brow for ever and a day." Rather, its political functioning "depends on the network of social and ideological relations" it participates in.[39] Text writing, reading, and use can be retrogressive or progressive (and sometimes some combination of both) depending on the social context. Textbooks can be fought against because they are part of a system of moral regulation. They can be fought for both as providing essential assistance in the labor of teaching or as part of a larger strategy of democratization.

What textbooks do, the social roles they play for different groups, is then *very complicated*. This has important implications not only for the politics of how and by whom textbooks are used, but for the politics of the internal qualities, the content and organization, of the text. Just as crucially, it also has an immense bearing on how people actually read and interpret the text, especially in a time of rightist resurgence. It is to these issues that I now turn.

The politics of cultural incorporation

We cannot assume that because so much of education has been linked to processes of gender, class, and race stratification[40] that all of the knowledge chosen to be included in texts simply represents relations of, say, cultural domination, or only includes the knowledge of dominant groups. This point requires that I speak theoretically and politically in this section of my argument, for all too many critical analyses of school knowledge—of what is included and excluded in the overt and hidden curricula of the school—take the easy way out. Reductive analysis comes cheap. Reality, however, is complex. Let us look at this in more detail.

It has been argued in considerable detail elsewhere that the selection and organization of knowledge for schools is an ideological process, one that serves the interests of particular classes and social groups.[41] However, as I just noted, this does not mean that the entire corpus of school knowledge is "a mirror reflection of ruling class ideas, imposed in an unmediated and coercive manner." Instead, "the processes of cultural incorporation are dynamic, reflecting both continuities and contradictions of that dominant culture and the continual remaking and relegitimation of that culture's plausibility system."[42] Curricula aren't imposed in countries like the United States. Rather, they are the products of often intense conflicts, negotiations, and attempts at rebuilding hegemonic control by actually incorporating the knowledge and perspectives of the less powerful under the umbrella of the discourse of dominant groups.

This is clear in the case of the textbook. As disenfranchised groups have fought to have their knowledge take center stage in the debates over cultural legitimacy, one trend has dominated in text production. In essence, little is usually dropped from textbooks. Major ideological frameworks do not get markedly changed. Textbook publishers are under considerable and constant pressure to include more in their books. Progressive *items* are perhaps mentioned, then, but are not developed in depth.[43] Dominance is partly maintained here through compromise and the process of "mentioning." Here, limited and isolated elements of the history and culture of less powerful groups are included in the texts. Thus, for example, a small and often separate section is included on "the contributions of women" and "minority groups," but without any substantive elaboration of the view of the world as seen from their perspectives. Neo-conservatives have been particularly good at doing this today.

Tony Bennett's discussion of the process by which dominant cultures actually become dominant is worth quoting at length here.

> Dominant culture gains a purchase not in being imposed, as an alien external force, onto the cultures of subordinate groups, but by reaching into these cultures, reshaping them, hooking them and, with them, the people whose consciousness and experience is defined in their terms, into an association with the values and ideologies of the ruling groups in society. Such processes neither erase the cultures of subordinate groups, nor do they rob "the people" of their "true culture": what they do do is shuffle those cultures on to an ideological and cultural terrain in which they can be disconnected from whatever radical impulses which may (but need not) have fuelled them and be connected to more conservative or, often, downright reactionary cultural and ideological tendencies.[44]

In some cases, "mentioning" may operate in exactly this way, integrating selective elements into the dominant tradition by bringing them into close association with the values of powerful groups. Thus, for instance, we will teach about AIDS, but only in the context of total abstinence or the sacredness of particular social constructions of the "traditional family." There will be times, however, when such a strategy will not be successful. Oppositional cultures may at times use elements of the dominant culture against such groups. Bennett goes on, describing how oppositional cultures operate, as well.

> Similarly, resistance to the dominant culture does not take the form of launching against it a ready-formed, constantly simmering oppositional culture—always there, but in need of being turned up from time to time. Oppositional cultural values are formed and take shape only in the context of their struggle with the dominant culture, a struggle which may borrow some of its resources from that culture and which must concede some ground to it if it is to be able to connect with it—and thereby with those whose consciousness and experience is partly shaped by it—in order, by turning it back upon itself, to peel it away, to create a space within and against it in which contradictory values can echo, reverberate and be heard.[45]

Some texts may, in fact, have such progressive "echoes" within them. There are victories in the politics of official knowledge, not only defeats.

Sometimes, of course, not only are people successful in creating some space where such contradictory values can indeed "echo, reverberate, and be heard," but they transform the entire social space. They create entirely new kinds of governments, new possibilities for democratic political, economic, and cultural arrangements. In these situations, the role of education takes on even more importance, since new knowledge, new ethics, and a new reality seek to replace the old. This is one of the reasons that those of us committed to more participatory and democratic cultures inside and outside of schools must give serious attention to changes in official knowledge in those nations that have sought to overthrow their colonial or elitist heritage. Here, the politics of the text takes on special importance, since the textbook often represents an overt attempt to help create a new cultural reality. The case of the creation of more democratic textbooks and other educational materials based on the expressed needs of less powerful groups in Granada during the years of the New Jewel Movement provides a cogent example here[46] even though it was partly destroyed by Reagan's invasion of Granada.

New social contexts, new processes of text creation, a new cultural politics, the transformation of authority relations, and new ways of reading texts, all of this can evolve and help usher in a positive rather than a negative sense of the power of the text. Less regulatory and more emancipatory relations of texts to real people can begin to evolve, a possibility made real in many of the programs of critical literacy that have had such a positive impact in nations throughout the world. Here people help create their own "texts," ones that signify their emerging power in the control of their own destinies.

However, we should not be overly romantic here. Such transformations of cultural authority and mechanisms of control and incorporation will not be easy.

For example, certainly, the ideas and values of a people are not directly prescribed by the conceptions of the world of dominant groups and just as certainly there will be many instances where people have been successful in creating realistic and workable alternatives to the culture and texts in dominance. Yet, we do need to acknowledge that the social distribution of what is considered legitimate knowledge *is* skewed in many nations. The social institutions directly concerned with the "transmission" of this knowledge, such as schools and the media, *are* grounded in and structured by the class, gender, sexual, and race inequalities that organize the society in which we live. The area of symbolic production is not divorced from the unequal relations of power that structure other spheres.[47]

Speaking only of class relations (much the same could be said about race, sex and gender), Stuart Hall, one of the most insightful analysts of cultural politics, puts it this way:

> Ruling or dominant conceptions of the world do not directly prescribe the mental content of the illusions that supposedly fill the heads of dominated classes. But the circle of dominant ideas *does* accumulate the symbolic power to map or classify the world for others; its classifications do acquire not only the constraining power of dominance over other modes of thought but also the initial authority of habit and instinct. It becomes the horizon of the taken-for-granted: what the world is and how it works, for all practical purposes. Ruling ideas may dominate other conceptions of the social world by setting the limit on what will appear as rational, reasonable, credible, indeed sayable or thinkable within the given vocabularies of motive and action available to us. Their dominance lies precisely in the power they have to contain within their limits, to frame within their circumference of thought, the reasoning and calculation of other social groups.[48]

In the United States, . . . there has been a movement of exactly this kind. Dominant groups—really a coalition of economic modernizers, what has been called the old humanists, and neo-conservative intellectuals—have attempted to create an ideological consensus around the return to traditional knowledge. The "great books" and "great ideas" of the "Western tradition" will preserve democracy. By returning to the common culture that has made this nation great, schools will increase student achievement and discipline, increase our international competitiveness, and ultimately reduce unemployment and poverty.

Mirrored in the problematic educational and cultural visions of volumes such as Bloom's *The Closing of the American Mind* and Hirsch's *Cultural Literacy*,[49] this position is probably best represented in quotes from former Secretary of Education William Bennett. In his view, we are finally emerging out of a crisis in which "we neglected and denied much of the best in American education." For a period, "we simply stopped doing the right things [and] allowed an assault on intellectual and moral standards." This assault on the current state of education has led schools to fall away from "the principles of our tradition."[50]

Yet, for Bennett, "the people" have now risen up. "The 1980's gave birth to a grass roots movement for educational reform that has generated a renewed commitment to excellence, character, and fundamentals." Because of this, "we have reason for optimism."[51] Why? Because

> the national debate on education is now focused on truly important matters: mastering the basics; . . . insisting on high standards and expectations; ensuring discipline in the classroom; conveying a grasp of our moral and political principles; and nurturing the character of our young.[52]

Notice the use of "we," "our," and "the people" here. Notice as well the assumed consensus on "basics" and "fundamentals" and the romanticization of the past both in schools and the larger society. The use of these terms, the attempt to bring people in under the ideological umbrella of the conservative restoration, is very clever rhetorically. However, as many people in the United States, Britain, and elsewhere— where rightist governments have been very active in transforming what education is about—have begun to realize, this ideological incorporation is having no small measure of success at the level of policy and at the level of whose knowledge and values are to be taught.[53]

If this movement has its way, the texts made available and the knowledge included in them will surely represent a major loss for many of the groups who have had successes in bringing their knowledge and culture more directly into the body of legitimate content in schools. Just as surely, the ideologies that will dominate the official knowledge will represent a considerably more elitist orientation than what we have now.

Yet, perhaps "surely" is not the correct word here. The situation is actually more complex than that, something we have learned from many of the newer methods of interpreting how social messages are actually "found" in texts.

Allan Luke has dealt with such issues very persuasively. It would be best to quote him at length here.

> A major pitfall of research in the sociology of curriculum has been its willingness to accept text form as a mere adjunct means for the delivery of ideological content: the former described in terms of dominant metaphors, images, or key ideas; the latter described in terms of the sum total of values, beliefs, and ideas which might be seen to constitute a false consciousness. For much content analysis presumes that text mirrors or reflects a particular ideological position, which in turn can be connected to specific class interests . . . It is predicated on the possibility of a one-to-one identification of school knowledge with textually represented ideas of the dominant classes. Even those critics who have recognized that the ideology encoded in curricular texts may reflect the internally contradictory character of a dominant culture have tended to neglect the need for a more complex model of text analysis, one that does not suppose that texts are simply readable, literal representations of "someone else's" version of social reality, objective knowledge and human relations. For texts do not always mean or communicate what they say.[54]

These are important points for they imply that we need more sophisticated and nuanced models of textual analysis. While we should certainly *not* be at all sanguine about the effects of the conservative restoration on texts and the curriculum, if texts don't simply represent dominant beliefs in some straight-forward way and if dominant cultures contain contradictions, fissures, and even elements of the culture of popular groups, then our readings of what knowledge is "in" texts cannot be done by the application of a simple formula.

We can claim, for instance, that the meaning of a text is not necessarily intrinsic to it. As poststructuralist theories would have it, meaning is "the product of a system of differences into which the text is articulated." Thus, there is not "one text," but many. Any text is open to multiple readings. This puts into doubt any claim that one can determine the meanings and politics of a text "by a straightforward encounter with the text itself." It also raises serious questions about whether one can fully understand the text by mechanically applying any interpretive procedure. Meanings, then, can be and are multiple and contradictory, and we must always be willing to "read" our own readings of a text, to interpret our own interpretations of what it means.[55] It seems that answering the questions of "whose knowledge" is in a text is not at all simple, though clearly the Right would very much like to reduce the range of meanings one might find.

This is true of our own interpretations of what is in textbooks. But it is also just as true for the students who sit in schools and at home and read (or in many cases don't read) their texts. I want to stress this point, not only at the level of theory and politics as I have been stressing here, but at the level of practice.

We cannot assume that what is "in" the text is actually taught. Nor can we assume that what is taught is actually learned. . . . Teachers have a long history of mediating and transforming text material when they employ it in classrooms. Students bring their own classed, raced, religious, and gendered biographies with them as well. They, too, accept, reinterpret, and reject what counts as legitimate knowledge selectively. As critical ethnographies of schools have shown, . . . students (and teachers) are not empty vessels into which knowledge is poured. Rather than what Freire has called "banking" education going on,[56] students are active constructors of the meanings of the education they encounter.[57]

We can talk about three ways in which people can potentially respond to a text: dominant, negotiated, and oppositional. In the dominant reading of a text, one accepts the messages at face value, in a negotiated response, the reader may dispute a particular claim, but accept the overall tendencies or interpretations of a text. Finally, an oppositional response rejects these dominant tendencies and interpretations. The reader "repositions" herself or himself in relation to the text and takes on the position of the oppressed.[58] These are, of course, no more than ideal types and many responses will be a contradictory combination of all three. But the point is that not only do texts themselves have contradictory elements, but that audiences *construct* their own responses to texts. They do not passively receive texts, but actively read them based on their own class race, gender and religious experiences—although we must always remember that there are institutional constraints on oppositional readings.

An immense amount of work needs to be done on student (and teacher) acceptance, interpretation, reinterpretation or partial and/or total rejection of texts. While there is a tradition of such research, much of it quite good, most of this in education is done in an overly psychologized manner. It is more concerned with questions of learning and achievement than it is with the equally as important and prior issues of whose knowledge it is that students are learning, negotiating, or opposing and what the sociocultural roots and effects are of such processes. Yet we simply cannot fully understand the power of the text, what it does ideologically and politically (or educationally, for that matter) unless we take very seriously the way students actually read them—not only as individuals but as members of social groups with their own particular cultures and histories.[59] For every textbook, then, there are multiple texts—contradictions within it, multiple readings of it, and different uses to which it will be put. Texts—be they the standardized, grade-level specific books so beloved by school systems, or the novels, trade books, and alternative materials that teachers either use to supplement these books or simply to replace them—are part of a complex story of cultural politics. They can signify authority (not always legitimate) or freedom. And critical teachers throughout many nations have learned a good deal about how we can employ even the most conservative material into a site for reflexive and challenging activity that clarifies with students the realities they (teachers and students) experience and construct. They can search out, as so many of them have, material and experiences that show the very possibility of alternative and oppositional interpretations of the world that go well beyond mere mentioning.[60] . . .

To recognize this, then, is also to recognize that our task as critically and democratically minded educators is itself a political one. We must acknowledge and understand the tremendous capacity of dominant institutions to regenerate themselves "not only in their material foundations and structures but in the hearts and minds of people." Yet, at the very same time—and especially now with the Right being so powerful and with their increasing attention to politics at the local, county, and state levels—we need never to lose sight of the power of popular organizations, of real people, to struggle, resist, and transform them.[61] Cultural authority, what counts as legitimate knowledge, what norms and values are represented in the officially sponsored curriculum of the school, all of these serve as important arenas in which the positive and negative relations of power surrounding the text will work themselves out. . . . And all of them involve the hopes and dreams of real people in real institutions, in real relations of inequality.

From all that I have said here, it should be clear that I oppose the idea that there can be one textual authority, one definitive set of "facts" that is divorced from its context of power relations. A "common culture" can never be an extension to everyone of what a minority mean and believe. Rather, and crucially, it requires not the stipulation and incorporation within textbooks of lists and concepts that make us all "culturally literate," *but the creation of the conditions necessary for all people to participate in the creation and re-creation of meanings and values.* It requires a democratic process in which all people—not simply those who see themselves as the intellectual guardians of the 'Western tradition"—can be involved in the deliberation of what is important.[62] It should go without saying that this necessitates the removal of the very real material obstacles (unequal power, wealth, time for reflection) that stand in the way of such participation.[63] Whether a more "moderate" administration can provide substantial spaces for countering the New Right and for removing these obstacles will take some time to see.

The very idea that there is one set of values that must guide the "selective tradition" can be a great danger, especially in contexts of differential power. Take, as one example, a famous line that was printed on an equally famous public building. It read, "There is one road to freedom. Its milestones are obedience, diligence, honesty, order, cleanliness, temperance, truth, sacrifice, and love of country." Many people may perhaps agree with much of the sentiment represented by these words. It may be of some interest that the building on which they appeared was in the administration block of the concentration camp at Dachau.[64]

We must ask, then, are we in the business of creating dead texts and dead minds? If we accept the title of educator—with all of the ethical and political commitments this entails—I think we already know what our answer should be. Critical literacy demands no less.

These struggles over the politics of official knowledge—over the text as both a commodity and a set of meaningful practices—are grounded in the history of previous conflicts and accords. Here, too, compromises were made. And here, too, dominant groups attempted to move the terms of the compromise in their direction. Yet, once again, the accord had cracks, spaces for action, but ones that were always in danger of being coopted, as this history will show. Perhaps the best way to document this is to go even deeper into the politics of the text by focusing our attention on the growth of the activist state, on how the government—as a site of conflicting power relations and social movements—entered into the regulation of official knowledge. Conservatives (and even some of those upwardly mobile "cosmopolitan elites") may have dominated here, but as we shall see, this is *not* the entire story.

Notes

1 This chapter is an expansion and refinement of the introductory chapter to Michael W. Apple and Linda Christian-Smith, eds., *The Politics of the Textbook* (New York: Routledge, 1991). Many of the essays in that volume are crucial to a more thorough understanding of the issues I raise here.
2 See John Willinsky, *The New Literacy* (New York: Routledge, 1990).
3 Janet Batsleer, Tony Davies, Rebecca O'Rourke, and Chris Weedon, *Rewriting English: Cultural Politics of Gender and Class* (New York: Methuen, 1985), 164–65. For an exceptional treatment of "political literacy" in theory and practice, see Colin Lankshear with Moira Lawler, *Literacy, Schooling and Revolution* (Philadelphia: Falmer, 1988).
4 John Fiske, Bob Hodge, and Graeme Turner, *Myths of Oz: Reading Australian Popular Culture* (Boston: Allen and Unwin, 1987), x.
5 John Fiske, *Reading the Popular* (Boston: Unwin Hyman, 1989), 149–50.
6 See, for example, Michael W. Apple and Lois Weis, eds., *Ideology and Practice in Schooling* (Philadelphia: Temple University Press, 1983).
7 For a current representative sample of the varied kinds of studies being done on the textbook, see Arthur Woodward, David L. Elliot, and Kathleen Carter Nagel eds, *Textbooks in School and Society* (New York: Garland, 1988). We need to make a distinction between the generic use of "texts" (all meaningful materials: symbolic, bodily, physical, etc., created by human, and sometimes "natural," activity) and text-books. My focus in this chapter is mostly on the latter, though many schools and many teachers are considerably more than standardized textbook material. Also, in passing, I am more than a little concerned that some people have overstated the case that the world is "only a text." See Bryan D. Palmer, *Descent into Discourse* (Philadelphia: Temple University Press, 1990).
8 Fred Inglis, *Popular Culture and Political Power* (New York: St. Martin's Press, 1988), 9.
9 Allan Luke, *Literacy, Textbooks and Ideology* (Philadelphia: Falmer, 1988), 27–29.
10 Michael W. Apple, *Ideology and Curriculum*, 2nd ed. (New York: Routledge, 1990); Michael W. Apple, *Education and Power* (New York: Routledge, rev. ARK ed., 1985); and Michael W. Apple, *Teachers and Texts: A Political Economy of Class and Gender Relations in Education* (New York and London: Routledge, 1988).
11 Michael W. Apple, "Redefining Equality: Authoritarian Populism and the Conservative Restoration," *Teachers College Record* 90 (Winter 1988): 167–84.
12 See, for example, Susan Rose, *Keeping Them Out of the Hands of Satan* (New York: Routledge, 1988).
13 Allen Hunter, *Children in the Service of Conservatism* (Madison: University of Wisconsin Institute for Legal Studies, 1988).
14 James Moffett, *Storm in the Mountains* (Carbonate: Southern Illinois University Press, 1988).

15 Raymond Williams, *The Long Revolution* (London: Chatto and Windus, 1961). See also Apple, *Ideology and Curriculum*.

16 Fred Inglis, *The Management of Ignorance: A Political Theory of the Curriculum* (New York: Basil Blackwell, 1985), 22–23.

17 Ibid., 23.

18 Miriam Schipper, "Textbook Controversy: Past and Present," *New York University Education Quarterly* 14 (Spring/Summer 1983): 31–36.

19 A. Graham Down, "Preface," in Harriet Tyson-Bernstein, *A Conspiracy of Good Intentions: America's Textbook Fiasco* (Washington, D.C.: The Council for Basic Education, 1988), viii.

20 Harriet Tyson-Bernstein, *A Conspiracy of Good Intentions*, 3.

21 Robert Darnton, *The Literacy Underground of the Old Regime* (Cambridge: Harvard University Press, 1982), 199.

22 The social roots of such adoption policies will be discussed in chapter four.

23 The issues surrounding cultural imperialism and colonialism are nicely laid out in Philip Altback and Gail Kelly, eds., *Education and the Colonial Experience* (New York: Transaction Books, 1984). For an excellent discussion of international relations over texts and knowledge, see Philip Altbach, *The Knowledge Context* (Albany: State University of New York Press, 1988).

24 See the analysis of such power relations in Bruce Fuller, *Growing Up Modern* (New York: Routledge, 1991) and Martin Carnoy and Joel Samoff, *Education and Social Transition in the Third World* (Princeton: Princeton University Press, 1990).

25 For some of the most elegant discussions of how we need to think about these "cultural silences," see Leslie Roman and Linda Christian-Smith with Elizabeth Ellsworth, eds., *Becoming Feminine: The Politics of Popular Culture* (Philadelphia: Falmer, 1988).

26 Marcus Raskin, *The Common Good* (New York: Routledge, 1986).

27 Inglis, *The Management of Ignorance*, 142.

28 Inglis, *Popular Culture and Political Power*, 4.

29 Ibid. I have placed "dark side" in quotation marks in the previous sentence because of the dominant tendency to unfortunately equate darkness with negativity. This is just one of the ways popular culture expresses racism. See Michael Omi and Howard Winant, *Racial Formation in the United States* (New York: Routledge 1986); and Edward Said, *Orientalism* (New York: Pantheon, 1978).

30 Darnton, *The Literary Underground of the Old Regime*, 13.

31 Batsleer, Davies, O'Rourke, and Weedon, *Rewriting English: Cultural Politics of Gender and Class.*

32 Lankshear with Lawler, *Literacy, Schooling and Revolution.*

33 Batsleer et al. *Rewriting English*, 5.

34 James W. Fraser, "Agents of Democracy: Urban Elementary School Teachers and the Conditions of Teaching," in Donald Warren, ed., *American Teachers: Histories of a Profession at Work* (New York: Macmillan, 1989), 128.

35 Apple, *Teachers and Texts.*

36 For further discussion of deskilling and reskilling, see Apple, *Education and Power.*

37 Margaret Haley, quoted in Fraser, "Agents of Democracy," 128.

38 Haley, quoted in Fraser, "Agents of Domcracy," 138.

39 Tony Bennett, "Introduction: Popular Culture and 'the Turn to Gramsci,'" in Tony Bennett, (Colin Mercer, and Janet Woollacott, eds., *Popular Culture and Social Relations* (Philadelphia: Open University Press, 1986), xvi.

40 The literature here is voluminous. For a more extended treatment see Apple, *Education and Power;* and Cameron McCarthy and Michael W. Apple, "Race, Class, and Gender in American Educational Research," in Lois Weis, ed., *Class, Race, and Gender in American Education* (Albany: State University Press, 1989).

41 See Apple, *Ideology and Curriculum;* and Linda Christian-Smith, *Becoming a Woman Through Romance* (New York: Routledge, 1991).

42 Luke, *Literacy, Textbooks and Ideology*, 24.

43 Tyson-Bernstein, *A Conspiracy of Good Intentions*, 18.

44 Tony Bennett, "The Politics of the 'Popular' and Popular Culture," 19.

45 Ibid.

46 See Didacus Jules, "Building Democracy," in Michael W. Apple and Linda Christian-Smith, eds., *The Politics of the Textbook* (New York: Routledge, 1991), 259–87.
47 Stuart Hall, "The Toad in the Garden: Thatcherism Among the Theorists," in Cary Nelson and Lawrence Grossberg, eds., *Marxism and the Interpretation of Culture* (Urbana: University of Illinois Press, 1988), 44.
48 Ibid.
49 Allan Bloom, *The Closing of the American Mind* (New York: Simon and Schuster, 1987); and E. D. Hirsch, Jr., *Cultural Literacy* (New York: Houghton Mifflin, 1986).
50 William Bennett, *Our Children and Our Country* (New York: Simon and Schuster, 1988), 9.
51 Ibid., 10.
52 Ibid.
53 Apple, "Redefining Equality."
54 Luke, *Literacy, Textbooks and Ideology*, 29–30. See also Allan Luke, "The Secular Word: Catholic Reconstructions of Dick and Jane," in Apple and Christian-Smith, eds., *The Politics of the Textbook*, 166–90.
55 Lawrence Grossberg and Cary Nelson, "Introduction: The Territory of Marxism," in Nelson and Grossberg, eds., *Marxism and the Interpretation of Culture*, 8.
56 Paulo Freire, *Pedagogy of the Oppressed* (New York: Herder and Herder , 1973).
57 See, for example, Paul Willis, *Learning to Labor* (New York: Columbia University Press, 1981); Angela McRobbie, "Working Class Girls and the Culture of Femininity," in Women's Studies Group, ed., *Women Take Issue* (London: Hutchinson, 1978), 96–108; Robert Everhart, *Reading, Writing and Resistance* (Boston: Routledge and Kegan Paul, 1983); Lois Weis, *Between Two Worlds* (Boston: Routledge and Kegan Paul, 1985); Bonnie Trudell, *Doing Sex Education* (New York: Routledge, in press); and Christian-Smith, *Becoming a Woman Through Romance.*
58 Tania Modleski, "Introduction," in Tania Modleski, ed., *Studies in Entertainment* (Bloomington: Indiana University Press, 1986), xi.
59 See Elizabeth Ellsworth, "Illicit Pleasures: Feminist Spectator and *Personal Best,*" in Roman, Christian-Smith, with Ellsworth, *Becoming Feminine*, 102–19; Elizabeth Ellsworth, "Why Doesn't This Feel Empowering?" *Harvard Educational Review* 59 (August 1989): 297–324; and Christian-Smith, *Becoming a Woman Through Romance.*
60 For an example of powerful and compelling literature for younger students, see the discussion in Joel Taxel, "Reclaiming the Voice of Resistance: The Fiction of Mildred Taylor," in Apple and Christian-Smith, eds., *The Politics of the Textbook*, 111–34.
61 Batsleer et al. *Rewriting English*, 5.
62 This is discussed in more detail in the new preface to the second edition of Apple, *Ideology and Curriculum.*
63 Raymond Williams, *Resources of Hope* (New York: Verso, 1989), 37–38.
64 David Horne, *The Public Culture* (Dover, NH: Pluto Press, 1986), 76.

CHAPTER 10

SOCIAL CLASS AND PEDAGOGIC PRACTICE

Basil Bernstein

The Structuring of Pedagogic Discourse, Volume IV: *Class, Codes and Control* (2003),
London: Routledge, pp. 63–93

I shall start this chapter[1] with an analysis of the basic social relation of any pedagogic practice. In this analysis I shall distinguish between pedagogic practice as a
cultural relay and pedagogic practice in terms of what that practice relays – in other
words, pedagogic practice as a social form and as a specific content. I shall argue
that the inner logic of pedagogic practice as a cultural relay is provided by a set of
three rules, and the nature of these rules acts selectively on the content of any pedagogic practice. If these rules constitute what can be called the 'how' of any practice,
then any particular 'how' created by any one set of rules acts selectively on the
'what' of the practice, the form of its content. The form of the content in turn acts
selectively on those who can successfully acquire. I shall examine in some detail the
social class assumptions and consequences of forms of pedagogic practice.

On the basis of the fundamental rules of any pedagogic practice I shall generate:

1   What are regarded as opposing modalities of pedagogic practice, usually referred
     to as conservative or traditional and progressive or child-centred.
2   What are regarded as oppositions within what is considered the same basic form.
     Here the opposition is between a pedagogic practice dependent upon the market
     place for its orientation and legitimation, a practice emphasizing the assumed rel-
     evance of vocational skills, and a pedagogic practice independent of the market
     place, claiming for itself an orientation and legitimation derived from the assumed
     autonomy of knowledge. It will be argued that the pedagogic practices of the new
     vocationalism and those of the old autonomy of knowledge represent a conflict
     between different elitist ideologies, one based on the class hierarchy of the mar-
     ket and the other based on the hierarchy of knowledge and its class supports.

The basic argument will be that whether we are considering the opposition between
conservative and progressive or the opposition between market and knowledge-
oriented pedagogic practice, present class inequalities are likely to be reproduced.

I shall start first with some thoughts about the inner logic of any pedagogic practice. A pedagogic practice can be understood as a relay, a cultural relay: a uniquely
human device for both the reproduction and the production of culture. As I have
said earlier, I shall distinguish between what is relayed, the contents, and how the
contents are relayed. That is, between the 'what' and the 'how' of any transmission.
When I refer to the inner logic of a pedagogic practice I am referring to a set of
rules which are prior to the content to be relayed (Figure 3).

Rules   Practices

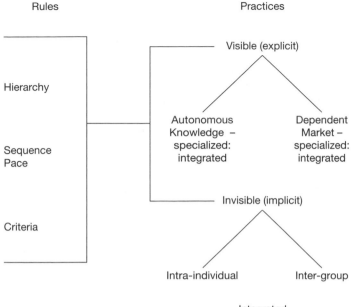

Figure 3 Pedagogic practices: generic forms and modalities. Whereas invisible pedagogies are always likely to relay integrated or embedded skills/subjects, visible pedagogies, especially of the autonomous type, are more likely to relay differentiated skills/subjects.

The relationship basic to cultural reproduction or transformation is essentially the pedagogic relation, and the pedagogic relation consists of transmitters and acquirers. I shall examine the internal logic of this relationship. In fact, I consider the fundamental logic of any pedagogic relation.

I have drawn a distinction here between what I call the fundamental logic of the practice and the various practices to which this logic can give rise. This is rather similar to language, itself: a finite set of rules which can generate a great number of other rule systems. I will examine some of the realizations of these practices and I will analyse the social class assumptions of these practices.

If we look at the relationship between transmitters and acquirers I shall assert that this is essentially, and intrinsically, an asymmetrical relation. There may be various strategies for disguising, masking, hiding the asymmetry. For example, in certain modalities of practice the acquirer is perceived as a transmitter, and, perhaps, the transmitter appears to be the acquirer, but these are essentially arabesques. This may seem a very cynical view but we shall see whether it is of any value. Now it is the case that although this relation is intrinsically asymmetrical the realization of the asymmetry may be very complex.

The rules of pedagogic practice as cultural relay

I shall propose that the essential logic of any pedagogic relation consists of the relationship essentially between three rules. And of these three rules,[2] the first is the dominant one. I would now like to outline concretely the three rules.

Hierarchical rule

In any pedagogic relationship the transmitter has to learn to be a transmitter and the acquirer has to learn to be an acquirer. When you go to the doctor you have to learn how to be a patient. It is no good going to the doctor and saying, 'I feel really bad today, everything is really grey.' He says, 'Don't waste my time,' because he has many patients. 'Where is the pain? How long have you had it? What kind of pain is it? Is it acute? Is it chronic? Is it sharp? Is it persistent?' After a bit you learn how to talk to your doctor. He teaches you to be an acquirer. But how he teaches you is the function of a much more general set of forces which we shall go on to discover.

The acquirer, then, has to learn to be an acquirer and the transmitter has to learn to be a transmitter. The process of learning how to be a transmitter entails the acquiring of rules of social order, character, and manner which became the condition for appropriate conduct in the pedagogic relation. It is these rules which are a prerequisite of any enduring pedagogic relation. In any one such relation the rules of conduct may to different degrees permit a space for negotiation. These rules of conduct will here be called hierarchical rules which establish the conditions for order, character, and manner.

Sequencing rules

Now if there is a transmission it cannot always happen at once. Something must come before and something must come after. If something comes before and after, there is a progression. If there is a progression, there must be sequencing rules. Every pedagogic practice must have sequencing rules, and these sequencing rules will imply pacing rules. Pacing is the rate of expected acquisition of the sequencing rules, that is, how much you have to learn in a given amount of time. Essentially, pacing is the time allowed for achieving the sequencing rules.

Criterial rules

Finally there are criteria which the acquirer is expected to take over and to apply to his/her own practices and those of others. The criteria enable the acquirer to understand what counts as a legitimate or illegitimate communication, social relation, or position.

The internal logic of any pedagogic relation consists of hierarchical rules, sequential/pacing rules, criterial rules. We can distinguish, at another level, two more general rules. The hierarchical rules will be called the *regulative* rules and the other rules of sequence/pace criteria will be called instructional or *discursive* rules. The fundamental rule is the regulative one. Later on we shall see why this is the case.[3] Briefly, all education is intrinsically a moral activity which articulates the dominant ideology(ies) of dominant group(s). On the basis of these rules, I want to generate, to begin with, two different kinds of practices, and I shall do so on the basis of an examination of these rules.

In any teaching relation, the essence of the relation is to evaluate the competence of the acquirer. What you are evaluating is whether the criteria that have been made available to the acquirer have been achieved – whether they are regulative criteria about conduct, character, and manner, or instructional, discursive criteria: how to solve this problem or that problem, or produce an acceptable piece of writing or speech.

On the basis of the above rules of regulative and discursive order I shall distinguish between two generic types or modalities of pedagogic practice. I must emphasize that these are types, and each can give rise to a range of practices, some of which will be discussed later in this chapter.

Generating modalities of pedagogic practice

Hierarchical rules

If we take, first of all, the hierarchical rules, these rules can be explicit but they can also be implicit. If they are explicit, then the power relations in the relationship are very clear. The relationship is one of explicit subordination and superordination. This creates an explicit hierarchy. But a hierarchy need not necessarily be explicit. A hierarchy can be implicit. Let me give an example.

In 1968 the French took to the streets and the English studied a government report (Plowden, 1967) on primary education. The report was called *Children and their Primary Schools* – not 'Children and Primary Schools' or 'Primary Schools and Children'. In this book there were thirty-six pictures. If you look at those thirty-six photographs, there are children playing creatively by themselves: individual, productive play. There are pictures of children playing in groups, there are children in the school corridors and in the gardens surrounding the school, but it is difficult to find a teacher. This is the context created by an implicit hierarchy. The more implicit the hierarchy, the more difficult it is to distinguish the transmitter. We can define an implicit hierarchy as a relationship where power is masked or hidden by devices of communication. In the case of an implicit hierarchy the teacher acts directly on the context of acquisition but indirectly on the acquirer. Thus hierarchy can be either explicit or implicit.

Sequencing rules

These rules can be explicit. If they are explicit, then it means that children of 5 years of age are expected to develop particular competences, to behave in a particular way, and at 6 years of age they are expected to have different competences. Explicit rules regulate the development of the child, usually in terms of age. This means that the child is always aware of what her/his expected state of consciousness is supposed to be. He or she may not like it, but it is clear. Explicit sequencing rules construct the temporal project of the child. They construct temporal dislocations. These sequencing rules may be inscribed in syllabuses, in curricula, in behavioural rules, in rules of punishment and reward, and are often marked by transition rituals. However, sequencing rules can be implicit. Where sequencing rules are implicit the child initially can never be aware of his or her temporal project. Only the transmitter is aware of the temporal project of the child. We have a difference here. In the case of explicit sequencing rules, the child has some awareness of its temporal project; in the case of implicit sequencing rules only the teacher or the transmitter can be so aware.

We have to ask ourselves what is the basis of such a relationship, because if the child is not aware of his or her temporal project, then the child lives only in the present. When the sequencing rules are explicit, the child has some awareness of her/his temporal project although he or she lives in the past. The grammatical tenses of these pedagogic practices are opposed to each other. One child lives in the past although he or she can see his/her future, whereas the other child lives in the present of its own doings. Sequencing rules reveal what may be called the ideology of tense.

	Stage	Active	Learning	Abstracted	Implicit hierarchy
Piaget	1	2	3	4	5
Freud (neo-Freudian)	1	2	3	4	5
Chomsky	1	2	3	4	5
Ethological theories of critical learning	1	2	3	4	–
Gestalt	–	2	3	4	5

Figure 4

How does this come about? If sequencing rules are implicit, then they will be drawn from a range of theories. The theories that I am going to put forward here are not the only ones, but others will be structurally similar where they apply to children. The theories are set out in Figure 4. They construct a pedagogic *bricolage*.

If we look at these theories we can see that although they are very different they have certain things in common. First, almost all the theories, with the exception of Gestalt, is a developmental theory. What is acquired has a meaning only in relation to a particular stage. (In the case of Freud there is the development from polymorphous perverse, the nirvana of babyhood, followed by oral, anal, phallic, and genital.) With one exception, all these theories are stage theories. Second, in every one of these theories the child is active in his or her own acquisition. Third, in all these theories the acquisition of the child cannot be readily modified by explicit public regulation, as learning is a tacit, invisible act. Fourth, in every one of these theories the child's institutional and cultural biography is excluded. The theories are asociological. At most the child has a family. Fifth, in every one of these theories, except the ethological, the relationship between the transmitter and the acquirer or the parent and the child is such that the socializer is potentially if not actually dangerous. These theories tend to be critical of the transmitter as an imposer of meaning. Every one of the theories, except the ethological, replaces domination by facilitation, imposition by accommodation.

The theories imply an implicit hierarchy. Now if you are going to apply this *bricolage* to the classroom as a teacher, or as a social worker, or as a counsellor, you have to have what is called a theory of reading. For in these theories the child is transformed into a text which only the transmitter can read. In other words, the teacher, the social worker, the psychotherapist is looking for certain signs, but the signs have meaning only to the teacher, and the child can never be aware of the meaning of its own signs, as their reading requires complex theories.

I was once in a classroom where a child was by himself. I happened to say that the child looked very unhappy, and the teacher said, 'Don't worry about that. He is just working through a problem.' The teacher, then, can read the child, and the teacher's behaviour to that child will depend on this reading, which in turn depends upon theories and upon how they have been transmitted, that is, recontextualized.

Sequencing rules can be implicit or explicit. Where rules are implicit the acquirer initially can never know the meaning of her/his sign, as the meaning is derived from complex theories and their recontextualizing, and so available only to the transmitter.

Criterial rules

Criteria can be explicit and specific. For example, in a school the child may be making some facsimile of a person, drawing a person, and the teacher comes along, looks at the drawing and says (it does not have to be repressive; explicit criteria do not have to be repressively realized), 'That's a lovely man, but he's only got three fingers,' or 'That's a very good house, but where is the chimney?' In other words, the pedagogy works by making available to the child what is missing in the product. Now if it works in this way, by showing what is missing in the product, the criteria will always be explicit and specific, *and the child will be aware of the criteria*. He or she may not like them, but they will be articulated. However, criteria can be implicit, multiple, and diffuse. Imagine we go to another classroom. The children have very big pieces of paper. A whole series of media are available through which their unique consciousness can be graphically realized. And the facilitator happens to glance at the image and says to the child, 'Tell me about it.' 'Oh, that's very exciting.'

In the case of implicit criteria, by definition, the child is not aware except in a very general way of the criteria she/he has to meet. It is as if this pedagogic practice creates a space in which the acquirer can create his/her text under conditions of apparently minimum external constraint and in a context and social relationship which appears highly supportive of the 'spontaneous' text the acquirer offers (Daniels, 1989).

We can now say that we have distinguished between pedagogic practices in terms of those which have explicit hierarchical rules, explicit sequencing/pacing rules, and explicit criteria and those with implicit hierarchical sequencing/pacing and criterial rules.[4]

Types of pedagogic practice: visible and invisible

I shall now define two generic types of pedagogic practice, as follows. If the rules of regulative and discursive order are explicit (hierarchy/sequence/pace) criteria, I shall call such a type a *visible* pedagogic practice (VP) and if the rules of regulative and discursive order are implicit I shall call such a type an *invisible* pedagogic practice (IP).

Visible pedagogies

A visible pedagogy (and there are many modalities) will always place the emphasis on the *performance* of the child, upon the text the child is creating and the extent to which that text is meeting the criteria. Thus acquirers will be graded according to the extent that they meet the criteria. A visible pedagogy puts the emphasis on the external product of the child,

Visible pedagogies and their modalities will act to produce differences between children: they are necessarily stratifying practices of transmission, a learning consequence for both transmitters and acquirers. It is here worth adding that because a visible pedagogy has explicit rules of regulative and discursive order it does not mean that there are no tacit rules or messages, only that their meaning must be understood in the context of a visible pedagogy.

Invisible pedagogies

In the case of an invisible pedagogy the discursive rules (the rules of order of instruction) are known only to the transmitter, and in this sense a pedagogic practice of this type is (at least initially) invisible to the acquirer, essentially because the acquirer appears to fill the pedagogic space rather than the transmitter. The concrete present of the acquirer is manifest rather than the abstract/abstracted past of the controlling discourse.

Invisible pedagogies are less concerned to produce explicit stratifying differences between acquirers because they are apparently less interested in matching the acquirer's text against an external common standard. Their focus is not upon a 'gradable' performance of the acquirer but upon procedures internal to the acquirer (cognitive, linguistic, affective, motivational) as a consequence of which a text is created and experienced. These *procedures of acquisition* are considered to be shared by all acquirers, although their realization in texts will create differences between acquirers.

But these differences do not signal differences in potential, as all acquirers are judged to share common procedures. Differences revealed by an invisible pedagogy are not to be used as a basis for comparison *between* acquirers, for differences reveal *uniqueness*. Thus whereas visible pedagogies focus upon an external gradable text, invisible pedagogies focus upon the procedures/competences which all acquirers bring to the pedagogic context. Invisible pedagogies are concerned to arrange that context to enable shared competences to develop realizations appropriate to the acquirer. Thus, in the case of invisible pedagogies, external non-comparable differences are produced by internal *commonalities* – that is, shared competences – whereas in the case of visible pedagogies external *comparable* differences are produced by internal differences in potential. In short, invisible pedagogies emphasize acquisition – competence and visible pedagogies transmission – performance.[5]

These differences in emphasis between visible and invisible pedagogies will clearly affect both the selection and the organization of what is to be acquired, that is, the recontextualizing principle adopted to create and systematize the contents to be acquired and the context in which it is acquired.

Different theories of instruction inhere in these two pedagogic types, which we illustrate in Figure 5 and, at the same time, show how modalities of the two types can be regarded as liberal, conservative, and radical practices.

In Figure 5 the vertical dimension refers to the object of change of the pedagogic practice. Thus the primary object may be to produce changes in the individual or the primary object may be to produce changes not in the individual but between social groups. The horizontal dimension refers to the focus of the pedagogic practice, which can be either upon the acquirer or upon the transmitter. Clearly the latter indicates a visible and the former an invisible pedagogy. If we take the top left-hand quadrant, intra-individual–acquisition, then this would indicate what is often regarded as 'progressive' pedagogic practice whose theories of instruction are likely to be drawn from those listed earlier. However, if we take the bottom left-hand quadrant, acquisition–intergroup, the primary object of this pedagogic practice is to produce changes *between* social groups, that is, how he acquirer comes to understand the relation between social groups and through this new appreciation change his/her practice. This would be a radical rather than a liberal–progressive practice, e.g. Freire and, through Freire, the pedagogy of liberation theology. It would also include neo-Marxist formulations such as those of Giroux (1989).

The top right-hand quadrant, intra-individual–transmission, is likely to select behaviourist or neo-behaviourist theories of instruction which, relative to those selected in the top left-hand quadrant, are often regarded as conservative. It is a matter of interest that this top right-hand quadrant is regarded as conservative but has often

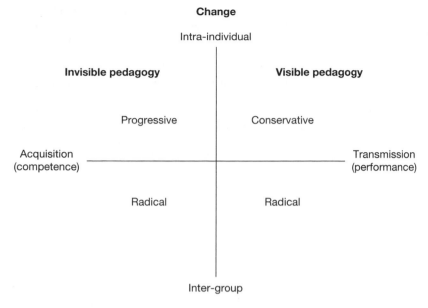

Figure 5

produced very innovative and radical acquirers. The bottom right-hand quadrant shows a radical realization of an apparently conservative pedagogic practice.

So far, then, we can see that these generic types can take either progressive, conservative, or radical modalities, and that theories of instruction will act selectively upon both the 'what' and 'how' of any pedagogic practice. Further, these different theories will act selectively upon 'what attributes of the acquirer become candidates for what labels. Finally, each theory will carry its own conditions of contestation, 'resistance', subversion.

I have proposed that it is important to distinguish between the fundamental grammar or ordering principles of a pedagogic practice and the forms of realization as pedagogic types. The ordering principles I have analysed as regulative (hierarchical) and instructional (selection, sequence/pace, and criteria). On the basis of this grammar I have generated two generic forms of pedagogic practice according to whether the ordering principles are explicit or implicit. These basic forms were shown to yield progressive, conservative, and radical modalities.

The next section will concentrate upon the social class assumptions of the generic types visible/invisible in their non-radical forms. We shall consider after this analysis two modalities of visible pedagogies, an autonomous modality and a market-oriented modality.

Social class assumptions of pedagogic practice

The fundamental proposition is that the same distribution of power may be reproduced by apparently opposing modalities of control. There is not a one-to-one relation between a given distribution of power and the modality of control through which it is relayed. In terms of this chapter, pedagogic practices are cultural relays of the distribution of power. Although visible and invisible pedagogies are apparently opposing types, it will be shown that both carry social class assumptions. However, these social class assumptions vary with the pedagogic type. The class assumptions of visible pedagogies are different from the class assumptions of invisible pedagogies. These class assumptions carry consequences for those children who are able to exploit the possibilities of the pedagogic practices. The assumptions of a visible pedagogy are more likely to be met by that fraction of the middle class whose employment has a direct relation to the economic field (production, distribution, and the circulation of capital). Whereas the assumptions of an invisible pedagogy are more likely to be met by that fraction of the middle class who have a direct relation not to the economic field but to the field of symbolic control and who work in specialized agencies of symbolic control usually located in the public sector. . . . For both these fractions education is a crucial means of cultural and economic reproduction, although perhaps less so for that fraction directly related to the economic field.[6]

Social class assumptions of visible pedagogies

Sequencing rules

I shall start by looking at the sequencing rules of a visible pedagogy. In the case of a visible pedagogy the sequencing rules are explicit and mark the future of the child in very clear steps or stages. At 5 you should know and be this, at 6 you should know and be that, and at 7 you should know and be something else. Now it is quite clear that if a child comes to school at 5 and cannot meet the initial requirements of the sequencing rules, it will have difficulty in meeting the requirements at 6. Gradually the child will fall further and further behind. Three strategies may be applied in this situation, or later in the life of the acquirer. Either a repair system will have to be introduced to cope with the children who have failed to meet sequencing requirements or the pacing rules will have to be relaxed so that the child is given more time to meet the requirements of the sequencing rules. Either strategy results in a stratification of acquirers. In the case of a repair system the stratification is explicit and public; in the case of relaxation of the pacing the stratification is implicit, and perhaps will not become explicit and public until later in the pedagogic life. A third strategy would be to maintain the pacing and sequencing rules but to reduce either the quantity or the quality of the contents to be acquired or both. All three strategies produce a more delicate system of stratification within an already stratifying pedagogic practice.

Early reading is crucial to a visible pedagogy and is an early requirement of the sequencing rules. Psychologists tell us that at a given age a child should be able to read. I am not certain I wholly accept this. The age by which a child should be able to read is a function of the sequencing rules of the pedagogic practice of the school. In the case of a visible pedagogy it is crucial that a child reads early, and this for many reasons.

Once a child can read, the book is there, and the book is the textbook or its equivalent. Once a child can read, independent solitary work is possible. He/she is also gradually introduced into a non-oral form of discourse, the rules of which are often at variance with oral forms. It is not only that reading involves the acquisition of a new symbolic relay but that *what* is relayed is itself different from the content of oral forms. Further, school reading is in many cases different from non-school reading. The difference is in what is relayed. In an important sense reading makes the child eventually less dependent upon the teacher and gives the acquirer access to alternative perspectives. Thus those children who are unable to meet sequencing rules as they apply to reading become more dependent upon the teacher and upon oral forms of discourse.

There is another aspect of sequencing rules which we should consider: the relation between the local, the here and now, the context-dependent, and the less local, the more distant, the more context-independent meanings. In pedagogic terms this refers to the acquisition of context-tied operations, on the one hand, and on the other to operations and understanding of principles and their application to new situations. In visible pedagogies there is usually a time interval between these different levels of discourse, in the sense that the local, context-dependent, context-tied operations come in the early stage of the pedagogic practice and the understanding and application of principles come at a later stage; the understanding of the principles of the principles even later. Visible pedagogies entail a distribution of expected age-related discourses.

However, if children cannot meet the requirements of the sequencing rules and are caught up in the strategies of the repair system, then these children, often the children of the lower working class (including other disadvantaged ethnic groups), are constrained by the local, context-dependent, context-tied skills; by a world of facticity. Children who can meet the requirements of the sequencing rules will eventually have access to the principles of their own discourse. These children are more likely to be middle class and are more likely to come to understand that the heart of discourse is not order but disorder, not coherence but incoherence, not clarity but ambiguity, and that the heart of discourse is the possibility of new realities.

We might ask ourselves, if this is the possibility of pedagogic discourse, why are the children of the dominant classes not demonstrating the possibilities of the discourses they have acquired? And the answer must be that socialization into a visible pedagogy tries, though not always successfully, to ensure that its discourse is safe rather than dangerous. In this way a visible pedagogy produces deformation of the children/students of both the dominant and the dominated social classes. In summary we can say that a visible pedagogy is likely to distribute different forms of consciousness according to the social class origin of acquirers. These different forms evolve from the sequencing rules.

Pacing rules: economy of pedagogic discourse

Pacing refers to the expected rate of acquisition, that is, the rate at which learning is expected to occur. Pacing is thus linked to sequencing rules and here refers to the rate at which the progression established by those rules is to be transmitted and acquired. Pacing rules, then, regulate the rhythm of the transmission, and this rhythm may vary in speed. Figure 6 illustrates pacing and sites of acquisition.

I shall propose that the schools' academic curriculum, if it is to be effectively acquired, always requires two sites of acquisition, the school and the home. Curricula cannot be acquired wholly by time spent at school. This is because the pacing of the acquisition is such that time at school must be supplemented by official pedagogic time at home, and the home must provide a pedagogic context and control of the pupil to remain in that context. There must be an official pedagogic discipline in the home. How does the school reproduce itself in the home? As the pupil gets older he/she is expected to do more and more school work in the home, and the family will be expected to ensure that the pupil has time at home for this work and will also have effective control over the peer-group practices of the child. The work the pupil is expected to do at home is, of course, homework. The basis of homework is usually a textbook. But the textbook requires a context, an official pedagogic

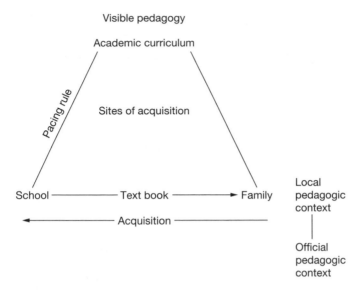

Figure 6

context in the home. That is, a space – a silent space – and this is not usually available in the homes of the poor. Nor is pedagogic time available for poor children, as often time is used to work for money – the curriculum practice of the street. Under these conditions there cannot be an effective second site of acquisition with an effective official pedagogic context and support. Without a second site, acquisition will not be possible, still less so as the child grows older. Failure becomes the expectation and the reality.

Where the catchment area of a school draws upon a lower working-class community it is likely, as we have seen, that the school will adopt strategies, or have strategies forced upon it, which will affect both the content and the pacing of the transmission. The content is likely to stress operations, local skills rather than the exploration of principles and general skills, and the pacing is likely to be weakened (Domingos, 1987). In this way children's consciousness is differentially and invidiously regulated according to their social class origin and their families' official pedagogic practice. In the case of a socially mixed catchment area where pupils are drawn from a variety of class backgrounds some schools, through a variety of strategies of stratification (sometimes including repetition), will stream (or 'set') pupils according to the school's estimate of their ability, and these different streams or sets will follow curricula varying in their content and/or pacing.

However, there is a more fundamental effect of strong pacing rules which affects the deep sociolinguistic rules of classroom communicative competence. With strong pacing, time is at a premium, and this regulates examples, illustrations, narratives which facilitate acquisition: regulates what questions may be put, and how many; regulates what counts as an explanation, both its length and its form. Further, strong pacing will tend to reduce pupils' speech and privilege teachers' talk, and this the pupils come to prefer, as time is scarce for the official pedagogic message. In this way the deep structure of pedagogic communication is itself affected. Pacing creates the rhythm of the communication, and rhythms of communication have different modalities. The rhythm of narrative is different from the rhythm of analysis. A strong pacing rule for the latter constructs a principle of communication very different from the inner structure of the communicative principle children use in everyday life. The dominant modality of human communication is not that of analysis but that of narrative. We tell each other stories. However, some families not only construct an official pedagogic context but also socialize their children into official pedagogic communication and the inner structure generated by its pacing rules: an inner structure which points towards analysis rather than narrative, non-linear rather than linear communicative competences. In this way the pacing rule not only affects the social relations of communication but regulates the inner logic of communication.

The strong pacing rule of the academic curriculum of the school creates the necessity of two sites of acquisition. It creates a particular form/modality of communication which does not privilege everyday narrative. In this structure children of the disadvantaged classes are doubly disadvantaged. There is no second site of acquisition and their orientation to language, narrative, is not privileged by the pedagogic communication of the school, either in form or in content, for only some narratives are permissible in school. Thus the pacing rule of the transmission acts selectively on those who can acquire the school's dominant pedagogic code, and this is a social class principle of selection. To weaken the pacing rule would require a change in the allocation of cultural capital and economic capital to the school. A change in cultural capital, because a weakened pacing rule sets up different classroom practice and communications which will require a change in the training of teachers and an increase in economic capital, because the transmission of the same information will now cost more. It is likely, however, that the costs of yearly repetition in some societies will most certainly be reduced, together with the costs of alienated youth. Currently the visible pedagogy of the school is cheap to transmit because it is subsidized by the middle-class family and paid for by the alienation and failure of children of the disadvantaged classes and groups.

We can now see that the pacing rule carries invisible social class assumptions which act selectively on those who can acquire the dominant pedagogic code of the school through the distributive consequences of the visible pedagogy's strong pacing and its regulation of the deep structure of sociolinguistic competences. Indeed, where pacing is strong we may find a *lexical* pedagogic code where one-word answers, or short sentences, relaying individual facts/skills/operations may be typical of the school class of marginal/lower working-class pupils, whereas a *syntactic* pedagogic code relaying relationships, processes, connections may be more typical of the school class of middle-class children, although even here pupil participation may be reduced.[7]

We can regard pacing rules as regulating the economy of the transmission and so these rules become the meeting point of the material, discursive, and social base of the transmission.

It is important to point out that a visible pedagogy is not intrinsically a relay for the reproduction of differential school achievement among children from different social classes. It is certainly possible to create a visible pedagogy which would weaken the relation between social class and educational achievement. This may well require a supportive pre-school structure, a relaxing of the framing on pacing and sequencing rules, and a weakening of the framing regulating the flow of communication between the school classroom and the community(ies) the school draws upon. Such relaxation of the framing of a visible pedagogy raises the cost of the transmission and has crucial implications for teacher training and school management. An invisible pedagogy, as we shall see later, is likely to create a pedagogic code intrinsically more difficult, initially at least, for disadvantaged social groups (from the perspective of formal education) to read and to control.

I have discussed the social class assumptions of visible pedagogies only in respect to sequencing rule and pacing. The discussion of the social class assumptions of hier- archical rules will be deferred for purposes of exposition until the discussion of the social class assumptions of invisible pedagogies. I must point out that what has been analysed is the implicit ideological basis of the pedagogic relay itself, that is, the *bias in the relay* which acts selectively upon those who can acquire what is relayed. Clearly what is relayed, the instructional contents, the values these presuppose, and the stan- dards of conduct, character, and manner which form the contents of the school's regulative discourse, carry cultural biases, including those of social class. These biases, the biases of what is relayed, are not the object of this analysis, as they are well documented in the literature.

Social class assumptions of an invisible pedagogy[8]

The class assumptions of an invisible pedagogy translate into cultural and economic prerequisites for the effective understanding and acquisition of this practice. I shall examine those assumptions with respect to the concept of space, the concept of time, and the concept of control. In the case of space and time I shall distinguish between economic and symbolic assumptions.

Space

Economic   The material costs of the space of an invisible pedagogy relative to a visible pedagogy is high. For an invisible pedagogy presupposes movement on the part of the child – indeed, considerable freedom of movement. In a school class organized for a visible pedagogy the amount of space per child would be the size of the table or, later, a desk and chair. Under these conditions the school class can hold, and often does, a large number of acquirers. However, if the same space were to be organized for an invisible pedagogy most of the tables or desks would have to be removed to allow each child freedom of movement. But now it would not be possible to put the same number of children in the same space. The number would have to be reduced if the invisible pedagogy were to realize its potential. This reduc- tion in the number of children necessarily increases the cost of the space. When the spatial requirement is translated into family space it is clear that the family cannot employ an invisible pedagogy where there are many members confined to a small space, as is the case with many working-class and lower working-class families, including, especially, disadvantaged families of minority ethnic groups. The spatial requirement is much more likely to be satisfied in the case of middle-class families.

Symbolic   The rules whereby space is constructed, marked, and ordered contain implicit cognitive and social messages. In the case of a family operating with a visible pedagogy each room has its own function; within rooms objects may well have fixed positions, spaces may be reserved for special categories of person. There are strong explicit rules regulating the movement of objects, practices, communication from one space to another. Such space is strongly classified and pollution is necessarily visible. However, such strong classification can often provide privacy within its specialized boundaries. In general, this organization of space is predicated on a user rule: 'Leave the space as you find it'. Such a spatial grid carries cognitive and social messages.

However, in the case of a family operating an invisible pedagogy the spatial grid is very different. Relative to a visible pedagogy space it is more weakly marked. The rules regulating movements of objects, persons, practices, communications are less constraining. Meals may be provided on a cafeteria system. Living is more open-plan. Paradoxically, with greater freedom there is less privacy. If a visible pedagogy spatial grid is based on the fundamental rule that 'Things must be kept apart', with the rule of use 'Leave the space as you find it', then the spatial grid of an invisible pedagogy is based on the rule 'Things must be brought together', with the rule of use 'Make your own mark'. That is, the spatial grid of the invisible pedagogy facilitates, encourages individual representations in the sense of showing, revealing, individual representations. Cognitive and social messages are carried by such a space, and such is unlikely to be available and constructed by families disadvantaged by class or ethnicity.

Time

Economic   If all children left school at 14 there would be no invisible pedagogies. An invisible pedagogy presupposes a long pedagogic life. Its relaxed rhythm, its less specialized acquisitions, its system of control (see later) entail a different temporal projection relative to a visible pedagogy for comparable acquisition. Indeed, this fact is explicitly taken into account by many middle-class families who favour this regime in the early years of their child's life before switching to a visible pedagogy at the secondary stage. Such favouring families often run a compensatory pedagogic programme dedicated to reading, writing, and counting whilst the child's creative potential may be facilitated by the invisible pedagogy of the infant school or pre-school.

Symbolic   A child socialized by a familial visible pedagogy is involved in a particular symbolic projection in which time is punctuated by a series of dislocations in her/his treatment and expected behaviour. Time is symbolically marked as the child progresses through a series of statuses which define her/his relation not only to parents but also to the other siblings. The implicit theory of instruction held by parents which regulates their practice constructs age-specific communications/acquisitions. The child is developed in, and by, a particular construction of time.

However, in the case of an invisible pedagogy, the child is developed by, and is constructed in, a differently specialized construction of time. The child is constructed by implicitly held theories of instruction derived from the theories discussed earlier. This construction of time appears to give priority to the child's time/space, rather than to the time/space of the parents; to the concrete present of the child, and age statuses give way to the unique signs of the child's own constructed development. In this sense the structuring of the child's time is through a different temporal grid. Visible and invisible pedagogies construct different concepts of the child's development in time which may or may not be consonant with the concept of development held by the school.

There are some implications of a visible pedagogy which I shall develop here. Where the child moves through a series of specialized statuses in time, his/her conduct, achievement, or aspiration is relative to a particular status and the child is subject to normative criteria. He/she is not measured against himself/herself but only against those sharing a similar temporal category. From this point of view the child competes only with those in a similar temporal category. In this way competition is reduced, for jealousies, envious feelings, operates towards his/her peers. This is not to say that the child does not direct negative feelings towards other than his/her peers, but that he/she is aware, or can be made aware of, a distributive rule which privileges older children; a rule which is not personal but public.

In the case of an invisible pedagogy, because statuses are relatively more weakly marked, because of the more individualized or, better, personalized realizations expected, the child, by apparently competing only with her/himself, competes with everybody. This may well be the charm of criteria referencing. Parents relate to the child in terms of the child's apparently unique showings and representations. Here the child, despite the apparent democracy of the pedagogic regime, is placed in a more competitive relation, as comparisons are less likely to be age-graded. Thus jealousies, envious feelings, aspirations are likely to be less specifically focused and so more difficult for both the parents and the child to deal with. From a cognitive and from a social point of view girls are less likely to be negatively constrained by invisible pedagogies than visible pedagogies. Conversely, for boys, under an invisible pedagogy practice, girls become successful competitors and a threat.

Control: hierarchical rules

Here I am concerned with how parents introduce and maintain principles of conduct, character, and manner – that is, concepts of social order, relation, and identity; in other words, with their regulative practice. In the case of a visible pedagogy the rules of social order are generally explicit and specific. The spatial and temporal grids provide an explicit structure, a grammar of proscriptions and prescriptions, and deviance is very visible. Once the child has acquired the implicit grammar of the spatial and temporal grids the problems of control are relatively reduced. Clearly, they do not evaporate. If the child disobeys, then privileges are withdrawn and explicit rules are articulated. In the extreme, strategies of exclusion and physical punishment may be used. I would like it to be clear that visible pedagogies are not necessarily 'authoritarian' but they are certainly positional. Control functions to clarify, maintain, repair boundaries. However, in the case of invisible pedagogies we can ask, where does the control lie in a context of weakened spatial and temporal grids, of encouraged personalized representations, especially in a context where we could reasonably expect a greater potential for issues of control to arise?

I want to propose that in this apparently relaxed familial context control lies almost entirely in inter-personal communication: a form of communication which works round the areas of motivation and intentionality as read by the parents. The communication is multi-layered. In order to facilitate this multi-layering of communication a progressive weakening takes place of the classification between the inside of the child and the outside. The parents encourage the child to make more of his/her inside public and facilitate the process. More of the child's feelings, fantasies, fears, and aspirations are expected to be made public. The surveillance of the child is total. In this sense it is difficult for the child to hide and also difficult for the parents to. The communication process works to make the invisible visible, through language, and this may carry its own pathology.

In the case of a visible pedagogy we said that one of the strategies of control is exclusion but that this strategy carries difficulties in the case of an invisible pedagogy. For if the child is excluded (or as a strategy of self-defence excludes him/herself by withdrawing), then the communication process is weakened and so is the means of control. This gives the child a powerful strategy for controlling the parents by withdrawing, by excluding him/herself, by not being there, symbolically or physically. The parents must then develop strategies of retrieval in order to return the child symbolically or physically to the communication system. In this way the child acquires a particular elaborated variant of communication which gives rise to an elaborate repertoire of manipulative skills.

Invisible pedagogies give rise to procedures of control based upon multi-layered class patterns of communication necessary to support and promote their concept and practice of social order. And the construction of these communicative competences is likely to be class-based. Where these competences are not made available in the family the child is less likely to be self-regulating in school, according to the requirements of its invisible pedagogy practice, and is likely to misread both the practice and its pedagogic context.

I have argued that the assumptions of invisible pedagogies as they inform spatial, temporal, and control grids are less likely to be met in class or ethnically disadvantaged groups, and as a consequence the child here is likely to misread the cultural and cognitive significance of such a classroom practice, and the teacher is likely to misread the cultural and cognitive significance of the child.

We have focused upon different pedagogic sites in our analysis of the social class assumptions of visible pedagogies and invisible pedagogies in their generic form. In the case of visible pedagogies we focused upon the school and in the case of invisible pedagogies we focused upon the family. This is because the *surface* features of a visible pedagogy can be understood by all, as it is a standard pedagogic form, whether or not its underlying principles and practices are reproduced in the family. Thus it was necessary to analyse the underlying ordering principles of the official – that is, the school's – pedagogic practice in order to show that the ordering principles may militate against the acquisition of this practice by class or ethnically disadvantaged groups. In the case of invisible pedagogies we focused on the family to show the supporting domestic pedagogic practice required if the classroom context and practice were to be understood for their pedagogic significance.

What we find, as I have pointed out before, is rarely a pure form of an invisible pedagogy but rather an embedded pedagogic practice where the invisible pedagogy is embedded in a visible pedagogy:

$$\frac{IP}{VP}$$

Here — indicates embedded. The specific specialized skills and attributes of a visible pedagogy are beneath the surface of an invisible pedagogy, or surface at special occasions. And this holds in the family. What is of interest is when the strong classification of a visible pedagogy emerges as a pedagogic form in itself or surfaces to interrupt an invisible pedagogy. It is clear that, even for ardent sponsors of invisible pedagogies, this practice is generally confined to the child's early years; certainly by the secondary level the demand is for a visible pedagogy, as it is this practice which leads to professional occupational placement. Given this situation, the socialization of a fraction of the middle class is perhaps unique as a modal type. We mean by modal that the form of socialization is not confined to individual families but is a publicly recognized form: a form in which the primary pedagogic socialization principles and practices are at variance with those of the secondary stage. Or where weak classification is embedded in a latent strong classification; and this, we suspect, has many complex consequences.

Whilst it is certainly not true to say that a visible pedagogy is a capitalist practice, it is the standard European pedagogic practice, in one form or another, of every elite secondary curriculum, whether in the East or the West. The strong classification of the visible pedagogy probably has its roots in the medieval university, in the major classification between the Trivium and the Quadrivium and in their sub-classifications, and the subordination of both to religion. The strong classification between mental and manual practice probably dates from the same period, when manual practice had its own specialized relays, either within the family or in specialized guilds, so creating the concept of the autonomous or abstract visible pedagogy. Such a visible pedagogy, autonomous with respect to control over its own practices, won its independence from the Church, but remained abstract in the sense that its discourse referred only to itself rather than to work. After gaining independence of the Church it became progressively regulated by the State. Whilst, in origin, the visible pedagogy as a relay is not itself a class product, *even though what it relayed was*, its institutionalization in either the private or the public sector led to a selective class-based acquisition.

In the case of the invisible pedagogy, certainly in the UK and probably elsewhere, the sponsors of this as a public form, its dissemination and construction as a practice, were members of that fraction of the middle class discussed earlier. Celia Jenkins (1989) has clearly shown that the members of the New Education Fellowship who were highly influential throughout the 1920s and 1930s in promoting and constructing the 'new education' were drawn almost entirely from professional agents of symbolic control functioning in specialized agencies of symbolic control. Those who opposed invisible pedagogies (other than pedagogues) were likely to be those members of the middle class whose work had a direct relation to the production, distribution, and circulation of capital.

The opposition between these fractions of the middle class is an opposition not over the distribution of power but over principles of social control. At economic and political levels the opposition is an opposition over the role of the State. On the whole the middle-class sponsors of invisible pedagogy support State intervention and the expansion of agents and agencies of symbolic control, and thus growth in public expenditure. For this is the ground and opportunity of their own reproduction and advancement, whereas the middle-class sponsors of visible pedagogy drawn from the economic sector and the entrepreneurial professions are opposed to growth in public expenditure. Thus there are opposing material and symbolic (discursive) interests.

We have so far discussed the class assumptions which act selectively on those who can achieve in visible and invisible pedagogies as generic types. We have earlier said that these generic types can generate a variety of modalities. We shall now consider two modalities of the visible pedagogy, modalities which are opposed to each other and which today are likely to be found in opposition in Europe and North and South America.

Autonomous and market-oriented visible pedagogies[9]

School systems and university systems are now more and more engaged in a struggle over what should be transmitted, over the autonomy of transmission, over the conditions of service of those who transmit, and over the procedures of evaluation of acquirers.

I shall conclude by looking, somewhat cursorily, at the present conflict between knowledge and market-oriented forms, that is, between 'autonomous' and 'dependent' forms of visible pedagogies. That is, between visible pedagogies justified by the intrinsic possibilities of knowledge itself and visible pedagogies justified by their market relevance. In a sense the autonomous visible pedagogy is both a sacred and a profane form, depending essentially upon one's position as either transmitter or acquirer. From an acquirer's point of view an autonomous visible pedagogy is instrumental to class placement through symbolic means. Yet it has the cover of the sacred. However, a market-oriented visible pedagogy is a truly secular form born out of the 'context of cost-efficient education', allegedly promoting relevant skills, attitudes, and technology in an era of large-scale chronic youth unemployment. The explicit rules of selection, sequence, pace, and criteria of a visible pedagogy readily translate into performance indicators of schools' staff and pupils, and a behaviourist theory of instruction readily realizes programmes, manuals, and packaged instruction. Specialization of curricula within a dominant market-oriented visible pedagogy allows for an almost perfect reproduction of the hierarchy of the economy within the school, or between schools (as in the case of 'magnet' schools), through the grading of curricula, e.g. managerial/administrative/business, through the various technological specializations, clerical, and imaginary trade apprenticeships for the lower working and marginal class groups. It is but a small step to encourage industry-based training and, as in Chile, State-sponsored privatized schools. Both autonomous and market-oriented visible pedagogies are relays of the stratification of knowledge, of social inequalities. However, the ideological base of the market-oriented visible pedagogy is more complex and, if I may be allowed, perhaps more sinister.

The autonomous visible pedagogy justifies itself by the intrinsic worthwhileness and value of the knowledge it relays and by the discipline its acquisition requires. Its arrogance lies in its claim to moral high ground and to the superiority of its culture, its indifference to its own stratification consequences, its conceit in its lack of relation to anything other than itself, its self-referential abstracted autonomy. The market-oriented visible pedagogy is ideologically a much more complex construction. It incorporates some of the criticism of the autonomous visible pedagogy, much of it originating from left-wing positions: criticism of the failure of the urban school, of the passivity and inferior status of parents, which combine to reduce their power over schools and teachers, of the boredom of working-class pupils and their conse-quent disruption of and resistance to irrelevant curricula, of assessment procedures which itemize relative failure rather than the positive strength of the acquirer. But it assimilates these criticisms into a new discourse: a new pedagogic Janus.

The explicit commitment to greater choice by parents and pupils is not a cele-bration of a participatory democracy but a thin cover for the old stratification of schools and curricula. New forms of assessment, profiling, criteria-referenced rather than norm-referenced assessment, allegedly to recognize and liberate individual qual-ities, allow of, and mark, greater control of assessment. At the same time periodic mass testing of pupils concentrates new distribution procedures for homogenizing acquisition and, at the same time, creates performance indicators of its effective-ness.[10] Vocationalism appears to offer the lower working class a legitimation of their own pedagogic interests in a manual-based curriculum, and in so doing appears to include them as significant pedagogic subjects, yet at the same time closes off their own personal and occupational possibilities.

The situation is indeed complex. At the same time as the economy is moving towards a greater concentration upon mergers and corporate growth, at a more micro level an entrepreneurial 'artisan' culture is being encouraged in the service sector. This is reflected in market-oriented visible pedagogies to develop imaginary appren-ticeships into the skills for this function, e.g. decorating, plumbing, carpentry for the self-employed. Even the pedagogic regimes are mixed, drawing on features of invis-ible pedagogy, e.g. in the 'negotiation' of pupils' profiles, life skill programmes.[11] The new pedagogic discourse recontextualizes and thus repositions within its own ideology features of apparently oppositional discourses.[12]

The market-oriented visible pedagogy, at least in the UK, creates apparently greater local independence for, and competition between, schools and teachers, yet at the same time the schools and teachers are tied more directly to State regulation. And finally we can detect that the State is now operating on quite different principles with respect to the principles and practices of the economy and the principles and practices of specialized agencies/agents of symbolic control, especially education. In the economy privatization rules but competition is reduced as mergers proceed apace. As the State reduces its control, corporations and multinationals take up the vacated space. In the sector of the specialized agencies of symbolic control, especially in education, we see that privatization, the local autonomies of agencies, are there to encourage greater competition between units. Indeed, we might say that the major site of competition is not the economy in total but increasingly within the sector of publicly regulated symbolic control. Yet despite the greater competition within this sector it is subject to greater and more complex forms of State regulation. Thus the essential shift which appears to be taking place is the shift of State regulation from the economy to symbolic control. Yet State management of symbolic control is accomplished more and more by the exclusion of its own agents and their replacement by managers, administrators, industrialists of the economy.

The ideological message of a market-oriented visible pedagogy is less the regulation and realization of the pedagogy of the new 'relevance' than the new regulation and realization of symbolic control in the transition to capitalism's latest transformation: communications.[13]

Addendum

This chapter is a revision of an earlier paper, 'Class and pedagogies: visible and invisible' (in *Class, Codes and Control*, vol. 3, revised edition 1977). It develops and extends the discussion of rules and their class assumptions and provides a more general model for generating types and modalities of pedagogic practices. Further, it includes a discussion of market-oriented pedagogies and speculations on their origin, function, and linkage to macro changes in the form of symbolic control. It does not. however, replace the earlier paper but extends and builds upon it. The chapter does show that the basic underlying logic of this and other papers can deal with the question of content, as well as linking macro and micro levels of analysis.

In terms of the general classification and framing analysis, much of the focus of the chapter in the discussion of specific pedagogic practices is upon framing rather than upon classification. It should be borne in mind that principles of classification are always invisibly present in any pedagogic practice in the sense that any context of that practice presupposes a relationship with other contexts, other pedagogic practices/communications, either within the institution or external to it. Further, principles of classification are visibly present within any pedagogic practice and are realized in the arrangement of acquirers, the distribution of tasks, and in the organizational features of the context. Thus principles of classification, as principles of framing, always have internal as well as external values.

Notes

1   This chapter has benefited from seminars held at CIDE, Santiago, Chile, in 1985, and at the University of Valle, Cali, Colombia, in 1986. The present form arose out of an invitation from Adelphi University, New York, to deliver the Robert Finkelstein Annual Lecture, 1987. I am grateful to Dr Alan Sadovnik of Adelphi University for comments and discussion, and also to Celia Jenkins, of the Department of the Sociology of Education, University of London Institute of Education, whose Ph.D. thesis investigated the social class basis of progressive education in Britain.

2   For the purposes of this chapter this logic has been reduced to three rules, but there is a fourth, a recontextualizing rule which creates the content to be transmitted. [. . .]

3 [. . .]
4 It is, of course, possible to have explicit hierarchical rules but degrees of implicitness of sequential/pacing rules, which indicate a weakening in the framing of these rules.
5 It is a matter of some interest that in the 1960s in the major disciplines of the human sciences, psychology, linguistics, and anthropology, the concept of competence underlined the structuralist theories of Piaget (child development), Chomsky (linguistics), and Lévi-Strauss (anthropology). Competence in all three theories refers to an in-built grammar. Chomsky's theory of syntax, Piaget's theory of the development and transformation of cognitive operations, Lévi-Strauss's theory of cultural assemblies and reassemblies are all competences triggered by interaction with non-culturally specific others. That is, competence arises out of two facilities, an in-built facility and an interactional facility. From this point of view competence-acquisition takes place, analytically speaking, at the level of the social, *not* the cultural, because acquisition is dependent not upon any cultural arrangement but upon *social* interaction.

Competence theories, then, integrate the biological with the social, but both are disconnected from the cultural. Competence theories point to competence-acquisition as entailing active participation on the part of the acquirer. Indeed, competence-acquisition arises out of the creative possibilities of the acquirer in inferring rules (Chomsky) in the process of accommodation (Piaget) in *bricolage* (Levi-Strauss). In a sense competence theories announce a fundamental democracy: all are equal in their acquisition, all actively participate in their acquisition, creativity is intrinsic to becoming social. Differences between individuals are then a product of culture. From this point of view competence theories may be regarded as critiques showing the disparity between what we are and what we become, between what we are capable of and our performance. However, this idealism is bought at a price: the price of severing the relation between power, culture, and competence, between meanings and the structures through which meanings become possible. The democracy of competence theories is a democracy removed from society.
6 An analysis of symbolic control, its agents, agencies, and its relation to the economic field may be found in Bernstein (1986). . . . For empirical study of differences in the socialization of adolescents whose parents function in the field of symbolic control and the economic field see Holland (1986), Aggleton and Whitty (1985), and Cohen (1981).
7 It is important to point out that what we have called 'lexical' and 'syntactic' pedagogic practices are within the general thesis that the privileging code of the school is elaborated. We may now be finding that this code is officially suspended and replaced by a 'lexical' pedagogic practice relaying less the exploration of principles than context-specific operations which develop low-level skills. In the past, the suspension of an elaborated code with respect to groups of pupils, usually lower working-class, including racially disadvantaged groups, was not official policy but came about because of the context that teachers and pupils alike found themselves in.
8 King (1978 and elsewhere) criticizes the analysis of invisible pedagogy on the grounds that his empirical study of primary schools found no evidence of its existence. As has been pointed out here and in the original paper it is more likely that what will be found is an embedded pedagogic practice, the invisible embedded in the visible. The pure form is more likely to be found in the private sector. Invisible pedagogy was institutionalized under the name of *dialog-pedagogike* in Sweden in the 1970s. Empirical support for the practice of invisible pedagogy in middle-class families may be found in the references cited in note 5, and at the level of the classroom in Daniels (1988, 1989). An enquiry into different forms of special school organization, pedagogic practice, and pupil discrimination is to be found in *CORE* 12, 2. See also Jenkins (1989).
9 'Autonomous' in the sense of independent is clearly *relative* to 'market-oriented' in the sense of dependent upon economy. Certainly in the United Kingdom (and, for that matter, elsewhere) all levels of the educational systems have for the past thirty years become more and more subject to central control. University research funding is now severely constrained both by the reduction in governmental funding (especially in the social sciences) and by governmental criteria regulating approved research.

Market-oriented visible pedagogies indicate a shift of focus of central government, both with respect to the knowledge which is transmitted and with respect to the change in the controlling agents, which now include industrialists. This shift of focus involves not only the development of specialized curricula but also the development of specialized schools.

10   I am indebted to Patricia Broadfoot (1986) for these points.

11   The discussion of invisible pedagogies has occurred in a context where such a practice is dominant within the institution (e.g. family, primary school, pre-school). It has been noted that an invisible pedagogy is less likely to appear in a pure form in the public sector but more likely to be embedded in a visible pedagogy. However, it is possible that features of invisible pedagogy will be found as specialized practices within a predominantly visible pedagogy modality. Here such a specialized practice is likely to be particular to a part of the curriculum (e.g. life skills), addressed to a particular social group (e.g. disadvantaged class or ethnic groups), or may even form part of an assessment procedure. In general invisible pedagogies and/or 'integrated' pedagogic practices are more likely to be formed at primary level or, if at secondary level, associated with disadvantaged social groups as means of their social control. In general, shifts towards invisible pedagogies or similar 'progressive' practices which imply a weakening of classification and framing are more likely to occur in times of 'economic buoyancy'. Such practices are more expensive, both with respect to the training of the transmitters and with respect to the cost of the transmission, than visible pedagogies. In times of economic boom/growth the demand side is less powerful than the supply side, and as a consequence hierarchies may well take a more indirect, less explicit form as well as being less able to be as selective with respect to ideas, personnel, and interests. However, in times of slump and chronic unemployment demand is more powerful than supply, hierarchies may be expected to become more explicit and directive, more selective of ideas, personnel, and interests. As a consequence, in general, classification and framing relations are likely to strengthen in conjunction with stronger central control. However, as pointed out earlier, specialized invisible pedagogic practices are still likely to be inserted as devices of social control.

In summary we could hypothesize that shifts in modal state pedagogic practices away from, or towards, weak classification and weak framing ('progressive' practices) are likely to be mediated by shifts in the economy which change the social basis of the influencing dominant agents of the state, the degree of explicitness of hierarchies, and the terms of supply of and demand for pedagogic practitioners. In the case of development/expansion of the economy, there is likely to be an increase in public expenditure on education, medical, and social services, and influencing dominant agents are likely to be drawn from agents of symbolic control specializing in agencies of symbolic control, whereas in the case of a downturn in the economy there is likely to be a reduction in public expenditure on education, medical, and social services, and influencing dominant agents of the state are likely to be drawn not from symbolic control but from the economic field.

12   Whilst it can be hypothesized that the more abstract the principles of the forces of division of labour then the more simple its social division of labour, because many of the lower (and increasingly the higher) functions are in information chains and feedback loops of the computer, it is also likely that, as the social division of labour of the economic field becomes both simplified and reduced, that of the field of symbolic control is likely to increase in complexity and size. Further, there is likely to be an attempt to develop an entrepreneurial service structure of the artesan type. Much of the vocational training of sections of the working class is directed towards this end.

13   The transition is linked to high levels of unemployment, changes in occupational functions and conditions, an increase in mergers, recurrent dangers of severe recession, which together may produce instabilities in the social order. The overall movement to greater state control in the field of symbolic control often announces itself through an ideology of the family and nation. This new individualism regulating the field of symbolic control contrasts sharply with the corporative potential of the communications revolution in the economic field.

References

Aggleton, P. and Whitty, G. (1985) 'Rebels without a cause? Socialization and subcultural style among children of the new middle classes', *Sociology of Education* 58, 1: 60–72.

Bernstein, B. (1975) 'Class and pedagogies: visible and invisible', in *Class, Codes and Control* 3: 116–56, London: Routledge; revised in the second edition, 1977.

—— (1986) 'On pedagogic discourse', J.G. Richardson (ed.) *Handbook of Theory and Research for the Sociology of Education*, New York: Greenwood.

Broadfoot, P. (1986) 'Whatever happened to inequality? Assessment policy and inequality: the UK experience', *British Journal of the Sociology of Education* 7, 2: 205–24.

Cohen, G. (1981) 'Culture and educational achievement', *Harvard Educational Review* 51, 2: 270–85.

Daniels, H.R.J. (1988) 'An enquiry into different forms of special school organization, pedagogic practice and pupil discrimination', *C.O.R.E.* 12, 2.

—— (1989) 'Visual displays as tacit relays of the structure of pedagogic practice', *British Journal of the Sociology of Education* 10, 2: 123–40.

Domingos, A.M. (1984) 'Social Class, Pedagogic Practice and Achievement in Science: a Study of Secondary Schools in Portugal' I. Ph.D. thesis, University of London; also in *C.O.R.E.* 11, 2 (1987).

Giroux, H.A. (1989) *Schooling for Democracy*, London: Routledge.

Holland, J. (1986) 'Social class differences in adolescents' conception of the domestic and industrial division of labour', *C.O.R.E.* 10, 1.

Jenkins, C. (1989) 'The Professional Middle Class and the Origins of Progressivism: a Case Study of the New Education Fellowship, 1920–50', Ph.D. thesis, University of London.

King, R. (1978) *All Things Bright and Beautiful? A Sociological Study of Infants' Classrooms*, Chichester: Wiley.

Plowden report (1967) *Children and their Primary Schools*, report of the Central Advisory Council for Education (England), London: HMSO.

PART 6

TEACHER

CHAPTER 11

THE RECONSTRUCTION OF PRIMARY TEACHERS' IDENTITIES

Peter Woods and Bob Jeffrey

British Journal of Sociology of Education (2002), 23 (1): 89–106

[. . .]

Introduction

The restructuring of education has brought about radical changes in primary teachers' work (Woods *et al.*, 1997). In previous publications, we have considered various different modes of teacher adaptation to these changes (Woods, 1995), and modifications to the teacher career (Troman & Woods, 2001). In this chapter, we wish to examine the implications for teacher identity.

We need to make clear at the outset our view of identity. We largely follow Snow & Anderson's (1987) construction, with some modifications, distinguishing among social identities, personal identities, and self-concept. Social identities are 'attributed or imputed to others in an attempt to place or situate them as social objects' (Snow & Anderson, 1987, p. 1347). These are largely 'imputations based primarily on information gleaned on the basis of appearance, behaviour, and the location and time of the action'. In the context of our research, we find the notion of an 'assigned social identity' (Ball, 1972) useful. These are imputations based on 'desired' or 'prescribed' appearance, etc. Personal identities refer to the 'meanings attributed to the self by the actor', and are 'self-designations and self-attributions brought into play during the course of interaction' (Ball, 1972). They may be consistent or inconsistent with social identities. The self-concept is the 'overarching view of oneself as a physical, social, spiritual, or moral being', and is 'a kind of working compromise between idealized images and imputed social identities' (Snow & Anderson, 1987, p. 1348). We shall be concerned with teachers' personal identities, which 'provide a glimpse of the consistency or inconsistency between social identities and self-concept' (p. 1348). We make a further distinction between 'substantial' and 'situational' identities. Ball (1972) used these terms to distinguish between more enduring identities and more transient ones given meaning by their contextual location. We shall refer to the combination of personal identity and self-concept as 'self-identity'.

In the years immediately preceding the restructuring of recent years, there seemed to be a great deal of consistency of social identity and self-concept among the majority of English primary teachers. Much of the literature of this period speaks of these teachers seeing their selves and social identities as isomorphic. Nias (1989), for example, writes:

The personal and occupational self may be so closely related that, in their own terms, they 'become' teachers: The persons they perceive themselves to be go to work and the teachers they feel they are come home, often to occupy their sleeping as well as their waking hours . . . Many teachers, for part or all of their working lives, invest their personal sense of identity in their work.

(pp. 224–225)

However, education has undergone a revolution since this was written. What challenges have teachers had to meet to their identities, and how have they dealt with them?

Giddens (1991) provides a useful reference point for current developments. He argues that, in the current state of 'late' or 'high modernity', as he calls it, global trends impact on the self in unprecedented ways. Daily life is reconstituted. Much of everyday life used to be based on a high degree of trust between people, but now trust is less personalized, and more invested in processes and abstract systems. We also live in a culture of high-consequence risks of global origin, which contain opportunity as well as danger. These developments have brought about the separation of time and space, and the 'disembedding' or 'lifting out' of 'social relations from local contexts and their articulation across indefinite tracts of time-space' (Giddens, 1991, p. 18). For the individual, the result is a challenge to the taken-for-grantedness of everyday life, to the erstwhile 'high level of reliability of the contexts of day-to-day social interaction', and to the 'ontological security' of the self (Giddens, 1991, p. 36). In education, these developments have been reflected in the growth of economic rationalism and technicism, an emphasis on marketability, efficiency and performativity, the growth of management systems and of audit accountability, and attacks on moral systems, such as child-centredness, which appear to run counter to these (Woods *et al.*, 1997). These processes demand attention, and teachers have been forced to reconsider their beliefs, values, roles, biographies, and ambitions in ways they had not anticipated. As Hargreaves (1994, p. 71) puts it, 'The fragile self becomes a continuous reflexive project. It has to be constantly and continuously remade and reaffirmed'.

According to Giddens (1991, pp. 189–196), the self in late modernity typically confronts four major dilemmas: (1) the degree to which the self is unified or becomes fragmented; (2) whether one appropriates the changes to one's own concerns, or feels powerless before the scale and depth of the changes; (3) the question of authority versus uncertainty; and (4) personalized versus commodified experience. However, although this is markedly different from the conditions pertaining to those of Nias' (1989) research, a substantial self-identity, Giddens feels, still appears to be at the heart of the resolution of these dilemmas. Giddens is keen to emphasize the role of agency, and the possibilities for integration as well as disintegration, for opportunity as well as risk. 'The ideal self', he says, 'is a key part of self-identity, because it forms a channel of positive aspirations in terms of which the narrative of self-identity is worked out' (Giddens, 1991, p. 68).

The reconstruction of teacher identities makes a useful test case for Giddens' theory, as well as providing an opportunity to consider identity theory in general. So far, humanist theories, emphasising the consistent and unitary self (and supported by, for example, Nias' research), have largely prevailed. But these have come under attack in recent years from poststructuralists, who argue that we have multiple selves and identities that change and shift according to different discourses. According to the latter view, there is no ideal, real or substantial self or identity. Individuals' negotiations through the rapid and radically changing events of recent years lend some support to this view. But we find both theories useful in understanding the reconstruction of teacher identities.

All of these processes are reflected in our research of recent years (Woods & Jeffrey, 1996; Woods *et al.*, 1997). In this chapter, we draw from our research during the period 1994–1999 into the effects on English primary teachers (teaching children aged 5–11) of the impact of school inspections carried out by the Office for Standards in Education (Ofsted), an organization established by the UK government in 1992 as part of its drive to raise standards of education (Jeffrey & Woods, 1998). These inspections were very traumatic, and brought to a head identity issues already stirred by Government legislation. In research terms, therefore, they constitute a 'critical case' (Hammersley & Atkinson, 1995). For the Ofsted research, we selected six primary schools, contrasting in size, location and pupil intake. We then studied the effects of the inspections on the teachers of these schools from two terms prior to the inspection (when schools were first given notice that they were to be inspected) to up to 1 year afterwards. We later returned to two of the schools where teachers were experiencing their second inspection 4 years after their first, enabling us to monitor adaptations in those schools over a period of 5 years. The main methods of data collection consisted of series of unstructured interviews with individual teachers, tape-recorded and transcribed, over the whole period, and observation in their schools at key points of the inspection process. Our full sample was over 90 teachers (consisting of 95% of the staff—a few were not willing to take part), 80% of whom were mid-career to late-career teachers whose educational values were established prior to the introduction of the National Curriculum. It is this latter population of teachers, therefore, who are chiefly represented in this chapter.

It was clear that these inspections were mounting the most significant challenge to teacher identities since they had begun teaching. We consider this challenge in this chapter, and how, in meeting it, teachers were negotiating new identities for themselves. We begin with a resume of typical features of the English primary teacher's self during the 1970s and 1980s as evidenced by our teachers.

The primary teachers' Plowden self-identity

The typical English primary teacher's self-identity of the 1970s and 1980s was strongly endorsed by government policy of the day, and educational and academic discourse, all epitomized in the Plowden Report (Central Advisory Council for Education in England, 1967). While we should be cautious about the extent to which Plowden ideals were operationalized in schools (Alexander, 1992), there is plenty of evidence to attest to its general influence among primary teachers (see, for example, Pollard, 1987; Nias, 1989; Osborn *et al.*, 2000). Consequently, those who began teaching in the 1970s had a strong sense of 'ontological security' and an almost taken-for-granted 'protective cocoon which stands guard over the self in its dealings with everyday reality' (Giddens, 1991, p. 3). Social and personal identities and self-concept were at one, and teachers had, for the most part, an integrated and consistent self-identity. It was based on two major sets of values—humanism and vocationalism—which we summarize here as illustrated by the teachers in our sample.

Humanism

This set of values centres around holism, person-centredness, and warm and caring relationships. The teacher is a whole and real person who could 'really be myself' and who could 'really feel at home' while teaching, rather than being someone who is 'really removed' (*Erica*). Teachers see children in holistic terms. Basic to this outlook is the child as person. They base their notion of 'good teaching' on child-centred principles, core features of which are full and harmonious development of the child, a focus on the individual learner rather than the whole class, an emphasis on activity and discovery, curriculum integration, and environmentally based learning (Sugrue, 1998). Teachers place a high priority on feelings in teaching and learning, and on making emotional connections with knowledge and with children (Woods & Jeffrey, 1996). Veronica, for example, believed that fun is a powerful educational tool, and was fond of playing educational games with her children, which she found highly motivational and very productive. Laura also felt that:

> If there's something that children are really, really enthusiastically interested in, it would be so silly to ignore it because the motivation's there, the eagerness, the drive to look at something, to find out about something. It's already there.

A humanist approach has close relationships as a central feature.

> It's the children as whole human beings that I worried about. I wanted to set them amongst their families and within their peer groups, I wanted to know how they felt about things and nurture them.
>
> (*Naomi*)

Marilyn emphasized the need for inter-personal skills, the need to communicate and for 'mutual respect'. This kind of relationship involves a high degree of trust. Erica felt that 'a warm, personal relationship wherein they can trust adults is important because children will feel that they can take risks, and not be rejected as people'. Their 'protective cocoon' is strengthened, not attacked. One of our head teachers was keen to develop a similar quality among the staff:

> I want them to be happy, to come in with enthusiasm and joy, and to take risks with children that will put a spark in them. You can only do this if you feel safe and secure and happy, and if children feel safe and happy with you, they are going to respond as independent learners because we're trusted, we're cared for, we're respected.
>
> (*Rachael*)

Trust is also important among teachers (Troman & Woods, 2001).

> It works informally because the relationships are such that you can go and talk to people. So you have respect for other people's professionalism. And you know if you need something, you know who to go to and you know you will get the kind of response you need to have, and you know the other person will give the time to help you. I think it's mutual trust and respect.
>
> (*Grace*)

Vocationalism

A second set of values revolves around the teacher's relationship with her work and job. Teachers exhibit various different degrees and types of commitment. For example, some can be quite instrumental, others more professional (Sikes *et al.*, 1985). The Plowden primary teacher, however, feels that teaching is a vocation. Our teachers had a mission to teach and ... I wanted to change the world and the only way I could do that was through changing individual children's futures. When parents say, 'My children turned out like this because of you', you think, 'Oh great!'.

(Angelina)

They have a strong emotional dedication to their work. Leila, for example, loves teaching:

I love being with the kids, being with a child when they actually achieve something. I could wax lyrical about it. I love being in my classroom with my kids and the door shut. Today the classroom was covered in paper and Calvin was talking to my new Somalie boy. I looked round and felt so excited.

These teachers have a strong moral and political investment in their work. Laura, for example, was

very much for the sort of world that is not patriarchal or matriarchal. I want a world where we live in some sort of mutual respect, and I want it for my sons and my daughter and for me and for all the children.

Their commitment was total:

You put so much into it, you can't switch off from it; you can't take a step back. In order to be good, you've got to be wholehearted and the children have got to see that you really care and you are committed.

(Carol)

Such commitment entails a 'feeling that you can never do enough for them'.

The importance of the fact that you are dealing with people never ceases to be at the back of your mind—the fact that you are instrumental in the growth of these children. However, you are always going to feel that you could have done a little more.

(Cloe)

Despite these feelings of frustration, to carry out their unified role teachers had to have 'an inner self-esteem. Nobody likes to think that they are not doing very well' *(Kirsty)*.

Challenges to the Plowden self-identity

The Plowden self-identity has been subject to challenges in recent years during the reconstruction of the educational system, primarily through criticisms of child-centred philosophy, the loss of 'elementary trust', and changes in the teacher role. At the heart of this is an 'assigned' social identity—one that the policy-makers wished teachers to adopt, and one under-written by sharply contrasting values to those of Plowden.

The assault on child-centred philosophy

This attack strikes at the heart of teachers' humanism. The marketization and managerialization of schooling (Ball, 1994), the subject orientation of the prescribed National

Curriculum, and new forms of assessment and inspection inform the new order. These developments are accompanied by government and inspectorial pressure on teachers to abandon child-centredness and adopt a more traditional approach to their classroom teaching. Cloe articulates the assault on humanism:

> We're not saying that the education system didn't need a review because I'm sure it did, but it has meant that children have become slots in a machine who have to come up with the right numbers and we're the ones that have got to make them come up with the right numbers whereas before you were dealing with the whole child. You were dealing with its emotions, you were dealing with its social life, you were dealing with its grandma, you were dealing with its physical development in a much more intense and bonding relationship than you do today. You had a real effect on these people and you felt that you were actually doing something that was worthwhile and they come back and see you and you're still 'Miss', you're still important to them. I was referred to as 'Miss' by a twenty nine-year-old. Being that important to other human beings is a real privilege, but that joy has been dampened until I don't think it's a privilege any more.

Veronica affirmed that children were 'not things to be shoved in little boxes, they're human beings, they have their good days and their bad days, they have their strengths and weaknesses'. There would soon be 'no individuality left in classrooms, no way to be with kids or to encourage them or direct them or lead them the way you feel is best'. One of the 'joys' of teaching for Victor, now disappearing, was 'feeling free to run with something . . . that sort of vibrant, really getting excited about it, really involving all the children . . . (which they) never forget that for the rest of their lives' (*Victor*).

The process of an Ofsted inspection reduced the complex, multiple qualities of Plowden teaching to a series of measurable criteria, ascertained in 20–30 minute assessments (Jeffrey & Woods, 1998) as to how well children had 'received' specific factual knowledge.

> My teaching is about the whole child, whether they're in the classroom, walking along the corridor, in assembly. It's the interactions that go on all the time that helps to bring that child 'together'. But my immediate reaction to the Ofsted inspector's questioning of the children was that it seemed like attack, attack, attack as they quizzed them on specific pieces of knowledge.
>
> (*Shula*)

Diminution of 'elementary trust'

Control of teachers has become 'tighter, largely through the codification and monitoring of processes and practices previously left to teachers' professional judgement, taken on trust or hallowed by tradition' (Dale, 1989, p. 132). Power (1994) argues that accountability in public services has become a substitute for trust, and that certainly seems to be born out in our research. Robina, a recently appointed Head of Department, felt this change after her department had been criticized by inspectors just as she was getting to grips with its problems:

> They're here all the time pushing for more and more and making you feel that you can't achieve, questioning your capability . . . You can't work like that because there's got to be a sense of trust if you've been given a job.

Veronica also observed that the demand for detailed and extensive records 'has left me with an even greater feeling of inadequacy than I had before . . . there's no trust that I am doing the job to the best of my ability'. Teachers are 'having to write down the hidden things that you take for granted'. Naomi illustrates the undermining of her sense of vocationalism, feeling that she had

> to chop the top off my head off and show somebody what's in it. 'Is it OK? You don't like what you see? Then I'll go and get another one'. The assumption is that teachers are inadequate. That's why I don't like this, it stinks! It thrives on inadequacy. What does this do for teachers' self-esteem? Why do I have to have all these people checking up on me? I just want to do my job— the job I used to love, I was there till 6 o'clock every night until I had my kids. Even then I used to take work home and kids home, take kids out for netball tournaments. I loved it, because people trusted me and I felt good about things. I don't feel good about anything I do anymore.

Local inspectors used to be collegial with teachers. However, since the 1986 Education Act and as a result of the Audit Commission' report (1989), local education authorities (LEAs) had been encouraged to adopt more of an Ofsted role, 'abandoning a long tradition of advice on curriculum developments and support of specialist curriculum areas' (Evans & Penney, 1994, p. 35).

> But when he [*the LEA Inspector*] came in on Wednesday, and acted differently from the way he has in the past, the atmosphere was totally different. People were tense, people were behaving differently, and they bolted things down in their class teaching. I almost got the feeling that he was slightly put out by this, that he thought that we should have been more relaxed because we knew him. But we said 'You were here as an Ofsted inspector'.
>
> *(Lauren)*

In most 'pre-modern' contexts, according to Giddens (1991), trust relations were localized and focused through personal ties. Audit accountability, in the post-Plowden order, places less emphasis on the local factors and more on universal strategies and practices, codified in written, standardized procedures:

> There seems to be a whole ethos of telling you rather than interacting with you and supporting you. It's 'how we view it from up here' rather than, 'how about looking at what we might be doing with this?' There's no real discussions about what are you doing here, why are you doing that, where you're going to, or what problems you're having. He's here just to look through the paperwork.
>
> *(Colin)*

The Plowden commitment is being undermined here. Deena said the LEA inspectors had been on their side to begin with, but had 'given up the fight'. In the end, 'you give up fighting for what you think is right'. Resolve is replaced by doubt:

> I just keep thinking, 'Am I going to feel good in my job afterwards? Am I going to be able to carry on? Am I going to be able to face parents when they see this report or have heard about it . . . and say 'Well I'm doing my best for you, I feel I'm a good enough teacher to teach your children?' And that worries me. I don't think I should feel that way because I think I am doing my best. It puts doubt in people's minds.
>
> *(Helen)*

Changes in the teacher role

From a notion of the 'good teacher' based on 'personal qualities' (Broadhead, 1987), the emphasis is now on teacher competencies, such as subject expertise, coordination, collaboration, management and supervision (Woods *et al.*, 1997). This is the new assigned social identity. But it is not one that our teachers welcome. It attacks their self-esteem 'saying that the teacher in all of this is not important. It's saying "well anybody can do it"' (*Shula*). It attacks teachers' personal philosophies, 'undervaluing exactly what teachers do. It's almost saying to us, "you haven't been doing it right, this is what you should be doing." . . . All the time there's a mismatch between what we think is best and what they're imposing. It's like you're being pulled in different directions' (*Cloe*).

The human element gives way to commodified experience—'there's nothing about what makes a "quality" teacher—rapport with the kids, interest in their life experiences, and enthusiasm in what they're teaching' (*Aileen*). This commodified discourse strikes at the roots of teacher commitment, giving 'a feeling of sickness about how it's all going' (*Toni*). It causes Freda to feel that 'As soon as that stuff outweighs the love of teaching, then that's the time when you are going to say "What's the point? Why have stress at work all day, and then come home and be stressed as well?"' Something central to the Plowden self-identity has to give way:

> I now put a lot of time and effort into school to the detriment of my own personal identity. I will do things like planning but I'm going to take a bit of time back for *me*. It is a process that puts you through so much stress and strain that you are no longer talking about yourself as a 'rounded person'. We're like cardboard cut outs.
>
> (*Shula*)

The new role thus appears to demand a radical change of identity: 'It's almost like telling us to change our personalities. If you say to somebody, 'you can't do that any more' after 24 years' teaching, it is completely and utterly demoralizing. It's so alien to the way we work' (*Carol*).

Within a child-centred discourse, the 'persona of perfection' (Hargreaves, 1994) was accepted as the moral basis of a humanistic and vocational professional life, even though it was understood that it was impossible to achieve. However, audit accountability seeks a perfection that *is* possible. Inspectors' grading of a teacher's work in quantitative terms and the setting of targets for pupil achievement levels exemplifies this conclusion. Success and failure are constructed through a 'discourse of derision' (Ball, 1990) and a continuous onslaught on teacher adequacy. Leticia found 'every paper you open tells you you're not good enough, that we are responsible for all society's ills'. Veronica found this 'slowly eroding away at your confidence till you're beginning to doubt nearly everything that you do. "God, if I do it that way what'll he say, and if it goes wrong how will he react?" No day's going to be perfect but you want it to be perfect. You want everything to be right'. Continuous criticism strikes at the heart of the self-identity:

> For all those years you've tried to do your very best and then to be told, 'You're not good here, you're not good there' is a blow to your pride isn't it? We are pretty engaged with the kids, so any criticism of your teaching is a criticism of *you*. It's bound to be, you can't separate them.
>
> (*Aileen*)

It affects the inside of you, working on people's guilt feelings, working on people's sense of inadequacy. It's hitting people in the ego but it's also pushing buttons in their unconscious, so it's getting to very deep places.

(Naomi)

To move towards the new assigned social identity makes you 'feel ashamed. It's like licking their boots' *(Diane)*. Shame 'bears directly on self-identity because it is essentially anxiety about the adequacy of the narrative by means of which the individual sustains a coherent biography' (Giddens, 1991, p. 65). The other side of shame is pride. However, pride is continually vulnerable to reactions to others, 'being naked in front of the gaze of the onlooker' (Giddens, 1991, p. 65); in this case, inspectors:

I felt degraded by it. We've talked as a staff about this feeling of being undressed by it, of being laid bare, being laid naked. It is very much a sort of professional rape if you like ... You *are* accountable for what goes on in your classroom, I don't hide away from that, but it's done in such a way as to make you feel like a victim.

(Cloe)

Teacher dilemmas

We can see how these challenges bring on, among our teachers, the four Giddens' dilemmas noted earlier typical of experiences of the self in late modernity.

1   The previously unified self is in danger of becoming fragmented in a number of ways. There is a yearning by teachers to retain the old values, but strong pressure on them to adopt a new persona. The holism of child-centredness is being splintered in the focus on the child as pupil, of knowledge by the focus on subjects, and of teacher identity by the focus on managerial and marketable aspects of the new teacher role.

2   There is an assault on teacher autonomy, and an introduction of far-reaching strongly prescribed changes, sustained over a period, leaving teachers with a feeling of powerlessness. Little attention is paid to their views. They are no longer trusted. They are under almost continuous surveillance.

3   A strong note of uncertainty has been introduced into teachers' minds about their work and about their selves. The constant pressure and criticism breeds uncertainty in teachers about their abilities, aims, relationships and commitment to teaching. In some instances, there is a feeling of anomie (see Jeffrey & Woods, 1998), all sense of reality and who they are being lost. Guilt, shame, and loss of confidence ensue.

4   We have seen how commodified has come to challenge personalized experience. Consumerism has replaced care. Measurable quantities have replaced immeasurable qualities in assessment. Audit accountability sidesteps the personal and local, putting emphasis on the abstract and the universal. Competencies have replaced personal qualities as criteria of the good teacher.

These dilemmas induced 'fateful moments', when:

the individual is likely to recognize that she is faced with an altered set of risks and possibilities. In such circumstances, she is called on to question routinised habits of relevant kinds; even sometimes those most closely integrated with self-identity.

(Giddens, 1991 pp. 131–132)

The Ofsted inspection certainly had this effect on Shula:

> We can't separate self from what we actually do within the classroom. The Ofsted team cannot come in and say, 'We're looking at your teaching practice', without saying, 'We're looking at you as a person'. The self is a complex thing, with many layers which is constantly evolving and changing and developing, but by encapsulating the assessment in one week they've tried to make the self stand still. That's not what people are about ... They strip all off these layers and you feel as if you haven't got any real substance ... It's building back that self that is necessary for us. I find myself thinking, 'What's my purpose, what's my role? What am I going to do?' It goes right down to where you see yourself in the scheme of things and what's important. I've never, ever, ever, had something that's really made me question something so big all at once. I feel lost ... It was really getting down and saying, 'Who are you Shula, and what are you doing?' And asking the question 'if you were feeling like this, what the hell are you doing to the kids? What hope are you giving to them?' I've lost me in it somewhere and I've got to find me, if I can.
>
> (*Shula*)

Aileen was also struggling in the search for self:

> I still am worried; I haven't found me yet. I haven't found myself because I do in fact care. I don't feel that I'm working *with* the children any more, I'm working *at* the children but it's not a very pleasant experience. You feel responsible for every part of the school during an inspection, whether you had anything to do with some departments or not but at the same time I feel alienated from the whole process, divorced from it all.

Carol, similarly, was at an impasse:

> I don't want to be seen to be good, but I don't want to be seen to be crap either, I just want to get by. I don't rate the process, but I don't want to be beaten by it. I don't quite know what to do ...

How did teachers go about resolving these dilemmas? How did they emerge from their 'fateful moments'?

Identity work: meeting the challenges

Teachers engaged in 'identity work', which Snow & Anderson (1987) define as 'the range of activities individuals engage in to create, present, and sustain personal identities that are congruent with and supportive of the self-concept' (p. 1348). As with their sample of the homeless, so our sample of teachers, challenged by the new assigned social identity already outlined and lacking the power to pursue other varieties of identity work, engaged in a great deal of 'identity talk', involving the 'verbal construction and assertion of personal identities' (Snow & Anderson, 1987, p. 1348). However, it was not just talk. As we shall see, teacher talk conveyed a great deal of feeling. This is important, as the strongly traumatic negative feelings induced by the assigning of the new social identity—those of guilt, shame, fear, shock, etc.—needed to be countered if the personal identity were to be salvaged. We find in teachers' expressions, therefore, among some, certainly, feelings of shock, resignation and despair, but among others a great deal of anger, feelings of injustice, fighting qualities, pride, determination and resolve, courage, spirit and hope. Like Snow and Anderson's homeless, they have been disempowered, and are trying here 'to generate identities that provide them with a measure of self-worth and dignity'.

The easiest identity work in securing a new substantial self-identity comes to those teachers whose self-concept most accords with the new social identity. They simply 'embrace' the new identity, but there is still some 'talking up' to be done, to ensure and almost to celebrate a close fit. Laura, for example, was rebellious as a young person but had a breakdown after the failure of a relationship and she decided she could not let it happen again. 'I suffered because I was against things so much. Now I go with the flow and I am much happier. Inspections are opportunities to perform'. She talked herself up 'about how fine I feel and how I enjoy the work'. Larry 'grabbed the inspectors as often as I could. I was keen to show them what the children could do ... It is up to you as to whether you want to jump through those hoops'. Toni felt that others should accept that 'You can't be an individual in this system at the moment', and used the currency of the inspection discourse to reinforce her self-identity, feeling 'There's something to be said for using numbers to show your worth, providing that you are influencing the interpretation'.

However, on the whole, teachers were made to work a good deal harder in negotiating some consistency between self-concept and social identity. We found two major patterns of response among them. The first was to do with 'self-positioning', teachers summoning up their own reserves to refuse to embrace the new social identity, and to assert the merits of their own favoured self-identity. This was largely emotional work, establishing a platform for the more intellectual work of 'identity strategies' by which teachers would attempt to resolve the dilemmas that confronted them. There were a number of these, but they all point to the same conclusion—the dismemberment of the old substantial self-identity, and its replacement by a more fragmented one.

Self-positioning

Most of our teachers showed a strong resolve to maintain the Plowden self-identity, rejecting the new assigned social identity.

Refusal. Carol had to maintain the same level of humanism:

> For all those years you've aimed to be good, you have tried to do your very best and then to be told 'No, you're not good here, you're not good there' is a blow. You have your pride. You want the children to do well and you want to show the children that you care about them. So you can't take a step back from the self. It's all or nothing, you've really got to put everything in.

This meant that, if pressed, she would leave teaching:

> I don't like what we are being asked to do. You have to fit in to what is being demanded of you. What I am actually good at, I can't do any more, so I might as well try and find something that I am happier doing even it means I am paid at a lower level. I want to go with my self-esteem intact.

Corrine did leave, in between the inspections, and thought that she was going to regret it, 'but I didn't, I prefer to come in and go voluntarily now. If I had to do

Ofsted now, I wouldn't cope. One of my children is doing Key Stage 3 exams (at age 14), and the other is doing Key Stage 1 (age 7). There is no way that I could cope and go home and help them. It nearly destroyed my family last time'. While her childcare values coincided with her teaching values she could cope, but once they diverged she chose to maintain her personal values. Stephanie had been teaching for 8 years, and her experience of her first Ofsted inspection was traumatic. Prior to her second inspection she had already decided to have a break from teaching, and this enhanced her second inspection performance and confidence in her own self:

> At first they put you off. I was so nervous with them sitting there and one of them said after the first lesson 'Be a bit more lively', and I just laughed, because I am a bit of a drama queen. After that I said 'Stuff it, I will just be myself'.

She had decided to reject the new assigned substantial identity and maintain her original self-identity. Bronwyn, a far more experienced teacher, took an equally strong stand:

> I will actually turn around and say something if we are criticized for not doing the best for the children. I will look them straight in the face this time and say 'I love my job, and I am doing my very best'. Ofsted are not going to make me change because that would mean being something that I am not ... I am what I am from 30 years of teaching.

Self-assertion. Faced with the dilemma of powerlessness versus appropriation, teachers summoned up all their resolve. Carol was:

> determined that I am actually going to get through this, no matter what it takes, because if I didn't, it would seem that the 26 years that I have been teaching have been wiped out. How could I answer the question, 'What have I done with my life?'.

 Sophie sustained self-esteem by thinking, 'They might be able to tell us all the theory and how it should be done, but I'd like to see them actually do it. So in some ways I feel a bit superior to them because I feel that our job is more important than theirs'. Toni similarly reflected on the first day of the inspection, 'I'm better than any of them on my worst day'. Becky said,

> Although you could make a complete hash of something you're good at when there's somebody else there, I don't feel inadequate. I believe I'm a good teacher and that my children do well. I think you've got to believe in yourself.

Sometimes, the feeling of superiority was not enough. Formal complaint was required. Elvira, for example:

> was so angry and I wanted to hit out, and then as the week went on I got to the stage where I thought, 'I don't care, it doesn't matter, I know that I'm good at my job so it doesn't matter'. Then I thought 'Blow me, it does!' and I put this letter together thinking, 'I will let them know how I feel because it's important to me'.

At other times, teachers developed a 'bottom line': 'My safety barrier is that I can walk out of the job and tell the inspectors what I think'. The exit option was one solution to too much pressure, again illustrating a weakening of the vocational link:

> I know what I am doing, wherever I am doing it, they should trust me. I think I am a valuable commodity. If people push me too far I will say 'OK, I am going'. Although I need the money, I also need my sanity; that is more important to me.
>
> *(Clare)*

Shula was upset by the inspection, but eventually concluded 'it might well have been a good thing, in the sense that it made me start to kick back and say, "No way, no way, I'm not sitting back and taking this"'.

Identity strategies

The strategies teachers deployed all involved some separation of the self from the new, assigned social identity. They necessitated the development of new personal identities, sufficient to meet the ostensible requirements (although not the spirit) of the new social identity, while reserving and cultivating what to them were more important aspects of the self for their private life outside the teacher role. In this sense, their erstwhile substantial self-identities have been dismembered, the 'substantial' element of aspects they hold most near and dear now being displaced to life outside teaching, while their personal identities within teaching have become more 'situational', constructed to meet different situations and purposes with which they might be presented, but in which they feel they cannot invest their full selves. Naomi expresses the problem:

> I can't come to terms with all this. I really cannot believe it. I do love the kids but I can't go on with all this. Angela will come in and say she's been working all weekend or all night. I know she spends hours and hours planning her lessons, but I think she is wasting her life and I'm not prepared to give my whole life. I'm 48 years old and I need to have some of my life for myself. I feel extremely vulnerable with all this going on, I might even crack up and have the week off. I don't owe my life to this institution.

Self-displacement. Teachers, like others, will engage in identity work to dissipate the harmful effects of any incongruity. Even when Cloe found out that one of the new inexperienced teachers had been graded 'excellent', whereas her own grading had been 'satisfactory', this did not affect her because

> as I told you, it wasn't me. It was somebody else they looked at. They can think what they like, as far as I am concerned, I just don't want to know. They can please themselves what they do; I don't care. I will do what I have got to do. I will smile when I have to smile, I will be somebody else, when I have to be somebody else but they aren't going to get to *me*.

In schools that had had a second Ofsted inspection, teachers had acquired a certain streetwise knowledge that was empowering, and enabled them to counteract 'expropriation processes'; like Ofsted inspections, which 'reach not only spheres of day-to-day life but the heart of the self' (Giddens, 1991, p. 192). Cloe regained control of her self-identity by detaching:

myself from my work and it made me feel good. It gave some power back to me, to who I was. If I hadn't they would have skinned me alive like they did last time when I had all my guts hanging out. My whole career, my whole life was laid on the line for that 'bloody inspection'.

Cloe is still committed to her work, but it is a commitment that reflects a new personal identity, that of mainly raising achievement levels. She retains her humanism but has lost her sense of vocation that was constituted by a unified self-identity.

Francis adopted temporary ambivalence, 'I'm not resisting it, I'm just not accepting it at the moment, because there is enough pressure elsewhere'. Others treated it like a life trauma. Leticia 'decided I've just got to get through it, like most unpleasant things in life, just pretend it's not happening, though I'm not sure I know how to do that'. Clare 'felt good doing playground duty today when five girls and boys came up to give me a hug and a kiss, I thought, "Yes! this is what it's all about". I love these kids and that's got to triumph and I'm not going to think about the bad vibes'.

Being praised by inspectors caused even more problems, for this was announcing an identity that the teacher might not want, especially in the eyes of their colleagues. When Amy received a commendation from Ofsted, she was concerned that it might threaten her relationship with a colleague. 'I phoned her and said "I feel dreadful" but she said that she knew that I had a greater loyalty to my friendship with her. I would have been really upset if it had made a difference'. Similarly with the rest of her colleagues:

> When I sit in a staff room and put forward an idea I don't want people to just value my commendation because that's not me, that's about Ofsted and their skewed values system. I do not want to be judged by the number that has been stuck on me.
>
> *(Amy)*

Game playing. Goffman (1959) has written of how one 'presents oneself' in order to control the conduct of others, especially their responsive treatment of one. In 'playing the game', teachers acted out the new assigned social identity in inspection situations. Amy's analysis indicated how successful it was, 'It's no accident that both Larry and I are adult trainers and both got commended. We know how to put on a performance'. Keith remarked 'I don't think I will be able to go my own way as when I was on teaching practice with Ofsted coming up, I think it is going to be a bit more of an act to act up to what is needed'.

Game-playing is a defence. It is not for real, but something that is being enacted outside the really important frame of one's life where the innermost self resides. Most teachers were caught unawares with the first Ofsted inspections. The Plowden self-identity in its integrity was all that was on show, and they were extremely vulnerable. Hence the highly traumatic reactions (Jeffrey & Woods, 1998). But they were more prepared second time round. When the National Inspectors arrived 4 years after their first inspection, Cloe was determined 'that they wouldn't get to *me* this time. I distanced my "self" from the operation. I played the game and I'm pleased and satisfied about the way I did it'. Cloe's strategy was:

> that they weren't going to know who I was as a person. I was hiding behind the face of the Year 6 teacher. I smiled when I had to smile, but they weren't going to get to me like the last time. I came out of this inspection, thinking 'got you', not because of the result, but because they hadn't affected me. I am exhausted, like we all are, but they didn't affect who I was this time.

While Cloe expresses some satisfaction here, as individuals and as would-be vocationally dedicated teachers the orientation is troubling, for this is not their real selves. Toni wondered how far she was in control: 'Am I identifying things that are really there or are they being identified for me and I'm playing the game? I'm not the person I was when I was younger; it's been stamped out of me'. Diane's reaction to her own game playing was self-critical, 'I told myself that I wasn't going to play the game, but I am and I know they know I am. I don't respect myself for it'.

Victor was aware that he had to construct a new personal identity by negotiating between the new assigned identity and his self. 'We shouldn't have to go through this. It is a process that says we don't trust you. But I will stay and fight for the profession. It means I must play the game and it's a very trying game but I can't complain, I chose to do this'. Cloe, prior to her first Ofsted inspection, questioned the effect that the strategy being forced on her by the new assigned social identity was having on her personal identity:

> I'm just really worried about my own personality and my own emotions and I know that even if I'm nearly dead next week, I'll be putting on a show. I'll be belting around here like no teacher's ever belted around, smiling and being wonderful but I wonder what the cost will have been in terms of whether I would feel that what I have to offer in the future is sufficient. Am I going to feel that 'I'm not good enough' and that I'm going to have to find something else to do?

Game-playing can leave teachers ambivalent (Casey, 1995) about their self-identity. In the face of authority and loss of trust, uncertainty occurs and creates yet another dilemma for teachers.

Realignment. Realignment involves recognition that the self-identity is no longer a harmonious, integrated whole, and that it is composed of separate parts that cannot be blended together, and that indeed some significant areas are in tension with each other. This necessitates teachers reviewing the balance of their selves and social roles, and re-prioritizing. In all instances, the self-concept is paramount. Social roles have to be meaningful in the light of the self-concept. A common strategy here was to separate out the personal identities of home and school. Teacher values of humanism and vocationalism (in the sense of heartfelt commitment) were sustained in the former, but came under adjustment in the latter. This was particularly true of vocationalism. There was thus less of what one might term the 'quality' self in the personal identity reconstructed for school.

Some insisted on maintaining a practical balance, not forsaking domestic and family affairs for the demands of an inspection, as many teachers have been wont to do (Jeffrey & Woods, 1998). The mother of Rachael, Mixstead's head teacher, for example, had a 90th birthday some 200 miles away on the Saturday prior to an Ofsted inspection beginning the following Monday, and she decided it had to go ahead. 'Ofsted is not the big thing in my life until Sunday night. I am going to spend a little time sorting out my assembly for Monday but most of my focus is on my mother's birthday'.

This was a way of keeping things evenly balanced. On the other hand, Frederica, with 30 years teaching experience, began distancing her personal self from her social identity between Ofsted inspections. Prior to her first inspection she had been resistant to the idea of change, or game-playing, or any other strategic device: 'I'm not going to change my way of working. If they can do better let them try'. However, after a prolonged absence due to ill health between inspections, she re-assessed her vocational commitment. Originally she saw herself as 'putting in a lot of energy, because I'm that sort of person anyway, I'll put 150% into anything I do'. However,

> Since I have been ill I have prioritized so much and I have realized what is valuable in life. So, with this inspection I thought 'What is the point of using energy on something that really can't be changed?'

Clare's commitment has very clearly changed from vocationalism to instrumentalism:

> I remember my first school in Brixton. I didn't have children of my own and those children were my life. I loved them, and the parents loved me. It was wonderful, it was so rewarding. They were the best years of my life as far as my professionalism is concerned. It was based on my interaction with the children and my own intellectual thought being imparted to the children. But I don't feel I have a career anymore, not at all. This is just a job, a means to an end to earn some money until I am retired. I have no commitment whatsoever, it has gone out the window. I am more important than my job, as are my family, my husband and my son. There is no feeling that this is my vocation, my way of life, that I was meant to do this.

In terms of career, Clare's unified self-identity has disintegrated. Her personal self now resides in her family situation, while her commitment to teaching has become purely instrumental. 'It's a job and I do it and I'm also *me*. But there's no place for *me* now'.

Teachers are practising a form of 'strategic compliance' (Lacey, 1977), wherein the individual accepts the prevailing system but entertains private reservations. The acceptance and the compliance, however, are made to differing degrees with differing feelings. Cloe, for example, 'decided to comply, to go along with it because otherwise you tear yourself in half if you're always working against what you believe in. I've shuffled my beliefs away in a back drawer somewhere'. In all, then, it is a very reluctant, grudging kind of compliance, with even more seething beneath the surface at times.

> I will cope with it, I will take it on board, I will do all the things I'm meant to do and I'll scrape and bow and I will back the head teacher and the school to the hilt. I won't let anybody down. But secretly inside myself I'm very, very angry that we're being made to go through this.
>
> (*Bronwen*)

In these cases, the new school personal identity is experienced as being in sharp conflict with the self-concept. The full-blown instrumentalism of the identity is at complete odds with the humanistic vocationalism of the self. The more the self is dedicated to the latter values, the more difficult is the resolution of this problem.

Conclusion

For primary school teachers, local trust relations have been reconstituted in terms of audit accountability, position in national and local league tables as decided by SATs and Ofsted inspection reports, and by grading by inspectors. The introduction of literacy and numerary programmes has further reduced teacher qualities to a short and narrow list of competences (Cox, 1998). The 'expert systems' behind these policies now define teachers' social identities by 'performativity' (Ball, 1998; Broadfoot, 1998). This is how they are known within the official educational world. But it is not how they are known to themselves. This has brought on severe identity crises for teachers. For the mid-career teachers of our researches, a unified self-identity had been unchallenged for many years. It was deep in the heart, but not in the forefront of their minds. The challenge has caused them much heart-searching, and has forced them to reconsider and reconstruct.

For most, their new self-identities show some key changes from those that pertained during the Plowden era. In general terms, our data suggest a retention of the humanistic values, most evident in teachers' resolution to remain dedicated to caring, to the child, and to holism, even though they are at some odds with the current rationalist discourse in education. There is a weakening, however, of the vocationalism. Certainly, the physical conditions described earlier by Nias (1989) of teaching occupying their 'sleeping as well as their working hours' may still apply to many, but then it was a matter of choice, of 'giving their all to work'; whereas now, it is a matter of weight of prescription, of 'work demanding all'. One involves integration of the self, the other disintegration. There is no easy resolution of Giddens' late modernity dilemmas.

In general, teachers have been forced to become more strategic and political in defending their self-identities against the countervailing inroads of the new teacher social identity. Their priorities have been to hold on to their values and their self-esteem, while adjusting their commitment and other aspects of the holistic approach. Current trends, therefore, appear to be working against the conception of primary education that Nias, for one, had in the 1980s:

> Primary teaching has a bottomless appetite for the investment of scarce personal resources, such as time, interest and energy. The more of these resources that individuals choose to commit to their work, the better for pupils, parents and fellow staff, and the more rewards the individual teacher is likely to reap, in terms of appreciation, recognition, self-esteem, and, perhaps, self-extension. Therefore, it could reasonably be argued that children, teachers, and parents will all benefit, if teachers are motivated to give more to their work than simply the physical presence and minimal level of competence required. . . .
>
> (1989, p. 208)

For education, this is clearly a serious matter. There is no direct route to changes in teaching and learning, restructuring education or raising educational standards. Such desired outcomes, however politically willed, have to be processed through teachers, who have feelings, values, beliefs, thoughts, cherished ideals; in short, identities. Before they can apply themselves to best effect, they have to work out how to organize a personal identity or identities congruent with the social identity and self-concept—to know who they are. As Snow & Anderson (1987, p. 1365) among others argue, in opposition to Maslow (1962), such concerns are just as important as physiological and safety needs. As a teacher told Riseborough (1981, p. 15): 'You know, if you take this (status) away, not all the money in the world will make him feel content with his job, and this is what teaching is all about. You've got to feel right'. In most cases, as we have seen, the identity work aimed toward such equanimity has involved the deployment of strategies to resist the new assigned social identity, to extol aspects of the old, to construct new personal identities congruent with the self-concept, and to disguise situational identities. Education is the loser here on two counts. First, identity work consumes enormous emotional and intellectual energy that might otherwise be dedicated to teaching. Second, the teacher's personal identity in the new order is partial, fragmented, and inferior to that of the old in that teachers retain a sense of the ideal self, but it is no longer in teaching. The personal identity of work has become a situational one, designed to meet the instrumental purposes of audit accountability. Teachers' real selves are held in reserve, to be realized in other situations outside school or in some different future within.

It is in this sense that the evidence presented here challenges the poststructural scepticism about an essential self (Maclure, 1993; Davies & Harré, 1994) and their championing of a multifaceted self, one that is not constant and constraining but which recreates itself anew in different social situations. Yet, in some ways, there is evidence here to support this view. The dilemmas are only partially resolved. Teachers have to live with them—there is no neat transition. Identities are thus in flux, there is no settled state. There are signs of multiple and situational identities that were not there before in the integrated self-identity. However, as Snow & Anderson (1987, p. 1364) point out, personal identities are not static, but alter with time. In the case of their sample, 'distancing' was more a feature of the early stages, evolving later into 'embracement'. Will teachers similarly grow more into the new assigned social identity? Some will, no doubt, especially younger teachers who are fashioning personal identities in teaching for the first time. For our mid-career teachers, it is more a matter of regaining control. Identity work goes on. There is no endpoint, no completion of task. The new self-identities are much more volatile than the old.

References

Alexander, R. (1992) *Policy and Practice in Primary Education* (London, Routledge).
Audit Commission (1989) *Assuring Quality in Education: the role of local authority inspectors and advisors* (London, HMSO).
Ball, D. (1972) Self and identity in the context of deviance: the case of criminal abortion, in: R.A. Scott & J.D. Douglas (Eds) *Theoretical Perspectives on Deviance* (New York, Basic Books).
Ball, S.J. (1990) *Politics and Policy Making in Education: explorations in policy sociology* (London, Routledge).
Ball, S.J. (1994) *Education Reform: a critical and post-structural approach* (Buckingham, Open University Press).
Ball, S.J. (1998) Performativity and fragmentation in 'Postmodern Schooling', in: J. Carter (Ed.) *Postmodernity and Fragmentation of Welfare* (London, Routledge).
Broadfoot, P. (1998) Quality standards and control in higher education: what price lifelong learning? *International Studies in Sociology of Education*, 8(2), pp. 155–181.
Broadhead, P. (1987) A blue print for the good teacher. The HMI/DES model of good primary practice, *British Journal of Educational Studies*, 35(1), pp. 57–72.
Casey, K. (1995) *Work, Self and Identity* (London, Routledge).
Central Advisory Council for Education in England (1967) *Children and Their Primary Schools* (The Plowden Report) (London, HMSO).
Cox, B. (Ed.) (1998) *Literacy is not Enough: essays on the importance of reading* (Manchester, Manchester University Press).
Dale, I.R. (1989) *The State and Education Policy* (Milton Keynes, Open University Press).
Davies, B. & Harré, R. (1994) Positioning, conversation and the production of selves, *Journal for the Theory of Social Behaviour*, 20(1), pp. 43–63.
Evans, J. & Penney, D. (1994) Whatever happened to good advice? Service and inspection after the Education Reform Act, *British Educational Research Journal*, 20(5), pp. 519–583.
Giddens, A. (1991) *Modernity and Self-Identity* (Cambridge, Polity).
Goffman, E. (1959) *The Presentation of Self in Everyday Life* (London, Penguin).

Hammersley, M. & Atkinson, P. (1995) *Ethnography: principles in practice* (London, Routledge).

Hargreaves, A. (1994) *Changing Teachers, Changing Times: teacher's work and culture in the postmodern age* (London, Cassell).

Jeffrey, B. & Woods, P. (1998) *Testing Teachers: the impact of school inspections on primary teachers* (London, Falmer).

Lacey, C. (1977) *The Socialization of Teachers* (London, Methuen).

Maclure, M. (1993) Arguing for your self: identity as an organizing principle in teachers' jobs and lives, *British Educational Research Journal*, 19(4), pp. 311–322.

Maslow, A.H. (1962) *Toward a Psychology of Being* (New York, Panthcon).

Nias, J. (1989) *Primary Teachers Talking* (London, Routledge).

Osborn, M., McNess, E. & Broadfoot, P. (2000) *What Teachers Do: changing policy and practice in primary education* (London, Continuum).

Pollard, A. (Ed.) (1987) *Children and Their Primary Schools* (Lewes, Falmer Press).

Power, M. (1994) *The Audit Explosion* (London, Demos).

Riseborough, G.F. (1981) Teacher careers and comprehensive education: an empirical study, *Sociology*, 15(3), pp. 352–381.

Sikes, P., Measor, L. & Woods, P. (1985) *Teacher Careers: crises and continuities* (Lewes, Falmer Press).

Snow, D. & Anderson, L. (1987) Identity work among the homeless: the verbal construction and avowal of personal identities, *American Journal of Sociology*, 92(6), pp. 1336–1371.

Sugrue, C. (1998) *Complexities of Teaching: child-centred perspectives* (London, Falmer).

Troman, G. & Woods, P. (2001) *Primary Teachers' Stress* (London, Routledge-Falmer).

Woods, P. (1995) *Creative Teachers in Primary Schools* (Buckingham, Open University Press).

Woods, P. & Jeffrey, B. (1996) *Teachable Moments: the art of teaching in primary schools* (Buckingham, Open University Press).

Woods, P., Jeffrey, B., Troman, G. & Boyle, M. (1997) *Restructuring Schools, Reconstructing Teachers* (Buckingham, Open University Press).

CHAPTER 12

TEACHERS DOING THEIR 'ECONOMIC' WORK

John Smyth and Geoffrey Shacklock

Re-making Teaching (1998), London: Routledge, pp. 77–106

An ideology of production or the production of an ideology?

In this chapter we want to explore the basis for much of the educational reform that has come to surround teachers' work in the past two decades or so. The case has been made from several quarters that since the 1960s there has been growing disaffection and disenchantment worldwide from parents and the wider community with schooling, such that: 'There exists today an "informed scepticism" about educational change that distinguishes the 1980s from the 1960s and has led to the declining appeal of grand principles and all-embracing educational theories' (OECD 1989: 136). The evidential basis for this alleged shift has been made less than clear on most occasions but, notwithstanding, significant changes have proceeded as if the claims had a solid foundation.

The three aspects of recent educational reform that have caught our attention are: (a) an infatuation with issues of relevance of schooling for the world of work, and its expression in the 'new vocationalism'; (b) the emergence of 'enterprise culture' as a convenient rallying point for conservative educational restorationists; and (c) from an earlier period, starting in the early 1980s, 'quality' as a dominant theme for educational policy discourse – one used with considerable force to advance the debate about what education should look like after what commentators on the New Right label the permissive and profligate 1960s and 1970s.

Probably the most pervasive and consistent themes and arguments put in respect of the need for the reform of teaching and education are that it is necessary in order to satisfy the requirements of a rapidly changing world of work. The argument is generally couched in terms of the alleged shift from Fordist to post-Fordist forms of organisation and production, most notably, the move to short production lines, niche marketing, teamwork and partnerships, flatter hierarchies, outsourcing, and the construction and management of images and impressions. (For an elaboration of this 'new work order', see Gee *et al*, 1996 and Kumar 1995; and, for more detailed accounts of how this is worked through in educational reforms, see Bowe *et al.* 1992; Ball 1994; Gewirtz *et al.* 1995; Hartley 1992; Welch 1996; Smyth 1996a.)

The 'new vocationalism' as an educational response

In respect of teaching, arguments about the so-called 'new work order' boil down to whether the wider forces of globalisation, international competitiveness and economic production are forcing and requiring the new marketised, consumerist and vocationalised relationships within schools and teaching we continually hear about, or whether there are other possible interpretations. One possibility that deserves consideration and exploration is that proffered by Moore (1987), who argues that what has become known as the 'new vocationalism' in schooling may in point of fact be more of a cover for, and not a direct response to, the economic forces at all – rather it is an expression of a:

> new 'hidden curriculum' of the possessive individualism of market economics [which] reflects political and ideological imperatives, rather than the immediate needs of the economy. The 'new vocationalism' is seen as an ideology of production regulating education rather than as an educational ideology servicing production.
>
> (p. 227)

Some compelling reasons can be advanced for this alternative explanation. Moore (1987) argues that:

> The term 'new vocationalism' can be taken as a convenient convention for glossing over a complex set of interrelated developments ranging [in the UK context] from the Technical and Vocational Education Initiative (TVEI), the Certificate of Pre-Vocational Education (CPVE), the Youth Training Scheme (YTS) and the General Certificate of Secondary Education (GCSE), to more specific practices such as profiling and wider institutional arrangements such as targeted funding, the interventions of the Manpower Services Commission (MSC) within the educational system and the National Council for Vocational Qualifications (NCVQ).
>
> (p. 228)

Constellations like these are bound together and held in place by:

> a general movement towards an occupationalist integration between the education system and the occupational system, mediated by a behavioural approach to skill training and supported by new institutional arrangements which construct, legitimate and enforce new definitions of knowledge.
>
> (p. 228)

Moore (1987) explains that the 'hidden curriculum' behind notions like the 'new vocationalism' can be captured in what MacPherson (1962, cited in Moore 1987: 231) labelled the 'political theory of possessive individualism'. Put simply, this view holds that individuals are composed of personal capacities made up of bundles of skills, and that they operate in society as 'proprietors of their own capacities' in exchange relationships with each other. The role of government is to provide for the protection of this property and facilitate the orderly conditions under which exchange can occur. In other words, the role of government is restricted to setting up pedagogical processes to enable the creation and delivery of skills modules and to provide for subsequent accreditation. Clearly, within such arrangements, education comprises processes both to promote 'possessive individualism' while also emphasising 'methodological individualism' – what Wellington (1993) calls the 'press for relevance', 'transferable and core skills', skills that prepare for 'rapid technological change', as well as processes that improve 'attitudes to work and industry' – ideas that all sound

decidedly old-fashioned, protectionist and outmoded in these new times of the unfettered and free reign of market forces!

Moore (1987) says a 'new hegemonic form' is thus created with which to restructure the educational field – 'its discourses, practices, institutional arrangements and
principles of power, control and legitimation' (p. 228). It is not so much that classroom and teaching practices are immediately and directly changed through official
proclamations or centrally produced materials and curricula (although that can happen
in the case of some individual teachers), but rather that teachers are likely selectively
and pragmatically to appropriate what they see as being useful to satisfy 'the specific
needs of particular groups of students at given times' (p. 228). In other words, 'There
is no simple top-down imposition of any particular approach or policy' (p. 228), but
rather a more gradual creation of:

> attempts to define the effective characteristics of an ideology which is in the
> process of acquiring a hegemonic position within the educational field and which,
> therefore, can both control the agenda of the educational debate and, by becoming
> the orthodoxy, force liberal and radical opponents into a heterodox position
> which undermines their credibility and legitimacy
>
> (p. 229)

'Enterprise culture' as the new educational organiser

Another good illustration of the emergence of a new hegemonic form is the concept
of 'enterprise culture' which has entered the educational discourse in recent times.
This new darling of the educational conservatives in the 1990s has supplanted vocationalism as the glitz word of the 1980s – a new signifier and organiser of all that
is considered virtuous and good educationally speaking. As Wellington (1993) notes,
this is in part a language game, as the phraseology and the lexicon shift effortlessly
from vocationalism to enterprise, with all of the connotations that the latter has
about increased emphasis on personal and individual qualities of: initiative, drive,
determination, self-monitoring, independence, autonomy, self-reliance, risk-taking,
decision making, flexibility and leadership.

Coffield (1990) says there is no consensus about the meaning of enterprise: 'We
are not dealing with a tightly defined concept but a farrago of hurrah words'
(Wellington 1993: 34). Vocationalism is 'out' because it is considered to place too
much emphasis on social and life skills preparation and focus around a collective
emphasis, and insufficient on 'competence' as a response to the need for enterprise
initiatives, which are on the ascendancy. One of the advantages of a confusing word
like 'enterprise' in education is that it is so ambiguous it can be accommodated to
all manner of divergent perspectives. As Watts (1993) shows, the political power of
a word like enterprise sits comfortably across the spectrum: with governments finding
the notion of 'entrepreneurship' acceptable because of the way it conjures up notions
of people sustaining activities on their own; with employers who are happy with
educating students to 'work in enterprises'; and, with progressives who resonate with
the adjectival meaning of 'enterprising skills' (p. 47). Indeed, enterprise is a very
potent political word because it can be 'unpacked and used for all sorts of different
purposes' (Watts 1993: 48). In Watts' (1993) view: 'there [is] something for everyone
in the notion of "enterprise". It ... provide[s] a rich base for education–business
partnerships supported by government, with each putting the frame they prefer ...
around it' (p. 48). It serves to reinforce the power of language, too: 'If you can find
words which have that degree of ambiguity, you can form alliances which you

wouldn't be able to form otherwise, building upon that ambiguity ... Ambiguous language can be enormously influential' (Watts 1993: 49).

'Quality' the longest-lasting educational aerosol word

'Quality' has for some time been a canopy or umbrella term within which officially to house a limited and constrained set of interpretations about the condition of education and schooling, and a basis upon which to warehouse an equally limiting, atomistic and impoverished set of prescriptions as to what ought legitimately to constitute the work of teachers and schooling. From its beginnings in the mid-1980s, quality has been used effectively as a necessary albeit decidedly ambiguous ingredient for a much needed educational restoration. Organisations like the OECD have featured prominently in propagating an international discourse about quality schooling – one that appears natural, common sense, and as having all the right hallmarks of institutional respectability about it. Documents like *The Teacher Today* (OECD 1990), following close on the heels of *Schools and Quality: An International Report* (OECD 1989), make the point repeatedly about the absence of 'quality' from schools, and how teachers need to be reconstructed so as to restore it or acquire more of it. The reason we cryptically describe quality as an aerosol word is that it has infiltrated the educational discourse in precisely the manner of an aerosol deodorant – it is sprayed around! Furthermore, its timely appearance – coinciding as it does with the fiscal retreat by governments around the world from universal and equitable provision of public education so as to allow the market to do its work – has meant that quality has the fragrance of a bouquet word used to cover up the slightly offensive odour surrounding the decay of the public provision of schooling.

A useful but by no means complete way of portraying the way quality has been constructed (and on some occasions contested) as a vehicle for carrying educational discourse, can be gleaned from *Schools and Quality*, and we intend to highlight some of its key themes and elements. We should offer a caveat at the outset – while we do not regard international consortia like the OECD as being the *only* or necessarily the most influential of players in framing educational reform, they have certainly been *one* of the more influential, and while we will never be able to ascertain accurately the full extent of educational policy borrowing from them by governments, we cannot be dismissive of what appears to be their likely widespread effects as policy disseminators and legitimators. Our thesis would be that the OECD has been an important rallying point since the mid-1980s as an international clearinghouse for a number of highly questionable 'solutions' to what is wrong with education – most of which, as it turns out, constitute little more than a slogan system under the umbrella of 'quality'. We will explain this in more detail in a moment.

While much play is made in the Introduction to *Schools and Quality* (OECD 1989) about the importance of not having 'a single, tight definition of "quality"', the need for 'a more detached perspective', a 'restrained aim [so as] to analyse differing interpretations of quality', wanting only to 'inform the debate' rather than 'provid[ing] policy makers with *the* right answers', or crafting 'a standard model or plan that can be implemented in a "top-down" fashion', and the difficulty of 'apply[ing] these goals across OECD countries', it seems to us that when the report is considered as a whole, this lamenting and handwringing has more to do with the conceptual and practical difficulties of imposing a view than it has to do with any deep-seated pre-disposition not to do it *per se*. The reason we say this is that in the latter sections of the report, once the messy conceptual issues are temporarily laid to rest, the writers get down in remarkably business-like fashion to what looks like a laying out of a quite specific cachet of 'particular policies and practices' (p. 11).

It seems that 'quality' was settled upon by the OECD as an organising construct for what needed to be *done to schools* (our deliberate choice of term) to emphasise the required shift in ideology from a focus on materialist expansion that had characterised the first three post-war decades, to a sharp break with that. Quality was used as a contradistinction to what was regarded (in the veiled terms of the report) as an overdue extension of the worldwide materialist extension of resources to schooling. Reference is made in the report to an earlier OECD document *Compulsory Schooling in a Changing World* (1983), in which the term 'quality' first appeared as counter to the continuation of 'tangible improvements'.

From the beginning, the emphasis on quality in *Schools and Quality* was, therefore, couched in terms of the need for 'reactions to the era of growth' (p. 15) – where there is only the feeblest of attempts by the writers of the report to disguise their endorsement of the view that as 'OECD economies faltered in the 1970s ... the simple formula "more education, more prosperity" had been found wanting ... The link between education and social mobility no longer appeared self-evident' (p. 16). In barely disguised glee, the report goes on to describe the fall in educational expenditures that occurred in OECD countries along with the questions being raised (we are not sure by whom) about 'value for money' and 'how efficient schools were'. From this oeuvre, we regard it as a relatively short step to the ideas the OECD sees as the preferred policy options, most notably:

- quality couched in terms of economic imperatives (p. 19);
- qualified support for the re-emergence of 'human capital' views (p. 20);
- the importance of education attending to the 'phenomenon of international competition' (p. 21); and,
- increased pressures on schools for greater accountability (p. 24).

While many of these are carefully hedged and qualified in the report it is hard not to form the opinion that the OECD was not altogether opposed to what it regarded as these self-evident and natural tendencies, and that indeed some of them might not only have been worthwhile but considerably overdue.

The key themes addressed in the report are conceptually and practically separated and fall into the categories of curriculum; teachers; school organisation; appraisal, assessment and monitoring; and resources. As with most policy positions, what is explicitly revealed, focused upon and included, is as revealing as the silences and what remains unspoken. In this document there is an overwhelming ideological and conceptual consistency about the frame factors considered necessary for an undeclared and preferable process of remaking teaching – it comes through in the tenor and the tone of the document and in its cultural portrayal of teaching as a subservient technical process. The remedy for the slippage in standards and rigour of teaching lies, it says, in the provision of an entitlement to the 'basics of curriculum for all – a core' (p. 55), in a context where there is greater 'relevance to modern society' (p. 55) through 'work-oriented and practical studies' (p. 61), and with an abiding emphasis on 'clear planning objectives and evaluation procedures' (p. 63). Teachers are to be brought back into line, it says, by 'attracting good recruits' (p. 72), preparing them 'effectively' with the right measure of balance between theory and practice, and by incorporating proper role models through 'lead teachers', 'induction', and ensuring this orientation is held in place with 'competency approaches', appropriate and continuing 'inservice' and 'career structures' (pp. 75–9).

School organisation is construed as a grab bag of items contributing to this overall policy thrust in the form of a focus on 'cycles of schooling and articulation between levels' (p. 86), 'staff/student ratios and class sizes' that are not necessarily at the lower end of the scale (p. 87), higher levels of 'time on-task' (p. 89), extended length of the school day and school year (p. 91), more attention to 'homework' (p. 91) and reduced student 'absenteeism' (p. 91) – all within a context of a 'selected and trained ... powerful principal' (p. 97), albeit exercising a 'participatory style' of decision making (p. 95) in circumstances where teaching draws on the manifest benefits of enhanced 'information technology' (p. 96). In many respects these are educational softeners for the essence of what the OECD regards as the *sine qua non* of 'evaluation', 'appraisal' and 'assessment' of teaching, learning, curriculum and the school (notwithstanding that the pursuit of these brings with it an acknowledged increase in costs). The 'search for efficiency' (p. 115) is not far below the surface here as 'school ethos' (p. 105), 'teacher appraisal' (p. 103), the 'performance of students' (p. 105) and 'the education system as a whole' (p. 122) are monitored through 'central inspectorates' (p. 109), 'national and international' statistical indicators (p. 110) and, if all that does not do the job, then 'parental choice' (p. 106) through marketisation. Resources are considered important, but mainly to 'maintain minimum standards' (p. 119) and to ensure a context of flexible delivery of 'educational aims' (p. 120).

The similarity and the overall tenor of these reforms bear a remarkable resemblance to a set of recommendations for educational reform proposed by the World Bank in its *Priorities and Strategies for Education* (World Bank 1995). Remembering that this organisation is working ostensibly for poor countries assisting them in development activities, it is interesting that many of the same remedies keep appearing. Quoting from Watson's (1996) critique of that review:

> As the Review says, 'Curricula and syllabi should be closely tied to performance standards and measures of outcome' (p. 7). It is also argued that standards would be improved if teachers have a good grasp of their subject, if the school year can be extended, and if the instructional time can be made more flexible ... and if homework could be set regularly. Above all it is felt that there should be greater institutional autonomy. Head teachers, parents and school governors should be given greater power to run their own institutions because this would involve the local community in ensuring that good standards are achieved. 'School based leadership ensures an effective climate for learning' (p. 8).
>
> (pp. 47–8)

It is hard not to reach the conclusion that this veritable cornucopia of educationally conservative elements of what is considered to constitute educational 'quality' are not somehow the vestiges of a now defunct corpus of 'teacher and school effectiveness' literature discredited and discarded some time ago (see Angus 1993; Proudford and Baker 1995). Like its sibling 'excellence', quality makes about as much sense to teachers as the Latin mottoes once emblazoned on school letterheads and school uniforms. Both are hurrah words that are used simultaneously as buzzwords and as criteria for success – herein lies their problem.

So far in this chapter we have argued that much of the ideology or restructuring that has affected teachers, at least in English-speaking countries, has been incubated in and through international organisations. The indirect effect has been the promotion of certain concepts which, while they seem fairly innocuous, bring with them some unfortunate baggage, mostly of an educationally conservative persuasion.

In the next part of this chapter we provide a way of 'reading' how dominant discourses of teaching are constructed through the language employed.

Developing a 'reading position' on teaching

Oppositional and resistant reading

When we speak of a 'reading position' (Hodge and Kress 1993: 180) we are referring to the act of adopting a declared political position with respect to how we regard teaching. This is not to say that we intend adopting some overt partisan political position, but rather to argue the importance of taking a considered, resistant and strategic stance in which the intent is to open up debate and discussion about the multiple pedagogical perspectives that inform and shape reaching. We believe it is important to attempt to break out of the official forms of totalising language and discourse currently operating to frame teaching as alluded to in the earlier part of this chapter, and to find instead new and more energising discourses, images and forms of signification. The way we produce social and psychological realities are sometimes referred to as 'discursive practices' (Bizzell 1992; Harre and Gillett 1994). Davies and Harre (1990) put it that:

> a discourse is to be understood as an institutionalised use of language and language-like sign systems. Institutionalisation can occur at the disciplinary, the political, the cultural and the small group level. There can also be discourses that develop around a specific topic . . . Discourses can compete with each other or they can create distinct and incompatible versions of reality. To know anything is to know it in terms of one or more discourses.
>
> (p. 45)

How we position ourselves reflects something about a range of aspects to which we attach value, as well as telling us about what we consider to be important:

> Once having taken up a position as one's own, a person inevitably sees the world from the vantage point of that position and in terms of the particular images, metaphors, story lines and concepts which are made relevant within the particular discursive practice in which they are positioned.
>
> (Davies and Harre 1990: 46)

What we are reacting against and resisting here are the impoverished forms of 'tunnel vision' and the 'failure of political imagination' (Walter 1996) that have currently come to paralyse what passes as 'official' discourses about education and teaching – the kind of ideas behind code words like 'quality', 'enterprise' and 'excellence'. Trying to move away from the dominant economistic, reductionist and exclusively resourced-based views currently holding sway in educational discussion means that we need to be much more tuned into the voices and forms of knowing that are pushed to the margins – that means, the least advantaged in our schools, including the voices of students, parents and teachers.

The oppositional and resistant reading (Kress 1985; Janks 1991) which we wish to bring to an understanding of the work of teaching emerges out of a critical approach to language awareness (Fairclough 1992a) – one that regards readers (as well as actors in particular social contexts) as being vulnerable and open to manipulation unless they understand how language constructs and locates individuals and groups in certain ways. The reason 'dominant' and 'dominated' discourses are important, Fairclough (1992b) argues, is that certain views get to be represented, sustained and maintained while others are relegated to the category of being subservient, unworthy, unimportant or irrelevant. Furthermore, while some views are naturalised and labelled as common sense, others are considered dangerous or deviant As Fairclough (1992b) puts it: 'The stake is more than "mere words"; it is controlling the contours of the political world, it is legitimising policy, and it is sustaining power relations' (p. 90).

To take an example; if the language in which teaching is spoken about is predominantly that of productivity improvement, value added, cost-efficiency and effectiveness, measurement of achievement, learning outcomes, flexible delivery, markets, and the like, then it should not be too surprising if this lexicon gradually begins to have the appearance of being credible natural, logical and a common-sense way of talking about what is important in teaching. What gets excluded or rendered inaudible are the indigenous discourses teachers use to represent their work. Again from Fairclough (1992b):

> if a discourse type so dominates an institution that dominated types are more or less entirely suppressed or contained, then it will cease to be seen as arbitrary (in the sense of being one among several possible ways of 'seeing' things) and will come to be seen as *natural*, and legitimate because it is simply *the* way of conducting oneself.
>
> (p. 91)

When dominant viewpoints do not completely encase or obliterate, they exist in relations of 'opposition' to a dominant one: 'The linguist Michael Halliday calls one type of oppositional discourse the anti-language. Anti-languages are set up and used as conscious alternatives to the dominant or established discourse types (Fairclough 1992b: 91).

While a reading position is crucial to us as researchers in order to have way of situating the violence being wreaked on teachers through so-called reform processes, it is equally important to us as well having regard to the fact that we are not ideologically innocent, either. In the kind of research we do into teachers' work we consider ourselves to be involved in a form of critical literacy that is something akin to 'reading and writing against the grain of academic discourse' (Kramer-Dahl 1995). In other words, we are constantly struggling with maintaining an awareness that we are confronted with a contradiction. The kind of up-close inquiry we engage in with teachers can simultaneously contribute to being 'a form of regulation and exploitation and a potential mode of resistance, celebration and solidarity' (Batsleer *et al.* 1985: 9–10). It is only if we continue to struggle with what Threadgold (1988) calls 'critical examination of our discursive positioning' (p. 329) that we are able to see how our own agenda as researchers contradicts and is implicated in reproducing stereo-typical representations of their work.

While it was an agonising process of travelling this far in coming to grips with our own positionality as researchers *vis-à-vis* teachers and learning, this paled by significance to the task of trying to find where to start the dialogue about the counter discourse of teaching. In the end, it seemed that Richard Pring (1996) provided the breakthrough we needed. He conceptualised dominant or hegemonic discourse as being concerned with 'defending standards' through the by now familiar 'site-based management with conditions for quality assurance, centralisation of control, . . . diminishing unit of resource, and quasi-market conditions with the attendant language of "performance indicators", "efficiency gains", etc.' (p. 139). Pring (1996) likens the counter-hegemonic to the 'affirmation of an ideal' – a moral framework for discussion and inquiry and from within which all students can receive an education according to age, ability and aptitude. There is a major contradiction here – research about matters committed to defending standards is 'perceived by those who endure them as an intrusion into a distinctively educational world, and perceived by those who promote them as the protection of educational standards [and, therefore] as proper' (p. 139). This impasse can only ever be resolved, Pring (1996) says, if research attempts to understand 'how children learn and behave and how teachers plan and teach and how schools reconcile the many demands upon them' (p. 139). These are important research questions, and much research may not be addressing them: 'That is why educational researchers must, by and large, be in close touch with educational practice' (p. 139).

Any informed discussion about teaching has to begin with an acknowledgment of the inherent complexity of the work. Pring (1996) again:

> Teaching is, as we all know, a very complex activity – made even more so by the social and institutional framework within which it takes place. Those who are not aware of that complexity and of the subtle ways in which interactions between teacher and learner, and between teacher and teacher take place, will try to impose tidy and simple categories to provide a framework ... which is manageable. But in doing so they will say something which will seem irrelevant to the world teachers inhabit.
>
> (pp. 139–40)

A starting point might be with what Kupferberg (1996) characterises as 'the rather disordered and unstructured everyday reality of teaching' (p. 227) – which is not meant to be insulting to teachers, but acknowledges that 'teachers spend their days in a social reality where the need to improvise and to be highly alert to unexpected events is [high]' (p. 229). This situation in which 'reflection-in-action' counts more than 'technical rationality' (Schon 1983) generates a confrontation. As Kremer-Hayon (1994) says of teachers' knowledge:

> technical rationality depends on the agreement of clear ends and means which cannot work in confusing and ambiguous situations, where conflicting paradigms and pluralistic views are accepted as inherently characteristic ... [P]rofessional practice has unpredictable elements which cannot be dealt with by systematic pre-planning.
>
> (pp. 54–5)

This is quite different to 'reflection-in-action' which is a real world activity based upon 'using knowledge, of thinking about something while doing it ... and is characterised by spontaneous and intuitive behaviour' (Kremer-Hayon 1994: 54–5). This need to craft teaching knowledge on-the-job and through experience is related to an understanding of the nature of students, why they are in classrooms and the

> very real problem of maintaining some kind of discipline among inherently unruly pupils who come to school for the many various reasons, most of which have little to do with the motive of learning as such.
>
> (Kupferberg 1996: 229–30)

[P]upils attend classes because they have to, not because they want to. Gradually individuals find reasons other than fear of reprisals for going to school, for instance, companionship, intellectual curiosity, boredom at home, etc. However, this does not turn the act of attending classes into a voluntary activity. It remains a duty, as does most social behaviour.

(Kupferberg 1996: 244)

The other important framing reality in teaching is that what counts in a classroom is more like a 'conversation' than it is like a carefully structured or scripted 'performance' (as in the case of a university lecture). While there are certainly routines followed in classrooms, there is less structured order (than in lecture halls). Therefore:

Emotional tensions are more pronounced and are only marginally related to the subject matter. The teacher's authority is constantly tested in the classroom and the teacher feels a need to address the class in a diffuse as well as a selective way.

(Kupferberg 1996: 244)

Teaching as 'readerly' or 'writerly' text

One way of approaching teaching is to think about it from a literary perspective as a kind of metaphorical 'text' – in the sense of a script or a document to be both written and read. It is in a continual process of being constructed, as well as understood, challenged and unveiled. Moore (1996), drawing upon Eagleton (1983), argues that some written texts, such as legal documents, 'are more "hardened" than others, and present as if they were timeless, neutral, beyond challenge and ultimately "intimidating"' (p. 204).

Bowe *et al.* (1992) in their *Reforming Education and Changing Schools: Case Studies in Policy Sociology* raise questions about the amenability of texts, especially those written *for* and *on behalf* of others. They draw on Roland Barthes' useful conceptual starting point about the extent to which text gives the reader a role or a function, or whether the reader is rendered idle and redundant. The question really comes down to whether a text is, in Roland Barthes' (1975) terms, 'readerly' or 'writerly'. Readerly text is one in which 'there is a minimum of opportunity for creative interpretation by the reader'. 'Writerly' texts, on the other hand, 'self-consciously invite the reader to "join in", to co-operate and co-author' (Bowe *et al.* 1992: 11). In their words:

'Making sense' of new texts leads people into a process of trying to 'translate' and make familiar the language and the attendant embedded logics. In this process they place what they know against the new. Readerly texts, however, presuppose and depend upon presumptions of innocence, upon the belief that the reader will have little to offer by way of an alternative.

(p. 11)

It is an interesting question, therefore, as to the extent to which the view of teaching currently being constructed through various educational reforms worldwide actually provides the opportunity for hearing voices, without closing down the spaces or the frontier for discussion. Trying to steer a path between the following sets of tensions, therefore, appears as a formidable challenge:

- trying to manage the work of teaching, without appearing to be impositional or top-down;
- producing a direction for education policy that connects it to wider trends in globalisation, while giving the appearance that this is a natural or inevitable trend;
- providing spaces from within which teachers can be constructed as participatory carriers of the prevailing ideology without, however, giving them so much space that they can develop a coherent undermining ideology.

In the next three sections of this chapter we examine the topics of 'skills', 'markets' and 'management' using notions of oppositional and resistant reading. We shall be trying to argue for a more 'writerly' and inclusive text for teaching, rather than one that is authoritatively prescriptive and definitive.

Discursive pedagogical skill construction in teaching

Hodge (1993) uses an interesting but not especially elegant term to describe the most important way teachers enact their work – he calls it 'teacherese' (p. 118). It refers to the preponderance of dialogue in the language-rich nature of teaching. Examining the linguistic nature of what teachers do tells us much about what they regard as important, as well as how they explicitly and implicitly construct and frame their work. The reason linguistic forms are so important in teaching is that they are the means through which teachers foster 'creativity' and handle expressions of 'resistance' from students, both of which constitute primary energy sources within classrooms. According to Hodge (1993) teacherese is not an especially natural form:

> No one speaks pure teacherese outside the classroom. All pupils are exposed to it and they can understand it passively from the outside, but it is very different to the active grasp that they must acquire when they become teachers themselves. The conscious effort that is required has its dangers. Like anyone learning a new language new teachers tend to over-correct, speaking teacherese better (more rigorously) than experienced teachers, though failing to see some of the subtleties and variations that are a part of the language in its fuller form ...
>
> There are two basic strategies for teacher-talk. One is deductive, a top-down, hypotactic approach, which starts from explicit, well-ordered descriptions of clear intentions (what to teach and how to teach it). It puts these into practice and then evaluates the results. The other approach is inductive, a bottom-up, paratactic approach. It scans teaching practice as a complex text, looking for regularities and anomalies. The generalisations it comes up with are paratactic. They may never be fully integrated with one another into a single theory of good teaching, but they connect more directly with experience.
>
> (p. 118)

Dialogue is, therefore, the exchange teachers use to keep the mobilisation of creativity in balance, so that the fine line between students acting creatively and impulsively for difference does not become so negative and oppositional that resistance to authority gets in the way of learning (Hodge 1993: 61). Teachers are thus continually acting in ways in which they harness the utterances of students so they become 'balanced and thoughtful responses' (p. 65) of a kind appropriate for open classroom discussion. That skill in teaching is to a large extent verbal and linguistic is given added poignancy by the way control and discipline are exercised in teaching, as Hodge (1993) indicates:

When you stand in front of your first class for the first time and see rows of eyes looking back at you, you know without question that teaching is a form of struggle in which the numerical advantage is undoubtedly with the enemy. At such a time, neophyte teachers commonly wish they had learned more about 'discipline' and ways of maintaining control, and less about theories of curriculum. In their later career they will often have days when they reflect ruefully on the meagre instruments of control that lie to hand, and the hell that follows when control has gone. Yet the exercise of power has its cost, and the time and effort taken up in its maintenance are a distraction from teaching and learning ... Different styles of teaching involve different attitudes to power and different levels of investment in its exercise, but for no one can it be the only virtue. The relationship between teacher and pupil necessarily involves an asymmetry of knowledge and power, but that asymmetry takes many forms and has to be negotiated in different ways.

(p. 24)

AST: indications of policy disjuncture

As a way of providing an *entrée* into teachers' voices about their work, we would like to turn our commentary to the framework of the policy agenda [. . .] – the AST. We find it more useful to give some broad brushstrokes before hearing the teachers' voices, because of the way in which this analysis brings out the macro issues discussed so far in this chapter.

A way into the policy disjuncture of an initiative that was supposed to elevate teachers' self-worth, but ended up being subverted to other ends, is to pose the question: what view of skill was behind the AST process?

Teaching is never innocent – it always includes some things, while excluding or denying others; celebrates some perspectives and actions while discouraging and denying others; co-opts, favours and promotes some ways of working with students, while punishing, ignoring or silencing other views of teaching. What constitutes legitimate teaching, therefore, depends on who is doing the defining, and their perception of the valued social end or purpose to which the teaching is directed. If the attempt is to contain, control or shape teaching to promote national economic imperatives, then teaching will become a tool of micro-economic reform and will look quite different than if teaching was a genuine attempt to formulate schooling as a more relevant curriculum response to the complex lives of contemporary youth. Teaching will look different again, if the primary interest is that of parents who want their children to succeed vocationally, or employers who want a literate, numerate and compliant workforce. These multiple and conflicting interpretations of teaching have to struggle to co-exist with each other and arrive at uneasy forms of settlement at particular historical moments. Which set of views gets to have preference over others is invariably a hotly contested political question, even though the real agenda may be obscured and not always overtly obvious.

In the case of the attempt to construct a view of what constituted 'advanced teaching skills' in Australian schools in the early 1990s, there were a number of competing interests and discourses: the official or policy aspirations; the lived realities of how the official aspirations were lived out at the level of the process of selecting the teachers; and, the accommodation, contestation and resistance displayed by teachers as they acted to give voice to their own local or indigenous definitions of skilful teaching. It was clear that these various constructions were not always heading in the same direction, nor were they one and the same thing.

The major point of departure was at the level of the paradigmatic view of teaching – official views endorsed a 'competencies' approach of displaying attributes, traits and behaviours consistent with a series of pre-formulated criteria; at the level of teachers, there was a regret that the impositional approach was not more nuanced and consistent with teachers' preferred ways that tended to favour storied and narrative styles of portrayal. Teachers often put this in terms of what they saw as skills that endorsed 'bureaucratically preferred ways'. Teachers became angry when these were ranked higher than what teachers themselves regarded as being most important. Some teachers claimed that when criteria of competent teaching were developed external to and at a distance from teaching, rather than being the consequence of any process that was up-close or internal to the understandings of what it meant to be a good teacher, then considerable damage was done. Accumulated wisdom acquired through many years of successful classroom teaching was denigrated because it did not necessarily or readily equate with the skill requirements embodied in the criteria: 'experience', 'commitment', 'status' and 'self-esteem' did not necessarily equal skilled teaching as measured through the application of criteria.

Accommodated and subjugated knowledges of teaching

The paradigmatic preference for what amounted to technicist ways of regarding teaching also manifested itself in other ways – for example, the strong emphasis in the AST selection process on evidence and what appeared to be a quasi-judicial process of an adversarial type, in which teachers were required to account for their skills in written form, supported by evidence from in-class observation, at interview, and in response to questioning by a panel. The verification of claims about personal teaching against the standards embodied in the AST criteria produced levels of tension and frustration that many teachers found difficult to live with.

At another level, teachers found the requirement of having to meet specified criteria as 'limiting the boundaries of admissible evidence'. They argued repeatedly that the process of 'narrowing down' teaching (some drew the parallel with 'dumbing down') to meet criteria produced a situation in which large and important aspects of teaching are made deliberately 'invisible'.

For some teachers this whole approach smacked too much of having to jump through criterial hoops, displaying just the right amount of policy gloss in terms of familiarity with the latest government ideology, in order to receive a meagre reward. Teachers regarded this as akin to using school sites as conduits for the latest educational ideology, where being rewarded with an acknowledgement of AST amounted to being a carrier of this new ideology. Being successful, paradoxically, meant moving spiritually and linguistically away from the classroom, at least in terms of being able to converse freely in the jargon in order to demonstrate convincingly the ability to mouth the rhetoric. For teachers who were successful, this amounted to a form of policy assimilation of the new skills discourse of competencies. It was as if skill in teaching was somehow being used as a kind of ideological manoeuvre with which to produce policy conformity. This tended to take the form of the requirement to demonstrate knowledge of systems policy, and was further exacerbated as the 'gaze' of self-regulation was driven back into routine aspects of teaching. This led, teachers said, to a kind of self-imposed performance accountability of desirable visible teaching traits, which was ultimately corrupting. We would not want to deny, however, that there *can* also be a positive side to systemic policy concerns, for example, the way in which teachers enact policies of social justice in their classroom practices (see, for example: Queensland Department of Education 1996), but this was not, however, an issue that teachers spoke of in the AST study.

Teachers spoke frequently of the guilt they experienced in electing to undergo the process of being selected as an AST – to satisfy the requirements of putting together the very detailed written proposal (often taking weeks or months to prepare), they had to forego the dedicated attention they normally gave to their daily teaching duties – especially out-of-hours activities like evening and weekend marking of student assignment work. In order to become recognised as an AST it seemed they had to be prepared to become temporarily negligent.

The playing of 'language games' through the written application and the subsequent interview was seen as having the effect of devaluing the essence of the work of teaching – the relational aspects of classroom teaching did not appear to many teachers to be highly regarded – it was a case of being able to show that they were somehow competent classroom managers. Teachers experienced this separation of 'performance against criteria' from the wider lived totality of their self-worth as teachers as a kind of artificially constructed exposition of a 'performance facade'.

The presentation of evidence about their teaching to a panel and the associated interview process caused a lot of grief among teachers – one teacher described it as an 'ordeal by representation'. There was a widely held view that some teachers were better at the 'interview game' than others and that the combative nature of the process unnecessarily put many in the situation where fear of failure led to 'nervous omission, rather than complete and meaningful disclosure' of what they knew about teaching. The view was put that the kind of skill necessary was one that was about 'talking your way around the criteria' and 'impressing outsiders', rather than any genuine attempt to get at core understandings about real issues of teaching in complex contemporary circumstances.

There was almost universal condemnation of the situation of discomfort experienced by most teachers in having to engage with 'necessary forms of self-promotion' in order to manufacture and manage impression and performance during the selection process.

Fundamental questions were raised by teachers too about the value to the school and its wider community of a 'personal classification of skill'. For many teachers, teaching is no longer the isolated and insulated activity it used to be, and therefore, to reward individual teachers with an individual classification flies directly in the face of the collaborative reality of the way these teachers experience their work. This point was picked up repeatedly by teachers in the way they talked about the extraordinarily high levels of collegial support they received while enduring the selection process. Many made it clear that without the very tangible assistance of colleagues they would not have been able to proceed. This raises serious questions about why individual rewards are persisted with when schools themselves refuse to treat teachers as if they were islands. The competitive model is not only outdated – it may actually be highly counter-productive to schools.

With the allocation of rewards being such a public process, and so significantly related to the life of schools, this had its drawbacks too. For example, not only was there 'shame, humiliation, anger and loss of confidence at failure', but after years of positive peer and community affirmation, good teaching could be quickly shattered through a failure at criterial assessment – a situation exacerbated by a total absence of any official procedure for 'after-the-process' support for individuals who failed to meet up to arbitrarily set and administered standards of good teaching. The inextricable embeddedness of self-worth in teaching meant that failure produced huge emotional and social disjuncture.

Any teachers agreeing to putting themselves forward for selection as ASTs were placing themselves in a situation of considerable personal and professional vulnerability – the 'hidden costs' of being an applicant were not insignificant in a context where the fissure of misunderstanding over the meaning of competence was always a palpable reality. The literalistic discourse of skills continually rubbed abrasively against the oral tradition of teaching, a circumstance that was bound to produce a context of incongruence between 'professional' and 'criterial' notions of assessment. In brief, there was a deep and irresolvable confusion and tension throughout between the *alleged* 'celebration' of good teaching and its *actual* 'evaluation'.

The form of 'contrived collegiality' (Hargreaves 1994: 80) that was manufactured through having a colleague on the selection panel did not wash with most teachers; they were quick to see this shallow contrivance for what it was – an attempt to disguise traditional bureaucratic forms of evaluation. Well-meaning colleagues were often regarded as lacking credibility, from the vantage point of teachers who were more interested in the benefits derived from being part of a genuine learning community – exchanging ideas, trailing new teaching approaches and generally supporting one another.

While the overt and demonstrable aspects of being selected as an AST were often spoken about in less than edifying terms by teachers, there were also references to the not so easily seen aspects. Although teachers did not use the term, there was a feeling of complicity of peers in 'horizontal violence', as colleagues became implicated into forms of pseudo-ownership of the process through involvement on school-based selection panels.

Teachers' resistant discourses and readings of the AST

One theme that consistently emerged from the interviews was the oral, storied and discursive tradition of teaching as a site of resistance. The issues of what was admissible and inadmissible as evidence of advanced teaching skills, what was masked, opaque and therefore beyond dispute as criteria, were by no means settled in the eyes of teachers. They were troubled by the approach of dismantling their teaching into 'bits and pieces' as if such deconstruction were natural, common sense and inevitable; they resisted this in the ways they presented accounts that emphasised teaching in its totality. The relational aspect of teaching, which teachers insisted was at the core of their work, failed to feature prominently in the official criteria. While teachers were certainly keen to receive symbolic recognition of the significance of their work, they were unprepared to accept this without challenging the medium of representation especially if this was at the expense of artificiality. Contestation and politicisation were seen as the most effective antidotes to literal, detached and shallow renditions that failed to judge teaching in the milieu of its connected context. For example, requests throughout the AST process to provide evidence of how criteria were invisible carriers of systems policy, and how these were 'applied' in teaching, were responded to by teachers with instances of policy as being 'experienced in' or 'grounded in' and actively redefined through a shared experiential construction of a localised culture of teaching. In other words, teachers were continually engaging in reframing the discursive boundaries of their teaching in situations where sharing insights about their teaching was a normal part of a wider community-building process.

It seemed that in many respects the AST process was about producing a 'marketised' and 'managed' set of relationships in teaching. We turn our attention to these twin elements now, drawing our examples from New Zealand, the UK and the USA.

Marketised relationships in schools

The argument

Given the intention of governments to have schools managed like businesses, it is clear that the mechanism by which teachers are to be controlled is through techniques of business management. The consequence as Ball (1988) notes is that 'The task of schooling is increasingly subject to the logics of industrial production and market competition' (p. 292). Hatcher (1994) argues that 'market relationships are becoming the organising principle of the school system' (p. 42). As evidence of this he cites the experience from Britain of introducing new management regimes from the private sector incorporating:

> certain structural changes including devolved organisation, expanded role definitions for line managers, new forms of control systems and new forms of production system. Accompanying these structural changes there appear to have been certain 'cultural' changes such as new management styles designed to give renewed emphasis to customer orientation, innovation, enterprise and competitive edge.
>
> (p. 42)

According to Hatcher (1994) even the recent attempts of policy sociology to alter this have been less than successful because of a focus on the 'top' end of the 'top down' approach: 'Ordinary teachers are afforded the potential of an active oppositional role in their theoretical analysis, but they are largely absent from the empirical research' (p. 44).

The crucial linkage that is missing from the attempt to translate the new management regime from business to schools is the vastly different culture of schools (see Westoby 1988 for a full treatment), and furthermore, the 'new management regimes in the private sector takes [*sic*] place in a context in which the work process is directly governed by market relationships' (Hatcher 1994: 45).

The topic of markets in schooling is of interest to us here primarily in the way it casts light on how teachers' work is shaped pedagogically. We do not offer an exhaustive treatment of the notion of markets in education, but refer instead to others who have treated the topic in detail such as Bowe *et al.* (1992), Keep (1992), Kenway *et al.* (1993; 1994), Gewirtz *et al.* (1995) and Marginson (1995; 1997).

The idea that markets should be the primary organising and motivating feature of schooling has been central to educational reforms in the UK, New Zealand, Australia and the USA for a decade or more. The argument in which teachers are constructed as 'providers', principals as 'managers', parents as 'employers', and students as 'consumers', is overly simplistic, but it goes something like this: poor school performance lies at the root of national economic under-performance; teachers have for too long had a monopoly over the content and direction of educational decisions; they have occupied a position of 'producer capture' and engaged in 'feather bedding' as a way of protecting their own self-interests; what is required to rectify this is the introduction of market-led reforms in which schools and teachers are required to compete against each other; what will happen as a consequence is that schools and teachers will either lift their game and become more efficient, or go out of business as parents exercise their choice of schools; 'if protectionism is lifted and competition encouraged, products will sink or swim depending on their ability to compete' (Sullivan 1994: 4).

While the key theoretical assumptions may be clear enough, namely that 'self-management will ensure that schools are able to match their services directly to student need and that market forces will ensure that "standards" are raised as schools compete for students and seek to stabilise or maximise their income' (Ball and Bowe 1992: 58), what is far from clear is how this reaches down into the work of teaching to make teachers more efficient and effective; the 'black box' of the classroom has been studiously ignored in all of this theorising about market relationships in schools.

Management for all seasons: managing teaching through market consent

Structural changes to teachers' work

Questions about how teachers in schools are (or should be) managed are never far off the public agenda. The persistence of this desire to control teachers seems to be caught up with the wider desire to apportion blame for the economic demise while, at the same time, attempting to proffer solutions as to what should be done to fix the situation. We do not intend to rehearse any more the scapegoating of teachers that has occurred worldwide with such vehemence (see Lingard *et al.* 1993; Hargreaves 1994; Berliner and Biddle 1995; Woods *et al.* 1997). But, appreciating the effects of the hostility of this attack on teachers becomes important in understanding the most recent attempts (at least in England and in New Zealand, and increasingly in Australia) to control teachers through market-driven forms of educational policy. It is only when we take account of the importance of teachers' work culture and the centrality to teachers of concepts like co-operation, work ethic, commitment to children's learning, and the intrinsic worth of teaching itself (Smyth 1992), that we can come to see the reluctance of teachers to embrace and deliver on the market agenda 'and thus it is that management comes to assume such significance' (Nicholls 1995: 3). Nicholls (1995) explores how in 'hitherto market-insulated primary schools' (p. 1) in the UK the 'rhetorical and ideological force of marketisation, together with the shifts in management–workforce relations that it fosters' (p. 3), produce a set of circumstances in which 'it is in this sphere of management–workforce relations that the market rhetoric does its "real" work' (p. 3). He claims that the steering of the educational market in the UK has come about largely through devolution of responsibility and function as schools have been provided with funds according to 'success', and where success is defined in terms of attracting students and funding (Ball 1993: 109). The logic of the constructed educational market is such that schools are encouraged 'to seek potentially successful pupils, while other pupils, with low market value or expensive needs, are not targeted' (Nicholls 1995: 4). Importantly:

> the steered education market is characterised by differentiation and stratification, though the rhetoric is that of choice, diversity, responsiveness and flexibility. This rhetoric is also abundant in the description of the emergent forms of teaching labour force, and similarly conceals stratification and segmentation, as well as the market's tendency to reinforce inequality.
>
> (p. 4)

The way this came about in England was through the 'occupational re-structuring' of the teaching force – through (a) direct regulation of pay and promotion for teachers, and (b) the deregulation and devolution of financial control to schools allowing them greater flexibility in employing teachers. The first of these worked through the abolition of teachers' negotiating rights, the fixing of pay scales, and giving principals the power to 'reward for good performance as measured against indicators' (Nicholls 1995: 5). The second occurred through governing councils being able to appoint teachers according to budget, the rise of ancillary and auxiliary teachers, and the 'virtual disappearance of financial support for inservice training [which] means that teachers fund their own professional development' (p. 5). All of this operates in England to produce an increasingly differentiated and segmented teaching force, where previously it had exhibited 'all of the characteristics of unalienated, integrated labour' (Nicholls 1995: 6).

The 'same' but 'different' situations of teachers in the UK and USA

Lawn (1995: 347) makes the point that restructuring of teaching in the USA and the UK have what appear to be similarities in that they both have pursued the touchstones of 'decentralisation of school management' and the 'development of quasi-markets in education' – but these surface similarities belie more substantive differences. While this is not the place to go into elaborate comparative analyses of reforms in the respective countries (see Weiler 1989; Hess 1992; Lawton 1992b; Nias *et al.* 1992; Murphy and Hallinger 1993), Lawn (1995) says that while some of the same language is used in relation to the reforms in both countries – collaboration, collegiality, responsibilities beyond the classroom, a professional view of teaching, delivery of national curriculum, greater involvement in school-wide policy – there are quite different sets of forces operating in the two countries. In the USA the thrust has come from attempts to move teaching beyond allegedly inefficient educational bureaucracy, trying to garner teacher involvement and empowerment from a situation in which teachers had historically been treated punitively and in teacher-proofing ways – in a phrase, the attempt was to promote more 'teacher professionalism'. In the UK, while the touchstones were the same, the history and the circumstances were quite different; teacher exclusion from the reform process; a shift away from existing partnerships between teachers and government; a greater emphasis on privatisation; more individual responsibility; greater centralisation and regulation (Lawn 1995). In summary, while the rhetoric of 'collegiality and collaboration' have been used on both sides of the Atlantic to frame teacher reforms, in the UK it was being driven out of a push to create a market ideology for education, while in the USA it was an attempt to ameliorate the worst effects of bureaucratic forms of management (Lawn 1995: 349). It has to be said that the reforms in the USA, beyond the appearances of enhanced professionalism for teachers, were fundamentally also about introducing market forces through 'consumer' choice.

The effect on teachers in both places has been similar – 'a differentiated, flexible workforce in teaching'. In the UK the emphasis has been upon 'pay flexibility' – freeing-up teachers from centralised salary and promotions structures, giving school governors the power to set pay scales, and through 'workforce pliability' (Lawn 1995: 355) involving skilled, semi-skilled and unskilled teachers with differing tasks, modes of training and entry, and varying supervisory responsibilities. As Lawn (1995) put it: 'New kinds of teachers and classroom assistants are appearing in England who have the potential to act ... as low-skilled workers alongside the new core workers, the multi-skilled teachers' (p. 358). 'The idea of a professional standard of work can be seen to be moving from a collective responsibility to an individual's performance and from a definition created by the teacher (or, more accurately, teachers) to that created by management' (p. 352).

Managing teaching through the 'new management discourses'

Nicholls (1995) studied twelve primary schools in the UK and focused on their responses to marketisation, particularly parental choice, competition between schools, and the significance of image management. His research is of particular significance (and will be examined in detail) for the light it casts on how marketisation works through the construction of new management relationships in schools. Nicholls (1995) found that 'despite the absence of classically defined markets, there is evidence that primary school managers feel obliged to act as though they were competitive business managers ... and felt they must hold down costs' (p. 10).

The integration of the ideology of the market and managerial sets of relationships, and their effect on teachers through the way teams of senior managers acted in the schools Nicholls studied, can be summarised thus:

> Pressure on schools to be accountable to clients and to attract clients through performance levels increases the monitoring and surveillance functions of these teams. Because schools must attract to survive, the pressure on such teams to eradicate problems and establish smooth production is correspondingly greater. Deviations from, or variations on, school policy seem less likely to be tolerated. The status of the class teacher is threatened by the quasi-managerial function of post-holders and the growth of supervisory functions implicit in collegiality. Indeed the connections and relationships between the growth of supervisory functions in teaching, which may 'extend' professionalism of a particular kind to some, and the deskilling of other educational workers, especially women and part-timers, connects to current debates about the changing nature of the workforce in Western 'post-industrialist' societies and in particular to the emergence of core and flexible workers.
>
> (p. 10)

Furthermore, this was given particular expression in the primary schools studied:

> there is evidence of considerable development in the practice of primary schools in terms of important areas of activity, including 'client' awareness, market research, image and impression management, unofficial selection, and the development of a visible 'mission' or ethos encapsulated in the school development plan.
>
> (p. 11)

Nicholls (1995) argues that there are strong surface similarities between some of the features of primary-school work cultures – collegiality, flat management structures, flexible work arrangements, teamwork, and the like – and the precepts of Human Resource Management (HRM) that 'may assist in the manufacturing of consent' (p. 17). He warns, however, of making too much of this apparent connection on the grounds that to do that would be to misunderstand the nature of the new forms of management. The marketisation ideology operates through two mechanisms: (a) the notion of the 'flexible firm' (or organisation), and, (b) the discourses of HRM and Total Quality Management (TQM). We have already seen how flexibility works in the UK through the creation of internal labour markets in schools based on fragmentation of the work of teaching, functional flexibility for schools, the breakdown of a 'homogenous labour force' (p. 7), and constructing new jobs for some requiring additional skills and tasks. What is produced is a 'threat of visible job substitution' (p. 7) in a circumstance where: 'workers live with the shadow of their use-value firmly attached to remind all other workers of the disciplining operation of the labour market' (p. 7).

Workplace discipline 'which had traditionally been embodied in the form of management, supervision and bureaucracy is translated from an organisational contrivance to a seemingly external imperative derived from the very nature of the economic system which lies beyond the firm' (p. 7).

Some understanding of how the dual discourses of TQM and HRM have seeped into schools, particularly in the UK, but also extensively in other countries, is important (for an elaboration, see Smyth 1991; Smyth 1995d). Nicholls (1995) encapsulated the essence of TQM when he says that it 'raises the level of measurable quality in outputs by introducing the previously external relationships between customer and producer into the workplace through the employment relationship' (p. 7). It is a particularly smart arrangement because of the way it 'draws the principles of the market directly into the shop floor with the discipline of the "customer's gaze" installing an ever-watchful eye on the workforce' (p. 8). Through its emphasis on teamwork and measurable targets TQM, therefore, establishes a new pattern of relationships among workers where 'colleagues remain attentive to their tasks and aware of each other's level of contribution to the productive effort' (p. 8). HRM operates out of a broadly similar crucible emphasising a cachet that underscores the importance of 'individual employee identity' and 'evaluation on the basis of individual performance' (p. 8), where the stress on 'competitive individualism' and the extirpation of third party intervention resonate nicely with 'the language of the market place' as embodied in notions like 'teamwork', 'enterprise culture' and 'cohesive workforce' (that avoids solidarity) (p. 8). There are tensions here in HRM, but they are over-ridden by an 'enabling' and 'empowering' commitment of management to 'integrated', 'co-ordinated' and 'target-driven activity' within a 'flat/flexible' organisational structure of clearly articulated 'shared purposes' (Nicholls 1995: 8–9).

In this chapter we have looked at some of the more proximate sources of educational policy options via international agencies like the OECD, and discussed the way in which they framed a particular kind of discourse about the nature of schools. In contradistinction, we explained the importance of developing an oppositional reading to these positions and gave some preliminary insights into what transpired in the AST initiative in Australia – framed by a consideration of the changed marketised and managed relationships increasingly coming to characterise teaching in other places as well. [. . .]

References

Angus, L. (1993). The sociology of school effectiveness. *British Journal of Sociology of Education*, 14(3): 333–45.

Ball, S. (1988). Staff relations during the teachers' industrial action: context, conflict and proletarianisation. *British Journal of Sociology of Education*, 9(3): 289–306.

—— (1993). Education policy, power relations and teachers' work. *British Journal of Educational Studies*, 41(2): 106–21.

—— (1994). *Education Reform: A Critical and Post-Structural Analysis*. Milton Keynes: Open University Press.

—— and Bowe, R. (1992). Education, markets and professionalism: some recent reflections on recent policy developments in England and Wales. *Melbourne Studies in Education*, 56–62.

Batsleer, J., Davis, T., O'Rourke, R. and Weedon, C. (1985). *Rewriting English*. New York: Methuen.

Berliner, D. and Biddle, B. (1995). *The Manufactured Crisis: Myths, Fraud and the Attack on America's Public Schools*. Reading, MA: Addison-Wesley.

Bizzell, P. (1992). What is a 'discourse community'? In P. Bizzell (ed.), *Academic Discourse and Critical Consciousness* (pp. 222–37). Pittsburgh: University of Pittsburgh Press.

Bowe, R., Ball, S. and Gold, A. (1992). *Reforming Education and Changing Schools: Case Studies in Policy Sociology*. London and New York: Routledge.

Coffield, F. (1990). From the decade of the enterprise culture to the decade of the TECs. *British Journal of Education and Work*, 4(1): 59–78.

Davies, B. and Harre, R. (1990). Positioning: conversation and the production of selves. *Journal for the Theory of Social Behaviour*, 20(1): 43–63.

Eagleton, T. (1983). *Literary Theory: An Introduction*. Oxford: Blackwell.

Fairclough, N. (1992a). *Critical Language Awareness*. New York: Longman.

—— (ed.) (1992b). *Language and Power*. London: Longman.

Gee, J., Hull, G. and Lankshear, C. (1996). *New Work Order: Behind the Language of the New Capitalism*. St Leonards: Allen & Unwin.

Gewirtz, S., Ball, S. and Bowe, R. (1995). *Markets, Choice and Equity in Education*. Milton Keynes: Open University Press.

Gordon, L. (1992). Educational reform in New Zealand: contesting the role of the teacher. *International Studies in the Sociology of Education*, 2(1): 23–42.

—— (1995). Reflections on the social market: an investigation of school choice in a social policy context. Unpublished MS, University of Canterbury.

Hargreaves, A. (1994). *Changing Teachers, Changing Times: Teachers' Work and Culture in the Postmodern Age*. London: Cassell.

Harre, R. and Gillett, G. (1994). *The Discursive Mind*. Thousand Oaks, CA: Sage.

Hartley, D. (1992). *Teacher Appraisal: A Policy Analysis*. Edinburgh: Scottish Academic Press.

Hatcher, R. (1994). Market relationships and the management of teachers. *British Journal of Sociology of Education*, 15(1): 41–61.

Hess, G. (1992). Chicago and Britain: experiments in empowering parents. *Journal of Education Policy*, 7(2): 155–71.

Hodge, B. (1993). *Teaching as Communication*. London and New York: Longman.

—— and Kress, G. (1993). *Language as Ideology*. 2nd edn, London and New York: Routledge.

Janks, H. (1991). A critical approach to the teaching of language. *Educational Review*, 43(2): 191–9.

Keep, E. (1992). Schools in the market place? Some problems with private sector models. *British Journal of Education and Work*, 5(2): 43–56.

Kenway, J., Bigum, C., Fitzclarence, C. and Coillier, J. (1993). Marketing education in the post-modern age. *Journal of Education Policy*, 8(2): 105–22.

——, ——, —— and Tragenza, R. (1994). The rise and rise of markets in education. *Changing Education*, 1(1): 1 and 6–7.

Kramer-Dahl, A. (1995). Reading and writing against the grain of academic discourse. *Discourse: Studies in the Cultural Politics of Education*, 16(1): 21–38.

Kremer-Hayon, L. (1994). The knowledge teachers use in problem solving situation: sources and forms. *Scandinavian Journal of Educational Research*, 38: 63.

Kress, G. (1985). *Linguistic Processes in Sociocultural Practice*. Geelong: Deakin University Press.

Kumar, K. (1995). *From Post-Industrial to Post-Modern Society: New Theories of the Contemporary World*. Oxford: Blackwell.

Kupferberg, F. (1996). The reality of teaching: bringing disorder back into social theory and the sociology of education. *British Journal of Sociology of Education*, 17(2): 227–47.

Lawn, M. (1995). Restructuring teaching in the USA and England: moving towards the differentiated, flexible teacher. *Journal of Education Policy*, 10(4): 347–60.

Lawton, D. (1992b). Why restructure? An international survey of the roots of reform. *Journal of Education Policy*, 7(2): 139–54.

——, O'Brien, P. and Knight, J. (1993). Strengthening Australia's schools through corporate federalism. *Australian Journal of Education*, 37(3): 231–47.

Marginson, S. (1995). Markets in education: a theoretical note. *Australian Journal of Education*, 39(3): 294–312.

—— (1997). *Markets in Education*. Sydney: Allen & Unwin.

Moore, A. (1996). 'Masking the fissure': some thoughts on competencies, reflection and 'closure' in initial teacher education. *British Journal of Educational studies*, 44(2): 200–11.

Moore, R. (1987). Education and the ideology of production. *British Journal of Sociology of Education*, 8(2): 227–42.

Murphy, J. and Hallinger, P. (eds) (1993). *Restructuring Schooling: Learning from Ongoing Efforts*. Newbury Park, CA: Corwin Press.

Nias, J., Southworth, G. and Campbell, P. (1992). *Whole School Curriculum Development in the Primary School*. London: Falmer Press.

Nicholls, P. (1995). *Manufacturing consent through the market: the case of the service sector*. Paper presented at the Research Seminar Series, Murdoch University.

OECD (1989). *Schools and Quality: An International Report*. Paris: OECD.

OECD (1990). *The Teacher Today*. Paris: OECD.

Pring, R. (1996). Editorial. *British Journal of Educational Studies*, 44(2): 139–41.

Proudford, C. and Baker, R. (1995). Schools that make a difference: a sociological perspective on effective schooling. *British Journal of Sociology of Education*, 16(3): 277–92.

Smyth, J. (1991). International perspective on teacher collegiality: a labour process discussion based on teachers' work. *British Journal of Sociology of Education*, 12(4): 323–46.

—— (1992). Teachers' work and the politics of reflection. *American Educational Research Journal*, 29(2): 267–300.

—— (1995d). What's happening to teachers' work in Australia? *Educational Review*, 47(2): 189–98.

—— (1996a). Evaluation of teacher performance: move over hierarchy here comes collegiality! *Journal of Education Policy*, 11(2): 185–96.

Strain, M. (1995). Autonomy, schools and the constitutive role of community: towards a new moral and political order for education. *British Journal of Educational Studies*, 43(1): 4–20.

Sullivan, K. (1992). The myth of partnership: educational reform and teacher disempowerment. *New Zealand Annual Review of Education*, 2: 151–65.

—— (1994). The impact of educational reform on teachers' professional ideologies. *New Zealand Journal of Educational Studies*, 29(1): 3–20.

Threadgold, T. (1988). The genre debate. *Southern Review*, 21: 315–30.

Walter, J. (1996). *Tunnel Vision: The Failure of Political Imagination*. St Leonards, NSW: Allen & Unwin.

Watson, K. (1996). Banking on key reforms for educational development: a critique of the World Bank Review. *Mediterranean Journal of Educational Studies*, 1(1): 43–61.

Watts, T. (1993). Connecting curriculum to work: past patterns, current initiatives and future issues. In J. Wellington (ed.), *The Work Related Curriculum: Challenging the Vocational Imperative* (pp. 40–53). London: Kogan Page.

Weiler, H. (1989). Why reforms fail: the politics of education in France and the Federal Republic of Germany. *Journal of Curriculum Studies*, 21(4): 291–305.

Welch, A. (1996). *Australian Education: Reform or Crisis*. St Leonards: Allen & Unwin.

Wellington, J. (ed.) (1993). *The Work Related Curriculum: Challenging the Vocational Imperative*. London: Kogan Page.

Westoby, A. (ed.) (1988). *Culture and Power in Educational Organization*. Milton Keynes: Open University Press.

Woods, P., Jeffrey, B., Troman, G. and Boyle, M. (1997). *Restructuring Schools, Reconstructing Teachers: Responding to Change in the Primary School*. Milton Keynes: Open University Press.

World Bank (1995). *Priorities and Strategies for Education*. Washington, DC: A World Bank Review.

PART 7

STUDENTS AND CLASSROOM

SCHOOLS, FAMILIES AND ACADEMICALLY ABLE STUDENTS

Contrasting modes of involvement in secondary education

Sally Power, Geoff Whitty, Tony Edwards and Valerie Wigfall

British Journal of Sociology of Education (1998), 19 (2): 157–77

[. . .]

Introduction

This chapter draws on our ESRC-funded research into the educational biographies of nearly 350 young people. Although our sample is an opportunistic one, originally drawn for a different purpose, all of our students had been identified as 'academically able' at age 11. In that earlier research (Edwards *et al.*, 1989), they, and many of their parents, were interviewed while they were in the early stages of their secondary schooling. The 18 schools they attended ranged from inner-city comprehensives to some of the most prestigious and selective schools in the private sector. Now they are in their mid-twenties, we have used questionnaires and interviews to trace them through their secondary and, in most cases, higher education into their early occupational careers.

In relation to other studies on educational progressions, the biographies of our students are relatively homogeneous inasmuch as the majority pursued what Roberts (1993) calls the 'prime trajectory' for young people, through A-levels into higher education and then out into professional/managerial employment. Similarly, most would fall into Bynner *et al.*'s (1997) category of those who are 'getting on'. However, this apparent homogeneity hides significant and subtle differences. Firstly, not all our students followed that 'prime trajectory'. Secondly, the biographies of those who did reveal variations not just in terms of routes and destinations, but also in their orientations to schooling. A few (8%) left school with only a few GCSEs, but most stayed on in full-time education. The majority (over 80%) then went on to university, although a few (18) started a degree but then dropped out. A significant minority (14%) carried on with their studies beyond their first degree. A small proportion (11%) are now unemployed, while seven of our respondents were already earning in excess of £30,000 per annum at the time they were questioned. In terms of more qualitative dimensions, some have a clear sense of where they are going, but for others the future seems uncertain and opaque. And, while many look back on their time at school with affection, others feel bitter and disillusioned by their experience.

In order to make sense of these varying educational biographies, we have been exploring some recent work in social-class analysis and particularly in investigations of transitions of young people from school to work. Much writing in both these areas seems to reflect a move away from the theories of socio-cultural determinism that dominated the field in the 1970s and 1980s. For example, Saunders (1996, 1997) argues from his re-analysis of data from the National Child Development Survey that socio-cultural factors are now less significant in determining upward mobility than are individual attributes of ability and motivation. Although recognising the perpetuation of class-related patterns in educational careers, Goldthorpe (1996) and Breen & Goldthorpe (1997) also claim that these are inadequately explained by 'culturalist' approaches—particularly that developed by Bourdieu (e.g. Bourdieu, 1973). Class cultures, they argue, are only relevant in so far as they are 'the sedimented balance-sheets of past rational action, providing short-cut guides to future decision-making' (Breen & Goldthorpe, 1997). Instead, they propose an explanation based on Boudon's (1974) Rational Action Theory in which individuals make decisions about educational progression on the basis of calculations of costs, benefits and probabilities of success (in relation to subsequent economic returns and social status) of various options. Class differences in choices, even for children of the same academic ability, result from different evaluations of the benefits of education, rather than class cultural differences in values.

Coming from a rather different direction, some sociologists of education exploring transitions from school to work are also critical of what they see as the determinism of research which they believe concentrates too heavily on social and structural determinants. For example, Hodkinson & Sparkes (1997, p. 38) argue that even the term 'career trajectory' 'implies a subtle determinism about choices made and that the pathways embarked upon are somehow set and predictable'. Their own research led them to conclude that these pathways are not set and predictable, but often fluid and unpredictable. They put forward the alternative notions of 'horizons for action' (Hodkinson et al., 1996) and 'careership' through which occupational and other choices are 'not predetermined but subject to change' (Hodkinson & Sparkes 1997, p. 41). MacDonald & Coffield (1991, p. 93) also comment negatively on the determinism of research on trajectories that shows 'little regard to the active cultural role played by people in the construction of their own individual biographies'.

Although these shifts away from strong socio-cultural explanations may reflect the current *zeitgeist* of individualism, we want to argue that 'the sedimented balance-sheets' played down by Breen & Goldthorpe (1996) continue to provide a powerful explanatory framework for understanding both predictable *and* unpredictable biographies. Whatever the weaknesses of Bourdieu's approach, there may be other forms of analysis of cultural transactions between home and school that can throw light on both continuity and discontinuity in educational progressions. Some of the early writing of Basil Bernstein, in particular, seems to provide a way forward in helping us clarify the various experiences and outcomes of our sample of young people. In order to explore the usefulness of this work, we will examine the contrasting modes of involvement at two of our 18 research schools that exemplify different institutional cultures.[1]

Sources of consensus and disaffection in education

Bernstein (1966) argues that the sources of consensus and disaffection in education are to be understood through exploring the relationship between the culture of the school and the orientation of the family to that culture. Although the relationship between the school and the family is not straightforward, being mediated by such variables as the child's ability and friendship groups, Bernstein provides us with a typology through which complex orientations and outcomes can be unravelled along a number of dimensions.

The culture of the school: instrumental and expressive orders

In terms of the culture of the school, Bernstein (1966) identifies two distinct but interrelated complexes of behaviour embodied within the school. The expressive order is the complex of behaviour and activities to do with conduct, character and manner. The instrumental order is concerned with the acquisition of specific skills and bodies of knowledge. Within individual schools, there can be variation in the relative strengths of each of these orders—and there is often, argues Bernstein, considerable tension between them. In addition, there is another dimension to the culture of the school that needs to be considered when categorising individual institutions. Both the instrumental and the expressive order tend towards being 'open' or 'closed'—leading to social relations within the school that are respectively 'differentiated' or, 'stratified' (Bernstein *et al.*, 1966).

King's (1976, 1981) research led him to conclude that Bernstein's distinction between 'open' and 'closed' schools is insufficiently clear-cut to provide an adequate basis for categorisation. But the survey methods he used may have been an inappropriate strategy for testing Bernstein's propositions. Defending Bernstein against King's criticism, Tyler (1988) goes so far as to argue that:

> ... Bernstein's structural interpretation of school organisation is so differently conceived from other theories of the school, it does not lend itself easily to conventional empirical testing. Not only does it reconstitute the elements of a theory of school organisation, it also generates its own methodological principles which make any 'objective' empirical test to some degree self-validating. Since the instrumentation of empirical research is an aspect of coding practices, an inappropriate choice of a method could produce a very distorting result.
>
> (1982, pp. 159–160)

While Tyler may somewhat overplay the untestability of Bernstein's analysis, it is probable that identification of the organising principles of institutions and the cultures they seek to transmit will require something more sensitive than survey methods. We were able to draw on a range of data to position the schools that our informants had attended. In addition to contemporary school literature, visits to the schools and interviews with the head teachers, we have also used parental and student impressions gathered by interview during their initial years at the school.[2] Based on the independent judgements of each of the researchers, Fig. 7 locates the relative positions of the 18 schools along two continua representing the strength of the instrumental and expressive orders.

The instrumental order was dominant in the grammar (g1 and g2) and several private (p2, p3, p5 and p8) schools—particularly those that were ex-direct grant schools. Those schools where the expressive order was more pronounced than the instrumental order tended to be comprehensive schools (c1, c3, c4 and c5), although some of these schools were relatively weak in both dimensions (c2, c6 and c7). We also found that, in many of these schools, the contrasting emphasis on the instrumental and the expressive was also connected to degrees of openness and closure. Those schools positioned highest on the instrumental side tended to be 'closed' and

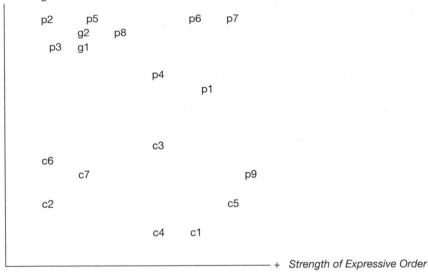

Figure 7 The culture of the 18 research schools (c = comprehensive, g = state grammar, p = private).[3]

to show strong stratificatory structures. Conversely, most of the schools tending to emphasise the expressive order were structured more along principles of differentiation. Those private schools with long-established foundations, often still referrered to as 'public schools', occupied a wider range of positions. Some (p4, p6 and p7) appeared to be strong in both orders. Two (p1 and p9), certainly during the early to mid-1980s, placed greater emphasis on the expressive order. But, unlike the comprehensives, this dimension tended to emphasise hierarchy and competition through activities such as team games and army cadet corps.[4]

For the purposes of this exploration, we will be taking two schools—Archbishop Ambrose's Grammar School for Boys[5] (g2) and Vicarage Road Comprehensive (c5)— to represent two contrasting school cultures. Although the former is not the most selective school in our sample and the latter is not a typically 'inner-city' comprehensive, these schools provide useful comparison as they are located towards opposing ends of the spectrum presented here, both in terms of the relative emphasis placed on the instrumental and the expressive, and the extent to which the social relations within the school were stratified or differentiated.

Archbishop Ambrose's Grammar School for Boys

Archbishop Ambrose was an LEA-maintained grammar school for boys. Although it has subsequently become grant maintained and undergone extensive refurbishment, during the mid-1980s it had the dilapidated but austere atmosphere of the old county grammar school. At the time when our respondents were there, it had 850 students aged 11–18. Most of its 300 sixth-formers proceeded to higher education, including a considerable number to Oxbridge. The school could be clearly identified in terms of its pronounced overt emphasis on the instrumental side. For instance, the school prospectus from the time of our students' entry concentrated on a list of subjects and options alongside much more abbreviated information about extra-curricular activities and disciplinary procedures. In terms of the indicators Bernstein provides, the instrumental order was constructed along lines of closure and competition. A highly selective intake was then subdivided by subject-based ability. Homework requirements were heavy and examination performance was emphasised, although (as noted later) not to the exclusion of other activities.

Like the instrumental order, the expressive order could also be classified as being strongly stratified and closed both internally and externally. On the expressive side, relations between staff and students, and among students, were clearly demarcated. There were various age and sex differentiating rituals (Bernstein *et al.*, 1966). For example, the uniform was altered as students progressed through the school. In the fifth year (Year 11), a different badge had to be worn on the blazer. In the upper sixth, the colour and badge of the blazer changed again. The marking-off of Archbishop Ambrose students from other schoolboys and contemporary youth culture in general was evident in the strict guidelines on appearance concerning, for instance, footwear ('not suede'), scarves ('only of regulation colour') and hair ('will be of reasonable bulk', 'sideburns will not extend below the earlobe'). Extra-curricular activities also emphasised hierarchy, regimentation and competition. In addition to inter-house competitions, students could participate in the Venture Scout unit and general-knowledge competitions.

Archbishop Ambrose attempted to provide a relatively totalising environment that 'protected' students from potentially 'unhelpful' peer group pressures. Although the head teacher complained that he did not have the same 'hold' over his boys' time as a neighbouring private school, the demands of the school in terms of homework, sporting activities and, often, long travelling distances between home and school, effectively served to isolate students from 'outside' influences. It was certainly difficult to make and maintain friendships outside the school.

Vicarage Road Comprehensive

Vicarage Road is a mixed comprehensive school which had approximately 950 students aged 11–16 in the mid-1980s. As a former secondary modern school, it had made vigorous attempts to throw off the negative association of that status and to recruit aspiring and particularly middle-class parents—both in the borough and in the adjacent LEA. By comparison with Archbishop Ambrose, Vicarage Road was far weaker on the instrumental side and stronger on the expressive side. In addition, unlike Archbishop Ambrose, both dimensions tended to be structured along lines of openness rather than closure—contributing to differentiated rather than stratified social relations within the school.

The instrumental order was much less prominent in school literature and in the comments of the then headteacher. It was also less closely bounded. The school was more heterogeneous in terms of teaching units than Archbishop Ambrose. Comprehensive rather than academically selective, it was coeducational rather than single sex. But there also appears to have been less screening and categorising of students within the school. Many classes, at least in the initial stages, were taken as tutor groups constructed to offer a range of ability. Again, at least in the earlier years, traditional subject specialisms were less pronounced. The curriculum was organised largely into subject *areas* such as humanities, creative studies and communication skills. There was less closure to outside influences than at Archbishop Ambrose. As the headteacher commented: 'We offer a very much wider curriculum and the social education and the youngsters who actually emerge are far better prepared for the sort of life they are going to lead'. The school was then involved in the TVEI (Technical and Vocational Education Initiative) scheme and was experimenting with a modular curriculum in some areas.

In terms of the expressive order, there was less pronounced emphasis on the forms of discipline favoured at Archbishop Ambrose and those which did exist were not visibly based on hierarchical control. The prospectus advertised the 'encouragement of self-discipline, tolerance, co-operation and mutual respect and the promotion of positive attitudes and values . . .' and the headteacher stated that 'our discipline aims to be positive far more often than negative'. The lack of age- and sex-differentiating rituals was also evident in the more flexible uniform requirements. These stipulated what colours should be worn and were generally less restrictive and more open to interpretation. Ties were not essential for boys or girls, and students were not required to display their school affiliation outside through the wearing of blazers. Indeed, unlike Archbishop Ambrose, the openness to parents and the wider community was emphasised and celebrated in documentation.

Some of the differences between the two schools are evident in the aggregated questionnaire responses of our students (see Table 3). The strong emphasis on the instrumental order at Archbishop Ambrose and its stratified nature are reflected in the fact that nearly three-quarters of the Archbishop Ambrose students remembered being worried about 'not being able to keep up with the work', whereas at Vicarage Road the majority were 'never' worried on this account. Indeed, the lack of hierarchy and the inclusiveness of Vicarage Road might be reflected in the fact that students were more likely to worry about other students thinking they were *too* clever. This was true of half the Vicarage Road respondents as opposed to just over one fifth of the Archbishop Ambrose students.

While such aggregated responses may give something of a flavour of each school, they hide a variety of individual responses to the culture of the school that suggest different modes and levels of student involvement. These are influenced by many factors, among which the family's orientations towards the school culture is potentially crucial.

The family effect

In order to facilitate a high level of student involvement, the family has to accept the ends *and* understand the means of the expressive and instrumental orders. The ability and inclination to understand and accept are likely to be dependent on the socio-economic location and cultural orientation of the family. Drawing on Merton's framework for analysing suicide, Bernstein identifies a range of possible relations that the family may have with the school, which are illustrated in Fig. 8. As Bernstein

Table 3 Worries over schoolwork and ability at Archbishop Ambrose and Vicarage Road

	Not being able to keep up with the work		Other pupils thinking you were too clever	
	Archbishop Ambrose	Vicarage Road	Archbishop Ambrose	Vicarage Road
Worried you *a lot*	1	0	0	1
Worried you *a little*	12	8	4	9
Never worried you	5	12	14	10

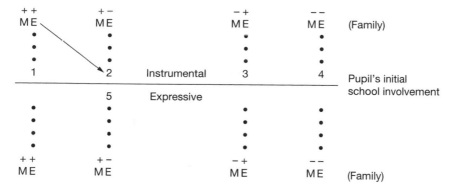

Figure 8 The family's effect on the student's involvement in school (from Bernstein, 1966). M = *understanding of the means; E = acceptance of the ends; 1, understanding of means, acceptance of ends; 2, understanding of means, non-acceptance or rejection of ends; 3, no or little understanding of means, but acceptance of ends; 4, no or little understanding of means, non-acceptance or rejection of ends; 5, understanding of means of both orders, acceptance of ends of instrumental order but rejection of ends of expressive order.*

notes, it is the aim of the school to move students towards Position 1—where they understand and accept the means and ends of the school. However, this is likely to be more or less easy according to the family's initial orientation to the school. Although the eventual form of student role involvement cannot be read off from parental perceptions because other experiences and influences come into play throughout the school career, the orientation of the family, and any tensions between the culture of the family and that of the school, is likely to have strong effects at least on students' initial location.

Student involvement

Bernstein (1966) outlines five potential positions for student role involvement. The positions of commitment and alienation need the least explanation. While these are often the only positions given serious attention in some research (for example, Willis, 1977; Corrigan, 1979), Bernstein offers us three further types of involvement—detachment, estrangement and deferment. Detachment arises when the student both understands and accepts the instrumental order but rejects the expressive order of the school. Conversely, estrangement occurs when the student understands and accepts the expressive order and also accepts the ends of the instrumental order but fails to understand the means. Deferment is when the student's involvement is suspended—'watching the state of play' (Bernstein, 1977, p. 45).[6]

There are strong parallels here between Bernstein's categories and those developed by Woods (1977) and Wakeford (1969), who also draw on Merton's schema. However, while Woods' adaptation has the advantage of providing a wider range of possibilities within each position (for instance, he identified a number of variants of 'conformity'), he does not provide a means of distinguishing between school types. Certainly, for our research, given the wide variety of markedly different institutions with which we are dealing, classification of school cultures has been a starting point in the analysis.

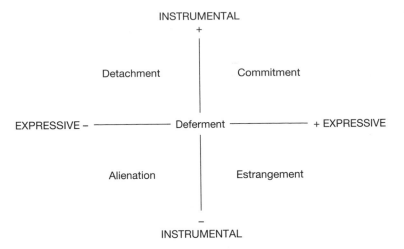

Figure 9 Types of involvement in the role of the student (Bernstein, 1977, p. 50).

In the next section, we draw on biographical data from the project to examine the extent to which these interconnections can be identified and used to explain apparently idiosyncratic stories of success and failure, consensus and disaffection at the two schools. We have drawn on a range of data to categorise family orientation to the culture of the school and ultimate student involvement.[7] Family involvement has been ascertained from the initial interviews with students[8] and many of their parents in the early years of secondary schooling. Given the different purposes of the original research, we do not have full and relevant data from all our respondents' parents. We have indicated in Tables 4 and 5 where there are insufficient data to establish orientation. Student role involvement has been established through responses to the questionnaire survey and, in many cases, through individual interviews. In identifying positions of student involvement we need to bear in mind the retrospective nature of the data. However, while some relate to informants' perceptions after leaving school, we also asked them about their actual participation in school activities and about any positions of responsibility they had held. There is also supporting evidence from recent longitudinal research (Andersson, 1997) of a remarkable degree of continuity between attitudes expressed by students while at school and those elicited several years after leaving.

Student involvement at Archbishop Ambrose

Evidence from the initial interviews in the early 1980s indicates conflicting orientations towards the culture of this school. While there was an unambiguously positive orientation towards the instrumental order, irrespective of social class background, there were varying degrees of enthusiasm for the expressive order (see Table 4). Bernstein's (1977) analysis of class and pedagogies provides a valuable framework for interpreting this variation. He identifies two large subgroups of the middle class—the 'old' middle class who are generally located within the economic (e) field of production, and the 'new' middle class who are agents within the symbolic (s) field of production. Both the old middle class and the working class tend to be antagonistic to the progressivism of the post-war period that is manifest throughout the

Table 4 Family orientation[9] and student involvment at Archbishop Ambrose

	Parents' class	Orientation to IO	Orientation to EO	A-level results	Student involvement
Kapelko	mc (e)	positive	no data	AAB	committed
Grant	mc (e)	positive	positive	CCD	committed
Stephens	mc (e)	positive	positive	BBC	committed
Weston	mc (e)	positive	positive	CNN	estranged
Slocombe	mc (e)	positive	positive	none	estranged
Finch	mc (e/s)	positive	positive	BCC	committed
Beasley	mc (e/s)	positive	no data	ACD	committed
Pachul	mc (e/s)	positive	ambivalent	AAAA	detached
Drainsfield	mc (e/s)	positive	positive	BCDE	estranged
Korecki	mc (s[a]/e)	positive	no data	BBDD	committed
Fellowes	mc (s)	positive	hostile	AAAA	committed
Leventhal	mc (s)	positive	ambivalent	BCD	detached
Pearson	mc (s)	ambivalent	ambivalent	none	detached
Glynn	lmc (s)	positive	positive	DDE	detached
Emerson	lmc (s)	no data	no data	CCC	detached
Moore	lmc (e)	positive	ambivalent	CCE	committed
Povey	wc	positive	positive	AAB	committed
Andrews	wc	positive	indifferent	DEE	detached

[a]Father died when student was 11.

symbolic field and which was particularly evident in education during recent decades. For both groups, the ambiguity and interpersonal dimension of progressive modes of education threatened their own mode of socialisation and cultural reproduction. For the new middle class, however, successful socialisation is to some extent dependent upon ambiguity—a loosening of visible hierarchy and explicit control. However, as Bernstein also points out, this group of parents is confronted with a dilemma. Faced with 'the grim obduracy of the division of labour and of the narrow pathways to its positions of power and prestige' (Bernstein, 1977, p. 126), the new middle class needs to ensure access to more traditional and hierarchically ordered forms of schooling at secondary stage. Of course, the new middle class itself is not homogeneous. There are elements within it that are ideologically predisposed towards traditional modes of education. Members of what Bernstein terms 'regulators' (the legal system, police, prison service, church), 'repairers' (medical/psychiatric services, social services) and 'executors' (civil service, bureaucrats) are likely to be more conservative than 'shapers' (creators of symbolic forms in arts and sciences), 'diffusers' (mass and specialised media) and 'reproducers' (teachers).

The various dispositions are identified in Table 4 and then connected with the ultimate positions of student involvement at Archbishop Ambrose. In general, middle-class parents located unambiguously within the economic field of production (Kapelko, Grant, Stephens, Weston and Slocombe) tended to be more positively oriented towards both the instrumental and expressive orders of the school.

For these middle-class students there was often close involvement with the school—between the school and the parents and between the school and the student. In terms of family involvement, these parents understood and accepted the means and the ends of the instrumental and expressive orders of Archbishop Ambrose (position 1, Fig. 8). There would appear to be a strong connection between these parents' positive perceptions of the school and their children's level of commitment. Although not always outstandingly successful academically relative to the overall profile of Archbishop Ambrose, these students often held key positions of responsibility within the school, were heavily involved in school sports and look back on their time at school with affection. Many still keep in touch with the school through dropping in to talk to teachers and joining the 'old boys' association, Stephens provides a typical example of a committed student. His parents, with whom he is still very close, were positively oriented towards the school and kept a 'careful watch' on him throughout his school years. While at school he was Head Boy ('in charge of 20 odd prefects and having to sort them out every day'), head of house and captain of rugby. He also participated in cricket, athletics, drama and debating. As he reminisces: 'I had a thoroughly good time there. Thoroughly enjoyed it and they gave you some marvellous opportunities which as long as you're willing to take them and push yourself ... [not just] in academic work, but in music, sport, across the board.'

However, even though there may have been continuity between the culture of the school and the orientation of these middle-class families, student involvement was not always characterised by commitment. It is also possible to identify students who became 'estranged' from the school. Although these shared the values of the school, they did not have the means to succeed—either because of the heavy academic demands of such an academically oriented school and/or inappropriate cultural resources within the home. As Bernstein (1977, p. 46) notes, 'the blighted aspirations, combined with a low stream, coupled with his loyalty to the school, may make his school experience particularly painful and damaging'. Although it is possible to speculate that a position of commitment to the school may be engineered through the expressive order, this is problematic in a school in which the stratification of students by academic achievement is so visible.

One such estranged student is Weston. His parents (father, general manager of an engineering company; mother, housewife) were positively disposed towards both the instrumental and expressive orders of Archbishop Ambrose. However, they did not seem to have fully understood the means by which they could ensure his commitment (Position 3, Fig. 8). Perhaps because neither had undertaken any higher education themselves, they appeared to believe that passing the entrance test was enough and their subsequent support was passive rather than active. As Weston puts it 'they were far too removed'. This created a potential source of danger as the influence of peer groups tended to outweigh that of parents and school:

> There seemed to be the people whose parents really pushed them ... My parents didn't really push me that hard. I mean I was quite well behaved as a child and I was doing my homework, But I would kind of just drift along and do what I could. So I just sort of did as best as I could and that always seemed to be enough.

He recalls, for instance, how he made 'silly choices' at GCSEs, made on the basis of what his friends were doing. He only passed one of his A-levels and, after retakes, just scraped a place at a College of Higher Education.

Drainsfield provides us with a different variant of estrangement. His parents were positively disposed towards both the instrumental and expressive orders of the school and, unlike Weston, would appear to have had the necessary understanding to facilitate his full commitment to this school. However, for reasons which he believed included a precarious placing in 'advanced' streams, Drainsfield was unable to realise the instrumental ends. Although he did participate fully in the expressive activities of the school (athletics, choir, orchestra, drama, rowing) and held minor positions of responsibility (house prefect and deputy music prefect), his relative failure on the instrumental side was a cause of much anxiety for him and his parents.

> ... I think that the third and fourth year was the toughest year because that was when we had to do everything in two years ... at the time there was nothing more that I wanted than to go into the A stream, be up with the best. Crazy really and I think my parents were right behind me as well ... But as soon as I went into that class, I was with a much stronger group of boys ... Sort of ranking it was, dropped miles down the class, I was almost down the bottom from being at the top. Ranking was very important to me at the time.

Despite struggling to keep up with the rest, Drainsfield maintained his ambition to go on to an elite university—the aim of many Archbishop Ambrose boys. At sixth-form level, which he reached a year early, he finally realised his ambition might not be easily attainable: 'My marks weren't as good as they had been and I don't think I was able to work out why or what I could do about it ... I deferred my application till I was eighteen ... Then I put down Cambridge ... Bristol, very sort of top places'. When he finally failed to get the grades, he found it difficult to face the humiliation of attending a less prestigious higher education institution:

> I just wanted to stop studying and get out of it all and I just got a job instead ... All the way through school my only ambition was to go to Cambridge ... And I didn't get it and I didn't want to do anything else.[10]

Although he now wishes he had continued his education, much to his parents' disappointment, he gave it up, got married and found employment as a bank cashier.

As noted earlier, while middle-class parents located in the symbolic field of production were generally positive about the means and ends of the instrumental order of Archbishop Ambrose, some were more ambivalent and even hostile towards the expressive order. Mrs Fellowes, for instance, was quite clear in her dislike of the 'the ethos and attitudes' of Archbishop Ambrose and claimed to be 'very antagonistic to the system of division in general'. Her son provides an interesting example of someone who became committed to the school despite the ambivalence of his parents. He illustrates a process of removal from the values of his family as dramatic in many ways as that reported by the upwardly mobile students of Jackson & Marsden's (1966) research. Born into a typically new middle-class family (father, television editor; mother, social worker) one might have expected Fellowes to have preserved some of his parents' ambivalence and hostility towards at least the expressive order of Archbishop Ambrose. However, Fellowes has detached himself from his parents' values and was fully committed to the ethos and principles of a school to which he expressed 'this strong sense of attachment'. Unlike his parents, Fellowes is 'very pro grammar schools'.

His position is somewhat exceptional, however. More often, where there is rejection of the expressive order of the school, the student will take on a position of 'detachment'. Bernstein notes that such a position is often taken by working-class students who realise that incorporation into the expressive order of the school will take them away from the values of the home. However, detachment is also evident in some of our students with one or more parents working in the symbolic field of production. These potential recruits into the new middle class came from a background that enabled them to achieve academically but caused resistance to being integrated into the expressive culture of the school.

Pachul provides a clear case of this form of detachment. His father is a financial adviser and his mother a teacher, both graduates. Despite his unambiguous academic success, Pachul's involvement with the school became increasingly disconnected as he progressed. In addition to the ambivalence of his parents towards Archbishop Ambrose, his lack of involvement was exacerbated by his ethnic identity. Born of an Italian mother and an Indian father, he found it difficult to find a group of fellow students with whom he could identify. His experiences at primary school 'made me discard the Indian part of me and when I was at Archbishop Ambrose I began defending myself by saying that I was Italian ... It seemed easier because Indians seemed to have a negative image ... At Archbishop Ambrose I never had anything to do with Asian pupils until the last 2 years. Prior to that I tried to keep more in with the English. Being half Italian and half Indian and living in England, I've always felt split. I don't feel English'.

But one key factor behind his detachment appears to have been his (and his family's) rejection of the expressive ends of the school when it appeared they might jeopardise the instrumental ends. For instance, as an athletic student Pachul was much in demand for 'millions of events'. The perceived pressure of these demands eventually led to a substantial rift between the school and his family. When he refused to play cricket on the day before his GCSEs, he was, as he puts it, 'in their bad books'. Looking back he speaks of the teachers with some bitterness, saying that he wished 'they had sacked half of them'. His ultimate desire would be to 'to get my own back on the teachers'. Perhaps the strength of the instrumental order at Archbishop Ambrose, and Pachul's willingness and propensity to perform well in that dimension, meant that he was able to carry on at the school without that detachment turning to alienation.

In accounting for the different forms of involvement between Fellowes and Pachul, we need to look beyond family orientation and academic ability because both sets of parents expressed ambivalence towards the school and both students were high achievers. It is probable that the difference can be explained by the mediating influence of friendship groups. While Pachul felt isolated within the school, Fellowes seems to have formed close and continuing relationships with other Archbishop Ambrose boys whose commitment to it was high.

This is not the case with Pearson, who provides an example of detachment that comes much closer to alienation. Pearson's parents were ambivalent, although not hostile, towards both the expressive and instrumental orders. His father, in particular, valued the idea of Archbishop Ambrose—'it was the thought of his son going to Archbishop Ambrose and it would stand me in good stead for the future as some kind of symbol of me being really intelligent'. But in other ways they were out of step with the culture of the school. Of all our Archbishop Ambrose sample, Pearson's family comes closest to position 4 (Fig. 8). His father, a musician and computer programmer, and his Austrian mother, an antiques dealer and furniture restorer, had appeared somewhat exotic compared to other Archbishop Ambrose parents: '... my dad was a little flamboyant, had a big Mercedes and things, despite the fact that it was on hire purchase ... they knew he was a musician and had had a record in the charts'. Pearson's somewhat 'alternative' socialisation led him to be antagonistic towards both the instrumental and expressive sides—in similar ways to Aggleton's (1987) 'rebels without a cause': 'I didn't really like schooling ... I was very critical at the time and vocal about it, that I don't really believe in exams. I don't think they measure the right things.' At 16, he decided he wanted to be a musician like his father: 'I didn't like exams and things and just wanted out'. He left school and pursued his career through informal networks, in particular those of his father and computing friends he had made while at school.

For middle-class students it is often unwillingness to take on the expressive dimension of the school that leads to detachment. With students of lower socio-economic status, it may be a lack of understanding or lack of means to fulfil this dimension as much as unwillingness. This may well be the case for Glynn and Emerson, who come from lower-middle-class homes with no history of higher education, and Andrews, who comes from an unambiguous working-class background.

Emerson, for instance, found the high academic expectations 'more of a hindrance' than a help and struggled with his schoolwork. While this may reflect a position of estrangement, he seems detached inasmuch as he seems to have rejected the ethos of the school. Most of his friendship groups were formed outside Archbishop Ambrose and he disliked what he saw as its 'arrogance': 'My personal opinion of it now is that it was quite a snobbish school. It was quite a macho school. My friends outside were probably more important to me than my friends at school. My social life outside school was more important to me . . .' Andrews similarly struggled with his schoolwork and also found himself unable to slot into any of the elite sporting groups. His lack of commitment to the school is evident in his attempts to leave the school—always overruled by his mother: '. . . by the time I got to the last few years I found the regime was too disciplined and it was too enforced and then they try to inflict things on you when you're 16, 17 and 18 . . . I resented being there.' Again the influence of friendship groups is important: 'half of my friends in the final 2 years had left during that period and went to sixth-form colleges. And already I wanted to leave before I'd started so it wasn't a nice 2 years. I didn't enjoy it and I wished I wasn't there'. Only the fact that Andrews *did* remain at school to complete his A-levels prevents us from categorising him as 'alienated'.

Student involvement at Vicarage Road

The profile of the parents from our sample of Vicarage Road students indicates a cross-section of social class similar to that of Archbishop Ambrose, although with the larger number of working-class parents that would be expected from evidence of the disproportionate representation of middle-class parents at grammar and 11–18 schools (Kerckhoff *et al.*, 1997). There was also a larger number of middle-class parents who can be unambiguously located within the symbolic field of production. This may well reflect the 'new middle class' preference for differentiated, rather than stratified, modes of socialisation discussed earlier. However, as Table 5 shows, many of these parents were ambivalent or even negatively disposed towards the instrumental and expressive orders at Vicarage Road.

In the main, the ambivalence expressed towards the instrumental order involved an acceptance of the instrumental ends of the school, but scepticism over the means of achieving them. It is notable that Vicarage Road had not been the first choice of school for nine of these families. As discussed earlier, the transition from primary to secondary school is often the point at which new middle-class parents choose to introduce their children to more stratified modes of education that appear to offer more certain routes to higher education and occupational success. Some of these parents had unsuccessfully applied for places at a neighbouring single-sex girls' comprehensive or assisted places at nearby independent schools. There was less ambivalence towards the expressive order of the school, perhaps because of its more inclusive nature.

Table 5 Family orientation and student involvement at Vicarage Road

	Parents' class	Orientation to IO	Orientation to EO	A-level results[a]	Student involvement
Vanessa	mc (e)	ambivalent	positive	CDD	committed
Claire	mc (e)	no data	no data	none	committed
Barbara[b]	mc (e)	ambivalent	negative	none	alienated
Kristof	mc (e)	positive	no data	CCD	detached
Christine[b]	mc (e/s)	ambivalent	ambivalent	BCD	detached
Beatrice	mc (s/e)	positive	positive	D	committed
Bethany	mc (s)	positive	positive	AAB	detached
Georgia	mc (s)	no data	no data	AAC	committed
Jeremy	mc (s)	positive	positive	ACC	committed
Chloe[b]	mc (s)	negative	negative	BBC	committed
Bridget[b]	mc (s)	ambivalent	positive	BCU	committed
William	mc (s)	ambivalent	positive	none	committed
Mark[b]	mc (s)	ambivalent	positive	BBC	committed
Helen[b]	wc	ambivalent	ambivalent	BBC	committed
Bernadette	wc	positive	positive	BBC	committed
Bryan[b]	wc	positive	negative	ABEU	estranged
Melissa[b]	wc	no data	no data	EE	committed
Parva	wc	ambivalent	positive	BBD	committed
Graham[b]	wc	ambivalent	ambivalent	AABB	committed
Cheryl	wc	no data	positive	BBB	committed

[a]As Vicarage Road is an 11–16 school, A-levels were studied elsewhere, usually the local further education college, but occasionally nearby independent sixth forms.

[b]Parents initially wanted to place their children at other schools.

Responses towards the school by parents and by ex-students are, in general, less clear-cut than for Archbishop Ambrose. Perhaps because Archbishop Ambrose promoted a more unambiguously and visibly defined culture, it evoked stronger reactions—both of attachment and hostility. As mentioned earlier, Vicarage Road offered a less totalising environment in which the boundaries between school and outside tended to be blurred. There was also less congruity between the instrumental and expressive orders, and this appeared in the responses of our informants. As academically able students, they are likely to have experienced a somewhat more stratified and less therapeutic schooling than their schoolmates in lower sets, for whom the framing of knowledge may be weakened (Bernstein, 1971). Another dimension of differentiated schools such as Vicarage Road is that they are likely, at least at the official level, to promote the adoption of invisible pedagogies (Bernstein, 1977). Although these will reorient students to the school in particular ways, their significance may not be recognised and understood by all students.

Thus, while there are many students who have left Vicarage Road who can be characterised as having a relationship of 'commitment' with the school, this is frequently less pronounced than that expressed by Archbishop Ambrose students and covered a wider range of shades. Nevertheless, there are some, like Jeremy, who exhibit strong commitment to both the instrumental and expressive orders. Jeremy's parents, both teachers, were very positive about the culture of Vicarage Road and maintained a close involvement through the school: 'Mum was a member of the PTA and supported all the fund raising events ... But I think that the school enjoyed strong support from both of them.'

Jeremy clearly thrived on the less hierarchical relations at Vicarage Road. Indeed, he claims: 'I probably related better to many of the staff than I did to people of my own age'. Moreover he claims the 'more relaxed' and adult atmosphere enabled him not only to achieve good results at school, but also to perform well at university where he achieved a first-class honours degree:

> I've always maintained that Vicarage Road was an absolutely smashing school to attend. I thoroughly enjoyed my time there and it was probably the atmosphere that was so conducive to bringing out the best in everybody. That's what I think helped people to come out with such good results from that school . . . at Vicarage Road we were always treated with more responsibility and maturity than pupils from other schools. I think that has 'rubbed of'; particularly during my university years. I think I had the additional responsibility and maturity handed to me at an earlier age than some of the other students, and that can only have been because of Vicarage Road.

But it is the expressive side that he placed most value on, again in keeping with the values of the school. He claimed the most useful experience he took from Vicarage Road was:

> . . . mixing with people and forming relationships with people, especially with people in authority, such as the teachers when I was at school. I enjoy a good relationship with people who some of my friends would be terrified of. I've never been particularly daunted or frightened by people in more superior positions. I think that was because the Vicarage Road environment was so friendly, warm, welcoming, interested and concerned. I think that is probably the single biggest contribution that school made to my subsequent life.

Many others whom we have categorised as committed were similarly positive about the expressive order of the school, but more ambivalent about its instrumental side. Although their uncertainty was not expressed in terms of disillusionment or disappointment that might lead to estrangement, several of them mentioned the lack of 'push' from the school. It may be that these students, because of their early socialisation, were unable to penetrate the underlying principles of invisible pedagogies in which the rules of criteria, hierarchy and pace of learning are largely implicit. Those students who seemed unable to grasp these principles were often those from old middle-class or working-class backgrounds, in contrast to Jeremy whose parents were 'reproducers' within the new middle class.

Bernadette (father, production supervisor; mother, childminder) valued 'mixing with so many different people . . . not everyone was rich and intelligent' but believes that having the right attitude was more important than hard work: 'I think like academically you had to show that you were trying, that you weren't sitting back and moaning. You had to sort of be able to mix with students from the different academic levels . . . because I was up there and I could keep up. If I'd been willing to learn but not as able, I don't know . . . I don't remember ever actually them saying "you must sit down and do this"'.

Some students felt that the emphasis on the expressive dimension jeopardised the instrumental ends, or at least those supported by themselves and their parents. Where the ends and means of the expressive order were rejected by families, the potential for detachment arose. This was the case for Christine (father, sales manager; mother, health visitor) who said she disliked the way that 'if you were quiet it was frowned upon'. Detachment is also evident in Kristof. His parents came from Turkey, to which his father (a geophysicist for a private company) and his twin brother have since returned. His father was initially interested in sending the boys to private school but decided that he could get 'as good an education' at Vicarage Road. However, Kristof's subsequent experience did not obviously endorse this confidence. Kristof concedes that: 'When I was at Vicarage Road I think I did quite well. But it wasn't because of Vicarage Road School itself', it was because I was willing to do good work for myself. Vicarage Road didn't actually encourage me to work hard. It encouraged me to attend and to be socially active, but it was never a challenge. They were more concerned that people could get the same kind of grades more than anything else, rather than helping people who were more able to do achieve more.' At 16, his parents placed him at private school to complete his A-levels, an option that Kristof now believes would have been better taken at age 11 rather than later.

It is not possible to explain detachment through the values of home and school being out of step in the case of Bethany (father, architect; mother, lecturer), whose antipathy to the school is such that the only thing she liked about her school was leaving it, and the thing she wishes most about it is that it had burned down before she arrived. Given the high emphasis placed upon the expressive dimension, it may be that students who prefer more cloistered approaches to learning are seen as somehow inadequate. Bethany describes herself feeling 'introvert', 'non-conformist' 'unconfident' and 'intellectual' during her time at Vicarage Road.[11]

In one case, where the instrumental order was clearly not understood by the student, it is possible to see the only position of estrangement evident among our sample from Vicarage Road, and even here it does not appear to have carried with it quite so much humiliation as that experienced at Archbishop Ambrose. Bryan came from a working-class background (father, police constable; mother, dinner lady). His father had high hopes for him and originally wanted him to attend private school: 'It was from a young age, I remember my dad saying "you've got to do well at school, you've got to do well at school"'. However, it does not appear that his parents were able to offer Bryan any specific help with what 'doing well' might involve. As he progressed through the school he found the work increasingly hard— a problem he resolved through missing lessons: 'Twenty-five percent I suppose, I used to miss a lot of lessons ... when it got hard I suppose the better way of coping with it was not going, which was completely wrong'. His other strategy for coping was to revise hard just before the exams: 'I still felt that I had it in me to pass exams. Because I am very good at revising ... But it didn't pay off.' Despite his disappointment academically, Bryan remains committed to the expressive aspects of Vicarage Road—in particular, its inclusivity: 'The most impressive thing I got out of it was the social outlook. I can still look back through now, I can relate quite heavily to it and think I have learnt about the people while at the Vicarage Road because you are, just chucked in there ... What I got the most, the most, the feel for either different classes, different type of people that are around.'

Discussion

In this exploration, we have attempted to show that the cultural interplay between family and home continues to be an important factor in understanding orientation to school and, in some respects, academic achievement. While unravelling the various aspects of this interaction does not allow us to predict levels of student involvement in any simplistic way, we want to argue that it provides a means of looking at educational progressions and their apparent idiosyncrasies that continues to be valid, despite the criticisms of 'culturalism' and 'determinism' that have been levied at this kind of approach.

We have indicated that Bernstein's framework, in particular, enables us to unravel in a systematic way some of the connections between educational involvement, social-class background and school culture that would be left out of the probabilistic equations of Rational Action Theory or marginalised within the constructivist approaches adopted in some recent research into school to work transitions. This does not mean that Bernstein's framework enables us easily to formulate strategies whereby the incidence of estrangement, detachment and alienation might be reduced. It may seem probable that children from 'old' middle-class parents are less likely to become detached if they attend 'old' middle-class schools such as Archbishop Ambrose, but they also run the risk of estrangement if they are committed to the values but unable to do the work. Similarly, children from 'new' middle-class families might seem well advised to attend 'differentiated' schools such as Vicarage Road; but, while they may be less likely to become detached or estranged, the more open nature of these schools may provide more distractions from the narrow path towards high status higher education. Thus, while differentiated comprehensive schools may increase levels of commitment among some students, they may do so at the expense of focusing on measures of school performance that remain a prerequisite to entering higher education. Many of our committed Vicarage Road students obtained lower examination results than our estranged or detached Archbishop Ambrose boys.

The situation of the students from lower socio-economic backgrounds is particularly interesting. The two working-class and two lower-middle-class students at Archbishop Ambrose display contrasting modes of involvement, with two categorised as committed and two detached. Of the seven working-class students at Vicarage Road, only one is not classified as committed. Although these numbers are small, they do call into question claims that academically selective schools provide the best means for gaining commitment to education from academically able working-class children. However, the suggestion that comprehensive schools, particularly those that are organised along principles of differentiation, provide a safer route for 'bright' working-class children raises other issues about Bernstein's analytical framework. Given the proposed connection between social class and pedagogies (Bernstein, 1997), it might have been anticipated that the working-class students would have greater difficulty in becoming committed at a school like Vicarage Road. That they did not, may indicate the possibility of becoming at least partially committed to the expressive and instrumental ends without fully understanding the means. As we mentioned earlier, there were marked differences in degrees of commitment at Vicarage Road that could reflect differences in the degrees to which students were able to penetrate the principles of the pedagogic discourse. On the other hand, this may reflect the relative incongruity between the instrumental and expressive orders at Vicarage Road, particularly for academically able students, that provided a variety of means through which commitment could be generated. Again, however, we need to note that forms of commitment do not closely mirror levels of attainment.

It could be argued that school performance is more important than student involvement, in that it does not matter how students *feel* about their education as long as they end up with the necessary qualifications. But it appears from our evidence that, even where the level of involvement is not linked to attainment in any straightforward way, it has an important bearing on future educational pathways and prospects. The nature of students' involvement in their higher education appears to be more or less problematic according to their involvement at school. Moreover, in the longer term, the relationship between the student and the school is likely to have implications for their future decisions about education, both generally in terms of preferences for particular policy changes, and personally in terms of where they choose to send children of their own. As we have seen, even high academic achievement does not generate loyalty to a particular form of schooling, and many of those who were detached or estranged from their schools were quite insistent that they would not send any of their children to such an institution even when they themselves would have appeared, to an outsider, to have gained attainment benefits. Given the relatively high number of less than committed students from Archbishop Ambrose, their ambivalence may raise interesting questions about the future supporters of state-maintained, academically selective, single-sex schools. On the other hand, their doubts about this kind of schooling may disappear when they, like their parents, are also faced with 'the grim obduracy of the division of labour and of the narrow pathways to its positions of power and prestige' (Bernstein, 1977, p. 126).

In conclusion, although the analysis we have presented is exploratory, we believe it illustrates the usefulness of Bernstein's framework for making sense of contrasting modes of involvement in schooling. If the conclusions drawn from the analysis are tentative, this is not only or even mainly because of the necessarily small numbers of informants in a project dependent on extended interviews. It is largely because the evidence indicates the complexity of the influences shaping students' school experiences. Bernstein's theoretical approach though, unlike some that are currently in vogue, invites us to unravel such complexity rather than ignore it or use it to celebrate indeterminacy uncritically.

Acknowledgements

We are grateful to the Economic and Social Research Council for supporting the research project 'Destined for Success? The educational biographies of academically able pupils' (Grant R000235570). We would also like to thank The British Council and Consejo de Investigaciones Científicas y Technológicas de la Provincia de Córdoba for funds to enable Sally Power to participate in the course 'Basil Bernstein: Desarollos teoricos y su aplicacion a estudios empiricas. Analisis espistimologico' at the Facultad de Filosofia y Humanidades, Universidad Nacional de Córdoba, Argentina. It was here that the usefulness of the theoretical framework for our data was first explored.

Notes

1 In other papers, we have looked at the broader patterns of educational attainment across all our students (Edwards *et al.*, 1997), theoretical issues relating modes of sponsorship (Edwards *et al.*, 1996), the strengths and weaknesses of political arithmetic and biographical approaches, particularly in relation to our female respondents (Power *et al.*, 1996), and the relationship between academic achievement and gender identification amongst our male respondents (Power *et al.*, 1998).

2 For a fuller account of these data, see Edwards *et al.* (1989).

3 The key to these schools can be found in the Appendix.

4 The precise components of each complex of behaviour and the way they interconnect will not only vary across institutions, but also over time. It would be interesting to explore how they have been affected by recent policies that may have brought about an increasing emphasis of the instrumental order. These policies were only just beginning to be implemented while our respondents were at school.

5 These pseudonyms are the same as those used in reports of the earlier research project. A gazetteer of the schools can be found at the end of Edwards *et al.* (1989).

6 This position is of only passing interest to us here, given the longitudinal and retrospective nature of our respondents' biographies and the temporary nature of deferment.

7 As with all categorisation, the location of particular students and families was based on the researchers' judgements. It is worth noting, however, that there was a high degree of consistency in the categorisation of both schools and students between us and academics from the University of Córdoba, Argentina, despite differences in language and culture.

8 In academically selective schools, students were selected randomly. In comprehensive schools, students who were deemed to have been capable of gaining a place at an academically selective school, either on the basis of tests or teacher assessment, were identified by the school.

9 As with schools, student and family names are pseudonyms.

10 There are strong parallels with Edward (See Power *et al.*, 1998), who attended Nortown Grammer—similar in many ways to Archbishop Ambrose.

11 Although gender does not appear to be a significant factor in categorising students within this particular typology of involvement, we need to explore more fully in the future the ways in which these self-perceptions are gendered. Holland's (1996) work is clearly relevant to this issue and suggests that within each field of production, girls were socialised into weaker classification systems than boys.

References

Andersson, B.E. (1997) Young people look back on their school situation in senior high school. Paper presented at the *European Conference on Educational Research*, Johann Wolfgang Goethe-Universität, Frankfurt am Main, Germany, 24–27 September.

Aggleton, P. (1987) *Rebels Without a Cause? Middle class youth and the transition from school to work* (London, Falmer).

Bernstein, B. (1966) Sources of consensus and disaffection in education, *Journal of the Association of Assistant Mistresses*, 17, pp. 4–11.

Bernstein, B. (1971) On the classification and framing of educational knowledge, in: M.F.D. Young (Ed.) *Knowledge and Control: new directions in the sociology of education* (London, Collier-Macmillan).

Bernstein, B. (1977) *Class, Codes and Control Volume 3: towards a theory of education transitions*, 2nd (London, Routledge and Kegan Paul).

Bernstein, B., Elvin, L. & Peters, R. (1966) Ritual in education, *Philosophical Transactions of the Royal Society of London*, Series B, 251 (772).

Boudon, R. (1974) *Education, Opportunity and Social Inequality* (New York, John Wiley).

Bourdieu, P. (1973) Cultural reproduction and social reproduction, in: R. Brown (Ed.) *Knowledge, Education and Cultural Change* (London, Tavistock).

Breen, R. & Goldthorpe, J. (1997) Explaining Educational Differentials: towards a formal rational action theory, *Rationality and Society*, 9(3), pp. 275–305.

Bynner, J., Ferri, E. & Shepherd, P. (1997) *Twenty-something in the 1990s* (Aldershot, Ashgate).

Corrigan, P. (1979) *Schooling the Smash Street Kids* (London, Macmillan).

Edwards, T., Fritz, J. & Whitty, G. (1989) *The State and Private Education: an evaluation of the assisted places scheme* (London, Falmer Press).

Edwards, T., Power, S. & Whitty, G. (1996) Selected for success? State sponsorship of academically able children. Paper presented at the *European Conference on Educational Research*, Seville, Spain, 25–28 September.

Edwards, T., Wigfall, V., Whitty, G. & Power, S. (1997) Sponsorship, selection and common schooling: educational biographies of academically able pupils. Paper presented at the *European Conference on Educational Research*, Johann Wolfgang Goethe-Universität, Frankfurt am Main, Germany, 24–27 September.

Goldthorpe, J. (1996) Class analysis and the reorientation of class theory: the case of persisting differentials in educational attainment, *British Journal of Sociology*, 47(3), pp. 481–505.

Hodkinson, P. & Sparkes, A.C. (1997) Careership: a sociological theory of career decision-making, *British Journal of Sociology of Education*, 18(1), pp. 29–44.

Hodkinson, P., Sparkes, A.C. & Hodkinson, H. (1996) *Triumph or Tears: young people, markets and the transition from school to work* (London, David Fulton).

Holland, J. (1986) Social class differences in adolescents' conceptions of the domestic and industrial division of labour, *CORE*, 10, p. 1.

Jackson, B. & Marsden, D. (1966) *Education and the Working Class* (Harmondsworth, Penguin).

Kerckhoff, A., Fogelman, K. & Manilove, J. (1997) Staying ahead: the middle class and school reform in England and Wales, *Sociology of Education*, 70 (January), pp. 19–35.

King, R. (1976) Bernstein's sociology of the school: some propositions tested, *British Journal of Sociology*, 27, pp. 430–443.

King, R. (1981) Bernstein's sociology of the school—a further testing, *British Journal of Sociology*, 32, pp. 259–265.

MacDonald, R. & Coffield, F. (1991) *Risky Business: youth and the enterprise culture* (Lewes, Falmer Press).

Power, S., Edwards, T. & Whitty, G. (1996) Political arithmetic versus biography: analysing the educational trajectories of 24 academically able girls. Paper presented to *CEDAR*, University of Warwick, April.

Power, S., Whitty, G., Edwards, T. & Wigfall, V. (1998) Schoolboys and schoolwork: gender identification and academic achievement, *International Journal of Inclusive Education*, 2(2) pp. 135–153.

Roberts, K. (1993) Career trajectories and the mirage of increased social mobility, in: I. Bates & G. Riseborough (Eds) *Youth and Inequality* (Buckingham, Open University Press).

Saunders, P. (1996) *Unequal but Fair? A Study of Class Barriers in Britain* (London, Institute of Economic Affairs, Choice and Welfare Unit).

Saunders, P. (1997) Social mobility in Britain: an empirical evaluation of two competing explanations, *Sociology*, 31(2), pp. 261–288.

Tyler, W. (1988) *School organization: a sociological perspective* (London, Croom Helm).

Wakeford, J. (1969) *The Cloistered Elite: a sociological analysis of the English public boarding school* (London, Macmillan).

Willis, P. (1977) *Learning to Labour* (Farnborough, Saxon House).

Woods, P. (1977) *The Pupil's Experience, E202 Schooling and Society* (Milton Keynes, Open University Press).

Appendix

c1	Frampton Comprehensive School
c2	Cherry Tree Comprehensive School
c3	Shirebrook Comprehensive School
c4	Rowton Comprehensive School
c5	Vicarage Road Comprehensive School
c6	Moorside Comprehensive School
c7	Parkside School for Girls
g1	Highgrove County School for Girls
g2	Archbishop Ambrose Grammar School for Boys
p1	Bankside College
p2	Milltown Grammar School for Boys
p3	Milltown High School for Girls
p4	Dame Margaret's High School
p5	Nortown Grammar School
p6	St. Hilda's Girls' School
p7	Cathedral College
p8	Nortown High School for Girls
p9	Weston School

CHAPTER 14

TOWARDS A SOCIOLOGY OF LEARNING IN PRIMARY SCHOOLS

Andrew Pollard

British Journal of Sociology of Education (1990), 11 (3): 241–56

[. . .]

The limitations of disciplinary boundaries

One could argue that the division of labour between the academic disciplines which make up the social sciences has justified itself over the years by the quality of descriptions and depth of analyses which have been produced. There are processes of research, publication and debate which foster such refinement. Thus, within each discipline, dominant perspectives tend to come and go as development takes place and each decade witnesses new 'taken for granteds' and discrete progress within the disciplines.

However, the demarcations between disciplines must be seen as socio-historical products, maintained by people and institutions who had, and have, enormous personal, cultural and material investments in them and who must respond to the specific circumstances which they face. This throws up the danger that the reliance on detailed intra-disciplinary development could result in the establishment of theoretical perspectives and empirical procedures which in fact fail to engage with the more complex and enduring realities of social processes and phenomena. Indeed, I would argue that, as our understanding of the social world becomes more sophisticated, it is becoming increasingly apparent that the validity of the study of many issues cannot be maximised unless each of the relevant disciplines is drawn on in sustained study.

Interestingly, such more complex and enduring issues are often those which are regarded as being particularly important by practitioners—by the people who live out the processes which academic analysts study—and, indeed, by policy makers—people who have to make decisions of great significance with whatever information and understanding is available to them at the time. From the perspective of such groups, social scientists are often seen as myopic pedants, locked into their theoretical thought-worlds with little grasp of 'practical realities'. The underlying message here, on offer to those who are actively listening, is that the lack of an integrated analysis, comparable to the integrated nature of experience, denies the validity and thus the credibility of the academic account.

At the same time though, it would be a churlish observer of the social sciences who did not recognise that each discipline has particular strengths for addressing particular social phenomena and issues. It might thus be concluded that ways of drawing on such strengths should be found and, in the first place, it might reasonably be argued that academics should cooperate across disciplinary boundaries. Only this can begin to ensure that the issues which we address are tackled in more valid and transferable ways.

The issue of learning in primary schools provides a case in point.

Learning in primary schools

A review of the sociology primary schooling and of the psychology of young children's learning over the past twenty years or so reveals a curious picture. On the one hand, sociologists have continued, in one way or another, to focus their attention on issues of social differentiation. Certainly the emphasis has developed from that of social class to include increasing attention to issues of race and gender, and theoretical refinements have accumulated too. However, the overriding impression left by work such as Hartley (1985), Pollard (1985), Sharp & Green (1975), Lubeck (1985), King (1978) and King (1989), is that learning processes are, at best, tangential to issues such as typification, group formation and the consequences of differentiation. Returning over a decade earlier, and to a different theoretical perspective, reveals a similar story—as is illustrated by the way in which Dreeben's *On What is Learned in School* (1968) concerns itself with socialisation of children into norms but makes no attempt to consider the sociological factors which influence the learning of knowledge, concepts and skills.

Sociologists' focus on differentiation in the past has, until recently, been matched by the naive individualism of much child psychology which derived from the work of Piaget. Piaget's work was directed, in an overarching sense, towards the study of 'genetic epistemology', but the route towards this analysis was through many detailed studies of children's thinking and behaviour. Careful development and use of the clinical method over many years enabled Piaget to generate a model of learning processes based on the interaction between individuals and their environment and involving development through successive stages of equilibration, each of which was taken to be associated with particular capacities and ways of thinking. This model was powerfully adopted by primary school teachers in the UK in the years following the Plowden Report (CACE, 1967) and was used as a professional legitimation for 'progressive' classroom practices which, ostensibly, gave children a large degree of control over their learning.

However, whilst it is impossible to overestimate Piaget's influence within developmental psychology over the past decades, it is also true to say that Piaget's ideas have increasingly been modified by the gradual emergence of a new paradigm—'social constructivism'.

Thus, the previously dominant model, which implicitly conceptualised children as *individual* 'active scientists', has begun to be superseded by an image of children as *social* beings who construct their understandings (learn) from social interaction within specific socio-cultural settings. They are thus seen as intelligent social actors who, although their knowledge base may be limited in absolute terms, are capable in many ways. For instance, processes of 'intellectual search' have been identified in young children (Tizard & Hughes, 1984) as have children's capacities to develop sophisticated forms of representation for meaning and understanding. Such findings are being found with younger and younger children as research goes on.

The theoretical basis of such psychological research is strongly influenced by Vygotsky (1962, 1978). Of particular importance is his comparative work on the interrelations of thought, language and culture and, at another level, on the role of adults in scaffolding children's understanding across the 'zone of proximal development'—the extension of understanding which can be attained with appropriate support

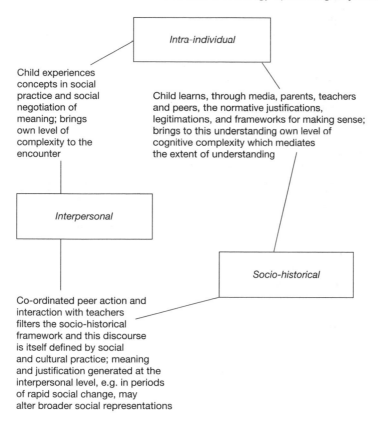

Figure 10 The relationship between intra-individual, interpersonal and socio-historical factors in learning.
Source: Haste (1987, p. 175).

from others. According to Bruner & Haste (1987), this social constructivist approach has brought about a 'quiet revolution' in developmental psychology in the last decade and this is certainly borne out by the impact in education of work such as that by Donaldson (1978), Hughes (1986), Bruner (1986) and Edwards & Mercer (1987).

A key thrust of such new approaches is to recognise the way in which the social context influences perspectives and behaviour. One particularly interesting way of conceptualising this has been provided by Helen Haste (1987) in her model of 'intra-individual', 'interpersonal' and 'socio-historical' factors affecting learning (Fig. 10).

The intra-individual domain is the province of the cognitive psychologists who have accumulated so many insights into the ways in which individuals assimilate experiences and construct understanding. The interpersonal is the domain of social interaction—the area in which meanings are negotiated and through which cultural norms and social conventions are learned. The socio-historical is the domain of culturally defined and historically accumulated justification and explanation. It is a socio-historical resource for both interpersonal interaction and intra-individual reflection.

Such conceptualisation of factors and domains affecting learning begins to make it possible to break out of the individualist assumptions which have been common in child psychology, so that wider social issues can be addressed. Sociologists could have much to offer here for, as Apple (1986) has argued:

> We do not confront abstract 'learners' in schools. Instead, we see specific classed, raced and gendered subjects, people whose biographies are intimately linked to the economic, political and ideological trajectories of their families and communities, to the political economies of their neighbourhoods.
>
> (1986, p. 7:5)

In other words, intra-individual learning cannot really be understood without reference to both interpersonal experiences and socio-historical circumstances.

I suspect that there is some way to go in the development of working relationships and analytical tools before psychologists and sociologists concerned with children's learning are able to take on the full import of Haste's framework and Apple's suggestion in detailed empirical investigations. However, a growing consensus about the inter-relatedness of such factors does seem to be emerging and this is underpinned, not just by theory and empirical research, but also by the common-sense and lived experiences of millions of children, teachers, parents and others. If we are to investigate the issue of learning in valid ways, then our first problem, as social scientists, is really to find ways of bridging the artificial disciplinary boundaries which dissipate our energies.

I want to suggest that one way of developing such collaborative work could be through the linking of social constructivist psychology and symbolic interactionist sociology.

These approaches share a basic assumption that people are active and make decisions on the basis of meanings. However, whilst social constructivist work has begun to identify the processes by which people 'make sense' in social situations, and thus come to 'know', symbolic interactionist studies promise to provide more detailed and incisive accounts of the dynamics and constraints of the contexts in which learning takes place. The two approaches are, arguably, complementary.

Some years ago I began to toy with this potential sociological contribution through the publication of a collection of papers which highlighted the influence of social contexts in schools on children's thinking and learning (Pollard, 1987). This collection of case studies includes material from 3–12 year olds and provides a degree of 'thick description' which invites further theorisation regarding the nature of such complementarity—a task which I have begun through the work on an ethnography and which is reflected in this chapter.

However, before addressing the study and the theoretical issue directly, it is appropriate to place the topic of 'learning in primary schools' in the context of recent policies in England and Wales and in relation to other approaches to classroom teaching/learning processes. In particular, I will have regard below to the work of Neville Bennett because of the sustained quality and impact of his research into classroom teaching and learning over many years.

Policy and substantive contexts

In recent years, major thrusts of Government policy in England and Wales have been directed towards the streamlining of the management of schools, increasing the effectiveness and accountability of teachers and restructuring the curriculum (e.g. Education Act, 1986; Education Reform Act, 1988). We do not yet know whether such initiatives will achieve their aims in terms of the delivery of the curriculum. However, irrespective of this, it can be argued that far too little attention has been paid to the actual reception of the curriculum by learners. Indeed, by focusing on the issue of learning, one could claim to be anticipating a policy debate of the future—a claim based on the proposition that when the dust of reforms of teacher and curriculum management has settled and we are still chasing that ever-receding Holy Grail of 'educational standards', more detailed attention to learning and the learners in schools will be perceived as necessary.

The issue also has implications for teachers in primary schools in a more general way concerning the theoretical underpinning of practice. Over the past decade or so, there has been a gradual erosion of the primacy of the Plowden Report's (CACE, 1967) philosophy of 'child centredness', which underpinned much primary school practice. As Piaget's work has been questioned and research evidence has accumulated about actual classroom behaviour, so primary school practice has begun to be seen to lack a theoretical base' (Sylva, 1987). I would suggest that a fusion of social-constructivism and symbolic-interactionism, suitably applied, has the potential to offer a new legitimation—indeed, I think there are many forms of innovative curriculum practice which, perhaps unwittingly, appear to be based on such precepts.

In the past twenty years a considerable amount of research has been conducted with the aim of identifying factors which enable teachers to be 'effective'. However, as Bennett (1987) has argued, whilst the initial work, emphasising teaching styles, identified some interesting patterns and descriptions, it lacked explanatory power and made few connections with actual practice. It was superseded in the mid-70s by an 'opportunities to learn' model in which the teacher was seen as the manager of the attention and time of the pupils. A key indicator became the amount of time which the pupil was 'on task'. More recently the focus has also turned to the analysis of what is termed 'quality' of classroom tasks—defined in terms of the degree of appropriate match with children's capacities (e.g. Bennett *et al.*, 1984).

Neville Bennett's work represents a sustained and consistent attempt to develop and test a model of teaching and learning. His successive studies have focused on different parts of an emerging model and his work continues through his present Leverhulme Project on the quality of teacher's subject knowledge and ability to diagnose learning difficulties.

Bennett, and his co-author, Joy Kell, express the model particularly clearly below:

> Teaching is, we argue, a purposeful activity: teachers provide tasks and activities for their children for good reasons. These reasons or, as we call them in the model, teacher intentions, will inform the teacher's selection of tasks/activities. Once chosen these are presented to children in some way, e.g. to individuals, groups or the whole class, together with the necessary materials. The children then get on with their work, demonstrating, through their performances, their understanding (or misconceptions) of it. When they have completed their activity it might be expected that the teacher will assess it in some way in order to judge children's developing competencies, and it might also be expected that the information gained from those assessments will inform the teacher's next intentions.

The very important point which Bennett has empirically documented is that breakdowns can and do occur regularly between each stage in the 'task process cycle' and it is unfortunate that this can sometimes come across as an unappreciative critique of teachers. Rather, I would suggest that it should be seen, more constructively, as providing a detailed testimony of just how difficult the job is.

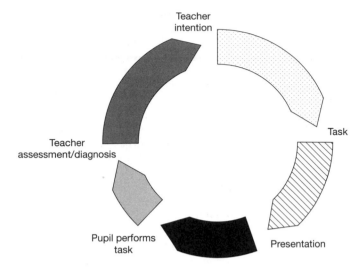

Figure 11 A model of classroom task processes.
Source: Bennett & Kell (1989, p. 27).

Having said that though, I would also argue that such work seriously underplays the importance of the socio-cultural situation in which teaching and learning take place and fails to trace the full impact of the subjectivity of the participants. There is no specific emphasis on learners with reference to their responses to the social influences and teaching/learning situations which they experience. The model thus appears as a technical model of teaching—one which is dominated by the teacher, with pupils 'performing' to externally determined tasks.

In terms of the issues raised by Helen Haste, Bennett's analysis is very partial. It is worthwhile and necessary, but it is not sufficient and should be complemented by other work—work which is more informed by sociological perspectives.

Among other related issues which have emerged regularly in recent research and in HMI surveys has been that of the routine nature of many of the activity structures and classroom tasks in which children engage—particularly in the 'basic' curriculum areas (Alexander, 1984). In an attempt to address this issue and to be appreciative to the concerns of teachers, Woods (1990) has drawn on coping strategies theory (e.g. Pollard, 1982) to identify problems of the limited 'opportunities to teach' in classrooms. These are constrained by the inadequate resourcing of schools and by the enormous current expectations of teachers.

However, it is also clear that the routinisation of tasks and activity structures is not simply the result of a transmission process for which teachers are solely responsible. Indeed, Doyle (1979) has suggested that many pupils seek tasks which are 'low risk' and 'low ambiguity' and both the ORACLE researchers' identification of 'intermittent working' and 'easy riding' (Galton *et al.*, 1980) and my own identification of pupil 'drifting' (Pollard & Tann, 1987) suggest that pupils' learning stances and strategies could be of considerable significance. Arguably, this is particularly important in the context of the national concern for improvement in the level of learning achievements, given the psychological evidence on the contribution of risk-taking to learning (Claxton, 1984) and Dweck's socio-cognitive research on motivation (1986). As Galton's (1987) review of the field in the last twenty years concludes:

... if advances (in our understanding) are to be made, there will (need to) be greater concentration on the social factors affecting pupil learning and (on) the ways in which teachers can create classroom climates which allow situations of 'high risk' and 'high ambiguity' to be coped with successfully.

(1987, p. 44)

This statement underlines a key point in social constructivist models of learning about control of the learning process. Since understanding can only be constructed in the mind of the learner, it is essential that learners exercise a significant degree of control of the process—a point to which I will return below.

I turn now though, to introduce the empirical study around which my thinking on this topic has developed.

A longitudinal ethnography

In 1987 I began a research programme, a longitudinal ethnography, which was designed to explore the potential for linking social interactionism and social constructivism.

I aimed to monitor the primary school careers of a small cohort of ten children at one primary school by using a variety of qualitative methods and I started from the children's entry to the school at the age of four. I particularly focused on the social factors which were likely to influence the children's stance, perspectives and strategies regarding learning. Data was thus collected from parents about family life, sibling relationships and the children's emergent identities; from peers and playground contexts concerning peer-group relations; and from teachers with regard to classroom behaviour and academic achievements.

At the heart of the study was regular classroom observation so that the progression of organisation, activity structures and routine tasks in each class which the children passed through could be documented—together with the responses of the children to such provision. The main sources of data were: field-notes from participant-observation, interviews, teacher records, parent diaries, school documents, photographs, video recordings, sociometry and examples of children's work.

This work built on the sociological studies of teacher/pupil coping strategies in schools which has developed over a number of years (e.g. Woods, 1977; Hargreaves, 1978; Pollard, 1982; Beynon, 1985; Scarth, 1987), with its strong influence of symbolic interactionism. Since that work has been generally accepted as a means of conceptualising and analysing macro-micro linkages as they affect school processes, I judged that it might also prove to be capable of bearing the weight of analysis of socio-historical factors in learning, as raised by Helen Haste (see Fig. 10), in addition to the interpersonal factors which are the more obvious provenance of symbolic interactionism.

I also hoped that the study would develop existing work on coping strategies substantively because of the focus on children as pupils developing through schools. This focus was designed to complement the considerable amount of work which is now available on teacher strategies and careers (Ball & Goodson, 1985; Sikes *et al.*, 1985; Nias, 1989). Additionally, of course, the study was intended to provide a more explicit focus on learning than is evident in previous sociological work, which, as I argued earlier, has tended to be primarily concerned with differentiation.

The main aims of the study were thus:

1   to trace the development of a cohort of young children's stances, perspectives and strategies regarding learning, through consideration of home, playground and classroom settings;

2   to investigate pupil career, in terms of emergent identities and the influences on them, as children move through different teachers and classrooms within their school;

3   to develop the analytic potential of combining social constructivist models of children's learning and symbolic interactionist models of school processes.

In the course of gathering data, I attempted to code and analyse it with the intention of generating grounded theoretical models and concepts (Glaser & Strauss, 1967; Hammersley & Atkinson, 1985) which could contribute to both professional and academic debate. In keeping with other, earlier work, I do not aspire to 'prove' relationships, believing this to be inappropriate with regard to such subtle issues (or indeed to many aspects of social science more generally). However, through the detailed analysis of the data, I aimed to highlight the most significant issues and patterns in the social relationships which seem to affect pupil learning and career. Others can then relate this analysis to their own circumstances.

This paper represents my first public attempt to begin to make sense of work. It remains tentative in many respects, but certainly indicates the direction in which my thinking is leading.

By the Spring of 1990, I had studied nine children (one child had moved schools) over their first three school years with regard to three major social settings (classroom, playground, home). I had collected a large amount of data and faced analytical problems which I aimed to address through the comparison of the nine cases which the children represented.

Before I focus directly on the emerging analysis, an indication of the data is provided below by a brief illustrative account of the educational experiences, over their first two school years, of just two of the children whom I studied.

This is a highly condensed 'account', in almost narrative form, and was written initially for an audience of governors and parents (Pollard, 1990). The judgements expressed in it rest on a detailed analysis of data, but the main point which I wish to make requires a holistic understanding, for which narrative documentary is a proven vehicle. I thus hope that the account below serves its purpose in highlighting the importance of contextual factors in learning and in providing a bridge to the theoretical analysis in the final section of this chapter. More complete substantive documentation and analysis will appear in due course.

Learning and developing an identity

The two children on whom this illustration is based began their school careers together, with twenty-four others, in the same 'reception' class.

The first child, a girl called Sally, was the youngest of the two children of the school caretaker. Her mother also worked in the school as a School Meals Services Assistant and as a cleaner. Her parents had always taken enormous pleasure and pride in Sally's achievements. They celebrated each step as it came but did not seem to overtly press her. Life, for them, seemed very much in perspective. Sally was physically agile and had a good deal of self-confidence. She had known the school and the teaching staff for most of her life. She felt at home. She was very sensitive to 'school rules' and adult concerns and she engaged in each new challenge with zest. Over the years, with her parents' encouragement, she had developed a considerable talent for dancing and had won several competitions. In school she had also taken a leading role in several class assemblies and had made good progress with her reading and other work. The teachers felt she was a delightful and rewarding child to teach—convivial and able, but compliant too. Her friends were mainly girls though she mixed easily. She was at the centre of a group which was particularly popular in the class and which, over the years since playgroup, had developed strong internal links and friendships through shared interests, for instance, in 'My Little Pony', playing at 'mummies and daddies' and reciprocal home visits.

The second child, Daniel, was the fifth and youngest in his family. His father was an extremely busy business executive and his mother had devoted the previous sixteen years to caring for their children, which she saw as a worthwhile but all-absorbing commitment. She was concerned for Daniel who had had some difficulties in establishing his identity in the bustle of the family with four older children. She also felt that he had 'always tended to worry about things' and was not very confident in himself. For many years he had tended to play on being the youngest, the baby of the family, a role which seemed naturally available. At playgroup he was particularly friendly with a girl, Harriet, who was later to be in his class at school. However, over their first year at school, distinct friendships of boys and girls began to form. It became 'sissy' to play with girls. Daniel, who had found the transition from the security of home hard to take and who had to begin to develop a greater self-sufficiency, thus found the ground-rules of appropriate friendships changing, as the power of child culture asserted itself. He could not play with Harriet because she was a girl, but nor was he fully accepted by the dominant groups of boys.

This insecurity was increased when he moved from the structured and 'motherly' atmosphere of his reception class into the more volatile environment of his 'middle infant' class. There were now thirty one children in his class, most of whom were from a parallel reception class—within which a group of boys had developed a reputation for being 'difficult'. The new teacher thus judged that the class ... 'needed a firm hand to settle them down after last year' and, as a caring but experienced infant teacher, decided to stand no nonsense. It also so happened that this teacher was somewhat stressed, as a lot of teachers in England and Wales have been in the late 1980s. She sometimes acted a little harshly and in other ways which were against her own better judgement.

The environment which Daniel experienced was therefore one which was sometimes a little unpredictable. Whilst he was never one of the ones who 'got into trouble', he was very worried by the possibility that he might 'upset Miss'. Daniel would thus be very careful. He would watch and listen to the teacher, attempting to 'be good' and do exactly what was required. He would check with other children and, on making a first attempt at a task, try to have his efforts approved before proceeding further. Occasionally, at work with a group and with other children also pressing, the teacher might wave Daniel away. He would then drift, unsure, watching to take another opportunity to obtain the reinforcement which he felt he needed. As the year progressed, Daniel became more unhappy and increasingly unwilling to go to school.

Daniel's mother was torn as this situation developed—was the 'problem' caused by Daniel's 'immaturity' or was it because he was frightened of the teacher? She felt it was probably a bit of both but school-gate advice suggested that discussion in school might not go easily. She delayed and the situation worsened, with Daniel making up excuses to avoid school, insisting on returning home for lunch and becoming unwilling to visit the homes of other children. Daniel's mother eventually and tentatively visited the school where the issues were aired.

Over the following weeks the teacher worked hard to support Daniel and to help him settle. Daniel's confidence improved a little, particularly when he found a new friend, a boy, from whom he then became inseparable. Even so, as his mother told me towards the end of the year, 'we are holding on and praying for the end of term'.

These two children attended the same school and were part of the same classes—yet as learners they had quite different characteristics. Whilst Sally was confident, keen to 'have a go' and would take risks, Daniel was insecure, fearful lest he 'got things wrong' in a world in which he felt evaluated and vulnerable. The accident of birth into a small or large family may have been an influence too, with Sally having had the psychological space to flourish and the day to day support of both her parents all around her, whilst Daniel had to establish his place in a large family in which both parents faced considerable pressure in their work—be it in an office or domestically. Perhaps too, Daniel's initial solutions to his position, which had carried him in good stead in his infancy, whilst at home, would simply not transfer into the less bounded environment of school.

Towards an analytical framework

The data which underpins an account such as that reviewed above is highly complex and, in attempting to make sense of it, one can easily lose direction or become distracted. For the purposes of this study, it was crucial to retain the focus on identity and learning whilst also structuring the comparison of cases across settings—with 27 interrelated data sets formed by the nine children and three major settings. Building on what I take to be key interactionist and constructivist principles, I evolved a simple analytical formula which I found to be powerful and which could be applied to data and cases derived from any setting.

Figure 12 Individual, context and learning: an analytic formula.

The relationship between self and others expresses the key symbolic interactionist focus, with its recognition of the importance of social context in the formation of meaning and self. A sense of control in social situations is seen as a product of this. It is an indication of the success, or otherwise, of a child's coping strategies in the politico-cultural context of any particular social setting—home, classroom, playground—and thus reflects the interplay of interests, power, strategies and negotiation. However, it is also a necessary element of the learning process as conceived by social constructivist psychologists. Only children themselves can 'make sense', understand and learn. They may be supported and instructed by others, but, once their understanding has been scaffolded in such ways, it must stand on its own foundations—foundations which can only be secure when the child has been able to control the construction itself.

Teaching and other forms of support by adults are necessary, but they are not sufficient. Learning also requires conditions which enable each child to control the assembly and construction of their understanding.[1]

I have elaborated below, a model by Rowland (1987) in order to express this point.

Figure 13 A social constructivist model of the teaching/learning process.

It is worth dwelling a little on the importance of the role of an adult as a 'reflective agent' in this model, providing meaningful and appropriate guidance and extension to the cognitive structuring and skill development arising from the child's initial experiences. This, it is suggested, supports the child's attempts to 'make sense' and enables them to cross the zone of proximal development (ZPD).

Their thinking is thus *restructured* in the course of further experiences. Of course, the concept of 'reflective agent' is not unrelated to that of 'reflective teaching' (Pollard & Tann, 1987), which is becoming a new orthodoxy in terms of course rationales for teacher education in the UK. However, as with sociology of education, present work on reflective teaching is relatively weak on the issue of learning itself.[2] Of great interest too, is the fact that carrying out the role of a reflective agent effectively is dependent on sensitivity *and* accurate knowledge of each child's needs. It thus places a premium on formative, teacher assessment (TGAT, 1988) and could be greatly facilitated in England and Wales by the requirements of new legislation—if it is appropriately implemented, a condition which, unfortunately, we cannot take for granted.

To recap—in Fig. 13 above, we see the need for appropriate adult support and instruction and its relationship to children's control over their learning. The two are not contradictory. Indeed, I would argue that both are necessary but neither is sufficient for high quality learning. In the cases of Sally and Daniel, Sally was able to negotiate, control and cope with the variety of domestic, classroom and playground settings which she encountered with relative ease. She was confident in tackling new learning situations and achieved a great deal. Daniel found things much more difficult in each setting, but particularly in the classroom. He developed two key strategies regarding this learning. First, to watch, check and recheck to make sure that he 'was doing it right' so that he could avoid 'trouble with Miss'. Second, to stay away from school. His learning achievements over the two years were relatively modest.

Of course, the simple formula (Fig. 12) and the social constructivist model of interaction in learning (Fig. 13) express only a small part of the story, and I have developed them further to begin to reflect on the outcomes and consequences of the learning process.

This model expresses the recursive nature of experience. Self-confidence, together with other attributes and other contextual factors (e.g. Bennett's work on the quality of tasks set), produces particular learning outcomes—successful or otherwise—and with them associated perspectives. These, it is suggested, contribute cumulatively to each child's sense of identity and to their learning stance, and it is with these which, for better or worse, they enter the next setting. Over time, as this cycle moves forward, it tends to develop in patterned ways into what can be identified more clearly as 'pupil career'.

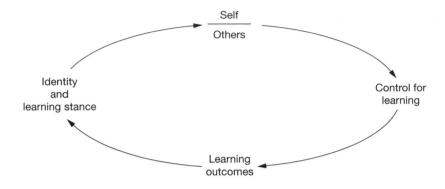

Figure 14 A model of teaming and identity.

Thus, in the case of Sally and Daniel, we might speculate that Sally's pupil career will go from strength to strength, founded on the confidence of her learning stance, whilst Daniel's progress may be more halting. In fact, of course, such speculation is premature. Time will bring new social contexts and experiences and the factor of social class may influence the children's development. This is where the longitudinal design of the study should be significant.

Whatever the empirical outcomes, the nature of the patterns in pupil learning and career is of consequence for both psychologists and sociologists. For psychologists, it highlights processes of learning in context. For sociologists, it begins to relate factors such as social class, gender and race, through the processes of learning and identity formation, and on to long term social differentiation, career and life chances.

I am attempting to apply the basic formula, Fig. 12, above, in relation to the settings of classrooms, playground and the home, through the application of some key elements of the model of coping strategies which I developed some years ago (Pollard, 1985). Four important aspects of this are:

1   An individual's structural position: their power, influence and capacity to take active decisions.
2   An individual's interests-at-hand: the immediate concerns of a person in processes of interaction, given their goals and structural position within a particular social setting.
3   The working consensus: the social rules and understandings which tend to become established in any particular setting as a result of interaction. Such understandings often involve a negotiated 'trade-off' between the participants.
4   Strategic action: strategies used by individuals as a means of coping with different settings. These include conformity, negotiating and rejecting and may or may not be transferred across different settings.

In the case of both the children illustrated, we see the influence of each of the three major social settings and significant others in their lives—family, peers and teachers.

For Sally, the particular, overlapping configuration of the self/other relationship between home and school gave her self-confidence on which she was able to build in her relationships with her peers and which enabled her to exercise considerable control over her classroom learning. Other data clearly shows how this control was obtained, in large part, through her social awareness and negotiating skills. She contributed directly to the working consensus in both classes. Her structural position was strong, her interests-at-hand could be accommodated within teacher goals and she acted with skill and strategic awareness to achieve expected learning outcomes and a positive identity—despite the risks associated with life in her second class.

For Daniel, the situation was more difficult. His structural position was weak both in his family and then, almost as a knock-on effect of his strategies in the home setting, amongst his peers. He felt insecure, in one way or another, in each of the three main settings in his life and he thus developed relatively defensive strategies in order to protect his interests. At its most obvious, this involved trying to avoid coming to school but, once there, it was manifested by extreme caution in his dealings with teachers and a reluctance to take any sort of risk or exercise control over his learning. Preferring to keep a low profile, he participated little in the establishment of classroom understandings and the working consensus. Learning outcomes were affected and with them, Daniel's identity began to develop and to be registered with both his teachers, parents and peers.

Of course, these patterns are related to the particular classroom settings in which Daniel worked and to the teachers concerned and, unfortunately, the teacher of Daniel's middle infant class seemed to compound some of his difficulties. It remains perfectly possible that Daniel will develop more poise and belief in himself as he gets older and he has many abilities and social advantages. The question is an empirical one about which, for the moment, we must be open-minded.

The story of these two children is not just about learning in a narrow academic sense. Additionally, it is about the ways in which Sally and Daniel began to develop their identities as people. As was suggested by Fig. 14, identity and self-confidence in stances towards future learning develop alongside skills, knowledge and other learning outcomes. They thus feed back, recursively, into future actions and experiences and as the biography and career of each child is gradually constructed.

This brief illustration of the cases of Sally and Daniel demonstrates the importance of the social context in which learning takes place and suggests that it will impact on children irrespective of their individual capabilities. Interestingly, it also reinforces the suggestion that there is no necessary connection between social class factors or income levels and the quality of the learning environment which parents can provide.

There are many further aspects of this attempt to generate theoretical models of the social factors affecting learning which could be discussed. However, in a chapter such as this there is little space to do them justice and they must therefore await elaboration elsewhere.

Summary and conclusion

In this chapter I firstly suggested that many social phenomena require interdisciplinary analysis if they are to be studied in ways which are valid—and thus practically useful. Learning in primary schools provided a case in point and I reflected on the strange absence of a sociological account and on the partial nature of other analyses because of this omission. I then began to explore the potential for drawing on symbolic interactionism and social constructivism to construct an integrated analysis and showed how I have attempted to begin this through the analysis of data gathered from a longitudinal ethnography of a small group of children in one school.

This analysis has significant policy implications for parents, teachers and school governors since they bear very heavy responsibilities for children's learning and careers. This is so because children develop their perspectives, strategies and, thus, identities in response to their need to cope with circumstances which such adults control. If adults fail to co-operate, to liaise, to negotiate or to think their actions through, then it is the children who will suffer. Their lives are, literally, an ongoing test of the continuity and support which adults provide. Certainly such vulnerability deserves our attention and can, I would argue, best be addressed by focusing on the nature of the learning provision in different settings and by recognising the integrated nature of experience.

It is interesting that, at the present time in England and Wales, such issues are far down the educational agenda—an agenda which is dominated by curriculum, assessment, accountability and management issues. One day, when policies are sought with a more secure foundation on learning processes, it is to be hoped that sociologists will be able to contribute to the available understanding about this extremely important issue.

Acknowledgements

I would like to thank all the children, parents, teachers and governors of the school from whom case-study data is drawn in this chapter. Without their consistent trust, openness and support the study on which this work is based would not have been possible.

I am grateful to Bristol Polytechnic for supporting this project over several years and to Cassell for permission to publish some material from my book, *Learning in Primary Schools* (1990).

I would also like to thank Charles Desforges, Peter Kutnick and Peter Woods for their helpful comments on the design of this project and Neville Bennett and two anonymous BJSE referees for useful comments on a draft of this chapter.

Notes

1   Neville Bennett, in helpfully commenting on a draft of this chapter (personal communication, May, 1990), has advised that he 'knows of no data which would argue that pupil choice of work is more positively related to elaborated schema than, say, teacher given work'. I am still thinking about this statement because at first sight it appears to beg the issue of motivation and its relationship to learning. Clearly more discussion is necessary to clarify this important issue.
2   In the case of my own book with Sarah Tann (*Reflective Teaching in the Primary School*, Cassell, 1987), a new edition [. . . 1993 should] correct this.

References

Apple, M. (1986) *Teachers and Texts* (London, Routledge).
Ball, S. & Goodson, I. (1985) *Teachers' Lives and Careers* (Lewes, Falmer Press).
Bennett, N. (1987) 'The search for the effective primary school teacher', in: S. Delamont (Ed.) *The Primary School Teacher* (Lewes, Falmer Press).
Bennett, N. *et al.* (1984) *The Quality of Pupil Learning Experiences* (London, Lawrence Erlbaum).
Bennett, N. & Kell, J. (1989) *A Good Start? Four Year Olds in Infant Schools* (Oxford, Basil Blackwell).
Beynon, J. (1985) *Initial Encounters in the Secondary School* (Lewes, Falmer Press).
Bruner, J. (1986) *Actual Minds, Possible Worlds* (London, Harvard University Press).
Bruner, J. & Haste, H. (1987) *Making Sense* (London, Methuen).
Cace (1967) *Children and their Primary Schools* (the Plowden Report) (London, HMSO).
Claxton, G. (1984) *Live and Learn* (London, Harper & Row).
Donaldson, M. (1978) *Children's Minds* (London, Fontana).

Doyle, W. (1979) 'Classroom tasks and student abilities', in: P. Peterson & H. Walberg (Eds) *Research on Teaching: concepts, findings and implications* (Berkeley, CA, McCutchan).

Dreeben, R. (1968) *On What is Learned in School* (London, Harvard).

Dweck, C. (1986) 'Motivational processes affecting learning', *American Psychologist*, October, pp. 1040–1048.

Edwards, D. & Mercer, N. (1987) *Common Knowledge* (London, Methuen).

Galton, M., Simon, B. & Croll, P. (1980) *Inside Primary Schools* (London, Routledge).

Glaser, B. & Strauss, A. (1967) *The Discovery of Grounded Theory* (Chicago, Aldine).

Hammersley, M. & Atkinson, P. (1983) *Ethnography: principles into practice* (London, Tavistock).

Hargreaves, A. (1978) 'The significance of classroom coping strategies', in: L. Barton & R. Meighan (Eds) *Sociological Interpretations of Schooling and Classrooms* (Driffield, Nafferton).

Hartley, D. (1985) *Understanding Primary Schools* (London, Croom Helm).

Haste, H. (1987) 'Growing into rules', in: J. Bruner & H. Haste (Eds) *Making Sense* (London, Methuen).

Hughes, M. (1986) *Children and Number* (Oxford, Basil Blackwell).

King, R.A. (1978) *All Things Bright and Beautiful* (London, Wiley).

King, R.A. (1989) *The Best of Primary Education* (Lewes, Falmer Press).

Lubeck, S. (1985) *Sandbox Society* (Lewes, Falmer Press).

Nias, J. (1989) *Primary Teacher's Talking* (London, Routledge).

Pollard, A. (1982) 'A model of coping strategies', *British Journal of Sociology of Education*, Vol. 3, No. 1, pp. 19–37.

Pollard, A. (1985) *The Social World of the Primary School* (London, Cassell).

Pollard, A. (1987a) *Children and their Primary Schools, A New Perspective* (Lewes, Falmer Press).

Pollard, A. (1990) *Learning in Primary Schools* (London, Cassell).

Pollard, A. & Tann, S. (1987b) *Reflective Teaching in the Primary School* (London, Cassell).

Rowland, S. (1987) 'Child in control', in: A. Pollard (Ed.) *Children and their Primary Schools* (Lewes, Falmer Press).

Scarth, J. (1987) 'Teacher strategies: a review and critique', *British Journal of Sociology of Education*, Vol. 8, No. 3, pp. 245–262.

Sharp, R. & Green, A. (1975) *Education and Social Control* (London, Routledge).

Sikes, P., Measor, L. & Woods, P. (1985) *Teacher Careers: crisis and continuities* (Lewes, Falmer Press).

Sylva, K. (1987) 'Plowden: history and prospect—research', *Oxford Review of Education*, Vol. 13, No. 1, pp. 3–11.

Task Group on Assessment and Testing (1988) *National Curriculum Report* (London, Department of Education and Science).

Tizard, B. & Hughes, M. (1987) 'The intellectual search of young children', in: A. Pollard (Ed.) *Children and their Primary Schools: a new perspective* (Lewes, Falmer Press).

Vygotsky, L. (1962) *Thought and Language* (New York, Wiley).

Vygotsky, L. (1978) *Mind in Society* (London, Harvard).

Woods, P. (1977) 'Teaching for survival', in: P. Woods & M. Hammersley (Eds) *School Experience* (London, Croom Helm).

Woods, P. (1990) *Teacher Skills and Strategies* (Lewes, Falmer Press).

Journal of Education Policy

EDITORS
Stephen Ball, *University of London, UK*
Ivor Goodson, *University of East Anglia, UK*

The *Journal of Education Policy* aims to discuss, analyse and debate policymaking, policy implementation and policy impact at all levels of and in all facets of education. It offers a forum for theoretical debate, and historical and comparative studies, as well as policy analysis and evaluation reports. The journal also analyses key policy documents and reviews, relevant texts and monographs.

Journal of Education Policy is essential reading for policy analysts and researchers, teachers, educational administrators, educational managers and sociologists of education.

This journal is also available online. Please connect to www.tandf.co.uk/online.html for further information.

To request a sample copy please visit: **www.tandf.co.uk/journals**

SUBSCRIPTION RATES
2003 - Volume 18 (6 issues)
Print ISSN 0268-0939 Online ISSN 1464-5106
Institutional rate: US$501; £304 (includes online access)
Personal rate: US$249; £151 (print only)

Carfax Publishing
Taylor & Francis Group

tedp

For further information, please contact Customer Services at either:
Taylor & Francis Ltd, Rankine Road, Basingstoke, Hants RG24 8PR, UK
Tel: +44 (0)1256 813002   Fax: +44 (0)1256 330245 Email: enquiry@tandf.co.uk
Website: www.tandf.co.uk
Taylor & Francis Inc, 325 Chestnut Street, 8th Floor, Philadelphia, PA 19106, USA
Tel: +1 215 6258900 Fax: +1 215 6258914 Email: info@taylorandfrancis.com
Website: www.taylorandfrancis.com